WEBMASTER IN A NUTSHELL

WEBMASTER IN A NUTSHELL

Second Edition

Stephen Spainhour and Robert Eckstein

O'REILLY®

Beijing · Cambridge · Farnham · Köln · Paris · Sebastopol · Taipei · Tokyo

Webmaster in a Nutshell, Second Edition
by Stephen Spainhour and Robert Eckstein

Published by O'Reilly & Associates, Inc., 101 Morris Street, Sebastopol, CA 95472.

Editor: Linda Mui

Production Editor: Mary Anne Weeks Mayo

Printing History:

October 1996: First Edition.

June 1999: Second Edition.

ISBN: 1-56592-325-1 [8/00]
[M]

Table of Contents

Part IV: JavaScript

Part V: CGI and Perl

Part VI: PHP

Part VII: HTTP

Part VIII: Server Configuration

Preface

This book is for everyone who works on the content end of the World Wide Web. Do you author or maintain web documents? Do you write CGI scripts? Are you a programmer developing web-based client or server applications? Are you the administrator of a web site, responsible for maintaining and updating the server software?

There are innumerable books and online resources for learning web-related skills. What this book does is pare them down to a single desktop-sized volume for easy reference. You may be a whiz at CGI programming but forget the syntax for sending cookies. You may know HTML fairly well but can never remember the correct syntax for creating tables. You might forget the directive for creating directory aliases on your server or how to enforce password protection on documents.

By no means is this book a replacement for more detailed books on the Web. But when those books have been digested and placed on your bookshelves with pride, this one will remain on your desktop.

Contents

This book is separated into eight distinct subject areas.

Chapter 1, *Introduction*
: Introduces the book and the Web in general.

Part I: HTML

Chapter 2, *HTML Overview*
: Gives a brief background to HTML syntax and introduces the features of the latest specification, HTML 4.0.

Chapter 3, *HTML Reference*
: Lists the current set of HTML tags and their attributes.

Chapter 4, *Frames*
Shows how to use HTML frames.

Chapter 5, *Tables*
Shows how to use HTML tables.

Chapter 6, *Forms*
Shows how to create HTML forms.

Chapter 7, *Character Entities*
Lists the special characters recognized by HTML.

Chapter 8, *Color Names and Values*
Lists the names accepted by HTML and CSS attributes for color values.

Part II: CSS

Chapter 9, *Cascading Style Sheets*
Provides an overview and reference to the Cascading Style Sheets specification for HTML documents.

Part III: XML

Chapter 10, *XML*
Provides an introduction and reference to XML.

Part IV: JavaScript

Chapter 11, *JavaScript*
Provides a reference for the JavaScript language.

Part V: CGI and Perl

Chapter 12, *CGI Overview*
Gives a general overview to the Common Gateway Interface, or CGI.

Chapter 13, *Server Side Includes*
Describes SSI, listing directives and environment variables and demonstrating their use.

Chapter 14, *The CGI.pm Module*
Provides a reference to the Perl module CGI.pm, which simplifies CGI programming.

Chapter 15, *Web Server Programming with mod_perl*
Provides a reference to *mod_perl*, an Apache module that can significantly enhance CGI performance.

Part VI: PHP

Chapter 16, *PHP*
Lists the syntax and functions of PHP, a server-side, HTML-embedded scripting language.

Part VII: HTTP

Chapter 17, *HTTP*
: Provides an overview and reference to the Hypertext Transfer Protocol.

Part VIII: Server Configuration

Chapter 18, *Apache Configuration*
: Lists the configuration directives used by the Apache server.

Chapter 19, *Apache Modules*
: Lists the modules that you can use with Apache.

Chapter 20, *Server Performance*
: Describes 10 areas where you can improve the performance of your server.

Conventions Used in This Book

The following typographical conventions are used in this book:

`Constant width`
: Indicates headers, directives, attributes, code examples, and HTML tags.

`Constant width italic`
: Indicates variables in examples that should be replaced with user-supplied values.

Italic
: Indicates variables, filenames, directory names, URLs, and comments in examples.

You will also see the following icons: ⓘ and Ⓝ. These icons indicate compatibility with Microsoft's Internet Explorer browser or Netscape's Navigator browser, respectively.

How to Contact Us

We invite you to help us improve this book. If you have an idea that could make this a more useful quick reference, or if you find a bug in an example program or an error in the text, let us know by writing:

O'Reilly & Associates, Inc.
101 Morris Street
Sebastopol, CA 95472
1-800-998-9938 (in the United States or Canada)
1-707-829-0515 (international/local)
1-707-829-0104 (fax)

You can also send us messages electronically. To be put on the mailing list or request a catalog, send email to:

info@oreilly.com

To ask technical questions or comment on the book, send email to:

bookquestions@oreilly.com

We have a web site for this book, where we'll list examples, errata, and any plans for future editions. You can access this page at:

http://www.oreilly.com/catalog/webmaster2/

For more information about this book and others, see the O'Reilly web site:

http://www.oreilly.com

Acknowledgments

Some chapters in this book were researched from other books and some were contributed outright by other authors. We'd like to thank David Flanagan, Chuck Musciano, Bill Kennedy, and Clinton Wong for giving us permission to use their material as the basis for much of this one. We'd also like to thank Rasmus Lerdorf and Patrick Killelea for providing the chapters on PHP and server performance, respectively.

We'd especially like to thank the reviewers of this book, who did it on short notice and on a very short schedule. They are: Chris Maden, Chuck Musciano, John Ackermann, and Matthew Rechs.

In addition, we'd like to thank Linda Mui, the developmental editor of this book; Paula Ferguson, editor of the JavaScript and PHP chapters; Tim O'Reilly, the editor of the "in a Nutshell" series; and Val Quercia, for shepherding the book through the additions, updates, and reviews.

Special thanks to the production staff at O'Reilly who got this book out speedily, while allowing us to tweak it long after we promised we'd stay away.

CHAPTER 1

Introduction

This book is a compilation of some fairly diverse reference material. What links these topics is that they are crucial knowledge for today's webmaster in a Unix environment.

In this chapter, we give the world's quickest introduction to web technology and the role of the webmaster who breathes life into each web document. If you want to learn more about the history of the Web, how to make your web pages "cool," the social impact of the Internet, or how to make money online, this is the wrong book.

This is a book by impatient writers for impatient readers. We're less interested in the hype of the Web than we are in what makes it actually tick. We'll leave it to the pundits to predict the future of the Web or to declare today's technology already outdated. Too much analysis makes our heads spin; we just want to get our web sites online.

The Web in a Nutshell

We've organized this book in a roughly "outside-in" fashion—that is, with the outermost layer (HTML) first and the innermost layer (the server itself) last. But since it's a good idea for all readers to know how everything fits together, let's take a minute to breeze through a description of the Web from the inside-out: no history, no analysis, just the technology basics.

Clients and Servers

The tool most people use on the Web is a *browser*, such as Netscape Navigator, Internet Explorer, Opera, Mosaic, or Lynx. Web browsers work by connecting over the Internet to remote machines, requesting specific documents, and then formatting the documents they receive for viewing on the local machine.

The language, or *protocol*, used for web transactions is Hypertext Transfer Protocol, or HTTP. The remote machines containing the documents run HTTP *servers* that wait for requests from browsers and then return the specified document. The browsers themselves are technically HTTP *clients*.

Uniform Resource Locators (URLs)

One of the most important things to grasp when working on the Web is the format for URLs. A URL is basically an address on the Web, identifying each document uniquely (for example, *http://www.oreilly.com/products.html*). Since URLs are so fundamental to the Web, we discuss them here in a little detail. The simple syntax for a URL is:

```
http://host/path
```

where:

host
: The host to connect to—e.g., *www.oreilly.com* or *www.altavista.com*. (While many web servers run on hosts beginning with *www*, the *www* prefix is just a convention.)

path
: The document requested on that server. This is not the same as the filesystem path, as its root is defined by the server.

Most URLs you encounter follow this simple syntax. A more generalized syntax, however, is:

```
scheme://host/path/extra-path-info?query-info
```

where:

scheme
: The protocol that connects to the site. For web sites, the scheme is `http`; for FTP, the scheme is `ftp`.

extra-path-info and *query-info*
: Optional information used by CGI programs. See Chapter 12, *CGI Overview*, for more information.

HTML documents also often use a "shorthand" for linking to other documents on the same server, called a *relative URL*. An example of a relative URL is *images/webnut.gif*. The browser knows to translate this into complete URL syntax before sending the request. For example, if *http://www.oreilly.com/books/webnut.html* contains a reference to *images/webnut.gif*, the browser reconstructs the relative URL as a full (or *absolute*) URL, *http://www.oreilly.com/books/images/webnut.gif*, and requests that document independently (if needed).

Often in this book, you'll see us refer to a URI, not a URL. A URI (Universal Resource Identifier) is a superset of URL, in anticipation of different resource naming conventions being developed for the Web. For the time being, however, the only URI syntax in practice is URL; so while purists might complain, you can safely assume that "URI" is synonymous with "URL" and not go wrong (yet).

Web Content: HTML, XML, CGI, JavaScript, and PHP

While web documents can conceivably be in any format, the universal standard is Hypertext Markup Language (HTML), a language for creating formatted text interspersed with images, sounds, animation, and hypertext links to other documents anywhere on the Web. Chapter 2, *HTML Overview*, through Chapter 8, *Color Names and Values*, cover the most current version of HTML.

In 1996, a significant extension to HTML was developed in the form of Cascading Style Sheets (CSS). Cascading Style Sheets allow web site developers to associate a number of style-related characteristics (such as font, color, spacing, etc.) with a particular HTML tag. This enables HTML authors to create a consistent look and feel throughout a set of documents. Chapter 9, *Cascading Style Sheets*, provides an overview of and a reference to CSS.

While HTML remains the widespread choice for web site development, there is also an heir apparent called XML (Extensible Markup Language). XML is a metalanguage that allows you to define your own document tags. While XML's development remains highly volatile, Chapter 10, *XML*, gives you the basics.

When static documents aren't sufficient for a web site's needs, you can use tools such as CGI, JavaScript, and PHP. CGI is a way for the web server to call external programs instead of simply returning a static document. Chapter 12 through Chapter 15, *Web Server Programming with mod_perl*, are intended for CGI programmers using the Perl programming language. JavaScript and PHP are both programming languages embedded directly into HTML documents, but that's where the similarities end: JavaScript is used primarily for client-side scripting, and PHP is used primarily for database access. See Chapter 11, *JavaScript*, and Chapter 16, *PHP*.

The HTTP Protocol

In between clients and servers is the network, which uses TCP (Transmission Control Protocol) and IP (Internet Protocol) to transmit data and find servers and clients. On top of TCP/IP, clients and servers use the HTTP protocol to communicate. Chapter 17, *HTTP*, gives details on the HTTP protocol, which you must understand for writing CGI programs, server scripts, web administration, and just about any other part of working with a server.

Web Server

The runaway leader among Unix-based web servers is Apache. Chapter 18, *Apache Configuration*, deals with configuring Apache, while Chapter 19, *Apache Modules*, discusses the various Apache modules. Regardless of the type of server you're running, there are various measures you can take to maximize its efficiency. Chapter 20, *Server Performance*, describes a number of these server optimization techniques.

Who Are the Webmasters?

So if that's the Web in a nutshell, who are the webmasters? The title "webmaster" vaguely means a person who works on the content end of the web. When you examine what webmasters actually do, there are many different definitions.

On a typical web site, the responsibilities can be broken into four general groups:

- *Content providers* work on the data itself—creating or editing HTML documents, incorporating images and forms, and maintaining the integrity of the links.
- *Designers* create the images and also define the "look" of the site.
- *Programmers* write CGI, Java, JavaScript, and other programs for incorporation into the web site.
- *Administrators* make sure that the server is running properly and efficiently at all times. They might also be responsible for establishing new content development areas, writing new scripts, and maintaining the security of sensitive documents and of the site in general.

On a large site, you might have a staff of 50 content providers, a group of five designers, three or four programmers, and two administrators. On a small site, one person might do it all herself.

Each of these people might justifiably call themselves "webmasters." And while a programmer may not be especially interested in HTML syntax or server configuration, and someone who works only in HTML markup may not need to know anything about HTTP, this book should be useful to all.

Recommended Books

This is a reference book for looking up things you already know. But what if you don't already know it?

Much of the material in this book is adapted from other books already published by O'Reilly & Associates, or very near publication. At the risk of blatant self-promotion, we really do recommend these books:

- Web content providers will find *HTML: The Definitive Guide*, written by Chuck Musciano and Bill Kennedy, to be an essential reference. *Dynamic HTML: The Definitive Guide* by Danny Goodman contains just about everything you need to know to create dynamic web content.
- Designers who are getting started on the Web will find the basics of creating graphics and simple web pages in *Web Design in a Nutshell*, by Jennifer Niederst.
- Programmers on web sites should flock to *CGI Programming with Perl* by Scott Guelich, Shishir Gundavaram and Gunther Birznieks; *Perl in a Nutshell* by Ellen Siever, Stephen Spainhour, and Nathan Patwardhan; as well as two books by David Flanagan: *Java in a Nutshell* and *JavaScript: The Definitive*

Guide. For a Perl tutorial, we recommend *Learning Perl* by Randal Schwartz; for more complete Perl documentation, we recommend the classic "Camel" book, *Programming Perl*, by Larry Wall, Tom Christiansen, and Randal L. Schwartz. Programmers at Apache sites should also check out *Writing Apache Modules with Perl and C* by Lincoln Stein and Doug MacEachern.

- Web-site administrators might also consider the following references for their shelves: *Apache: The Definitive Guide* by Ben Laurie and Peter Laurie, *Web Security and Commerce* by Simson Garfinkel (with Gene Spafford), and *Web Performance Tuning* by Patrick Killelea.

PART I

HTML

CHAPTER 2

HTML Overview

Hypertext Markup Language (HTML) is the language that encodes World Wide Web documents. It is a document-layout and hyperlink-specification language that defines the syntax and placement of special, embedded directions that aren't displayed by a web browser but tell it how to display the contents of the document, including text, images, and other supported media. The language also tells you how to make a document interactive through special hypertext links, which connect your document with other documents on your local system, the World Wide Web, and other Internet resources such as FTP and Gopher.

The basic syntax and semantics of HTML are defined in the HTML standard. The HTML standard and all other web-related standards issues are developed under the authority of the World Wide Web Consortium (W3C). Standards specifications and drafts of new proposals can be found at *http://www.w3.org*.

The latest HTML specification approved by the W3C is HTML 4.0. The most popular browsers have implemented the new standard almost fully in their latest releases. Although some support is still buggy, very few features of the specification remain unsupported. Nonstandard extensions still exist, however, creating a few areas of incompatibility between browser platforms.

This section of the book summarizes the current state of HTML in seven chapters, as listed below. For more information on HTML, we recommend O'Reilly's *HTML: The Definitive Guide, 3rd Edition*, by Chuck Musciano and Bill Kennedy.

- The current chapter introduces you to the background and general syntax of HTML.
- Chapter 3, *HTML Reference*, describes the syntax of HTML tags and documents with descriptions of all the HTML tags in current use.
- For authors who want to use frames in HTML, Chapter 4, *Frames*, covers the frame tags in more detail and shows examples of using them.

- For authors using tables, Chapter 5, *Tables*, covers the table tags in more detail.
- Chapter 6, *Forms*, covers the form tags and shows examples of how to use them.
- Chapter 7, *Character Entities*, lists common character entities recognized in HTML documents.
- Chapter 8, *Color Names and Values*, contains listings of valid color values (for tags with attributes for specifying color).

HTML Document Structure

An HTML document consists of text, which comprises the content of the document, and tags, which define the structure and appearance of the document. The structure of an HTML document is simple, consisting of an outer <html> tag enclosing the document header and body:

```
<html>
<head>
<title>Barebones HTML Document</title>
</head>
<body>
<p>
This illustrates in a very <i>simple</i> way,
the basic structure of an HTML document.
</p>
</body>
</html>
```

Each document has a *head* and a *body*, delimited by the <head> and <body> tags. The head is where you give your HTML document a title and where you indicate other parameters the browser may use when displaying the document. The body is where you put the actual contents of the HTML document. This includes the text for display and document control markers (tags) that advise the browser how to display the text. Tags also reference special-effects files like graphics and sound, and indicate the hot spots (*hyperlinks* or *anchors*) that link your document to other documents.

HTML Syntax

For the most part, HTML document elements are simple to understand and use. Every HTML element consists of a tag *name*, sometimes followed by an optional list of *attributes*, all placed between opening and closing brackets (< and >). The simplest elements are nothing more than the tag name enclosed in brackets, such as <head> and <i>. More complicated tags have attributes, which may have specific values defined by the author to modify the behavior of an element.

Attributes belong after the tag name, each separated by one or more tab, space, or return characters. The order of attributes in a single tag is not important. An attribute's value, if it has one, follows an equal sign after the attribute name. If an attribute's value is a single word or number, you may simply add it after the equal sign. All other values should be enclosed in single or double quotation marks, especially if they contain several words separated by spaces. The length of an attribute's value is limited to 1024 characters. Here are some examples of tags with attributes:


```
<a href="http://www.ora.com/catalog.html">
<ul compact>
<input name=filename size=24 maxlength=80>
<link title="Table of Contents">
```

Tag and attribute names are not case-sensitive, but attribute values can be. For example, it is especially important to use the proper capitalization when referencing the URLs of other documents with the `href` attribute.

Most HTML elements consist of start and end tags that enclose text and other parts of a document. An end tag is the same as a start tag except it has a forward slash (/) before the tag name. End tags never contain attributes. For example, to italicize text, you enclose it within the `<i>` tags:

```
<i>This text in italics.</i>
```

You should take care when nesting elements in a document. You must end nested elements starting with the most recent one and work your way back out. In this example, a phrase in bold (`<b>`) appears in the text of a link (`<a href=...>`) contained in some body text:

```
<body>
This is some text in the body, with a
<a href="another_doc.html">link, a portion of which
is <b>set in bold</b></a>
</body>
```

There are a handful of HTML elements that do not have end tags because they are standalone elements. For example, the image element (`<img>`) inserts a single graphic into a document and does not require an end tag. Other standalone elements include the line break (`<br>`), horizontal rule (`<hr>`), and others that provide information about a document that doesn't affect its displayed content such as `<meta>` and `<base>`.

JavaScript Event Handlers

One of the most important features provided by JavaScript is the ability to detect and react to events that occur while a document is loaded, rendered, and used. The JavaScript code that handles these events may be placed within the `<script>` tag, but more commonly, it is associated with a specific tag via one or more special tag attributes.

For example, you might want to invoke a JavaScript function when the user passes the mouse over a hyperlink in a document. The JavaScript-aware browsers support a special "mouse over" event-handler attribute for the `<a>` tag called `onMouseOver` to do just that:

```
<a href=doc.html onMouseOver="document.status='Click me!'; return true">
```

When the mouse passes over this example link, the browser executes the JavaScript statements. (Notice that the two JavaScript statements are enclosed in quotes and separated by a semicolon, and that single quotes surround the text-message portion of the first statement.)

While a complete explanation of this code is beyond our scope, the net result is that the browser places the message "Click me!" in the status bar of the browser window. Commonly, HTML authors use this simple JavaScript function to display a more descriptive explanation of a hyperlink, in place of the often cryptic URL the browser traditionally displays in the status window.

HTML supports a rich set of event handlers through related "on" event tag attributes. The value of any of the JavaScript event handler attributes is a quoted string containing one or more JavaScript statements separated by semicolons. Extremely long statements can be broken across several lines, if needed. Care should also be taken when using entities for embedded double quotes in the statements, to avoid a syntax error when processing the attribute value.

Standard Event Handler Attributes

Table 2-1 presents the current set of event handlers as tag attributes. Most are supported by the popular browsers. Browsers also support a variety of nonstandard event handlers as well; these are tagged with asterisks in the table.

Table 2-1: Event Handlers

Event Handler	*HTML Tags*
onAbort	<img>*
onBlur	<a>
	<area>
	<body>*
	<button>
	<frameset>*
	<input>
	<label>
	<select>
	<textarea>
onChange	<input>
	<select>
	<textarea>
onClick	Most tags
onDblClick	Most tags
onError*	<img>
onFocus	<a>
	<area>
	<body>*
	<button>
	<frameset>*

Table 2-1: Event Handlers (continued)

Event Handler	*HTML Tags*
	<input>
	<label>
	<select>
	<textarea>
onKeyDown	Most tags
onKeyPress	Most tags
onKeyUp	Most tags
onLoad	<body>
	<frameset>
	<img>*
onMouseDown	Most tags
onMouseMove	Most tags
onMouseOut	Most tags
onMouseOver	Most tags
onMouseUp	Most tags
onReset	<form>
onSelect	<input>
	<textarea>
onSubmit	<form>
onUnload	<body>
	<frameset>

We put the event handlers into two categories: user- and document-related. The user-related ones are the mouse and keyboard events that occur when the user handles either device on the computer. User-related events are quite ubiquitous, appearing as standard attributes in nearly all the HTML tags (even though they may not yet be supported by any browser), so we don't list their associated tags in Table 2-1. Instead, here are the HTML 4.0 standard tags that do not accept these event attributes:

```
<applet>    <font>      <iframe>    <style>
<base>      <frame>     <isindex>   <title>
<basefont>  <frameset>  <meta>
<bdo>       <head>      <param>
<br>        <html>      <script>
```

Some events, however, occur rarely, and they have special tags. These relate to the special events and states that occur during the display and management of an HTML document and its elements by the browser.

Mouse-Related Events

The onClick, onDblClick, onMouseDown, and onMouseUp attributes refer to the mouse button. The onClick event happens when the user presses down and then quickly releases the mouse button, unless the user quickly clicks the mouse button a second time. In the latter case, the onDblClick event gets triggered in the browser.

If you need to detect both halves of a mouse click as separate events, use onMouseDown and onMouseUp. When the user presses the mouse button, the onMouseDown event occurs. The onMouseUp event happens when the user releases the mouse button.

The onMouseMove, onMouseOut, and onMouseOver events happen when the user drags the mouse pointer. The onMouseOver event occurs when the mouse first enters the display region occupied by the associated HTML element. After entry, onMouseMove events are generated as the mouse moves about within the element. Finally, when the mouse exits the element, onMouseOut occurs.

For some elements, the onFocus event corresponds to onMouseOver, and onBlur corresponds to onMouseOut.

Keyboard Events

Only three events currently are supported by the HTML 4.0 standard relating to user keyboard actions: onKeyDown, onKeyPress, and onKeyUp. The onKeyDown event occurs when the user depresses a key on the keyboard; onKeyUp happens when the key is released. The onKeyPress attribute is triggered when a key is pressed and released. Usually, you'll have handlers for either the up and down events or the composite keypress event, but not for both.

Document Events

Most of the document-related event handlers relate to the actions and states of HTML form controls. For instance, onReset and onSubmit happen when the user activates the respective reset or submit button. Similarly, onSelect and onChange occur as users interact with certain form elements. Please consult Chapter 6 for a detailed discussion of these HTML forms-related events.

There also are some document-related event handlers that occur when various document elements get handled by the browser. For instance, the onLoad event may happen when a frameset is complete or when the body of an HTML document gets loaded and displayed by the browser. Similarly, onUnload occurs when a document is removed from a frame or window.

JavaScript URLs

You can replace any conventional URL reference in a document with one or more JavaScript statements. The browser then executes the JavaScript code, rather than downloading another document, whenever the browser references the URL. The result of the last statement is taken to be the "document" referenced by the URL and is displayed by the browser accordingly. The result of the last statement is not the URL of a document; it is the actual content to be displayed by the browser.

To create a JavaScript URL, use `javascript` as the URL's protocol:

```
<a href="javascript:generate_document()">
```

In the example, the JavaScript function *generate_document()* gets executed whenever the hyperlink gets selected by the user. The value returned by the function, presumably a valid HTML document, is rendered and displayed by the browser.

It may be that the executed statement returns no value. In these cases, the current document is left unchanged. For example, this JavaScript URL:

```
<a href="javascript:alert('Error!')">
```

pops up an alert dialog box, and does nothing else. The document containing the hyperlink would still be visible after the dialog box gets displayed and is dismissed by the user.

See Chapter 11, *JavaScript*, for a complete reference on JavaScript.

CHAPTER 3

HTML Reference

This section lists the known HTML tags and attributes currently available for use in web documents. There are many different browsers out there, and they do not all support the same set of tags.

Most up-to-date browsers implement nearly all of HTML 4.0. However, there are still some browser-specific tags and attributes that are not contained in the standard. The tag descriptions in this chapter use icons to indicate if an element is supported by either browser with respect to the standard (i.e., tags not contained in the standard but supported by both browsers will indicate as such). The two most popular browsers are considered here: Netscape Navigator, currently at Version 4.0 (N), and Microsoft's Internet Explorer, Version 4.0 (I).

Core Attributes

Prior to HTML 4.0, there were few attributes that could be used consistently for all HTML tags. HTML 4.0 changes this, defining a set of 16 core attributes that can be applied to almost all the tags in the language. For brevity, we list these core attributes in this section and spare you the redundancies in the table that follows:

`class=`*name*
: Specify a style class controlling the appearance of the tag's contents.

`dir=`*dir*
: Specify the rendering direction for text, either left to right (`ltr`) or right to left (`rtl`).

`id=`*name*
: Define a reference name for the tag that is unique in the document.

`lang=`*language*
: Specify the human language for the tag's contents with an ISO639 standard two-character name and optional dialect subcode.

`onclick=`*applet*

Specify an applet to be executed when the user clicks the mouse on the tag's contents display area.

`ondblclick=`*applet*

Specify an applet to be executed when the user double-clicks the mouse button on the tag's contents display area.

`onkeydown=`*applet*

Specify an applet to be executed when the user presses down on a key while the tag's contents have input focus.

`onkeypress=`*applet*

Specify an applet to be executed when the user presses and releases a key while the tag's contents have input focus.

`onkeyup=`*applet*

Specify an applet to be executed when the user releases a pressed key while the tag's contents have input focus.

`onmousedown=`*applet*

Specify an applet to be executed when the user presses down on the mouse button when pointing to the tag's contents display area.

`onmousemove=`*applet*

Specify an applet to be executed when the user moves the mouse in the tag's contents display area.

`onmouseout=`*applet*

Specify an applet to be executed when the user moves the mouse off the tag's contents display area.

`onmouseover=`*applet*

Specify an applet to be executed when the user moves the mouse into the tag's contents display area.

`onmouseup=`*applet*

Specify an applet to be executed when the user releases the mouse button when in the tag's contents display area.

`style=`*style*

Specify an inline style for the tag.

`title=`*string*

Specify a title for the tag.

A small handful of tags do not accept all of these attributes. They are:

`<applet>`	`<embed>`	`<html>`	`<marquee>`	`<script>`
`<base>`	`<font>`	`<iframe>`	`<meta>`	`<server>`
`<basefont>`	`<frame>`	`<ilayer>`	`<multicol>`	`<spacer>`
`<bdo>`	`<frameset>`	`<isindex>`	`<nobr>`	`<style>`
` `	`<head>`	`<keygen>`	`<noembed>`	`<title>`
`<comment>`	`<hr>`	`<layer>`	`<param>`	`<wbr>`

In the reference section, we list all the attributes supported by these special tags, including the common ones. For all other tags, assume the common attributes in the preceding list apply. Note, however, that the popular browsers do not support all the HTML standard 4.0 attributes, common or not.

HTML Tag and Attribute Descriptions

<a>

<a> . . . </a>

Create a hyperlink (`href` attribute) or fragment identifier (`name` attribute) within a document.

Attributes

`accesskey=`*char*
Define the hot-key character for this anchor.

`charset=`*encoding*
Specify the character set used to encode the target.

`coords=`*list*
Specify a list of shape-dependent coordinates.

`href=`*url*
Specify the URL of a hyperlink target (required if not a name anchor).

`hreflang=`*language*
Specify the language encoding for the target.

`name=`*string*
Specify the name of a fragment identifier (required if not a hypertext reference anchor).

`rel=`*relationship*
Indicate the relationship from this document to the target.

`rev=`*relationship*
Indicate the reverse relationship of the target to this document.

`shape=`*shape*
Define the region's shape to be `circ`, `circle`, `poly`, `polygon`, `rect`, or `rectangle`.

`tabindex=`*value*
Define the position of this anchor in the document's tabbing order.

`target=`*name*
Define the name of the frame or window to receive the referenced document.

`type=`*type*
Specify the MIME type of the target.

Example

To create an anchor named `info` at some point in a document called *doc.html*, use the <a> tag with the `name` attribute:

→

```
<a name="info">Information</a>
```

To provide a hyperlink to that point in *doc.html*, use the <a> tag with the href attribute appending the anchor name to the filename using a hash mark (#):

```
<a href="doc.html#info">Link to information</a>
```

<abbr>

<abbr> . . . </abbr>

The enclosed text is an abbreviation.

<acronym>

<acronym> . . . </acronym>

The enclosed text is an acronym.

<address>

<address> . . . </address>

The enclosed text is an address.

<applet>

<applet> . . . </applet>

Define an executable applet within a text flow.

Attributes

align=*position*
: Align the <applet> region to either the top, middle, bottom (default), left, right, absmiddle, baseline, or absbottom of the text in the line.

alt=*string*
: Specify alternative text to replace the <applet> region within browsers that support the <applet> tag but cannot execute the application.

archive=*url*
: Specify a class archive to be downloaded to the browser and then searched for code class.

class=*name*
: Specify a style class controlling the appearance of the tag.

code=*class*
: Specify the class name of the code to be executed (required).

codebase=*url*
: URL from which the code is retrieved.

→

height=*n*
: Specify the height, in pixels, of the <applet> region.

hspace=*n*
: Specify additional space, in pixels, to the left and right of the <applet> region.

id=*name*
: Define a name for this applet that is unique to this document.

mayscript
: N If present, allows the applet to access JavaScript within the page.

name=*string*
: Specify the name of this particular instance of the <applet>.

object=*data*
: Specify a representation of the object's execution state.

style=*style*
: Specify an inline style for this tag.

title=*string*
: Provide a title for the applet.

vspace=*n*
: Specify additional space, in pixels, above and below the <applet> region.

width=*n*
: Specify the width, in pixels, of the <applet> region.

<area>

```
<area>
```

Define a mouse-sensitive area in a client-side image map.

Attributes

accesskey=*char*
: Define the hot-key character for this area.

alt=*string*
: Provide alternative text to be displayed by nongraphical browsers.

coords=*list*
: Specify a comma-separated list of shape-dependent coordinates that define the edge of this area.

href=*url*
: Specify the URL of a hyperlink target associated with this area.

nohref
: Indicate that no document is associated with this area; clicking in the area has no effect.

notab
: This area should not be included in the tabbing order.

→

onblur=*applet*
Specify an applet to be run when the mouse leaves the area.

onfocus=*applet*
Specify an applet to be run when the mouse enters the area.

shape=*shape*
Define the region's shape to be either circ, circle, poly, polygon, rect, or rectangle.

tabindex=*value*
Define the position of this area in the document's tabbing order.

taborder=*n*
Specify this area's position in the tabbing order.

target=*name*
Specify the frame or window to receive the document linked by this area.

<b>

<b> . . . </b>

Format the enclosed text using a **bold** typeface.

<base>

<base>

Specify the base URL for all relative URLs in this document.

Attributes

href=*url*
Specify the base URL.

target=*name*
Define the default target window of all <a> links in the document (mostly used for redirecting a link to other frames). There are four special values _blank, _parent, _self, and _top. These values are described in Chapter 4, *Frames*.

<basefont>

<basefont>

Specify the font size for subsequent text.

Attributes

color=*color*
Specify the base font's color.

face=*name*
Specify the local font to be used for the base font.

→

`id=`*name*
: Define a name for this tag that is unique to this document.

`name=`*name*
: ⓘ Specify the local font to be used for the base font.

`size=`*value*
: Set the basefont size from 1 to 7 (required; default is 3).

<bdo>

`<bdo> . . . </bdo>`

Bidirectional override; changes the rendering direction of the enclosed text.

Attributes

`class=`*name*
: Specify a class style controlling the appearance of this tag.

`dir=`*direction*
: Specify the rendering direction for text, either left to right (`ltr`) or right to left (`rtl`).

`id=`*name*
: Define a name for this tag that is unique to this document.

`lang=`*language*
: Specify the language used for this tag's contents using a standard two-character ISO language name.

`style=`*style*
: Specify an inline style for this tag.

`title=`*string*
: Specify a title for this tag.

<bgsound>

`<bgsound>`

ⓘ Define background audio for the document.

Attributes

`loop=`*value*
: Set the number of times to play the audio; *value* may be an integer or the value `infinite`.

`src=`*url*
: Provide the URL of the audio file to be played.

<big>

`<big> . . . </big>`

Format the enclosed text using a bigger typeface.

<blink>

`<blink> . . . </blink>`

Cause the enclosed text to blink.

<blockquote>

`<blockquote> . . . </blockquote>`

The enclosed text is a block quotation.

Attributes

`cite=`*url*
Specify the source URL of the quoted material.

<body>

`<body> . . . </body>`

Delimit the beginning and end of the document body.

Attributes

`alink=`*color*
Set the color of active hypertext links in the document.

`background=`*url*
Specify the URL of an image to be tiled in the document background.

`bgcolor=`*color*
Set the background color of the document.

`bgproperties=`*value*
When set to `fixed`, prevent the background image from scrolling with the document content.

`leftmargin=`*value*
Set the size, in pixels, of the document's left margin.

`link=`*color*
Set the color of unvisited hypertext links in the document.

`onblur=`*applet*
Specify an applet to be run when the mouse leaves the document window.

`onfocus=`*applet*
Specify an applet to be run when the mouse enters the document window.

`onload=`*applet*
Specify an applet to be run when the document is loaded.

→

`onunload=`*applet*

N O Specify an applet to be run when the document is unloaded.

`text=`*color*

Set the color of regular text in the document.

`topmargin=`*value*

O Set the size, in pixels, of the document's top margin.

`vlink=`*color*

Set the color of visited links in the document.

`<br>`

Break the current text flow, resuming at the beginning of the next line.

Attributes

`class=`*name*

Specify a style class controlling the appearance of this tag.

`clear=`*margin*

Break the flow and move downward until the desired margin, either `left`, `right`, or `all`, is clear.

`id=`*name*

Define a name for this tag that is unique to this document.

`style=`*style*

Specify an inline style for this tag.

`title=`*string*

Specify a title for this tag.

<button>

`<button>`

Create a push-button element within a `<form>`.

Attributes

`accesskey=`*char*

Define the hot-key character for this button.

`disabled`

Disable the button, preventing the user from clicking it.

`name=`*name*

Specify the name of the parameter to be passed to the form-processing application if the input element is selected (required).

`onblur=`*applet*

Specify an applet to be run when the mouse moves out of the button.

→

onfocus=*applet*
: Specify an applet to be run when the mouse moves into the button.

type=*type*
: Specify the button type, either button, submit, or reset.

tabindex=*n*
: Specify this element's position in the tabbing order.

value=*string*
: Specify the value of the parameter sent to the form-processing application if this form element is selected (required).

<caption>

<caption> . . . </caption>

Define a caption for a table.

Attributes

align=*position*
: N I For Netscape, set the vertical position of the caption to either top or bottom. Default is top, centered. For Internet Explorer, set the horizontal alignment of the caption to either left, center, or right, or the vertical position to top or bottom. The default is top, centered. You cannot set both the horizontal and vertical position with this attribute alone.

valign=*position*
: I Set the vertical position of the caption to either top or bottom. Default is top. Use this with a horizontal specification to align to set both vertical and horizontal caption positions.

See Chapter 5, *Tables*, for more information on using tables.

<center>

<center> . . . </center>

Center the enclosed text.

<cite>

<cite> . . . </cite>

The enclosed text is a citation.

<code>

<code> . . . </code>

The enclosed text is a code sample.

<col>

`<col>`

Set properties for a column (or columns) within a `<colgroup>` of a table.

Attributes

`align=`*value*
: Specify alignment of text in the cells of a column. Value can be `center`, `left`, or `right`.

`char=`*character*
: Specify the alignment character for text in these cells.

`charoff=`*value*
: Set the offset within the cell at which the alignment character will be placed.

`span=`*n*
: Specify the number of columns to be affected by the `<col>` settings.

`valign=`*position*
: Set the vertical alignment of text within the column to either `top`, `middle`, or `bottom`.

`width=`*n*
: Set the width of the column, in pixels or as a percentage.

<colgroup>

`<colgroup>`

Set properties for designated column or columns within a table. Also indicates where vertical rules will be drawn when `rules=`*groups* is set in the `<table>` tag.

Attributes

`align=`*value*
: Specify alignment of text in the cells of columns in the `<colgroup>`. Values can be `center`, `left`, or `right`.

`char=`*character*
: Specify the alignment character for text in these cells.

`charoff=`*value*
: Set the offset within the cell at which the alignment character will be placed.

`span=`*n*
: Specify the number of columns in the `<colgroup>`.

`valign=`*position*
: Set the vertical alignment of text within the columns to either `top`, `middle`, or `bottom`.

→

`width=`*n*
Set the width, in pixels or as a percentage, of each column in the group.

<comment>

`<comment> . . . </comment>`

◐ Place a comment in the document. Comments will be visible in all other browsers. Comments can be placed within `<!--` *comment text* `-->` for all browsers.

<dd>

`<dd> . . . </dd>`

Define the definition portion of an element in a definition list.

<del>

`<del> . . . </del>`

Delineate a deleted section of a document.

Attributes

`cite=`*url*
Cite a document justifying the deletion.

`datetime=`*date*
Specify the date and time of the deletion.

<dfn>

`<dfn> . . . </dfn>`

Format the enclosed text as a definition.

<dir>

`<dir> . . . </dir>`

Create a directory list containing `<li>` tags.

Attributes

`compact`
Make the list more compact if possible.

`type=`*bullet*
N ◐ Set the bullet style for this list to either `circle`, `disc` (default), or `square`.

<div>

```
<div> . . . </div>
```

Create a division within a document.

Attributes

`align=`*type*
: Align the text within the division to `left`, `center`, or `right`.

`nowrap`
: Ⓘ Suppress word wrapping within this division.

<dl>

```
<dl> . . . </dl>
```

Create a definition list containing `<dt>` and `<dd>` tags.

Attributes

`compact`
: Make the list more compact if possible.

<dt>

```
<dt> . . . </dt>
```

Define the definition term portion of an element in a definition list.

<em>

```
<em> . . . </em>
```

Format the enclosed text with additional emphasis.

<embed>

```
<embed> . . . </embed>
```

Embed an application into the document.

Attributes

`align=`*position*
: Ⓝ Align the applet area to either the `top` or `bottom` of the adjacent text, or to the `left` or `right` margin of the page, with subsequent text flowing around the applet.

`border=`*n*
: Ⓝ Specify the size, in pixels, of the border around the applet.

→

height=*n*
Specify the height of the area the embedded object will occupy.

hidden
N I If present, hide the applet on the page.

hspace=*n*
N Define, in pixels, additional space to be placed to the left and right of the applet.

name=*name*
N I Provide a name for the applet.

palette=*value*
N I In Netscape, a value of **foreground** causes the applet to use the foreground palette in Windows only; **background** uses the background palette. In Internet Explorer, provides the foreground and background colors for the applet, specified as two color values separated by a vertical bar (|).

pluginspage=*url*
N Provide the URL of the page containing instructions for installing the plug-in associated with the applet.

src=*url*
N I Supplies the URL of the data to be fed to the applet.

type=*type*
N Specify the MIME type of the plug-in to be used.

units=*type*
N I Set the units for the height and width attributes to either **pixels** (the default) or **en** (half the text point size).

vspace=*n*
N Define, in pixels, additional space to be placed above and below the applet.

width=*n*
N I Specify the width, in pixels, of the applet.

<fieldset>

<fieldset> . . . </fieldset>

Create a group of elements in a form.

<font>

<font> . . . </font>

Set the size, color, or typeface of the enclosed text.

Attributes

class=*name*
Specify a style class controlling the appearance of this tag.

→

`color=`*color*
: Set the color of the enclosed text.

`dir=`*dir*
: Specify the rendering direction for text, either left to right (`ltr`) or right to left (`rtl`).

`face=`*list*
: Set the typeface of the enclosed text to the first available font in the comma-separated list of font names.

`id=`*name*
: Define a name for this tag that is unique to this document.

`lang=`*language*
: Specify the language used for this tag's contents using a standard two-character ISO language name.

`size=`*value*
: Set the size to an absolute value (1 to 7), or relative to the `<basefont>` size using `+n` or `-n`.

`style=`*style*
: Specify an inline style for this tag.

`title=`*string*
: Specify a title for this tag.

<form>

`<form> . . . </form>`

Delimit a form.

Attributes

`accept-charset=`*list*
: Specify a list of character sets accepted by the server processing this form.

`action=`*url*
: Specify the URL of the application that will process the form. The default is the current URL.

`enctype=`*encoding*
: Specify how the form element values will be encoded.

`method=`*style*
: Specify the parameter-passing style, either `get` or `post`. The default is `get`.

`name=`*name*
: [N] Supply a name for this form for use by JavaScript.

`onreset=`*applet*
: Specify an applet to be run when the form is reset.

→

onsubmit=*applet*
Specify an applet to be run when the form is submitted.

target=*name*
Specify the name of a frame or a window to receive the results of the form after submission.

HTML

<frame>

<frame> . . . </frame>

Define a frame within a frameset.

Attributes

bordercolor=*color*
N Set the color of the frame's border to *color*.

class=*name*
Specify a style class controlling the appearance of this tag.

frameborder=*value*
If *value* is yes (Netscape only) or 1 (Netscape and Internet Explorer), enable frame borders. If *value* is no (Netscape only) or 0 (Netscape and Internet Explorer), disable frame borders.

id=*name*
Define a name for this tag that is unique in the document.

longdesc=*url*
Provide the URL of a document describing the contents of this frame.

marginheight=*n*
Place *n* pixels of space above and below the frame contents.

marginwidth=*n*
Place *n* pixels of space to the left and right of the frame contents.

name=*string*
Define the name of the frame.

noresize
Disable user resizing of the frame.

scrolling=*type*
Always add scrollbars (yes), never add scrollbars (no), or add scrollbars when needed (auto).

src=*url*
Define the URL of the source document for this frame.

style=*style*
Specify an inline style for this tag.

title=*string*
Specify a title for this tag.

See Chapter 4 for more information on using frames.

<frameset>

`<frameset> . . . </frameset>`

Define a collection of frames or other framesets.

Attributes

`border=`*n*
: Set size in pixels of frame borders within a frameset. Default border width is five pixels.

`bordercolor=`*color*
: Set the color for frame borders in a frameset.

`cols=`*list*
: Specify the number and width of frames within a frameset.

`frameborder=[yes|no]`
: Enable or disable the displaying of 3D borders or regular borders for frames. The default is `yes` (3D borders).

`frameborder=[1|0]`
: Enable or disable the displaying of 3D borders for frames within a frameset. The default is `1` (borders on).

`framespacing=`*n*
: Add additional space between adjacent frames in pixels.

`onblur=`*applet*
: Specify an applet to be run when the mouse leaves this frameset.

`onfocus=`*applet*
: Specify an applet to be run when the mouse enters this frameset.

`onload=`*applet*
: Specify an applet to be run when this frameset is loaded.

`onunload=`*applet*
: Specify an applet to be run when this frameset is unloaded.

`rows=`*list*
: Specify the number and height of frames within a frameset.

See Chapter 4 for more information on using frames.

<h*n*>

`<hn> . . . </hn>`

The enclosed text is a level *n* header; for level *n* from 1 to 6.

Attributes

`align=`*type*
: Specify the heading alignment as either `left` (default), `center`, or `right`.

<head>

<head> . . . </head>

Delimit the beginning and end of the document head.

Attributes

dir=*dir*
: Specify the rendering direction for text, either left to right (ltr) or right to left (rtl).

lang=*language*
: Specify the language used for this tag's contents using a standard two-character ISO language name.

profile=*url*
: Provide the URL of a profile for this document.

<hr>

<hr>

Break the current text flow and insert a horizontal rule.

Attributes

align=*type*
: Specify the rule alignment as either left, center (default), or right.

class=*name*
: Specify a style class controlling the appearance of the rule.

color=*color*
: Define the color of the rule.

id=*name*
: Define a name for this tag that is unique to this document.

noshade
: Do not use 3D shading to render the rule.

onclick=*applet*
: Specify an applet to be executed when the mouse button is clicked on this tag.

ondblclick=*applet*
: Specify an applet to be executed when the mouse button is double-clicked on this tag.

onkeydown=*applet*
: Specify an applet to be executed when a key is pressed down while this tag has input focus.

onkeypress=*applet*
: Specify an applet to be executed when a key is pressed and released while this tag has input focus.

→

`onkeyup=`*applet*
: Specify an applet to be executed when a key is released while this tag has input focus.

`onmousedown=`*applet*
: Specify an applet to be executed when a mouse button is pressed down on this tag.

`onmousemove=`*applet*
: Specify an applet to be executed when the mouse is moved over this tag.

`onmouseout=`*applet*
: Specify an applet to be executed when the mouse moves out of this tag's display area.

`onmouseover=`*applet*
: Specify an applet to be executed when the mouse moves into this tag's display area.

`onmouseup=`*applet*
: Specify an applet to be executed when a mouse button is released while over this tag.

`size=`*pixels*
: Set the thickness of the rule to an integer number of pixels.

`style=`*style*
: Specify an inline style for this tag.

`title=`*string*
: Specify a title for this tag.

`width=`*value*
: Set the width of the rule to either an integer number of pixels or a percentage of the page width.

<html>

```
<html> . . . </html>
```

Delimit the beginning and end of the entire HTML document.

Attributes

`dir=`*dir*
: Specify the rendering direction for text, either left to right (`ltr`) or right to left (`rtl`).

`lang=`*language*
: Specify the language used for this tag's contents using a standard two-character ISO language name.

`version=`*string*
: Indicate the HTML version used to create this document.

<i>

```
<i> . . . </i>
```

Format the enclosed text in an *italic* typeface.

<iframe>

```
<iframe> . . . </iframe>
```

Define an inline frame.

Attributes

`align=`*type*
Align the floating frame to either the `top`, `middle`, `bottom` (default), `left`, or `right` of the text in the line.

`class=`*name*
Specify a style class controlling the appearance of the frame contents.

`frameborder=[1|0]`
Enable or disable the display of borders for the frame. Default is `1`, which inserts the border. The value `0` turns the border off.

`height=`*n*
Specify the height of the frame in pixels or as a percentage of the window size.

`id=`*name*
Define a name for this tag that is unique to this document.

`longdesc=`*url*
Provide the URL of a document describing the contents of the frame.

`marginheight=`*n*
Place *n* pixels of space above and below the frame contents.

`marginwidth=`*n*
Place *n* pixels of space to the left and right of the frame contents.

`name=`*string*
Define the name of the frame.

`scrolling=`*type*
Always add scrollbars (`yes`), never add scrollbars (`no`), or add scrollbars when needed (`auto`).

`src=`*url*
Define the URL of the source document for this frame.

`style=`*style*
Specify an inline style for this tag.

`title=`*string*
Specify a title for this tag.

→

`width=`*n*
: Specify the width of the frame in pixels.

See Chapter 4 for more information on using frames.

<ilayer>

`<ilayer> . . . </ilayer>`

[N] Define an inline layer.

Attributes

`above=`*name*
Place this layer above the named layer.

`background=`*url*
Specify a background image for the layer.

`below=`*name*
Place this layer below the named layer.

`bgcolor=`*color*
Specify the background color for the layer.

`class=`*name*
Specify a style class controlling the appearance of this tag.

`left=`*n*
Define, in pixels, the position of the layer's left edge from the containing line of text.

`name=`*name*
Provide a name for the layer.

`src=`*url*
Supply the content of the layer from another document.

`style=`*style*
Specify an inline style for this tag.

`top=`*n*
Define, in pixels, the position of the layer's top edge from the containing line of text.

`visibility=`*value*
Determine whether to `show` the layer, `hide` the layer, or `inherit` the visibility attribute from a containing layer.

`width=`*n*
Define the width, in pixels, of the layer.

`z-index=`*n*
Specify the layer's position in the stacking order.

<img>

`<img>`

Insert an image into the current text flow.

Attributes

`align=`*type*
: Align the image to either the `top`, `middle`, `bottom` (default), `left`, or `right` of the text in the line. For Netscape Navigator, additionally align to the `texttop`, `absmiddle`, `absbottom`, or `baseline` of the text.

`alt=`*text*
: Provide descriptive text for nonimage-capable browsers, tool tips, telephone browsers, and search engines.

`border=`*n*
: Set the pixel thickness of the border around images contained within hyperlinks.

`controls`
: [I] Add playback controls for embedded video clips.

`dynsrc=`*url*
: [I] Specify the URL of a video clip to be displayed.

`height=`*n*
: Specify the height of the image in pixels.

`hspace=`*n*
: Specify the space, in pixels, to be added to the left and right of the image.

`ismap`
: Indicate that the image is mouse-selectable when used within an <a> tag.

`longdesc=`*url*
: Provide the URL of a document describing the image.

`loop=`*value*
: [I] Set the number of times to play the video; *value* may be an integer or the value `infinite`.

`lowsrc=`*url*
: [N] Specify a low-resolution image to be loaded by the browser first, followed by the image specified by the <src> attribute.

`src=`*url*
: Specify the source URL of the image to be displayed (required).

`name=`*name*
: [N] Provide a name for the image for use by JavaScript.

`onabort=`*applet*
: [N] Provide an applet to be run if the loading of the image is aborted.

→

onerror=*applet*

Provide an applet to be run if the loading of the image is unsuccessful.

onload=*applet*

Provide an applet to be run if the loading of the image is successful.

start=*start*

Specify when to play the video clip, either `fileopen` or `mouseover`.

usemap=*url*

Specify the map of coordinates and links that define the hypertext links within this image.

vspace=*n*

Specify the vertical space, in pixels, added at the top and bottom of the image.

width=*n*

Specify the width of the image in pixels.

<input>

<input type=button>

Create a push-button element within a `<form>`.

Attributes

accesskey=*char*

Define the hot-key character for this element.

disabled

Disable this control, making it inactive.

name=*name*

Specify the name of the parameter to be passed to the form-processing application if the input element is selected (required).

notab

Specify that this element is not part of the tabbing order.

onblur=*applet*

Specify an applet to be run when the mouse leaves this control.

onfocus=*applet*

Specify an applet to be run when the mouse enters this control.

tabindex=*n*

Specify this element's position in the tabbing order.

taborder=*n*

Specify this element's position in the tabbing order.

value=*string*

Specify the value of the parameter sent to the form-processing application if the input element is selected (required).

<input>

`<input type=checkbox>`

Create a checkbox input element within a `<form>`.

Attributes

`accesskey=`*char*
: Define the hot-key character for this element.

`checked`
: Mark the element as initially selected.

`disabled`
: Disable this control, making it inactive.

`name=`*string*
: Specify the name of the parameter to be passed to the form-processing application if the input element is selected (required).

`notab`
: Specify that this element is not part of the tabbing order.

`readonly`
: Prevent user modification of this element.

`tabindex=`*n*
: Specify this element's position in the tabbing order.

`taborder=`*n*
: Specify this element's position in the tabbing order.

`value=`*string*
: Specify the value of the parameter sent to the form-processing application if this form element is selected (required).

See Chapter 6, *Forms*, for more information on using forms.

<input>

`<input type=file>`

Create a file-selection element within a `<form>`.

Attributes

`accept=`*list*
: Specify list of MIME types that can be accepted by this element.

`accesskey=`*char*
: Define the hot-key character for this element.

`disabled`
: Disable this control, making it inactive.

`maxlength=`*n*
: Specify the maximum number of characters to accept for this element.

→

`name=`*string*
: Specify the name of the parameter that is passed to the form-processing application for this input element (required).

`notab`
: Specify that this element is not part of the tabbing order.

`onblur=`*applet*
: Specify an applet to be run when the mouse leaves this control.

`onchange=`*applet*
: Specify an applet to be run when the user changes the value of this element.

`onfocus=`*applet*
: Specify an applet to be run when the mouse enters this control.

`readonly`
: Prevent user modification of this element.

`size=`*n*
: Specify the number of characters to display for this element.

`tabindex=`*n*
: Specify this element's position in the tabbing order.

`taborder=`*n*
: Specify this element's position in the tabbing order.

`value=`*string*
: Specify the value of the parameter sent to the form-processing application if this form element is selected (required).

See Chapter 6 for more information on using forms.

<input>

`<input type=hidden>`

Create a hidden element within a `<form>`.

Attributes

`name=`*string*
: Specify the name of the parameter that is passed to the form-processing application for this input element (required).

`value=`*string*
: Specify the value of this element that is passed to the form-processing application.

See Chapter 6 for more information on using forms.

<input>

`<input type=image>`

Create an image input element within a `<form>`.

→

Attributes

accesskey=*char*
: Define the hot-key character for this element.

align=*type*
: Align the image to either the top, middle, or bottom of the form element's text.

alt=*string*
: Provide a text description for the image.

border=*n*
: Set the pixel thickness of the border of the image.

disabled
: Disable this control, making it inactive.

name=*string*
: Specify the name of the parameter to be passed to the form-processing application for this input element (required).

notab
: Ⓘ Specify that this element is not part of the tabbing order.

src=*url*
: Specify the source URL of the image (required).

tabindex=*n*
: Specify this element's position in the tabbing order.

taborder=*n*
: Ⓘ Specify this element's position in the tabbing order.

usemap=*url*
: Specify the URL of a map to be used with this image.

See Chapter 6 for more information on using forms.

<input>

<input type=*password*>

Create a content-protected text-input element within a <form>.

Attributes

accesskey=*char*
: Define the hot-key character for this element.

disabled
: Disable this control, making it inactive.

maxlength=*n*
: Specify the maximum number of characters to accept for this element.

name=*string*
: Specify the name of the parameter to be passed to the form-processing application for this input element (required).

→

`notab`
: ◐ Specify that this element is not part of the tabbing order.

`onblur=`*applet*
: Specify an applet to be run when the mouse leaves this control.

`onchange=`*applet*
: Specify an applet to be run when the user changes the value of this element.

`onfocus=`*applet*
: Specify an applet to be run when the mouse enters this control.

`onselect=`*applet*
: Specify an applet to be run when the user clicks this element.

`readonly`
: Prevent user modification of this element.

`size=`*n*
: Specify the number of characters to display for this element.

`tabindex=`*n*
: Specify this element's position in the tabbing order.

`taborder=`*n*
: ◐ Specify this element's position in the tabbing order.

`value=`*string*
: Specify the initial value for this element.

See Chapter 6 for more information on using forms.

<input>

`<input type=radio>`

Create a radio-button input element within a `<form>`.

Attributes

`accesskey=`*char*
: Define the hot-key character for this element.

`checked`
: Mark the element as initially selected.

`disabled`
: Disable this control, making it inactive.

`name=`*string*
: Specify the name of the parameter that is passed to the form-processing application if this input element is selected (required).

`notab`
: ◐ Specify that this element is not part of the tabbing order.

`readonly`
: Prevent user modification of this element.

→

tabindex=*n*
Specify this element's position in the tabbing order.

taborder=*n*
Ⓘ Specify this element's position in the tabbing order.

value=*string*
Specify the value of the parameter that is passed to the form-processing application if this element is selected (required).

See Chapter 6 for more information on using forms.

<input>

<input type=reset>

Create a reset button within a <form>.

Attributes

accesskey=*char*
Define the hot-key character for this element.

disabled
Disable this control, making it inactive.

notab
Ⓘ Specify that this element is not part of the tabbing order.

readonly
Prevent user modification of this element.

tabindex=*n*
Specify this element's position in the tabbing order.

taborder=*n*
Ⓘ Specify this element's position in the tabbing order.

value=*string*
Specify an alternate label for the reset button.

See Chapter 6 for more information on using forms.

<input>

<input type=submit>

Create a submit button within a <form>.

Attributes

accesskey=*char*
Define the hot-key character for this element.

disabled
Disable this control, making it inactive.

name=*string*
Specify the name of the parameter that is passed to the form-processing application for this input element (required).

→

notab

    ⓘ Specify that this element is not part of the tabbing order.

tabindex=*n*

    Specify this element's position in the tabbing order.

taborder=*n*

    ⓘ Specify this element's position in the tabbing order.

value=*string*

    Specify an alternate label for the submit button, as well as the value passed to the form-processing application for this parameter if this button is clicked.

See Chapter 6 for more information on using forms.

<input>

<input type=text>

Create a text input element within a <form>.

Attributes

accesskey=*char*

    Define the hot-key character for this element.

disabled

    Disable this control, making it inactive.

maxlength=*n*

    Specify the maximum number of characters to accept for this element.

name=*string*

    Specify the name of the parameter that is passed to the form-processing application for this input element (required).

notab

    ⓘ Specify that this element is not part of the tabbing order.

onblur=*applet*

    Specify an applet to be run when the mouse leaves this element.

onchange=*applet*

    Specify an applet to be run when the user changes the value of this element.

onfocus=*applet*

    Specify an applet to be run when the mouse enters this element.

onselect=*applet*

    Specify an applet to be run when the user clicks this element.

readonly

    Prevent user modification of this element.

size=*n*

    Specify the number of characters to display for this element.

→

`tabindex=`*n*

Specify this element's position in the tabbing order.

`taborder=`*n*

Ⓘ Specify this element's position in the tabbing order.

`value=`*string*

Specify the initial value for this element.

See Chapter 6 for more information on using forms.

<ins>

`<ins> . . . </ins>`

Delineate an inserted section of a document.

Attributes

`cite=`*url*

Specify the URL of the document justifying the insertion.

`datetime=`*date*

Specify the date and time of the insertion.

<isindex>

`<isindex>`

Create a "searchable" HTML document.

Attributes

`action=`*url*

Ⓘ Provide the URL of the program that will perform the searching action.

`class=`*name*

Specify a class style controlling the appearance of this tag.

`dir=`*direction*

Specify the rendering direction for text, either left to right (`ltr`) or right to left (`rtl`).

`id=`*name*

Define a name for this tag that is unique to this document.

`lang=`*language*

Specify the language used for this tag's contents using a standard two-character ISO language name.

`prompt=`*string*

Provide an alternate prompt for the input field.

`style=`*style*

Specify an inline style for this tag.

`title=`*string*

Specify a title for this tag.

<kbd>

`<kbd> . . . </kbd>`

The enclosed text is keyboard-like input.

<keygen>

`<keygen> . . . </keygen>`

[N] Generate key information in a form.

Attributes

`challenge=`*string*
: Provide a challenge string to be packaged with the key.

`name=`*name*
: Provide a name for the key.

<label>

`<label> . . . </label>`

Define a label for a form control.

Attributes

`accesskey=`*char*
: Define the hot-key character for this label.

`for=`*name*
: Specify the form element associated with this label.

`onblur=`*applet*
: Specify an applet to be run when the mouse leaves this label.

`onfocus=`*applet*
: Specify an applet to be run when the mouse enters this label.

<layer>

`<layer> . . . </layer>`

[N] Define a layer.

Attributes

`above=`*name*
: Place this layer above the named layer.

`background=`*url*
: Specify a background image for the layer.

`below=`*name*
: Place this layer below the named layer.

→

`bgcolor=`*color*
: Specify the background color for the layer.

`class=`*name*
: Specify a style class controlling the appearance of this tag.

`clip=`*edge*
: Define the layer's clipping region, in pixels. If `left` and `top` are 0, they may be omitted.

`left=`*n*
: Define, in pixels, the position of the layer's left edge from the containing line of text.

`name=`*name*
: Provide a name for the layer.

`src=`*url*
: Supply the content of the layer from another document.

`style=`*style*
: Specify an inline style for this tag.

`top=`*n*
: Define, in pixels, the position of the layer's top edge from the containing line of text.

`visibility=`*value*
: Determine whether to `show` the layer, `hide` the layer, or `inherit` the visibility attribute from a containing layer.

`width=`*n*
: Define the width, in pixels, of the layer.

`z-index=`*n*
: Specify the layer's position in the stacking order.

<legend>

```
<legend> . . . </legend>
```

Define a legend for a form field set.

Attributes

`accesskey=`*char*
: Define the hot-key character for this legend.

`align=`*position*
: Align the legend to the `top`, `bottom`, `left`, or `right` of the field set.

<li>

```
<li> . . . </li>
```

Delimit a list item in an ordered (`<ol>`) or unordered (`<ul>`) list.

→

Attributes

`type=`*format*
: Set the type of this list element to the desired format. For `<li>` within `<ol>`: `A` (capital letters), `a` (lowercase letters), `I` (capital Roman numerals), `i` (lowercase Roman numerals), or `1` (Arabic numerals; default). For `<li>` within `<ul>`: `circle`, `disc` (default), or `square`.

`value=`*n*
: Set the number for this list item to *n*.

<link>

`<link>`

Define a link in the document `<head>` between this document and another document. Currently this tag is implemented to provide links to style-sheet definition files and font definition files.

Attributes

`charset=`*charset*
: Specify the character set used to encode the target of this link.

`href=`*url*
: Specify the hypertext reference URL of the target document.

`hreflang=`*lang*
: Specify the language used for the target's contents using a standard two-character ISO language name.

`media=`*list*
: Specify a list of media types upon which this object can be rendered.

`rel=`*relation*
: Indicate the relationship from this document to the target. For Internet Explorer 3.0, `rel=`*style* indicates the existence of an external style sheet.

`rev=`*relation*
: Indicate the reverse relationship from the target to this document.

`type=text/css`
: Specify the MIME type for the linked document. Normally used in conjunction with links to style sheets, when the type is set to `text/css`.

<listing>

`<listing> . . . </listing>`

Same as `<pre width=`*n*`>` ... `</pre>`; deprecated: don't use.

<map>

`<map> . . . </map>`

Define a map containing hot spots in a client-side image map.

→

Attributes

name=*string*
Define the name of this map (required).

<marquee>

<marquee> . . . </marquee>

Create a scrolling-text marquee.

Attributes

align=*position*
Align the marquee to the top, middle, or bottom of the surrounding text.

behavior=*style*
Define marquee style to be scroll, slide, or alternate.

bgcolor=*color*
Set the background color of the marquee.

class=*name*
Specify a style class controlling the appearance of this tag.

direction=*dir*
Define the direction, left or right, the text is to scroll.

height=*value*
Define the height, in pixels, of the marquee area.

hspace=*value*
Define the space, in pixels, to be inserted to the left and right of the marquee.

loop=*value*
Set the number of times to animate the marquee; *value* is an integer or infinite.

scrollamount=*value*
Set the number of pixels to move the text for each scroll movement.

scrolldelay=*value*
Specify the delay, in milliseconds, between successive movements of the marquee text.

style=*style*
Specify an inline style for this tag.

vspace=*value*
Define the space, in pixels, to be inserted above and below the marquee.

width=*value*
Define the width, in pixels, of the marquee area.

<menu>

<menu> . . . </menu>

Define a menu list containing <li> tags.

→

Attributes

compact
: Make the list more compact.

type=*bullet*
: N O Set the bullet style for this list to either circle, disc (default), or square.

<meta>

<meta>

Provides additional information about a document.

Attributes

charset=*name*
: Specify the character set to be used with this document.

content=*string*
: Specify the value for the meta-information (required). For client pulls, content="*n*;*url*=*url*" tells the browser to load the specified *url* after *n* seconds. If no URL is specified, the source document will be reloaded. Must be used with http-equiv="refresh" within <meta>.

dir=*direction*
: Specify the rendering direction for text, either left to right (ltr) or right to left (rtl).

http-equiv=*string*
: Specify the HTTP equivalent name for the meta-information and cause the server to include the name and content in the HTTP header for this document when it is transmitted to the client.

  A value of refresh creates a "client-pull" within a document.

lang=*language*
: Specify the language used for this tag's contents using a standard two-character ISO language name.

name=*string*
: Specify the name of the meta-information.

scheme=*scheme*
: Specify the profile scheme used to interpret this property.

<multicol>

<multicol> . . . </multicol>

N Format enclosed HTML and text in multicolumn format. Text and elements will flow across specified number of columns to give them approximately equal length.

→

Attributes

`class=`*name*
: Specify a style class controlling the appearance of this tag.

`cols=`*n*
: Specify number of columns (required).

`gutter=`*n*
: Specify amount of space in pixels between columns. Default is 10 pixels.

`style=`*style*
: Specify an inline style for this tag.

`width=`*n*
: Specify width of columns in pixels.

<nobr>

```
<nobr> . . . </nobr>
```

No breaks allowed in the enclosed text.

<noembed>

```
<noembed> . . . </noembed>
```

Define content to be presented by browsers that do not support the `<embed>` tag.

<noframes>

```
<noframes> . . . </noframes>
```

Define content to be presented by browsers that do not support frames.

See Chapter 4 for more information on using frames.

<noscript>

```
<noscript> . . . </noscript>
```

Specify alternative content for browsers that do not support JavaScript. See Chapter 11, *JavaScript*, for more information on JavaScript.

<object>

```
<object> . . . </object>
```

Insert an object into the document. This tag is used to specify applets, OLE controls, and other media objects.

→

Attributes

`align=`*value*
: Specify how the object is aligned with other elements in the document. Values include `baseline`, `center`, `left`, `middle`, `right`, `textbottom`, `textmiddle`, and `texttop`.

`archive=`*list*
: Specify a list of URLs of archives containing resources used by this object.

`border=`*n*
: Set the width of the object's border if it is a hyperlink.

`classid=`*url*
: Identify the class identifier of the object. The syntax of the URL depends on the object type.

`codebase=`*url*
: Identify the URL of the object's codebase. The syntax of the URL depends on the object.

`codetype=`*codetype*
: Specify the media type of the code.

`data=`*url*
: Specify the URL of the data used for the object. The syntax of the URL depends on the object.

`declare`
: Declare an object without instantiating it.

`height=`*n*
: Specify the height of the object in pixels.

`hspace=`*n*
: Specify the amount of space in pixels between the sides of the object and the surrounding elements.

`name=`*url*
: Specify the name of the object.

`notab`
: Do not make this object part of the tabbing order.

`shapes`
: Indicate shaped hyperlinks in object.

`standby=`*message*
: Specify message to display during object loading.

`tabindex=`*n*
: Specify this object's position in the tabbing order.

`type=`*type*
: Specify the media type for data.

`usemap=`*url*
: Specify image map to use with object.

→

`vspace=`*n*
: Specify the amount of space, in pixels, above and below object.

`width=`*n*
: Specify object width.

<ol>

`<ol> . . . </ol>`

Define an ordered list containing numbered (ascending) `<li>` elements.

Attributes

`compact`
: Present the list in a more compact manner.

`start=`*n*
: Start numbering the list at *n*, instead of 1.

`type=`*format*
: Set the numbering format for this list to `A` (capital letters), `a` (lowercase letters), `I` (capital Roman numerals), `i` (lowercase Roman numerals), or `1` (Arabic numerals; default).

<optgroup>

`<optgroup> . . . </optgroup>`

Define a group of options within a `<select>` element.

Attributes

`disabled`
: Disable this group, making it inactive.

`label=`*string*
: Provide a label for this group.

<option>

`<option> . . . </option>`

Define an option within a `<select>` item in a `<form>`.

Attributes

`disabled`
: Disable this option, making it inactive.

`label=`*string*
: Provide a label for this option.

`selected`
: Make this item initially selected.

→

`value=`*string*
: Return the specified value to the form-processing application instead of the `<option>` contents.

See Chapter 6 for more information on using forms.

<p>

`<p> . . . </p>`

Start and end a paragraph.

Attributes

`align=`*type*
: Align the text within the paragraph to `left`, `center`, or `right`.

<param>

`<param> . . . </param>`

Supply a parameter to the `<applet>` or `<object>` surrounding this tag.

Attributes

`id=`*name*
: Define the unique identifier for this parameter.

`name=`*string*
: Define the name of the parameter.

`type=`*type*
: Specify the MIME type of the parameter.

`value=`*string*
: Define the value of the parameter.

`valuetype=`*type*
: Indicate the type of value. Can be one of three types: `data` indicates that the parameter's value is data (default); `ref` indicates that the parameter's value is a URL; `object` indicates that the value is a URL of another object in the document.

<plaintext>

`<plaintext>`

Render the remainder of the document as preformatted plain text.

<pre>

`<pre> . . . </pre>`

Render the enclosed text in its original, preformatted style, honoring line breaks and spacing.

→

Attributes

`width=`*n*
: Size the text, if possible, so that *n* characters fit across the display window.

HTML

<q>

```
<q> . . . </q>
```

Designate enclosed text as an inline quotation.

Attributes

`cite=`*url*
: Specify the URL of the source of the quoted material.

<s>

```
<s> . . . </s>
```

The enclosed text is struck through with a horizontal line.

<samp>

```
<samp> . . . </samp>
```

The enclosed text is a sample.

<script>

```
<script> . . . </script>
```

Define a script within the document.

Attributes

`charset=`*name*
: Specify the character set used to encode the script.

`defer`
: Defer execution of this script.

`language=`*lang*
: Specify the language used to create the script.

`src=`*url*
: Specify the URL of an outside file containing the script to be loaded and run with the document.

`type=`*type*
: Specify the MIME type of the script.

See Chapter 11 for more information on JavaScript.

<select>

`<select> . . . </select>`

Define a multiple-choice menu or scrolling list within a `<form>`, containing one or more `<option>` tags.

Attributes

`disabled`
: Disable this control, making it inactive.

`multiple`
: Allow user to select more than one `<option>` within the `<select>`.

`name=`*string*
: Define the name for the selected `<option>` values that, if selected, are passed to the form-processing application (required).

`onblur=`*applet*
: Specify an applet to be run when the mouse leaves this element.

`onchange=`*applet*
: Specify an applet to be run when the user changes the value of this element.

`onfocus=`*applet*
: Specify an applet to be run when the mouse enters this element.

`size=`*n*
: Display items using a pull-down menu for `size=1` (without `multiple` specified) and a scrolling list of *n* items otherwise.

`tabindex=`*n*
: Specify this element's position in the tabbing order.

See Chapter 6 for more information on using forms.

<server>

`<server> . . . </server>`

N Define a LiveWire script.

<small>

`<small> . . . </small>`

Format the enclosed text using a smaller typeface.

<spacer>

`<spacer>`

N Insert a whitespace element in a document.

→

Attributes

`type=`*type*
: Specify what type of spacer to use. `vertical` inserts space between two lines of text. `horizontal` inserts space between words or characters. `block` inserts a rectangular space such as an `<img>` object.

`size=`*n*
: Specify size in pixels for either width of `horizontal` spacer, or height of `vertical` spacer.

`width=`*n*
: Specify width in pixels of `block` spacer.

`height=`*n*
: Specify height in pixels of `block` spacer.

`align=`*value*
: Specify alignment of `block` spacer with surrounding text. Values are the same as for the `<img>` tag.

<span>

`<span> . . . </span>`

Specify style-sheet formatting to text between tags.

Attributes

`style=`*elements*
: Specify cascading style-sheet elements for text in the span.

<strike>

`<strike> . . . </strike>`

The enclosed text is struck through with a horizontal line.

<strong>

`<strong> . . . </strong>`

Strongly emphasize the enclosed text.

<style>

`<style> . . . </style>`

Define one or more document level styles.

Attributes

`dir=`*dir*
: Specify the rendering direction for the title text, either left to right (`ltr`) or right to left (`rtl`).

→

`lang=`*language*
: Specify the language used for this tag's title using a standard two-character ISO language name.

`media=`*list*
: Specify a list of media types upon which this object can be rendered.

`title=`*string*
: Specify a title for this tag.

`type=`*type*
: Define the format of the styles (i.e., `text/css`).

See Chapter 9, *Cascading Style Sheets*, for more information on styles and style sheets.

<sub>

```
<sub> . . . </sub>
```

Format the enclosed text as a subscript.

<sup>

```
<sup> . . . </sup>
```

Format the enclosed text as a superscript.

<table>

```
<table> . . . </table>
```

Define a table.

Attributes

`align=`*position*
: Align the table either `left` or `right` with the surrounding text flow.

`background=`*url*
: Ⓘ Specify an image to be tiled in the background of the table.

`bgcolor=`*color*
: Define the background color for the entire table.

`border=`*n*
: Create a border *n* pixels wide.

`bordercolor=`*color*
: Ⓘ Define the border color for the entire table.

`bordercolordark=`*color*
: Ⓘ Define the dark border-highlighting color for the entire table.

`bordercolorlight=`*color*
: Ⓘ Define the light border-highlighting color for the entire table.

→

`cellpadding=n`
: Place *n* pixels of padding around each cell's contents.

`cellspacing=n`
: Place *n* pixels of spacing between cells.

`cols=n`
: N I Specify the number of columns in this table.

`frame=[void|above|below|hsides|lhs|rhs|vsides|box|border]`
: I Specify which sides of a table's outer border will be drawn. `void` removes outer borders; `box` and `border` displays all. `hsides` draws horizontal sides; `vsides` draws vertical sides. `lhs` draws left side; `rhs` right side.

`height=n`
: N Define the height of the table in pixels.

`hspace=n`
: N Specify the horizontal space, in pixels, added at the left and right of the table.

`nowrap`
: I Supress text wrapping in table cells.

`rules=[all|cols|groups|none|rows]`
: I Turn off (`none`) or turn on rules between table cells by `cols`, `rows`, `groups`, or `all`.

`summary=string`
: Provide a description to summarize this table.

`vspace=n`
: Specify the vertical space, in pixels, added at the top and bottom of the table.

`width=n`
: Set the width of the table to *n* pixels or a percentage of the window width.

See Chapter 5 for more information on tables.

<tbody>

`<tbody> . . . </tbody>`

Create a row group within a table.

`align=position`
: Align the table body cell contents to the `left`, `center`, or `right`.

`char=char`
: Specify the cell alignment character for the body group.

`charoff=value`
: Specify the offset of the alignment position within the cells.

→

`valign=`*position*
: Vertically align the body group cells' contents to the `top`, `center`, `bottom`, or `baseline` of a cell.

<td>

`<td> . . . </td>`

Define a table data cell.

Attributes

`abbr=`*string*
: Specify an abbreviation for the cell's contents.

`align=`*type*
: Align the cell contents to the `left`, `center`, or `right`.

`axis=`*string*
: Provide a name for a related group of cells.

`background=`*url*
: ⓘ Specify an image to be tiled in the background of the cell.

`bgcolor=`*color*
: Define the background color for the cell.

`bordercolor=`*color*
: ⓘ Define the border color for the cell.

`bordercolordark=`*color*
: ⓘ Define the dark border-highlighting color for the cell.

`bordercolorlight=`*color*
: ⓘ Define the light border-highlighting color for the cell.

`char=`*char*
: Specify the cell alignment character.

`charoff=`*value*
: Specify the offset of the alignment position within the cell.

`colspan=`*n*
: Have this cell straddle *n* adjacent columns.

`headers=`*list*
: Provide a list of header cell names associated with this cell.

`height=`*n*
: Define the height, in pixels, for this cell.

`nowrap`
: Do not automatically wrap and fill text in this cell.

`rowspan=`*n*
: Have this cell straddle *n* adjacent rows.

`scope=`*scope*
: Define the scope of this header cell, either `row`, `col`, `rowgroup`, or `colgroup`.

→

valign=*type*

Vertically align this cell's contents to the top, middle, bottom, or baseline of the cell.

width=*n*

Set the width of this cell to *n* pixels or a percentage of the table width.

See Chapter 5 for more information on tables.

HTML

<textarea>

<textarea> . . . </textarea>

Define a multiline text input area within a <form>; content of the <textarea> tag is the initial, default value.

Attributes

accesskey=*char*

Define the hot-key character for this element.

cols=*n*

Display *n* columns of text within the text area.

disabled

Disable this control, making it inactive.

name=*string*

Define the name for the text-area value that is passed to the form-processing application (required).

onblur=*applet*

Specify an applet to be run when the mouse leaves this element.

onchange=*applet*

Specify an applet to be run if a user changes the value of this element.

onfocus=*applet*

Specify an applet to be run when the mouse enters this element.

onselect=*applet*

Specify an applet to be run if the user clicks this element.

readonly

Prevent user modification of this element.

rows=*n*

Display *n* rows of text within the text area.

tabindex=*n*

Specify this element's position in the tabbing order.

wrap=*style*

N Set word wrapping within the text area to off, virtual (display wrap, but do not transmit to server), or physical (display and transmit wrap).

See Chapter 6 for more information on forms.

<tfoot>

```
<tfoot>
```

Define a table footer.

Attributes

`align=`*position*
: Align the footer cell contents to the `left`, `center`, or `right`.

`char=`*char*
: Specify the cell alignment character.

`charoff=`*value*
: Specify the offset of the alignment position within the cell.

`valign=`*position*
: Vertically align the footer cells' contents to the `top`, `center`, `bottom`, or `baseline` of a cell.

<th>

```
<th> . . . </th>
```

Define a table header cell.

Attributes

`abbr=`*string*
: Specify an abbreviation for the cell's contents.

`align=`*type*
: Align the cell contents to the `left`, `center`, or `right`.

`axis=`*string*
: Provide a name for a related group of cells.

`background=`*url*
: Ⓘ Specify an image to be tiled in the background of the cell.

`bgcolor=`*color*
: Define the background color for the cell.

`bordercolor=`*color*
: Ⓘ Define the border color for the cell.

`bordercolordark=`*color*
: Ⓘ Define the dark border-highlighting color for the cell.

`bordercolorlight=`*color*
: Ⓘ Define the light border-highlighting color for the cell.

`char=`*char*
: Specify the cell alignment character.

`charoff=`*value*
: Specify the offset of the alignment position within the cell.

→

`colspan=`*n*
: Have this cell straddle *n* adjacent columns.

`headers=`*list*
: Provide a list of header cell names associated with this cell.

`height=`*n*
: Define the height, in pixels, for this cell.

`nowrap`
: Do not automatically wrap and fill text in this cell.

`rowspan=`*n*
: Have this cell straddle *n* adjacent rows.

`scope=`*scope*
: Define the scope of this header cell: `row`, `col`, `rowgroup`, or `colgroup`.

`valign=`*type*
: Vertically align this cell's contents to the `top`, `middle`, `bottom`, or `baseline` of the cell.

`width=`*n*
: Set the width of this cell to *n* pixels or a percentage of the table width.

See Chapter 5 for more information on tables.

<thead>

`<thead>`

Define a table heading.

Attributes

`align=`*position*
: Align the header cells' contents to the `left`, `center`, or `right`.

`char=`*char*
: Specify the cell alignment character for heading cells.

`charoff=`*value*
: Specify the offset of the alignment position within the cell.

`valign=`*positiona*
: Vertically align the header cells' contents to the `top`, `center`, `bottom`, or `baseline` of a cell.

<title>

`<title> . . . </title>`

Define the HTML document's title.

→

Attributes

`dir=`*dir*
: Specify the rendering direction for text, either left to right (`ltr`) or right to left (`rtl`).

`lang=`*language*
: Specify the language used for this tag's contents using a standard two-character ISO language name.

<tr>

```
<tr> . . . </tr>
```

Define a row of cells within a table.

Attributes

`align=`*type*
: Align the cell contents in this row to the `left`, `center`, or `right`.

`background=`*url*
: Specify an image to be tiled in the background of the cell.

`bgcolor=`*color*
: Define the background color for this row.

`border=`*n*
: Create a border *n* pixels wide.

`bordercolor=`*color*
: Define the border color for this row.

`bordercolordark=`*color*
: Define the dark border-highlighting color for this row.

`bordercolorlight=`*color*
: Define the light border-highlighting color for this row.

`char=`*char*
: Specify the cell alignment character for this row.

`charoff=`*value*
: Specify the offset of the alignment position with the cells of this row.

`nowrap`
: Disable word wrap for all cells in this row.

`valign=`*type*
: Vertically align the cell contents in this row to the `top`, `middle`, `bottom`, or `baseline` of the cell.

See Chapter 5 for more information on tables.

<tt>

```
<tt> . . . </tt>
```

Format the enclosed text in typewriter-style (monospaced) font.

<ul>

```
<ul> . . . </ul>
```

Define an unordered list of bulleted `<li>` elements.

Attributes

`compact`
: Display the list in a more compact manner.

`type=`*bullet*
: Set the bullet style for this list to either `circle`, `disc` (default), or `square`.

<var>

```
<var> . . . </var>
```

The enclosed text is a variable's name.

<wbr>

```
<wbr>
```

Indicate a potential word-break point within a `<nobr>` section.

<xmp>

```
<xmp> . . . </xmp>
```

Same as `<pre width=80>` ... `</pre>`; deprecated, do not use.

CHAPTER 4

Frames

Version 2.0 of Netscape Navigator introduced a new capability for web documents called *frames*. Frames allow you to divide the main browser window into smaller subwindows (frames), each of which simultaneously displays a separate document. Frame support has since been incorporated into Microsoft Internet Explorer as well.

Two tags are used to make frame documents: **<frameset>** and **<frame>**. The **<noframes>** element provides alternative content for nonframes browsers. This is a requirement for HTML 4.0 and should contain functional content, or a link to it, instead of telling someone to get a browser that supports frames.

A *frameset* is simply a collection of frames that occupy the browser's window. Column and row definition attributes for the **<frameset>** tag let you define the number and initial sizes for the columns and rows of frames. The **<frame>** tag defines what document—HTML or otherwise—initially goes into the frame, and is where you may give the frame a name to use for hypertext link targets.

Here is the HTML source for a simple frame document, which is displayed by the browser in Figure 4-1.

```
<html>
<head>
<title>Frames Layout</title>
</head>
<frameset rows="60%,*" cols="65%,20%,*">
  <frame src="frame1.html">
  <frame src="frame2.html">
  <frame src="frame3.html" name="fill_me">
  <frame scrolling=yes src="frame4.html">
  <frame src="frame5.html">
  <frame src="frame6.html">
  <noframes>
    You are using a browser that does not support frames.
    <a href="frame1.html">Take this link</a> to the first
```

```
    HTML document in the set.
  </noframes>
</frameset>
</html>
```


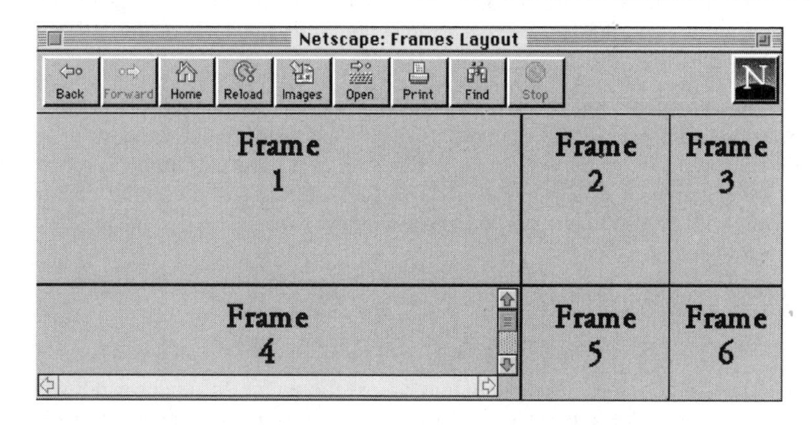

Figure 4–1: A simple six-panel frame layout in Netscape

The first thing to notice in the sample document is that Netscape fills the frames in the frameset in order across each row. Second, Frame 4 sports a scrollbar because we told it to, even though the contents may otherwise fit the frame without scrolling. (Scrollbars automatically appear if the contents overflow the frame's dimensions, unless explicitly disabled with `scrolling=no`.)

Another item of interest is the `name` attribute in Frame 3. Once named, you can reference a particular frame in which to display a hypertext-linked document. To do that, you add a special `target` attribute to the anchor (<a>) tag of the source hypertext link. For instance, to link a document called "new.html" for display in our example window Frame 3, which we've named "fill_me", the anchor looks like this:

```
<a href="new.html" target="fill_me">
```

If the user selects this link, say in Frame 1, the *new.html* document replaces the original *frame3.html* contents in Frame 3.

Frame Layout

The `<frameset>` tag defines the collection of frames or other framesets in a document. Framesets may be nested, providing a richer set of layout capabilities. The `<frameset>` tag replaces the `<body>` tag in a document. You may not include any other content except valid `<head>` and `<frameset>` content.

The `<frameset>` tag uses two attributes to let you define the size and number of columns (`cols`) and rows (`rows`) of either frames or nested framesets to display in the document window. These attributes divide a frameset in a grid-like or tabular format. Both attributes accept a quote-enclosed, comma-separated list of values that specify either the absolute or relative width (for columns) or height (for rows) for the frames. The number of attribute values determines how many rows or columns of frames the browser displays in the document window.

Each value in the `rows` and `cols` attributes can be specified in one of three ways: as an absolute number of pixels, as a percentage of the total width or height of the frameset, or as a portion of the space remaining after setting aside room for adjacent elements.

The browser matches the size specifications as closely as possible. However, the browser will not extend the boundaries of the main document window or leave blank space outside of frames. Space is allocated to a particular frame in reference to all other frames across the row or down the column, and the entire document window is filled. Also, the main document window for a frame document does not have scrollbars.

Here is an example of setting row heights in pixels:

```
<frameset rows="150,300,150">
```

This creates three frames, each stretching across the entire document window. The top and bottom rows are set to 150 pixels tall; the middle is set to 300 pixels. Unless the browser window is exactly 600 pixels tall, the browser automatically and proportionally stretches or compresses the top and bottom rows so that each occupies one-quarter of the window space. The middle row occupies the remaining half of the window. This frameset could be expressed with percentages like this:

```
<frameset rows="25%,50%,25%">
```

The percentages should add up to 100%, of course. If they don't, the browser resizes the rows proportionally to make them fit.

To make row and column sizing easier, you can use the asterisk (*) character. The asterisk represents one equal portion of the remaining window space, whatever it is. For example:

```
<frameset cols="50,*">
```

creates one fixed 50-pixel column down the left side of the window; the remaining space goes to the right column. The asterisk can also be used for more than one column or row. For example:

```
<frameset rows="*,100,*">
```

creates a 100-pixel-tall row across the middle of a frameset and rows above and below it that are equal in height.

If you precede the asterisk with an integer value, the corresponding row or column gets proportionally more of the available space. For example:

```
<frameset cols="10%,3*,*,*">
```

creates four columns: the first column occupies 10% of the overall width of the frameset. The second column then gets three-fifths of the remaining space, and the third and fourth columns each get one-fifth. Using the asterisk makes it easy to divide remaining space in a frameset.

Be aware that unless you explicitly tell it not to, the browser lets users manually resize the individual columns and rows in a frame document. To prevent this, use the `noresize` attribute for the `<frame>` tag.

HTML

Nested Framesets

You can achieve more complex layouts by using nested `<frameset>` tags. Any frame within a frameset can contain another frameset.

For example, Figure 4-2 shows a layout of two columns, the first with two rows and the second with three rows. This is created by nesting two `<frameset>` tags with row specifications within a top-level `<frameset>` that specifies the columns:

```
<frameset cols="50%,*">
  <frameset rows="50%,*">
    <frame src="frame1.html">
    <frame src="frame2.html">
  </frameset>
  <frameset rows="33%,33%,*">
    <frame src="frame3.html">
    <frame src="frame4.html">
    <frame src="frame5.html">
  </frameset>
</frameset>
```

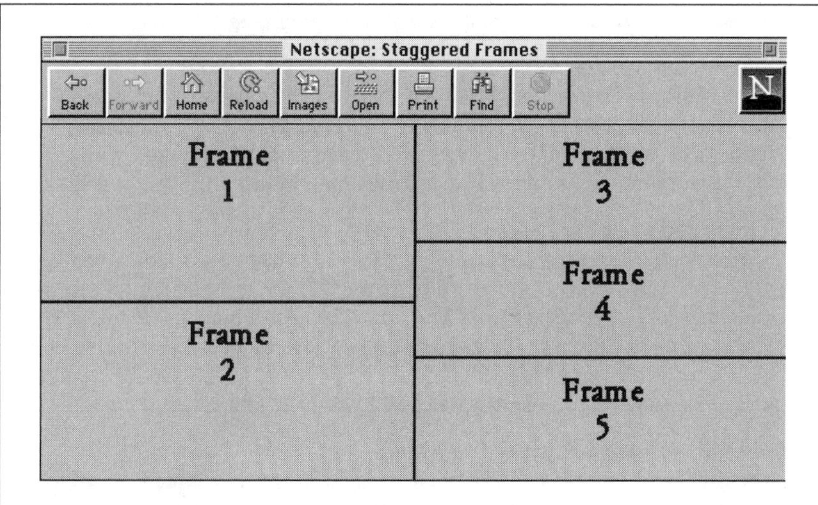

Figure 4-2: Staggered frame layouts using nested <frameset> tags

The <frame> Tag

A frame document contains no displayable content (except for the contents of the `<noframes>` tag, if applicable). The `<frame>` tags provide URL references to the individual documents that occupy each frame. `<frame>` tags are standalone elements and therefore, do not require a closing tag.

Frames are placed into a frameset column by column, from left to right, and then row by row, from top to bottom, so the sequence and number of `<frame>` tags inside a `<frameset>` are important.

Netscape displays empty frames for `<frame>` tags that do not contain an `src` document attribute and for those trailing ones in a frameset that do not have an associated `<frame>` tag. Such orphans, however, remain empty; you cannot put content into them later, even if they have a target `name` attribute for display redirection.

Listed below are the basic attributes that can be used in the `<frame>` tag.

`src=`*document_name*
: The value of the `src` attribute is a URL of the document that is to be displayed in the frame. The document may be any valid HTML document or displayable object, including images and multimedia. The referenced document may itself be another frame document.

`name=`*frame_name*
: The optional `name` attribute labels the frame for later reference by a `target` attribute in a hypertext link anchor `<a>` tag. If a link that targets a frame's name is selected, the document is displayed in the named frame. The value of the `name` attribute is a text string enclosed in quotes.

`noresize`
: Even though you may explicitly set their dimensions with attributes in the `<frameset>` tag, users can manually alter the size of a column or row of frames. To suppress this behavior, add the `noresize` attribute to the frame tags in the row or column whose relative dimensions you want to maintain.

`scrolling=[yes,no,auto]`
: Normally, the browser displays vertical and horizontal scrollbars for frames whose contents exceed the allotted space. If there is sufficient room for the content, no scrollbars appear. The `scrolling` attribute gives you explicit control over whether scrollbars appear. A value of `yes` turns the scrollbars on; `no` turns them off. The value of `auto` gives the default scrollbar behavior and is the same as not using the `scrolling` attribute at all.

`marginheight=`*height* `marginwidth=`*width*
: The browser normally places a small amount of space between the edge of a frame and its contents. Those margins can be manually set with the `marginheight` and `marginwidth` attributes, whose values are given in pixels. You cannot make a margin less than one pixel, nor so big that there is no room left for the frame's contents.

Frame Targets

The <frame> tag includes an attribute that allows you to name the frame. A hypertext link in another frame can load its referenced document into the named frame by using the target attribute in the <a> tag. For example:

```
<frame src="frame.html" name="display_frame">
```

describes a frame that displays frame.html and is named display_frame. If another frame or window (or even the same frame) contains this link:

```
<a href="file.html" target="display_frame">
```

and this link is selected, the file file.html replaces the file frame.html in the frame named display_frame. This is the basic use of targeting frames. A useful example is a book with a table of contents. The table of contents is loaded into a frame that occupies a narrow column on the left side of the browser window. The table of contents contains a list of links to each chapter in the book. Each chapter link targets the frame that occupies the rest of the window. You can then view the chapters while keeping the table of contents available for further navigation.

It can be tedious to specify a target for every hyperlink in your documents, especially when most are targeted at the same window or frame. To alleviate this problem, you can use the target attribute for the <base> tag in the <head> of your document. Adding a target to the <base> tag sets the default target for every hypertext link in the document that does not contain an explicit target attribute.

There are a couple of things to note about the use of targets and named frames:

- If a link without a target is contained within a frame, the referenced document replaces the current contents of the same frame if it is selected.
- If a link contains a target that does not exist, a new window is opened to display the referenced document, and the window is given the target's name. That window can thus be used by other links that target it.

Four reserved target names for special document redirection actions are listed below. They all begin with the underscore (_) character. You should not use the underscore character as the first letter of any name that you assign a frame, as it will be ignored by the browser.

_blank
: A linked document with target="_blank" is always loaded into a newly opened, unnamed window.

_self
: This target value is the default for all <a> tags that do not specify a target, causing the referenced document to be loaded in the same frame or window as the source document. The _self target is redundant and unnecessary unless used in combination with the target attribute of the <base> tag to override the default target value for all the links in the source document.

_parent
: The _parent target causes the document to load into the parent window or frameset containing the frame containing the hypertext reference. If the

reference is in a window or top-level frame, it is equivalent to the target _self.

_top
: This target causes the document to load into the window containing the hypertext link, replacing any frames currently displayed in the window.

Frame Border Attributes

Internet Explorer and Netscape Navigator both support tags that adjust the style of the borders that surround frames. Although they have the same functions, the attributes are slightly different for each browser.

Netscape uses the frameborder attribute to toggle between 3D borders and simple rules for borders. The default is to use 3D borders; a value of no gives simple borders. This attribute can be placed in either the <frameset> tag or in a <frame> tag. A setting in an individual <frame> overrides an outer <frameset> setting.

You can also set the color of the borders in both <frameset> and <frame> with the bordercolor attribute.

In the <frameset> tag, you can set the width of the borders in a whole frameset with the border attribute. The default width is 5 pixels. To achieve borderless frames in Netscape, set border=0 and frameborder=no.

Internet Explorer does all the same things, only with different attributes. It also uses frameborder in the <frameset> and <frame> tags, but the values are 1 for 3D borders and 0 for simple ones. In the <frameset> tag, you can set the amount of space between frames with the framespacing attribute. By setting framespacing=0 and frameborder=0, you can achieve borderless frames.

Another feature in Internet Explorer is the floating frame. This has all the abilities that a regular frame does, but it is placed within a document like an <img> would be. The tag for a floating frame is <iframe>, and it requires a closing tag. The attributes include all of the regular <frame> attributes, and the sizing, alignment, and placement attributes of <img>.

CHAPTER 5

Tables

HTML tables offer a detailed way to present tabular data, as well as a creative way to lay out the information in your web documents. The standard HTML model for tables is straightforward: a table is a collection of data arranged and related in rows and columns of cells. Most cells contain data values; others contain row and column headers that describe the data.

The HTML 4.0 table specification defines a number of tags and attributes for creating tables. Newly supported tags allow you to organize and display table data with great detail, and with the application of CSS style elements, table styles can be standardized across your documents.

The main tags that describe tables are: `<table>`, `<caption>`, `<tr>`, `<th>`, and `<td>`. The `<table>` tag surrounds the table and gives default specifications for the entire table such as background color, border size, and spacing between cells. The optional `<caption>` tag is placed within the `<table>` tags and provides a caption for the table. `<tr>` tags denote each row of the table and contain the tags for each cell within a row. `<th>` and `<td>` describe the table cells themselves, `<th>` being a header cell and `<td>` being a regular cell. `<th>` and `<td>` tags surround the information that is displayed within each table cell.

Table cells are defined across each row of a table. The number of cells in a row is determined by the number of `<th>` or `<td>` tags contained within a `<tr>`. If a table cell spans more than one row (using the `rowspan` attribute), the affected rows below it automatically accommodate the cell, and no additional cell tag is needed to represent it in those rows.

Figure 5-1 shows an HTML table rendered in two different browsers. Note how differently each browser displays the same table. You should keep these differences in mind when designing tables and test to see how your table looks in different browsers (as with all of your HTML documents).

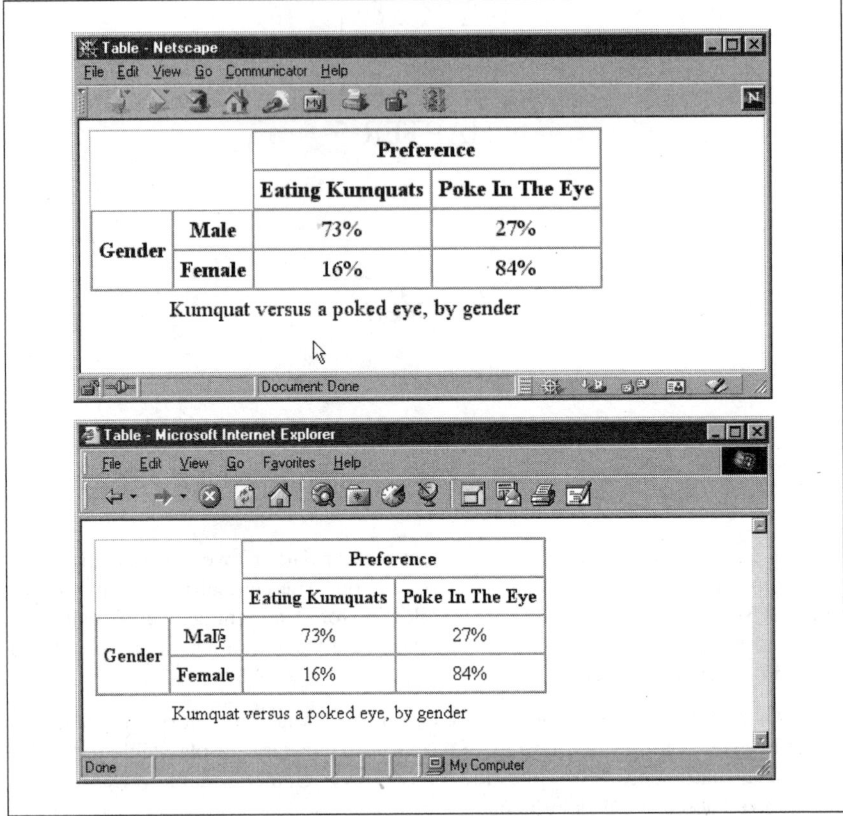

Figure 5-1: HTML table rendered by Navigator (top) and by Explorer (bottom)

Here is the code that renders the table:

```
<table border cellspacing=0 cellpadding=5>
  <caption align=bottom> Kumquat versus a poked
  eye, by gender</caption>
  <tr>
    <td colspan=2 rowspan=2></td>
    <th colspan=2 align=center>Preference</th>
  </tr>
  <tr>
    <th>Eating Kumquats</th>
    <th>Poke In The Eye</th>
  </tr>
  <tr align=center>
    <th rowspan=2>Gender</th>
    <th>Male</th>
    <td>73%</td>
    <td>27%</td>
  </tr>
  <tr align=center>
    <th>Female</th>
    <td>16%</td>
```

```
    <td>84%</td>
  </tr>
</table>
```

The contents of table cells may be any data that can be displayed in an HTML document. This can be plain text, images, tagged text, and other HTML structures. The table cells are sized according to their contents and in relation to other cells.

HTML

The <table> Tag

Tables are normally treated as floating objects within a browser window. They're aligned in the browser window to match the text flow, usually left-justified (or centered). Unlike inline images, however, text normally floats above and below a table but not beside it. Internet Explorer and Netscape allow you to set the alignment of a table and float text around it with the `align` attribute. `align` accepts two values, `left` and `right`. These values instruct the browser to align the table with either the left or right margin of the text flow around it. Text then flows along the opposite side of the table, if there is room.

The `hspace` and `vspace` attributes add extra space between the table and surrounding content. `hspace` adds space to the left and right sides of the table; `vspace` adds space above and below it. The value of each attribute is given as an integer number of pixels.

The `width` attribute can give you some control over the width of a table. Tables are normally rendered at the width that fits all the contents. The `width` attribute allows you to widen the table beyond the default size to occupy a set number of pixels or a percentage of the window's width. For example:

```
<table width="100%">
```

always stretches the table to the full width of the browser window. This is a conditional instruction, however. The size of a table cell is always determined by the size of the biggest "fixed" content, such as an image or a nonbreaking line of text. Therefore, a table may need to be wider than you wish it. If the table cells contain mostly wrapping text elements such as paragraphs (`<p>`), the browser usually accommodates your request.

The `border` attribute to `<table>` controls the borders within and around the table. Simply using `border` with no attributes adds default borders to a table, which are not rendered the same in any two browsers. You can set border width by giving the attribute an integer number of pixels as a value. The `border=0` setting turns table borders off completely.

The amount of space around each cell is controlled by the `cellpadding` and `cellspacing` attributes to the `<table>` tag. Each accepts an integer number of pixels as a value. `cellpadding` sets the space between a cell's contents and its edges, whether borders are on or off. `cellspacing` sets the space between adjacent table cells. If borders are turned on, `cellspacing` will add the space outside of the border (half on one side, half on the other). The border width is not included or affected by `cellspacing` or `cellpadding`.

The additional attributes to the <table> tag are supported only by Internet Explorer. The `rules` and `frames` attributes tell the browser where to draw the rules (or borders) in the table. These settings depend on the use of other tags for the table such as <colgroup> or <tfoot>, which group table cells into distinct sections. There are many different values for `rules` and `frames`, making this feature quite versatile. It is, however, not supported in other browsers.

The other <table> attributes exclusive to Internet Explorer set backgrounds and colors for 3D borders. They are also usable in the lower-level <tr>, <th>, and <td> tags. They are discussed presently.

The <caption> Tag

You can add a title or `caption` to your table by using a <caption> tag within a <table>. The default placement of the caption for Netscape and Internet Explorer is above the table and centered with it. The placement and alignment of the caption is controlled by special alignment attributes that differ between the browsers.

In Netscape and Mosaic, the `align` attribute accepts two values: `top` and `bottom`. These allow you to put the caption above or below the table. The default value is `top`.

Internet Explorer, on the other hand, uses the `align` attribute for horizontal placement of the caption. It accepts values of `left`, `right`, and `center` (the default). The vertical positioning of the caption in Internet Explorer is controlled by a special `valign` attribute, which accepts either `top` (the default) or `bottom`. Each browser ignores the attributes and values it does not accept.

The <tr> Tag

Every row in a table is created with a <tr> tag. Within the <tr> tag are one or more cells containing either headers, each defined with the <th> tag, or data, each defined with the <td> tag.

Every row in a table has the same number of cells as the longest row; the browser automatically creates empty cells to pad rows with fewer defined cells.

Attributes to the <tr> tag control behavior for every cell it contains. There are two commonly used attributes for this tag:

- `align` is used differently in <tr> than it is in <table> (where it is now deprecated). In a table row, `align` lets you change the default horizontal alignment of the contents of the cells within the row. The attribute accepts values of `left`, `right`, `center`, or `justify`. HTML 4.0 also allows the value `char`, which aligns the contents to a specified character. However, this attribute is not yet supported in Navigator or Explorer. The default horizontal alignment for header cells (<th>) is centered; for data cells (<td>) it is left-justified.
- The `valign` attribute allows you to specify the vertical alignment of cell contents within a row. Four values are supported: `top`, `bottom`, `baseline`, and `middle`. The default vertical alignment is the same as specifying `middle`.

The browser treats each table cell as though it were its own browser window, fitting the contents to the size of the cell by breaking lines and flowing text. You can restrict line breaks with the nowrap attribute.

Background colors can be set for the cells in a row with bgcolor. Additional attributes for the <tr> tag that can specify a background image and set 3D border colors are specific to Internet Explorer.

HTML

The <th> and <td> Tags

The <th> (table header) and <td> (table data) tags go inside the <tr> tags of an HTML table to create the cells and contents of each cell within a row. The two tags operate similarly, except that header cells are typically rendered in bold text and centered by default. <td> cell contents are rendered in the regular base font, left-justified.

The align, valign, and other attributes work the same in the cell tags as they do in the row tag. When specified for <th> and <td>, these attributes override the same behavior set in the upper-level tags for their specific cell.

The other attributes to the cell tags are very important to the layout of your table. The width attribute can set the width of a table cell and all cells within its column. As with the <table> tag, a value may be given in an integer number of pixels or a percentage of the width of the table. A width value may be ignored by the browser if contents within the column have a fixed width larger than the value (i.e., an image or nonbreaking line of text). You should use only one width value in the cells of the same column. If two width values are specified in the same column of cells, the browser uses the larger value.

The nowrap attribute, when included in a cell tag, disables regular linebreaking of text within a table cell. With nowrap, the browser assembles the contents of a cell onto a single line, unless you insert a <br> or <p> tag, which forces a break.

Cell Spanning

It is common to have table cells span several columns or rows. This behavior is set within the <th> and <td> tags with the colspan and rowspan attributes. Each value is given in an integer number of columns or rows the cell is to stretch across. For example:

```
<td colspan=3>
```

tells the browser to make the cell occupy the same horizontal space as three cells in rows above or below it. The browser flows the contents of the cell to occupy the entire space.

If there aren't enough empty cells on the right, the browser just extends the cell over as many columns as exist to the right; it doesn't add extra empty cells to each row to accommodate an over-extended colspan value.

Similar to the colspan attribute, rowspan stretches a cell down two or more rows in a table. You include the rowspan attribute in the <th> or <td> tag of the uppermost row of a table where you want the cell to begin and set its value equal to the number of rows you want it to span. The cell then occupies the same space as the current row and an appropriate number of cells below that row. The following code:

```
<td rowspan=3>
```

creates a cell that occupies the current row plus two more rows below that. The browser ignores overextended rowspan values and extends the current cell only down rows you've explicitly defined by other <tr> tags following the current row.

You may combine colspan and rowspan attributes to create a cell that spans both rows and columns. In our example table in Figure 5-1, the blank cell in the upper-left corner does this with the tag:

```
<td colspan=2 rowspan=2></td>
```

Border Color and Backgrounds

Internet Explorer accepts a number of additional attributes to its table tags. These attributes let you set images for the backgrounds and border colors of table elements. They can set values for the whole table, individual rows, and individual cells. Values can be set in a nested fashion, so that a specification for a single cell can override the broader setting for its row or the whole table.

Each attribute accepts a value specified as either an RGB color value or a standard color name, both of which are described in Chapter 8, *Color Names and Values.*

The background attribute allows you to set a background image for the entire table or individual cells. The image is tiled behind the appropriate table element automatically. The value of the background attribute is the URL of the image file.

Borders in Netscape and Internet Explorer create a 3D effect by using three differently colored strips. There is a thick center strip with much thinner strips on each side. One of the outer strips is colored darker than the center strip, and one is lighter, producing a shadowed effect. Internet Explorer allows you to set the colors for each of these elements when you have borders turned on with the border attribute in the <table> tag.

The bordercolor attribute sets the color of the main center strip of a border. The bordercolorlight attribute sets the color of the light strip of a border, the top- or left-most strip. bordercolordark sets the color of the dark strip, the bottom or right-most strip.

You needn't specify all three border colors. The default for Internet Explorer's table borders sets the lighter and darker strips about 25% brighter and darker than the main border color.

Advanced Table Tags

While it is easy to build a simple table quickly with the tags we have described, you may desire more advanced table control such as varying border styles, running headers and footers, and column-based layout. HTML 4.0 adds new tags to accomplish these tasks, which originally appeared as extensions for Internet Explorer 3.0. Although they are defined in the standard, the only browser that implements these tags currently is still Internet Explorer. When making a table with these tags, make sure your tables can still be accommodated on other browsers.

Table Section Tags

The three table section tags provide a way for you to break your table into logical sections: the header, body, and footer. You define the sections by placing the row tags `<tr>` within the `<thead>`, `<tbody>`, or `<tfoot>` tags. The usual attributes for controlling the placement of the contents can be used in these tags to set the alignment for the rows and cells they contain.

The main purpose for defining these sections is that when the table is printed or displayed in multiple sections, it will use consistent running headers and footers. Another benefit is that you can visibly delineate the sections by adjusting the size of the rules between them. Internet Explorer allows you to do this by supplying the `rules` attribute to the `<table>` tag with the values `groups`, `rows`, or `all`.

Column Grouping

Similar to the sectioning of tables by rows, you can also section tables by columns. You can define column groups to span a number of similar columns, or you can create them from dissimilar columns. Each column group is defined by the `<colgroup>` tag. `<colgroup>` tags should appear within `<table>` tags. They group columns specified by the table cell tags that appear in the rest of the table. Multiple column groups can be delineated with additional `<colgroup>` tags.

To create column groups of similar columns, use the `span` attribute to `<colgroup>`. For example:

```
<colgroup span=2 width="25%">
<colgroup span=4 width="75%">
```

Here we create two groups. The first has two columns; the second has four. We have also used the common width attribute to set the relative widths of the columns. Other common attributes can be used here as well.

For groups of similar columns, place a `<col>` element for each within a `<colgroup>`. This example creates the same groups as above:

```
<colgroup width="25%">
 <col>
 <col>
</colgroup>
<colgroup width="75%">
 <col>
```

```
  <col>
  <col>
  <col>
</colgroup>
```

By specifying columns with <col>, you can set specific attributes for the cells contained in that column.

To make the distinction between column groups when your table is displayed, use the `rules` attribute to draw rules between your groups. The values can be either `groups`, `cols`, or `all`.

CHAPTER 6

Forms

Most CGI programs use HTML forms to gather user input. Forms are comprised of one or more text-input boxes, clickable radio buttons, multiple-choice checkboxes, and even pull-down menus and clickable images, all placed inside the `<form>` tag. Within a form, you may also put regular body content, including text and images. The JavaScript event handlers can be used in various form elements as well, providing a number of effects such as testing and verifying form contents.

The <form> Tag

You place a form anywhere inside the body of an HTML document with its elements enclosed by the `<form>` tag and its respective end tag `</form>`. All of the form elements within a `<form>` tag comprise a single form. The browser sends all of the values of these elements—blank, default, or user-modified—when the user submits the form to the server.

The required `action` attribute for the `<form>` tag gives the URL of the application that is to receive and process the form's data. A typical `<form>` tag with the `action` attribute looks like this:

```
<form action="http://www.oreilly.com/cgi-bin/update">
...
</form>
```

The example URL tells the browser to contact the server named *www.oreilly.com* and pass along the user's form values to the application named *update*, located in the *cgi-bin* directory.

The browser specially encodes the form's data before it passes that data to the server so it does not become scrambled or corrupted during the transmission. It is up to the server to either decode the parameters or pass them, still encoded, to the application.

The standard encoding format is the media type named application/x-www-form-urlencoded. You can change that encoding with the optional enctype attribute in the <form> tag. If you do elect to use an alternative encoding, the only other supported format is multipart/form-data.

The standard encoding—application/x-www-form-urlencoded—converts any spaces in the form values to a plus sign (+), nonalphanumeric characters into a percent sign (%) followed by two hexadecimal digits that are the ASCII code of the character, and the line breaks in multiline form data into %0D%0A. (See Chapter 12, *CGI Overview*, for more information on URL encoding.)

The multipart/form-data encoding encapsulates the fields in the form as several parts of a single MIME-compatible compound document.

The other required attribute for the <form> tag sets the method by which the browser sends the form's data to the server for processing. There are two ways: the POST method and the GET method. See Chapter 12 for more information on GET and POST.

The <input> Tag

Use the <input> tag to define any one of a number of common form elements, including text fields, multiple-choice lists, clickable images, and submission buttons. Although there are many attributes for this tag, only the type and name attributes are required for each element (only type for a submission button). Each type of input element uses only a subset of the allowed attributes. Additional <input> attributes may be required based on the specified form element.

You select the type of element to include in the form with the <input> tag's required type attribute and name the field (used during the form-submission process to the server) with the name attribute.

The most useful (as well as the most common) form-input element is the text-entry field. A text-entry field appears in the browser window as an empty box on one line and accepts a single line of user input that becomes the value of the element when the user submits the form to the server. To create a text entry field inside a form in your HTML document, set the type of the <input> form element to text. You must include a name attribute as well.

The size and maxlength attributes allow you to dictate the width, in characters, of the text-input display box and how many total characters to accept from the user, respectively. The default value for size is dependent on the browser; the default value for maxlength is unlimited.

A text-entry field is usually blank until the user types something into it. You may, however, specify an initial default value for the field with the value attribute.

Password Fields

Password fields behave like a regular text field in a form, except that the user-typed characters don't appear onscreen. Rather, the browser obscures the characters in masked text to keep such things as passwords and other sensitive codes from prying eyes.

To create a password field, set the value of the `type` attribute to `password`. All other attributes and semantics of the conventional text field apply to the masked field. Note that a masked text field is not all that secure, since the browser transmits it unencrypted when the form is submitted to the server.

File-Selection Fields

The file-selection form field (introduced by Netscape Navigator) lets users select a file stored on their computer and send it to the server when they submit the form. Browsers present the file-selection form field to the user like other text fields, but it's accompanied by a button labeled "Browse." Users either type the pathname directly as text into the field or, with the Browse option, select the name of a locally stored file from a system-specific dialog box.

Create a file-selection field in a form by setting the value of the `type` attribute to `file`. Like other text fields, the `size` and `maxlength` of a file-selection field should be set to appropriate values.

Checkboxes

The checkbox element gives users a way to quickly and easily select or deselect an item in your form. Checkboxes may also be grouped to create a set of choices, any of which may be selected or deselected by the user.

Create individual checkboxes by setting the `type` attribute for each `<input>` tag to `checkbox`. Include the required `name` and `value` attributes. If the item is selected, it contributes a value when the form is submitted. If it is not selected, that element doesn't contribute a value. The optional `checked` attribute (no value) tells the browser to display a checked checkbox and include the value when submitting the form to the server, unless the user specifically clicks the mouse to deselect (uncheck) the box.

The browsers include the value of selected (checked) checkboxes with other form parameters when they are submitted to the server. The value of the checked checkbox is the text string you specify in the required `value` attribute.

By giving several checkboxes the same `name` attribute value, you create a group of checkbox elements. The browser automatically collects the values of a checkbox group and submits their selected values as a comma-separated string to the server, significantly easing server-side form processing.

Radio Buttons

Radio buttons are similar in behavior to checkboxes, except only one in the group may be selected by the user. Create a radio button by setting the `type` attribute of the `<input>` element to `radio`. Like checkbox elements, radio buttons each require a `name` and `value` attribute; buttons with the same name value are members of a group. One of them may be initially checked by including the `checked` attribute with that element. If no element in the group is checked, the browser automatically checks the first element in the group.

You should give each radio button element a different value, so the server can sort them after submission of the form.

Submission Buttons

The submit button (`<input type=submit>`) does what its name implies, setting in motion the form's submission to the server from the browser. You may have more than one submit button in a form. You may also include `name` and `value` attributes with a submit button.

With the simplest submit button (that is, one without a `name` or `value` attribute), the browser displays a small rectangle or oval with the default label "Submit." Otherwise, the browser labels the button with the text you include with the tag's `value` attribute. If you provide a `name` attribute, the `value` attribute for the submit button is added to the parameter list the browser sends to the server.

Reset Buttons

The reset type of form `<input>` button is nearly self-explanatory: it lets the user reset—erase or set to some default value—all elements in the form. By default, the browser displays a reset button with the label "Reset" or "Clear." You can change that by specifying a `value` attribute with your own button label.

Custom Buttons

With the image type of `<input>` form element, you create a custom button, one that is a "clickable" image. It's a special button made out of your specified image that, when clicked by the user, tells the browser to submit the form to the server, and includes the x,y coordinates of the mouse pointer in the form's parameter list. Image buttons require a `src` attribute with the URL of the image file, and you can include a `name` attribute. You may also include the `align` attribute to control image alignment within the current line of text, much like the `align` attribute for the `<img>` tag.

Hidden Fields

The last type of form `<input>` element we describe in this chapter is a way to embed information into your forms that cannot be ignored or altered by the browser or user. Rather, the `<input type=hidden>` tag's required `name` and `value` attributes automatically get included in the submitted form's parameter list. These serve to "label" the form and can be invaluable when sorting out different forms or form versions from a collection of submitted and saved forms.

The <textarea> Tag

The `<textarea>` tag creates a multiline text-entry area in the user's browser display. In it, the user may type a nearly unlimited number of lines of text. When the form is submitted, the browser sends the text along with the name specified by the required `name` attribute.

You may include plain text between the `<textarea>` tag and its end tag `</textarea>`. The browser uses that text as the default value for the text area.

You can control the dimensions of a multiline text area by defining the `cols` and `rows` attributes for the visible rectangular area set aside by the browser for multiline input.

Normally, text typed in the text area by the user is transmitted to the server exactly as typed, with lines broken only where the user pressed the Enter key. With the `wrap` attribute set to `virtual`, the text is wrapped within the text area for presentation to the user, but the text is transmitted to the server as if no wrapping had occurred, except where the user pressed the Enter key. With the `wrap` attribute set to `physical`, the text is wrapped within the text area and is transmitted to the server as if the user had actually typed it that way. To obtain the default action, set the `wrap` attribute to `off`.

The <select> Tag

Checkboxes and radio buttons give you powerful means for creating multiple-choice questions and answers, but they can lead to long forms that are tedious to write and put a fair amount of clutter onscreen. The `<select>` tag gives you two compact alternatives: pull-down menus and scrolling lists.

By placing a list of `<option>` tagged items inside the `<select>` tag of a form, you create a pull-down menu of choices.

As with other form tags, the `name` attribute is required and used by the browser when submitting the `<select>` choices to the server. Unlike radio buttons, however, no item is preselected, so if the user doesn't select any, no values are sent to the server when the form is submitted. Otherwise, the browser submits the selected item or collects multiple selections, each separated with commas, into a single parameter list and includes the `name` attribute when submitting `<select>` form data to the server.

To allow more than one option selection at a time, add the `multiple` attribute to the `<select>` tag. This causes the `<select>` to behave like an `<input type=checkbox>` element. If `multiple` is not specified, exactly one option can be selected at a time, just like a group of radio buttons.

The `size` attribute determines how many options are visible to the user at one time. The value of `size` should be a positive integer. If `size` is set to `1` and `multiple` is not specified, the `<select>` list is typically implemented as a pop-up menu, while values greater than 1 or specifying the `multiple` attribute cause the `<select>` to be displayed as a scrolling list.

Use the <option> tag to define each item within a <select> form element. The browser displays the <option> tag's contents as an element within the <select> tag's menu or scrolling list, so the content must be plain text only, without any other sort of markup.

Use the `value` attribute to set a value for each option the browser sends to the server if that option is selected by the user. If the `value` attribute has not been specified, the value of the option is set to the content of the <option> tag.

By default, all options within a multiple-choice <select> tag are unselected. Include the `selected` attribute (no value) inside the <option> tag to preselect one or more options, which the user may then deselect. Single-choice <select> tags preselect the first option if no option is explicitly preselected.

An Example Form

Figure 6-1 presents an HTML form showing as many form features as we can fit in the example.

The HTML used to create this form is shown here:

```
<html><head><title>Web Banking</title></head>
<body>
<h1>Web Banking</h1>
Welcome to our Web banking page!  No, you can't make
deposits or get cash ... but you can get balances, make
transfers, and list the most recent transactions on your account.
<form method="post" action="/cgi-bin/banking.pl">
<pre>
Account Number:    <input type="text" name="acct">
PIN:               <input type="password" name="pin" size=8>

Transaction:       <select name="transaction">
                   <option selected>Account balances
                   <option>Transfers
                   <option>Show recent transactions
                   <option>Stop payment on a check
                   </select>

<input type="radio" name="verify_by_mail" value="yes" checked> Mail me
a written verification
<input type="radio" name="verify_by_mail" value="no"> Do not mail me a
written verification

Mail me some information on:
   <input type="checkbox"name="info" value="cds"> Certificates of
deposit
   <input type="checkbox" name="info" value="mortgages"> Home mortgage
interest rates
   <input type="checkbox" name="info" value="autoloans"> Auto loan
interest rates


Tell us what you think about our Web services!
<textarea rows=5 cols=60 name="comments">
</textarea>
```

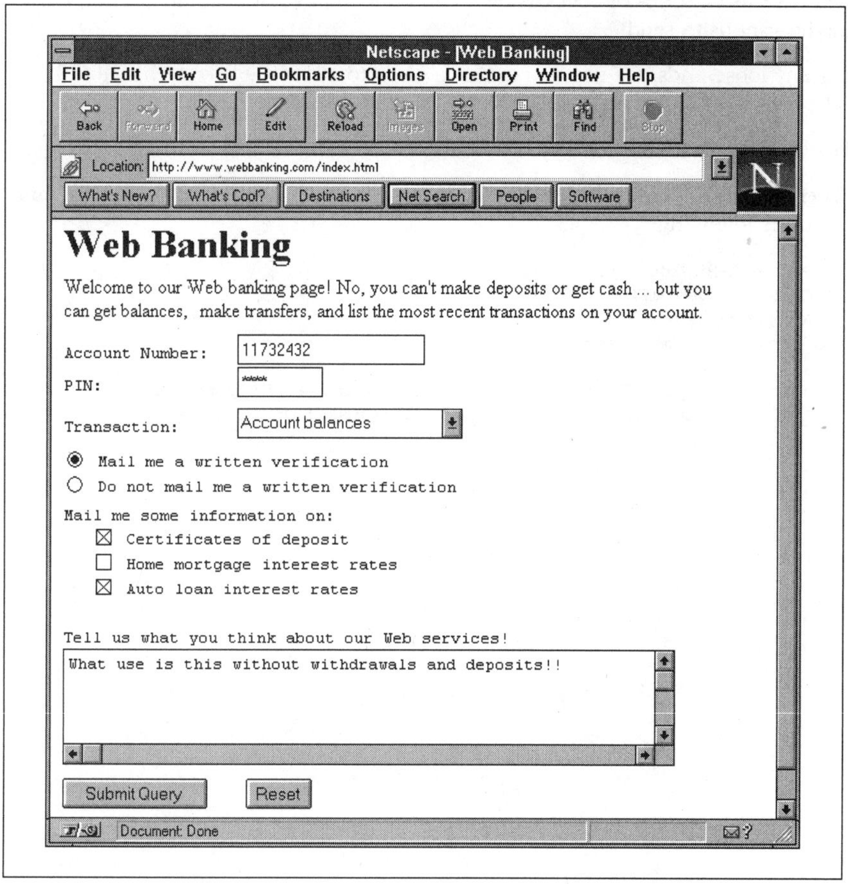

Figure 6-1: The completed form

```
<input type="submit">    <input type="reset">
</form>
</body></html>
```

First, we use an <input> text field to get the user's bank account number. For the user's Personal Identification Number (PIN), we use an <input> password field so that the numbers don't appear on screen. (In real life, this wouldn't be considered sufficient for protecting someone's PIN, since the data entered is sent unencrypted across the Internet.)

Next, we use a selection box to have the user choose a transaction. The user can choose to get account balances, transfer money, see a listing of the most recent transactions on that account, or stop payment on a check.

We use a radio box to let the user choose whether to get a written verification of this transaction. The default is to send written verification. In a radio box, the user can choose exactly one of the options. Notice that with radio boxes, each item needs to have the same name but different value attributes.

Next, we use a series of checkboxes to find out what additional information a user might want us to send.

For any loose ends, we use a **<textarea>** box to allow the user a chance to blow off steam.

Finally, we provide submit and reset buttons.

When the user submits this query, the browser sends a request to the server similar to the following:

```
POST /cgi-bin/banking.pl HTTP/1.0
Content-Length: 154
Accept: image/gif
          ... (more headers )

acct=11732432&pin=0545&transaction=Account+balances&verify_by_mail=YES
&info=cds,autoloans&comments=What+use+is+this+without+withdrawals+and+
deposits%21%21
```

CHAPTER 7

Character Entities

The following table collects the defined standard, proposed, and several nonstandard (but generally supported) character entities for HTML.

Entity names, if defined, appear for their respective characters and can be used in the HTML character-entity sequence `&name;` to define any character for display by the browser. Otherwise, or alternatively for named characters, use the character's three-digit numerical value in the sequence `&#nnn;` to specifically define an HTML character entity. Actual characters, however, may or may not be displayed by the browser depending on the computer platform and user-selected font for display.

Not all 256 characters in the ISO character set appear in the table. Missing ones are not recognized by the browser as either named or numeric entities.

To be sure that your documents are fully compliant with the HTML 4.0 standard, use only those named character entities whose conformance column is blank. Defy compliance by using the nonstandard (N) entities.

Numeric Entity	*Named Entity*	*Symbol*	*Description*	*Conformance*
` `			Horizontal tab	
`
`			Line feed	
`
`			Carriage return	
` `			Space	
`!`		!	Exclamation point	
`"`	`"`	"	Quotation mark	
`#`		#	Hash mark	
`$`		$	Dollar sign	
`%`		%	Percent sign	

Numeric Entity	*Named Entity*	*Symbol*	*Description*	*Conformance*
&	&	&	Ampersand	
'		'	Apostrophe	
(		(	Left parenthesis	
)		)	Right parenthesis	
*		*	Asterisk	
+		+	Plus sign	
,		,	Comma	
-		-	Hyphen	
.		.	Period	
/		/	Slash	
0 -9		0\n9	Digits 0–9	
:		:	Colon	
;		;	Semicolon	
<	<	<	Less than	
=		=	Equal sign	
>	>	>	Greater than	
?		?	Question mark	
@		@	Commercial "at" sign	
A - Z		A–Z	Letters A–Z	
[		[	Left square bracket	
\		\	Backslash	
]		]	Right square bracket	
^		^	Caret	
_		_	Underscore	
`		`	Grave accent	
a -z		a–z	Letters a–z	
{		{	Left curly brace	
			|	Vertical bar	
}		}	Right curly brace	
~		~	Tilde	
‚		‚	Rising single quote (low)	N
ƒ		*f*	Florin	N
„		„	Rising double quote (low)	N
…		...	Ellipsis	N
†		†	Dagger	N

Numeric Entity	Named Entity	Symbol	Description	Conformance
‡		‡	Double dagger	N
ˆ		ˆ	Circumflex	N
‰		‰	Permil	N
Š		_		N
‹		<	Left single angle bracket	N
Œ		Œ	Capital OE ligature	N
‘		‘	Left single quote	N
’		’	Right single quote	N
“		“	Left double quote	N
”		”	Right double quote	N
•		•	Bullet	N
–		–	En dash	N
—		—	Em dash	N
˜		˜	Tilde	N
™		™	Trademark	N
š		_		N
›		>	Right single angle bracket	N
œ		œ	Small oe ligature	N
Ÿ		Ÿ	Capital Y, umlaut	N
			Nonbreaking space	
¡	¡	¡	Inverted exclamation point	
¢	¢	¢	Cent sign	
£	£	£	Pound sign	
¤	¤	¤	General currency sign	
¥	¥	¥	Yen sign	
¦	¦	¦	Broken vertical bar	
§	§	§	Section sign	
¨	¨	¨	Umlaut	
©	©	©	Copyright	
ª	ª	ª	Feminine ordinal	
«	«	‵	Left angle quote	
¬	¬	∉	Not sign	
		–	Soft hyphen	
®	®	®	Registered trademark	
¯	¯	¯	Macron accent	
°	°	°	Degree sign	
±	±	±	Plus or minus	

Numeric Entity	*Named Entity*	*Symbol*	*Description*	*Conformance*
`²`	`²`	^{2}	Superscript 2	
`³`	`³`	^{3}	Superscript 3	
`´`	`´`	´	Acute accent	
`µ`	`µ`	µ	Micro sign (Greek mu)	
`¶`	`¶`	¶	Paragraph sign	
`·`	`·`	·	Middle dot	
`¸`	`¸`	¸	Cedilla	
`¹`	`¹`	^{1}	Superscript 1	
`º`	`º`	º	Masculine ordinal	
`»`	`»`	‹	Right angle quote	
`¼`	`¼`	¼	Fraction one-fourth	
`½`	`½`	½	Fraction one-half	
`¾`	`¾`	¾	Fraction three-fourths	
`¿`	`¿`	¿	Inverted question mark	
`À`	`À`	À	Capital A, grave accent	
`Á`	`Á`	Á	Capital A, acute accent	
`Â`	`Â`	Â	Capital A, circumflex accent	
`Ã`	`Ã`	Ã	Capital A, tilde	
`Ä`	`Ä`	Ä	Capital A, umlaut	
`Å`	`Å`	Å	Capital A, ring	
`Æ`	`Æ`	Æ	Capital AE ligature	
`Ç`	`Ç`	Ç	Capital C, cedilla	
`È`	`È`	È	Capital E, grave accent	
`É`	`É`	É	Capital E, acute accent	
`Ê`	`Ê`	Ê	Capital E, circumflex accent	
`Ë`	`Ë`	Ë	Capital E, umlaut	
`Ì`	`Ì`	Ì	Capital I, grave accent	
`Í`	`Í`	Í	Capital I, acute accent	
`Î`	`Î`	Î	Capital I, circumflex accent	
`Ï`	`Ï`	Ï	Capital I, umlaut	
`Ð`	`Ð`	Ð	Capital eth, Icelandic	
`Ñ`	`Ñ`	Ñ	Capital N, tilde	
`Ò`	`Ò`	Ò	Capital O, grave accent	
`Ó`	`Ó`	Ó	Capital O, acute accent	
`Ô`	`Ô`	Ô	Capital O, circumflex accent	
`Õ`	`Õ`	Õ	Capital O, tilde	
`Ö`	`Ö`	Ö	Capital O, umlaut	

Numeric Entity	*Named Entity*	*Symbol*	*Description*	*Conformance*
`×`	`×`	×	Multiply sign	
`Ø`	`Ø`	Ø	Capital O, slash	
`Ù`	`Ù`	Ù	Capital U, grave accent	
`Ú`	`Ú`	Ú	Capital U, acute accent	
`Û`	`Û`	Û	Capital U, circumflex accent	
`Ü`	`Ü`	Ü	Capital U, umlaut	
`Ý`	`Ý`	Ý	Capital Y, acute accent	
`Þ`	`Þ`	Þ	Capital thorn, Icelandic	
`ß`	`ß`	ß	Small sz ligature, German	
`à`	`à`	à	Small a, grave accent	
`á`	`á`	á	Small a, acute accent	
`â`	`â`	â	Small a, circumflex accent	
`ã`	`ã`	ã	Small a, tilde	
`ä`	`ä`	ä	Small a, umlaut	
`å`	`å`	å	Small a, ring	
`æ`	`æ`	æ	Small ae ligature	
`ç`	`ç`	ç	Small c, cedilla	
`è`	`è`	è	Small e, grave accent	
`é`	`é`	é	Small e, acute accent	
`ê`	`ê`	ê	Small e, circumflex accent	
`ë`	`ë`	ë	Small e, umlaut	
`ì`	`ì`	ì	Small i, grave accent	
`í`	`í`	í	Small i, acute accent	
`î`	`î`	î	Small i, circumflex accent	
`ï`	`ï`	ï	Small i, umlaut	
`ð`	`ð`	∂	Small eth, Icelandic	
`ñ`	`ñ`	ñ	Small n, tilde	
`ò`	`ò`	ò	Small o, grave accent	
`ó`	`ó`	ó	Small o, acute accent	
`ô`	`ô`	ô	Small o, circumflex accent	
`õ`	`õ`	õ	Small o, tilde	
`ö`	`ö`	ö	Small o, umlaut	
`÷`	`÷`	÷	Division sign	
`ø`	`ø`	ø	Small o, slash	
`ù`	`ù`	ù	Small u, grave accent	
`ú`	`ú`	ú	Small u, acute accent	
`û`	`û`	û	Small u, circumflex accent	

Numeric Entity	*Named Entity*	*Symbol*	*Description*	*Conformance*
`ü`	`ü`	ü	Small u, umlaut	
`ý`	`ý`	ý	Small y, acute accent	
`þ`	`þ`	þ	Small thorn, Icelandic	
`ÿ`	`ÿ`	ÿ	Small y, umlaut	

CHAPTER 8

Color Names and Values

With the popular browsers, you can prescribe the colors of various elements of your document via tag attributes or CSS style definitions.

You may specify the color value as a six-digit hexadecimal number that represents the red, green, and blue (RGB) components of the color. The first two digits correspond to the red component of the color, the next two to the green component, and the last two to the blue component. A value of 00 corresponds to the component being completely off; a value of FF (255) corresponds to the component being completely on. Thus, bright red is FF0000, bright green is 00FF00, and bright blue is 0000FF. Other primary colors are mixtures of two components, such as yellow (FFFF00), magenta (FF00FF), and cyan (00FFFF). White (FFFFFF) and black (000000) are also easy to figure out.

You use these values in a tag by replacing the color with the RGB triple, preceded by a hash (#) symbol. Thus, to make all visited links display as magenta, use this body tag:

```
<body vlink="#FF00FF">
```

Determining the hexadecimal value for more esoteric colors like "papaya whip" or "navajo white" is very difficult. You can go crazy trying to adjust the RGB triple for a color to get the shade just right, especially when each adjustment requires loading a document into your browser to view the result.

To make life easier, the HTML 4.0 standard defines 16 standard color names that can be used anywhere a numeric color value can be used. For example, you can make all visited links in the display magenta with the following attribute for the body tag:

```
<body vlink="magenta">
```

The color names and RGB values defined in the HTML standard are:

aqua (#00FFFF)	gray (#808080)	navy (#000080)	silver (#C0C0C0)
black (#000000)	green (#008000)	olive (#808000)	teal (#008080)
blue (#0000FF)	lime (#00FF00)	purple (#800080)	yellow (#FFFF00)
fuchsia (#FF00FF)	maroon (#800000)	red (#FF0000)	white (#FFFFFF)

The popular browsers go well beyond the HTML 4.0 standard and support the several hundred color names defined for use in the X Window System. Note that color names may contain no spaces; also, the word *gray* may be spelled *grey* in any color name.

Colors marked with an asterisk (*) represent a family of colors numbered one through four. Thus, there are actually four variants of blue, named blue1, blue2, blue3, and blue4, along with plain old blue. Blue1 is the lightest of the four; blue4 the darkest. The unnumbered color name is the same color as the first; thus, blue and blue1 are identical.

Finally, if all that isn't enough, there are 100 variants of gray (and grey) numbered 1 through 100. Gray1 is the darkest, gray100 is the lightest, and gray is very close to gray75.

The extended color names are:

aliceblue
antiquewhite*
aquamarine*
azure*
beige
bisque*
black
blanchedalmond
blue*
blueviolet
brown*
burlywood*
cadetblue*
chartreuse*
chocolate*
coral*
cornflowerblue
cornsilk*
cyan*
darkblue
darkcyan
darkgoldenrod*
darkgray
darkgreen
darkkhaki
darkmagenta
darkolivegreen*
darkturquoise
darkviolet
deeppink*
deepskyblue*
dimgray
dodgerblue*
firebrick*
floralwhite
forestgreen
gainsboro
ghostwhite
gold*
goldenrod*
gray
green*
greenyellow
honeydew*
hotpink*
indianred*
ivory*
khaki*
lavender
lavenderblush*
lawngreen
lemonchiffon*
lightblue*
lightcoral
lightseagreen
lightskyblue*
lightslateblue
lightslategray
lightsteelblue*
lightyellow*
limegreen
linen
magenta*
maroon*
mediumaquamarine
mediumblue
mediumorchid*
mediumpurple*
mediumseagreen
mediumslateblue
mediumspringgreen
mediumturquoise
mediumvioletred
midnightblue
mintcream
mistyrose*
moccasin
navajowhite*
navy
navyblue
oldlace
palevioletred*
papayawhip
peachpuff*
peru
pink*
plum*
powderblue
purple*
red*
rosybrown*
royalblue*
saddlebrown
salmon*
sandybrown
seagreen*
seashell*
sienna*
skyblue*
slateblue*
slategray*
snow*
springgreen*
steelblue*
tan*
thistle*
tomato*
turquoise*

darkorange*
darkorchid*
darkred
darksalmon
darkseagreen*
darkslateblue
darkslategray*

lightcyan*
lightgoldenrod*
lightgoldenrodyellow
lightgray
lightgreen
lightpink*
lightsalmon*

olivedrab*
orange*
orangered*
orchid*
palegoldenrod
palegreen*
paleturquoise*

violet
violetred*
wheat*
white
whitesmoke
yellow*
yellowgreen

PART II

CSS

CHAPTER 9

CSS

Cascading Style Sheets

Style sheets are the way publishing professionals manage the overall "look" of their publications—backgrounds, fonts, colors, etc. Most desktop publishing software supports style sheets, as do the popular word processors.

From its earliest origins, HTML focused on content over style. Authors were encouraged to provide high quality information, and leave it to the browser to worry about presentation. We strongly urge you to adopt that philosophy in your HTML documents.

However, while use of the HTML `<font>` tag and related attributes like `Wcolor` produce acute presentation effects, style sheets, when judiciously applied, bring consistency and order to documents. Style sheets let the HTML author control the presentation attributes for all the tags in a document or a whole collection of many documents, and from a single master style sheet.

In early 1996, the World Wide Web Consortium put together a draft proposal defining Cascading Style Sheets (CSS) for HTML. This draft proposal quickly matured into a recommended standard, which the commercial browser manufacturers were quick to exploit. Internet Explorer 4.0, introduced in the fall of 1997, implements most of the W3C standard. Netscape Navigator has some support for style sheets in Version 4.0, which was introduced in the spring of 1997. Style is fast achieving parity with content on the World Wide Web.

Since we realize that eventual compliance with the W3C standard is likely, we'll cover all the components of the standard in this section, even if they are not yet supported by any browser. We'll denote clearly what is real, what is proposed, and what is actually supported.

The Elements of Styles

At the simplest level, a style is nothing more than a rule that tells the browser how to display a particular HTML tag. Each tag has a number of properties associated with it, whose values define how that tag is rendered by the browser. A rule defines a specific value for one or more properties of a tag. For example, most tags have a color property, the value of which defines the color used to display that tag. Other properties include font attributes, line spacing, margins, and borders.

There are three ways to attach a style to a tag: inline styles, document-level styles, and external style sheets. You may use one or more style types in your documents. The browser either merges the style definitions from each style or redefines the style characteristic for a tag's contents. Styles from these various sources are applied to your document, combining and defining style properties that cascade from external style sheets through local document styles, ending with inline styles. This cascade of properties and style rules gives rise to the standard's name: Cascading Style Sheets.

Inline Styles

The inline style is the simplest way to attach a style to a tag—just include a `style` attribute with the tag, along with a list of properties and their values. The browser uses those style properties and values to render the contents of just this instance of the tag.

For instance, the following style tells the browser to display the level-one header text, "This is blue," in the `<h1>` tag style characteristic of the browser and also in the color blue and italicized:

```
<h1 style="color: blue; font-style: italic">This is blue</h1>
```

This type of style definition is called "inline" because it occurs with the tag as it appears in the document. The scope of the style covers the contents of that tag only. Since inline styles are sprinkled throughout your document, they can be difficult to maintain. Use the style attribute sparingly and only in those rare circumstances when you cannot achieve the same effects otherwise.

Style definitions are created with the name of the style attribute—`color` for example—followed by a colon and then the style's value. You will commonly supply a list of style definitions for a single element. In the list, each style definition is separated by a semicolon.

Document-Level Styles

The real power of style sheets dawns when you place a list of presentation rules within the head of an HTML document. Enclosed within their own `<style>` and `</style>` tags, "document-level" style sheets affect all the same tags within that document, except for tags that contain an overriding inline style attribute.

The `<style>` tag must appear within the `<head>` of a document. Everything between the `<style>` and `</style>` tags is considered part of the style rules to be applied to the document. To be perfectly correct, the content of the <style> tag is not HTML and is not bound by the normal rules for HTML content. The <style> tag, in effect, lets you insert foreign content into your HTML document that the browser uses to format your tags. Older browsers may not know how to handle this content, so it is common practice to place your style definitions inside an HTML comment (<!-- -->) within the style tag.

Style definitions in a style sheet begin with the name of the tag you are defining a style for. The style definitions are contained in braces following the tag name. For example, this document-level style sheet displays the contents of all <h1> tags as blue, italic text:

```
<head>
<title>All True Blue</title>

<style type="text/css">
  <!--
  /* make all H1 headers blue */

  H1 {color: blue; font-style: italic}

  -->
</style>
</head>

<body>
<h1>This is blue</h1>
<h1>Ever so blue</h1>
```

One important attribute for the `style` tag is the `type` attribute. The `type` attribute defines the types of styles you are including within the tag. Cascading style sheets always carry the type `text/css`; JavaScript style sheets use the type `text/javascript`. You may omit the `type` attribute and hope the browser figures out the kind of styles you are using. We prefer to include the `type` attribute so that there is no opportunity for confusion.

External Style Sheets

You may also place style definitions, like our document-level style sheet example for the <h1> tags, into a text file with the MIME type of `text/css` and import this style sheet into your HTML documents. Because an external style sheet is a file separate from the HTML document and is loaded by the browser over the network, you can store it anywhere, reuse it often, and even use others' style sheets. But most important, external style sheets give you the power to influence the display styles not only of all related tags in a single document, but for an entire collection of documents.

For example, suppose we create a file named *gen_styles.css* containing the style rule:

```
H1 {color: blue; font-style: italic}
```

For each and every one of the HTML documents in our collections, we can tell the browser to read the contents of the *gen_styles.css* file, which, in turn, colors all the <h1> tag contents blue and renders the text in italic. Of course, since style definitions cascade by nature, the style can be overridden by a document-level or inline style definition.

You can load external style sheets into your HTML document in two different ways: with the `<link>` tag for the `@import` style command.

Linked external stylesheets

One way to load an external style sheet is to use the `<link>` tag:

```
<head>
<title>Linked Style</title>

<link rel=stylesheet type="text/css"
      href="http://www.kumquats.com/styles/gen_styles.css"
      title="The blues">

</head>
```

The `<link>` tag creates a relationship between the current document and some other document on the Web. In the example, we tell the browser that the document named in the `href` attribute is a style sheet, and that its contents conform to the CSS standard, as indicated by the `type` attribute. We also provide a title for the style sheet, making it available for later reference by the browser.

The `<link>` tag must appear in the `<head>` of a document. The URL of the style sheet may be absolute or relative to the document's base URL. The type may also be `text/javascript`, indicating (for Netscape only) that the style rules are written in JavaScript instead of the CSS syntax.

Imported external style sheets

The second technique for loading an external style sheet imports the files with a special command within the `<style>` tag:

```
<head>
<title>Imported style sheet</title>

<style>
  <!--

    @import url(http://www.oreilly.com/styles/gen_styles.css);
    @import url(http://www.oreilly.com/styles/spec_styles.css);
    BODY: {background: url(backgrounds/marble.gif)}

  -->
</style>

</head>
```

The `@import` command expects a single URL parameter that names the network path to the external style sheet. The `url` keyword, parentheses, and trailing semicolon are all required elements of the `@import` command. The URL may be absolute or relative to the document's base URL. The `@import` command must appear before any conventional style rules, either in the `<style>` tag or in an external style sheet. Otherwise, the browser ignores the preceding style definitions. This ordering also means that subsequent style rules can override rules in the imported sheet, and indeed they do.

The `@import` command can appear in a document-level style definition or even in another external style sheet, letting you create nested style sheets.

Linked versus imported style sheets

At first glance, it may appear that linked and imported style sheets are equivalent, using different syntax for the same functionality. This is true if you use just one `<link>` tag in your document. However, special rules come into play if you include two or more `<link>` tags within a single document.

With one `<link>` tag, the browser loads the styles in the referenced style sheet and formats the document accordingly, with any document-level and inline styles overriding the external definitions. With two or more `<link>` tags, the browser presents the user with a list of all the linked style sheets. The user can then select one of the sheets, which is used to format the document. The other linked style sheets are ignored.

On the other hand, the styles-conscious browser merges, as opposed to separate, multiple imported style sheets to form a single set of style rules for your document. The last imported style sheet takes precedence if there are duplicate definitions among the style sheets. Imported styles also override linked external styles, just as document-level and inline styles override external style definitions.

Limitations of Current Browsers

Both Internet Explorer 4.0 and Netscape 4.0 allow you to use the `<link>` tag to apply an external style sheet to a document. Netscape ignores the `@import` command but continues to process other style rules within the `<style>` tag. Internet Explorer honors the `@import` command and also supports the `@import` command within external sheets, allowing sheets to be nested.

Neither Netscape nor Internet Explorer supports multiple linked style sheets as proposed by the CSS standard. Instead, they load all the linked style sheets, with rules in later sheets possibly overriding rules in earlier sheets.

We hope the standard will someday prevail so that style sheets, already mystifying to most, will become that much less confusing.

Style Comments

Comments are welcome inside the `<style>` tag and in external style sheets, but don't use a standard HTML comment; style sheets aren't HTML. Rather, enclose style comments beginning with the sequence `/*` and ending with `*/`. Use this comment syntax for both document-level and external style sheets. Comments may not be nested.

We recommend documenting your styles whenever possible, especially in external style sheets. Whenever the possibility exists that your styles may be used by other authors, comments make it much easier to understand your styles.

Style Syntax

The syntax of a style, as you may have gleaned from our previous examples, is fairly straightforward. A style rule is made up of at least three basic parts: a tag selector, which identifies the name of the tag that the style rule affects, followed by a curly brace ({}) enclosed, semicolon-separated list of one or more style property:value declaration pairs:

```
tag-selector {property1:value1; property2:value1 value2 value3; ...}
```

Properties require at least one value but may include two or more values. Separate multiple values with a space, as is done for the three values that define `property2` in the example. Some properties require that multiple values be separated with commas.

Styles-conscious browsers ignore letter case in any element of a rule. Hence, H1 and h1 are the same selector, and COLOR, color, ColOR, and cOLor are equivalent properties. Convention dictates, however, that tag names be all uppercase, and that properties and values be lowercase. We'll abide by those conventions throughout this book.

Any valid HTML tag name (a tag minus its enclosing < and > characters and attributes) can be a selector. You may include more than one tag name in the list of selectors, as we explain in the following sections.

Multiple Selectors

When separated by commas, all the tags named in the selector list are affected by the property values in the style rule. This can make life very easy for the HTML author. For instance:

```
H1, H2, H3, H4, H5, H6 {text-align: center}
```

tells the browser to center the contents of the header tag levels 1–6. Clearly, one line is easier to type, understand, and modify than six. And it takes less time and fewer resources to transmit across a network, as well.

Contextual Selectors

Normally, the styles-conscious browser applies styles to tags wherever they appear in your document, without regard to context. However, the CSS standard does define a way to have a style applied only when a tag occurs within a certain context within a document, such as when it is nested within other tags.

To create a contextual selector, list the tags in the order in which they should be nested in your document, outermost tag first, with *no* commas separating them. When that nesting order is encountered by the browser, the style properties is applied to the last tag in the list.

For example, here's how you might use contextual styles to define the classic numbering sequence used for outlines: capital letters for the outer level, uppercase Roman numerals for the next level, lowercase letters for the next, and Arabic numerals for the innermost level:

```
OL LI {list-style: upper-alpha}
OL OL LI {list-style: upper-roman}
OL OL OL LI {list-style: lower-alpha}
OL OL OL OL LI {list-style: decimal}
```

According to the example style sheet, when the styles-conscious browser encounters the <li> tag nested within one <ol> tag, it uses the upper-alpha value for the list-style property of the <li> tag. When it sees an <li> tag nested within two <ol> tags, the same browser uses the upper-roman list style. Nest an <li> tag within three and four <ol> tags, and you'll see the lower-alpha and decimal list-style used, respectively.

Similarly, you may impose a specific style on tags related only by context. For instance, this contextual style definition colors the emphasis tag's (<em>) contents red only when it appears inside a level-one header tag (<h1>), not elsewhere in the document:

```
H1 EM {color: red}
```

If there is potential ambiguity between two contextual styles, the more specific context prevails. Like individual tags, you may also have several contextual selectors mixed with individual selectors, each and all separated by commas, sharing the same list of style declarations. For example:

```
H1 EM, P STRONG, ADDRESS {color: red}
```

means that you'll see red whenever the <em> tag appears within an <h1> tag, or when the <strong> tag appears within a <p> tag, and for the contents of the <address> tag.

The nesting need not be exact to match the rule. For example, if you nest the <strong> tag within a <ul> tag within a <p> tag, you'll still match the rule for P STRONG that we defined above. If a particular nesting matches several style rules, the most specific rule is used.

Style Classes

There is one more feature of style sheets that we haven't mentioned yet: classes. Classes let you create, at the document level or in an external style sheet, several different styles for a single tag, each distinguished by a class name. To apply the style class, name it as the value of the class attribute in the tag.

Regular classes

In a technical paper you might want to define one paragraph style for the abstract, another for equations, and a third for centered quotations. None of the paragraph tags may have an explicit context in the HTML document so you could distinguish it from the others. Rather, you may define each as a different style class:

```
<style>
<!--

P.abstract {font-style: italic;
            left-margin: 0.5cm;
```

```
            right-margin: 0.5cm}

P.equation {font-family: Symbol;
            text-align: center}

H1, P.centered {text-align: center;
                left-margin: 0.5cm;
                right-margin: 0.5cm}

-->
</style>
```

Notice first in the example that defining a class is simply a matter of appending a period-separated class name as a suffix to the tag name as the selector in a style rule. The class name can be any sequence of letters, numbers, and hyphens but must begin with a letter. And classes, like all selectors, may be included with other selectors, separated by commas, as in the third example. The only restriction on classes is that they can't be nested: e.g., `P.equation.centered` is not allowed.

Accordingly, the first rule in the example creates a class of paragraph styles named "abstract" whose text is italic and indented from the left and right margins by a half centimeter. Similarly, the second paragraph style class "equation" instructs the browser to center the text and to use the Symbol typeface to display the text. The last style rule creates a style with centered text and half-centimeter margins, applying this style to all level-one headers, as well as creating a class of the <p> tag named centered with that style.

To use a particular class of a tag, you add the class attribute to the tag, as in this example:

```
<p class=abstract>
This is the abstract paragraph.  See how the margins are indented?
</p>

<h3>The equation paragraph follows</h3>

<p class=equation>
a = b + 1
</p>

<p class=centered>
This paragraph's text should be centered.
</p>
```

For each paragraph, the value of the class attribute is the name of the class to be used for that tag.

Generic classes

You may also define a class without associating it with a particular tag, and then apply that class selectively through your documents for a variety of tags. For example:

```
.italic {font-style: italic}
```

creates a generic class named *italic*. To use it, simply include its name with the class attribute. So, for instance, use <p class=italic> or <h1 class=italic> to create an italic paragraph or header.

Generic classes are quite handy and make it easy to apply a particular style to a broad range of tags. Generic classes are currently supported only by Netscape 4.0.

Using IDs as classes

CSS

Almost all HTML tags accept the id attribute, which assigns an identifier to the element that is unique within the document. This identifier can be the target of a URL, used by automated document processing tools, and can specify a style rule for the element.

To create a style class that can be applied with the id attribute, follow the same syntax used for style classes, except with a # character before the class name instead of a period. This style creates such classes:

```
<style>
<!--

#yellow { color : yellow}
H1#blue { color : blue}

-->
</style>
```

Within your document, you could use <h1 id=blue> to create a blue heading, or add id=yellow to almost any tag to turn it yellow. You can mix and match both class and id attributes, giving you a limited ability to apply two independent style rules to a single element.

There is a dramatic drawback to using classes defined this way: the value of the id attribute must be unique to exactly one tag within the document. You cannot legally reuse the class, although the browser might let you get away with it.

For this reason, we discourage creating and using these kinds of classes. Stick to the conventional style of classes to create correct, robust HTML documents.

Style pseudo-classes

In addition to conventional style classes, the CSS standard defines pseudo-classes, which allow you to define the display style for certain tag states. Pseudo-classes are like regular classes, with two notable differences: they are attached to the tag name with a colon instead of a period, and they have predefined names, not arbitrary ones you may give them.

There are five pseudo-classes, three of which are associated with the <a> tag. The other two can be used on any text element.

The browsers distinguish three special states for the hyperlinks created by the <a> tag: not visited, being visited, and visited. The browser may change the appearance of the tag's contents to indicate its state, such as underlining or changing the colors. Through pseudo-classes, the HTML author can control how these states get displayed by defining styles for A:link, A:active, and A:visited. The *link* pseudo-class controls the appearance of links that are not selected by the user and have not yet been visited. The *active* pseudo-class defines the appearance of links that are currently selected by the user and are being processed by the browser. The *visited* pseudo-class defines those links that have already been visited by the user.

To completely define all three states of the <a> tag, you might write:

```
A:link {color: blue}
A:active {color: red; font-weight: bold}
A:visited {color: green}
```

The two other pseudo-classes usually apply to the <p> element, and are named *first-letter* and *first-line.* As you might expect, these pseudo-classes control the appearance of the first letter and first line, respectively, of a paragraph and create effects commonly found in printed media, such as initial drop-caps and bold first lines. For example:

```
P:first-line {font-style: small-caps}
```

converts the first line of a paragraph to small capital letters. Similarly:

```
P:first-letter {font-size: 200%; float: left}
```

tells the browser to make the first letter of a paragraph twice as large as the remaining text and float the letter to the left, allowing the first two lines of the paragraph to float around the larger initial letter.

You may mix pseudo-classes with regular classes by appending the pseudo-class name to the selector's class name.

Class inheritance

Classes inherit the style properties of their generic base tag. For instance, all the properties of the plain <p> tag apply to a specially defined paragraph class, except where the class overrides a particular property.

Classes cannot inherit from other classes, only from the unclassed version of the tag they represent. In general, therefore, you should put as many common styles into the rule for the basic version of a tag, and create classes only for those properties that are unique to that class. This makes maintenance and sharing of your style classes easier, especially for large document collections.

Style Properties

At the heart of the Cascading Style Sheet specification are 53 properties that let you control how the styles-conscious browser presents your documents to the user. The standard collects these properties into six groups: fonts, colors and backgrounds, text, boxes and layout, lists, and tag classification. You'll find a summary of the style properties later in this chapter.

Property Values

There are five distinct kinds of property values: keywords, length values, percentage values, URLs, and colors.

Keyword property values

A property may have a keyword value that expresses action or dimension. For instance, the effects of underline and line-through are obvious property values. And you can express property dimensions with keywords like `small` and `xx-large`. Some keywords are even relational: `bolder`, for instance, is an acceptable value for the font-weight property. Keyword values are not case-sensitive: Underline, UNDERLINE, and underline are all acceptable keyword values. Keywords also cover such properties as font-family names.

Length property values

So-called length values (a term taken from the CSS standard) explicitly state the size of a property. They are numbers, some with decimals, too. Length values may have a leading + or - sign to indicate that the value is to be added to or subtracted from the immediate value of the property. Length values must be followed immediately by a two-letter unit abbreviation—with no intervening spaces.

There are three kinds of length-value units: relative, pixels, and absolute. Relative units specify a size that is relative to the size of some other property of the content. Currently, there are only two relative units: `em`, which is the height of the current font, and `x-height`, which is the height of the letter "x" in the current font (abbreviated `ex`). The pixels unit, abbreviated `px`, is equal to the size of a pixel on the browser's display. Absolute property value units are more familiar to us all. They include inches (`in`), centimeters (`cm`), millimeters (`mm`), points (`pt`, 1/72 of an inch), and picas (`pc`, 12 points).

All of the following are valid length values, although not all units are recognized by the styles-conscious browser:

```
1in
1.5cm
+0.25mm
-3pt
-2.5pc
+100em
-2.75ex
250px
```

Percentage property values

Similar to the relative length-value type, a percentage value describes a property size relative to some other aspect of the content. It has an optional sign and decimal portion to its numeric value and must have the percent sign (%) suffix. For example:

```
line-height: 120%
```

computes the separation between lines to be 120% of the current line height (usually relative to the text font height). Note that this value is not dynamic, though: changes made to the font height after the rule has been processed by the browser will not affect the computed line height.

URL property values

Some properties expect a URL as a value. The syntax for using a URL in a style property is different from conventional HTML:

```
url(service://server.com/pathname)
```

The keyword `url` is required, as are the opening and closing parentheses. Do not leave any spaces between `url` and the opening parenthesis. The `url` value may contain either an absolute or a relative URL. However, note that the URL is relative to the immediate style sheet's URL, the one in which it is declared. This means that if you use a `url` value in a document-level or inline style, the URL is relative to the HTML document containing the style document. Otherwise, the URL is relative to the imported or linked external style sheet's URL.

Color property values

Color values specify colors in a property. You can specify a color as a color name or a hexadecimal RGB triple, as is done for common HTML attributes, or as a decimal RGB triple unique to style properties. Both color names and hexadecimal RGB triple notation are described in Chapter 8, *Color Names and Values.*

Unlike regular HTML, style sheets will accept three-digit hexadecimal color values. The single digit is doubled to create a conventional six-digit triple. Thus, the color #78C is equivalent to #7788CC. In general, three-digit color values are handy only for simple colors.

The decimal RGB triple notation is a bit different:

```
rgb(red, green, blue)
```

The red, green, and blue intensity values are integers in the range 0 to 255 or integer percentages. As with a URL value, do not leave any spaces between `rgb` and the opening parenthesis.

For example, in decimal RGB convention, the color white is `rgb(255, 255, 255)` or `rgb(100%, 100%, 100%)`, and a medium yellow is `rgb(127, 127, 0)` or `rgb(50%, 50%, 0%)`.

Property Inheritance

In lieu of a specific rule for a particular tag, properties and their values for tags within tags are inherited from the parent tag. Thus, setting a property for the <body> tag effectively applies that property to every tag in the body of your document, except for those that specifically override it. So, to make all the text in your document blue, you need only say:

```
BODY {color: blue}
```

rather than create a rule for every tag you use in your document.

This inheritance extends to any level. If you later created a `<div>` tag with text of a different color, the styles-conscious browser displays all the text contents of the `<div>` tag and all its enclosed tags in that new color. When the `<div>` tag ends, the color reverts to that of the containing `<body>` tag.

CSS

CSS Reference

The remainder of this chapter lists all the properties defined in the World Wide Web Consortium's Recommended Specification for Cascading Style Sheets, Level 1 *(http://www.w3.org/pub/WWW/TR/REC-CSS1)*. All browsers do not implement all properties fully, and some simply do not work correctly. As in the HTML reference, we use the Netscape N and Internet Explorer I icons to show which browser supports that property. Properties with no icons are not currently supported by these browsers.

The following list includes each property's possible values, defined as either an explicit keyword (shown in constant width) or as one of these values:

color
: Either a color name or hexadecimal RGB value, as defined in Chapter 8, or an RGB triple of the form:

```
rgb(red, green, blue)
```

where red, green, and blue are either numbers in the range 0 to 255 or percentage values indicating the brightness of that color component. Values of 255 or 100% indicate that the corresponding color component is at its brightest; values of 0 or 0% indicate that the corresponding color component is turned off completely. For example:

```
rgb(27, 119, 207)
rgb(50%, 75%, 0%)
```

are both valid color specifications.

length
: An optional sign (either + or -), immediately followed by a number (with or without a decimal point) immediately followed by a two-character unit identifier. For values of zero, the unit identifier may be omitted.

The unit identifiers `em` and `ex` refer to the overall height of the font and to the height of the letter "x", respectively. The unit identifier `px` is equal to a single pixel on the display device. The unit identifiers `in`, `cm`, `mm`, `pt`, and `pc` refer to inches, centimeters, millimeters, points, and picas, respectively. There are 72.27 points per inch and 12 points in a pica.

number

An optional sign, immediately followed by a number (with or without a decimal point).

percent

An optional sign, immediately followed by a number (with or without a decimal point), immediately followed by a percent sign. The actual value is computed as a percentage of some other element property, usually the element's size.

url The keyword `url`, immediately followed (no spaces) by a left parenthesis, followed by a URL optionally enclosed in single or double quotes, followed by a matching right parenthesis. For example:

```
url("http://members.aol.com/htmlguru")
```

is a valid URL value.

Finally, some values are lists of other values and are described as a "list of" some other value. In these cases, a list consists of one or more of the allowed values, separated by commas.

The standard defines a default value for most properties. The default property is listed in the top syntax line for the property. Additional allowed values are listed beneath each description.

background

`background: list`

Composite property for the background-attachment, background-color, background-image, background-position, and background-repeat properties; *list* is any of these properties' values, in any order.

background-attachment

`background-attachment: scroll`

Determines if the background image is fixed in the window or scrolls as the document scrolls.

Accepted values: `fixed`, `scroll`

background-color

`background-color: transparent`

Sets the background color of an element.

Accepted values: *color*, `transparent`

background-image

`background-image: none`

N I Sets the background image of an element.

Accepted values: *url*, `transparent`

background-position

`background-position: percent`

I Sets the initial position of the element's background image, if specified; values are normally paired to provide x, y positions. Default position is `0% 0%`.

Accepted values: *length*, *percent*, `top`, `center`, `bottom`, `left`, `right`

background-repeat

`background-repeat: repeat`

N I Determines how the background image is repeated (tiled) across an element.

Accepted values: `repeat`, `repeat-x`, `repeat-y`, `no-repeat`

border

`border: list`

N I Sets all four borders on an element; value is one or more of a color, a value for border-width, and a value for border-style.

border-bottom

`border-bottom: list`

I Sets the bottom border on an element; value is one or more of a color, a value for border-bottom-width, and a value for border-style.

border-bottom-width

`border-bottom-width: medium`

N I Sets the thickness of an element's bottom border.

Accepted values: `medium`, *length*, `thin`, `thick`

border-color

`border-color: color`

N Sets the color of all four of an element's borders; default is the color of the element.

CSS

border-left

`border-left: list`

Ⓘ Sets the left border on an element; value is one or more of a color, a value for border-left-width, and a value for border-style.

border-left-width

`border-left-width: medium`

Ⓝ Ⓘ Sets the thickness of an element's left border.

Accepted values: *length*, `medium`, `thin`, `thick`

border-right

`border-right: list`

Ⓘ Sets the right border on an element; value is one or more of a color, a value for border-right-width, and a value for border-style.

border-right-width

`border-right-width: medium`

Ⓝ Ⓘ Sets the thickness of an element's right border.

Accepted values: *length*, `medium`, `thin`, `thick`

border-style

`border-style: none`

Ⓝ Ⓘ Sets the style of all four of an element's borders.

Accepted values: `none`, `dashed`, `dotted`, `double`, `groove`, `inset`, `outset`, `ridge`, `solid`

border-top

`border-top: list`

Ⓘ Sets the top border on an element; value is one or more of a color, a value for border-top-width, and a value for border-style.

border-top-width

`border-top-width: medium`

Ⓝ Ⓘ Sets the thickness of an element's top border.

Accepted values: *length*, `medium`, `thin`, `thick`

border-width

`border-width: medium`

[N][IE] Sets the thickness of all four of an element's borders.

Accepted values: *length*, `medium`, `thin`, `thick`

clear

`clear: none`

[N][IE] Sets which margins of an element must not be adjacent to a floating element; the element will be moved down until that margin is clear.

Accepted values: `none`, `both`, `left`, `right`

color

`color: *color*`

[N][IE] Sets the color of an element.

display

`display: block`

[N] Controls how an element is displayed.

Accepted values: `block`, `inline`, `list-item`, `none`

float

`float: none`

[N][IE] Determines if an element floats to the left or right, allowing text to wrap around it, or be displayed inline (using none).

Accepted values: `left`, `right`, `none`

font

`font: *list*`

[N][IE] Sets all the font attributes for an element; value is any of the values for font-style, font-variant, font-weight, font-size, line-height, and font-family, in that order.

font-family

`font-family: *list of font names*`

[N][IE] Defines the font for an element, either as a specific font or as one of the generic fonts serif, sans-serif, cursive, fantasy, or monospace.

font-size

`font-size: medium`

N O Defines the font size.

Accepted values: *length*, *percent*, `xx-small`, `x-small`, `small`, `medium`, `large`, `x-large`, `xx-large`, `larger`, `smaller`

font-style

`font-style: normal`

N O Defines the style of the face, either normal or some type of slanted style.

Accepted values: `italic`, `oblique`, `normal`

font-variant

`font-variant: normal`

O Defines a font to be in small caps.

Accepted values: `smallcaps`, `normal`

font-weight

`font-weight: normal`

N O Defines the font weight. If a number is used, it must be a multiple of 100 between 100 and 900; 400 is normal, 700 is the same as the keyword bold.

Accepted values: `bold`, `bolder`, `lighter`, *number*, `normal`

height

`height: auto`

N Defines the height of an element.

Accepted values: *length*, `auto`

letter-spacing

`letter-spacing: normal`

O Inserts additional space between text characters.

Accepted values: *length*, `normal`

line-height

`line-height: normal`

→

Sets the distance between adjacent text baselines.

Accepted values: *length*, *number*, *percent*, normal

list-style

list-style: *list*

Defines list-related styles using any of the values for list-style-image, list-style-position, and list-style-type.

list-style-image

list-style-image: none

Defines an image to be used as a list item's marker, in lieu of the value for list-style-type.

Accepted values: *url*, none

list-style-position

list-style-position: outside

Indents or extends (default) a list item's marker with respect to the item's content.

Accepted values: inside, outside

list-style-type

list-style-type: disc

Defines a list item's marker for either unordered lists (circle, disc, or square) or ordered lists (the rest).

Accepted values: circle, square, decimal, disc, lower-alpha, lower-roman, none, upper-alpha, upper-roman

margin

margin: *length*

Defines all four of an element's margins.

Accepted values: *length*, *percent*, auto

margin-bottom

margin-bottom: *length*

Defines the bottom margin of an element; default value is 0.

Accepted values: *length*, *percent*, auto

margin-left

`margin-left: length`

Defines the left margin of an element; default value is 0.

Accepted values: *length*, *percent*, `auto`

margin-right

`margin-right: length`

Defines the right margin of an element; default value is 0.

Accepted values: *length*, *percent*, `auto`

margin-top

`margin-top: length`

Defines the top margin of an element; default value is 0.

Accepted values: *length*, *percent*, `auto`

padding

`padding:list`

Defines all four padding amounts around an element.

padding-bottom

`padding-bottom: length`

Defines the bottom padding of an element; default value is 0.

Accepted values: *length*, `percent`

padding-left

`padding-left: length`

Defines the left padding of an element; default value is 0.

Accepted values: *length*, *percent*

padding-right

`padding-right: length`

Defines the right padding of an element; default value is 0.

Accepted values: *length*, *percent*

padding-top

`padding-top: length`

Defines the top padding of an element; default value is 0.

Accepted values: *length*, *percent*

text-align

`text-align: style`

Sets the text alignment style for an element. The default value is dependent on the element.

Accepted values: `center`, `justify`, `left`, `right`

text-decoration

`text-decoration: none`

Defines any decoration for the text; values may be combined.

Accepted values: `blink`, `line-through`, `none`, `overline`, `underline`

text-indent

`text-indent: length`

Defines the indentation of the first line of text in an element; default value is 0.

Accepted values: *length*, *percent*

text-transform

`text-transform: none`

Transforms the text in the element accordingly.

Accepted values: `capitalize`, `lowercase`, `none`, `uppercase`

vertical-align

`vertical-align: position`

Sets the vertical positioning of an element. The default setting is dependent on the element.

Accepted values: *percent*, `baseline`, `bottom`, `middle`, `sub`, `super`, `text-bottom`, `text-top`, `top`

word-spacing

`word-spacing: normal`

Inserts additional space between words.

Accepted values: *length*, `normal`

white-space

`white-space: normal`

N Defines how whitespace within an element is handled.

Accepted values: `normal`, `nowrap`, `pre`

width

`width: auto`

N I Defines the width of an element.

Accepted values: *length*, *percent*, `auto`

→

PART III

XML

CHAPTER 10

XML

XML

The Extensible Markup Language (XML) is a document processing standard proposed by the World Wide Web Consortium (W3C), the same group responsible for overseeing the HTML standard. Although the exact specifications have not been completed yet, many expect XML and its sibling technologies will replace HTML as the markup language of choice for dynamically generated content, including non-static web pages. Already several browser and word processor companies are integrating XML support into their products.

XML is actually a simplified form of Standard Generalized Markup Language (SGML), an international documentation standard that has existed since the 1980s. However, SGML is extremely bulky, especially for the Web. Much of the credit for XML's creation can be attributed to Jon Bosak of Sun Microsystems, Inc., who started the W3C working group responsbile for scaling down SGML to a form more suitable for the Internet.

Put succinctly, XML is a *meta-language* that allows you to create and format your own document markups. With HTML, existing markup is static: `<HEAD>` and `<BODY>`, for example, are tightly integrated into the HTML standard and cannot be changed or extended. XML, on the other hand, allows you to create your own markup tags and configure each to your liking: for example, `<HeadingA>`, `<Sidebar>`, or `<Quote>`, or even `<ReallyWildFont>`. Each of these elements can be defined through your own *document type definitions* and *stylesheets* and applied to one or more XML documents. Thus, it is important to realize that there are no "correct" tags for an XML document, except those you define yourself.

While many XML applications currently support CSS, a more extensible stylesheet specification exists called the *Extensible Stylesheet Language* (XSL). By using XSL, you ensure that your XML documents are formatted the same no matter which application or platform they appear on. This chapter documents portions of the XSL draft standard dated 16 December 1998, which marks a significant revision over its predecessors.

This chapter offers a quick overview of XML, as well as some sample applications that allow you to get started in coding. We won't cover everything about XML. In fact, much of XML is still in flux as this book goes to print. Consequently, creating a definitive reference at this point in XML's life seems a bit futile. However, after reading this chapter, we hope that the components that make up XML will seem a little less foreign to you.

XML Terminology

Before we move further, we need to standardize some terminology. An XML document consists of one or more *elements*. An element is marked with the following form:

```
<Body>This is text formatted according to the Body element</Body>
```

This element consists of two *tags*, an opening tag which places the name of the element between a less-than (<) and a greater-than (>) sign, and a closing tag which is identical except for the forward slash (/) that appears before the element name. Like HTML, the text contained between the opening and closing tags is considered part of the element and is formatted according to the element's rules.

Elements can have *attributes* applied to them, such as the following:

```
<Price currency="Euro">25.43</Price>
```

Here, the attribute is specified inside of the opening tag and is called "currency." It is given a value of "Euro", which is expressed inside quotation marks. Attributes are often used to further refine or modify the default behavior of an element.

In addition to the standard elements, XML also supports *empty elements*. An empty element has no text appearing between the opening and closing tag. Hence, both tags can (optionally) be merged together, with a forward slash appearing before the closing marker. For example, the following elements are identical:

```
<Picture src="blueball.gif"></Picture>
<Picture src="blueball.gif"/>
```

Empty elements are often used to add nontextual content to a document, or to provide additional information to the application that is parsing the XML. Note that while the closing slash may not be used in single-tag HTML elements, it is *mandatory* for single-term XML empty elements.

Unlearning Bad Habits

Whereas HTML browsers often ignore simple errors in documents, XML applications are not nearly as forgiving. For the HTML reader, there are a few bad habits that we should first dissuade you of:

Attribute values must be in quotation marks.
: You can't specify an attribute value such as `<picture src=/images/blueball.gif>`, which HTML browsers often overlooked. An attribute value must always be inside single or double quotation marks, or the XML parser will flag it as an error. Here is the correct way to specify such a tag:

```
<picture src="/images/blueball.gif">
```

An element must either have an opening and closing tag, or be an empty element.

Each element that specifies an opening tag must have a closing tag that matches it. If it does not, and it is not an empty element, the XML parser generates an error. In other words, you cannot do the following:

```
<Paragraph>
This is a paragraph.
<Paragraph>
This is another paragraph.
```

Instead, you must have an opening and closing tag for each paragraph element:

```
<Paragraph>This is a paragraph.</Paragraph>
<Paragraph>This is another paragraph.</Paragraph>
```

Tags must be nested correctly.

It is illegal to do the following:

```
<Italic><Bold>This is incorrect</Italic></Bold>
```

The closing tag for the `Bold` element should be inside the closing tag for the `Italic` element, to match the nearest opening tag and preserve the correct element nesting. It is essential for the application parsing your XML to process the hierarchy of the elements:

```
<Italic><Bold>This is correct</Bold></Italic>
```

These syntactic rules are the source of many common errors in XML, especially given that some of this behavior can be ignored by HTML browsers. An XML document that adheres to these rules (and a few others which we'll see later) is said to be *well-formed.*

An Overview of an XML Document

There are generally three files that are processed by an XML-compliant application to display XML content. They are:

The XML document

This file contains the document data, typically tagged with meaningful XML elements, some of which may contain attributes.

A stylesheet

The stylesheet dictates how document elements should be formatted when they are displayed, whether it be in a word processor or a browser. Note that you can apply different stylesheets to the same document, depending on the environment, thus changing its appearance without affecting any of the underlying data. The separation between content and formatting is an important distinction in XML.

Document Type Definition (DTD)

This file specifies rules for how the XML document elements, attributes, and other data are defined and logically related in an XML-compliant document.

A Simple XML Document

Example 10-1 shows a simple XML document.

Example 10-1: simple.xml

```
<?xml version="1.0" standalone="no"?>
<!DOCTYPE OReilly:Books SYSTEM "sample.dtd">
<!-- Here begins the XML data -->
<OReilly:Books xmlns:OReilly='http://www.oreilly.com/'>
  <OReilly:Product>Webmaster in a Nutshell</OReilly:Product>
  <OReilly:Price>24.95</OReilly:Price>
</OReilly:Books>
```

Let's look at this example line by line.

In the first line, the code between the `<?xml` and the `?>` is called an *XML declaration.* This declaration contains special information for the XML processor (the program reading the XML) indicating that this document conforms to Version 1.0 of the XML standard. In addition, the `standalone="no"` attribute informs the program that an outside DTD is needed to correctly interpret the document. (In this case, the DTD will reside in a separate file called *sample.dtd.*) On a side note, it is possible to simply embed the stylesheet and the DTD in the same file as the XML document. However, this is not recommended for general use, as it hampers reuse of both DTDs and stylesheets.

The second line is as follows:

```
<!DOCTYPE OReilly:Books SYSTEM "sample.dtd">
```

This line points out the *root element* of the document, as well as the DTD that validates each of the document elements that appear inside the root element. The root element is the outermost element in the document that the DTD applies to; it typically denotes the document's starting and ending point. In this example, the `<OReilly:Books>` element serves as the root element of the document. The `SYSTEM` keyword denotes that the DTD of the document resides in a separate local file named `sample.dtd`.

Following that line is a comment. Comments always begin with `<!--` and end with `-->`. You can write whatever you want inside a comment; they are ignored by the XML processor. Be aware that comments, however, cannot come before the XML declaration and cannot appear inside of an element tag. For example, this is illegal:

```
<OReilly:Books <!-- This is the tag for a book --!>>
```

Finally, `<OReilly:Product>`, `<OReilly:Price>`, and `<OReilly:Books>` are XML elements we invented. Like most elements in XML, they hold no special significance except for whatever document and style rules we define for them. Note that these elements look slightly different than those you may have seen previously because we are using *namespaces.* Each element tag can be divided into two parts. The portion before the colon (:) forms the tag's namespace, while the portion after the colon identifies the name of the tag itself.

Some XML terminology here: the `<OReilly:Product>` and `<OReilly:Price>` elements would consider the `<OReilly:Books>` element their *parent.* In the same manner, elements can be grandparents and grandchildren of other elements. However, we typically abbreviate multiple levels by stating that an element is either an *ancestor* or a *descendant* of another element.

Namespaces

Namespaces are a recent addition to the XML specification. The use of namespaces is not mandatory in XML, but it's often wise. Namespaces were created to ensure uniqueness among XML elements.

For example, let's pretend that the `<OReilly:Books>` element was simply named `<Books>`. When you think about it, it's not out of the question that another publisher would create its own `<Books>` element in its own XML documents. If the two publishers combined their documents, resolving a single (correct) definition for the `<Books>` tag would be impossible. When two XML documents containing identical elements from different sources are merged, those elements are said to *collide*. Namespaces help to avoid element collisions by scoping each tag.

In Example 10-1, we scoped each tag with the `OReilly` namespace. Namespaces are declared using the `xmlns:`*something* attribute, where *something* defines the ID of the namespace. The attribute value is a unique identifier that differentiates it from all other namespaces; the use of a URI is recommended. In this case, we use the O'Reilly URI `http://www.oreilly.com/` as the default namespace, which should guarantee uniqueness. A namespace declaration can appear as an attribute of any element, so long as the namespace's use remains inside that element's opening and closing tags. Here are some examples:

```
<OReilly:Books xmlns:OReilly='http://www.oreilly.com/'>
<xsl:stylesheet xmlns:xsl='http://www.w3.org/'>
```

You are allowed to define more than one namespace in the context of an element:

```
<OReilly:Books xmlns:OReilly='http://www.oreilly.com/'
               xmlns:Songline='http://www.songline.com/'>
</OReilly:Books>
```

If you do not specify a name after the `xmlns` prefix, the namespace is dubbed the *default namespace* and is applied to all elements inside the defining element that do not use a namespace prefix of their own. For example:

```
<Books xmlns='http://www.oreilly.com/'
       xmlns:Songline='http://www.songline.com/'>
    <Book>
        <Title>Webmaster in a Nutshell</Title>
        <ISBN>1-56592-229-8</ISBN>
    </Book>
    <Songline:CD>18231</Songline:CD>
</Books>
```

Here, the default namespace (represented by the URI `http://www.oreilly.com/`) is applied to the elements `<Books>`, `<Book>`, `<Title>`, and `<ISBN>`. However, it is not applied to the `<Songline:CD>` element, which has its own namespace.

Finally, you can set the default namespace to an empty string to ensure that there is no default namespace in use within a specific element:

```
<header xmlns=''
        xmlns:OReilly='http://www.oreilly.com/'
        xmlns:Songline='http://www.songline.com/'>
    <entry>Learn XML in a Week</entry>
    <price>10.00</price>
</header>
```

Here, the `<entry>` and `<price>` elements have no default namespace.

A Simple Document Type Definition (DTD)

Example 10–2 creates a simple DTD for our XML document.

Example 10–2: simple.dtd

```
<!-- DTD for sample document -->
<!ELEMENT OReilly:Books (OReilly:Product, OReilly:Price)>
<!ELEMENT OReilly:Product (#PCDATA)>
<!ELEMENT OReilly:Price (#PCDATA)>
```

The purpose of the this DTD is to declare each of the elements used in our XML document. All document-type data is placed inside a construct with the characters `<!`*something*`>`. Like the previous XML example, the first line is a comment because it begins with `<!--` and ends with the characters `-->`.

The `<!ELEMENT>` construct declares each valid element for our XML document. With the second line, we've specified that the `OReilly:Books` element is valid:

```
<!ELEMENT OReilly:Books (OReilly:Product, OReilly:Price)>
```

The parentheses group required child elements for the `<OReilly:Books>` element. In this case, the `<OReilly:Product>` element and the `<OReilly:Price>` element *must* be included inside our `<OReilly:Books>` element tags, and they must appear in the order specified. `<OReilly:Product>` and `<OReilly:Price>` are *children* of `<OReilly:Books>`.

Likewise, both the `<OReilly:Product>` and the `<OReilly:Price>` elements are declared in our DTD:

```
<!ELEMENT OReilly:Product (#PCDATA)>
<!ELEMENT OReilly:Price (#PCDATA)>
```

Again, parentheses specify required elements. In this case, they both have a single requirement, which is represented by `#PCDATA`. This is shorthand for *parsed character data*, which means that any characters are allowed, so long as they do not include other element tags or contain the characters `<` or `&`, or the sequence `]]>`. These characters are forbidden because they could be interpreted as markup. (We'll see how to get around this shortly.)

The XML data shown in Example 10–1 adheres to the rules of this DTD: it contains an `<OReilly:Books>` element, which in turn contains an `<OReilly:Product>` element, followed by an `<OReilly:Price>` element inside it (in that order). Therefore, if this DTD is applied to it with a `<!DOCTYPE>` statement, the document is said to be *valid*.

So far, we've structured the data but haven't paid much attention to its formatting. Now let's move on and add some style to our XML document.

A Simple XSL Stylesheet

The Extensible Stylesheet Language consists of a series of markups that can be used to apply formatting rules to each of the elements inside an XML document. XSL works by applying various style rules to the contents of an XML document, based on the elements that it encounters.

Let's add a simple XSL stylesheet to the example:

```
<?xml version="1.0"?>
<xsl:stylesheet xmlns:xsl="http://www.w3.org/TR/WD-xsl"
                xmlns:fo="http://www.w3.org/TR/WD-xsl/FO">
  <xsl:template match="/">
      <fo:block font-size="18pt">
        <xsl:apply-templates/>
      </fo:block>
  </xsl:template>
</xsl:stylesheet>
```

The first thing you might notice when you look at an XSL stylesheet is that it is formatted in the same way as a regular XML document. This is not a coincidence. In fact, by design XSL stylesheets are themselves XML documents, so they must adhere to the same rules as well-formed XML documents.

Breaking down the pieces, you should first note that all XSL elements must be enclosed in appropriate `<xsl:stylesheet>` tags. These tags tell the XSL processor that it is describing stylesheet information, not XML content itself. Between the `<xsl:stylesheet>` tags lie each of the rules that will be applied to our XML document. Each of these rules can be further broken down into two items: a *template pattern* and a *template action.*

Consider the line:

```
<xsl:template match="/">
```

This line forms the template pattern of the stylesheet rule. Here, the target pattern is the root element, as designated by `match="/"`. The `"/"` is shorthand to represent the XML document's root element (`<OReilly:Books>` in our case). Remember that if this stylesheet is applied to another XML document, the root element matched might be different.

The following lines:

```
<fo:block font-size="18pt">
  <xsl:apply-templates/>
</fo:block>
```

specify the template action that should be performed on the target. In this case, we see the empty element `<xsl:apply-templates/>` located inside a `<fo:block>` element. When the XSL processor formats the target element, every element that is inside the root element's opening and closing tags uses an 18-point font.

In our example, the `<OReilly:Product>` and `<OReilly:Price>` elements are enclosed inside the `<OReilly:Books>` tags. Therefore, the font size will be applied to the contents of those tags.

Example 10-3 displays a more realistic example.

Example 10-3: simple.xsl

```
<?xml version="1.0"?>
<xsl:stylesheet xmlns:xsl="http://www.w3.org/TR/WD-xsl"
                xmlns:fo="http://www.w3.org/TR/WD-xsl/FO">
                xmlns:OReilly="http://www.oreilly.com/">
  <xsl:template match="/">
      <fo:display-sequence>
        <xsl:apply-templates/>
      </fo:display-sequence>
  </xsl:template>
  <xsl:template match="OReilly:Books">
      <fo:block font-size="18pt">
        <xsl:text>Books:</xsl:text>
        <xsl:apply-templates/>
      </fo:block>
  </xsl:template>
  <xsl:template match="OReilly:Product">
      <fo:block font-size="12pt">
        <xsl:apply-templates/>
      </fo:block>
  </xsl:template>
  <xsl:template match="OReilly:Price">
      <fo:block font-size="14pt">
        <xsl:text>Price: $</xsl:text>
        <xsl:apply-templates/>
        <xsl:text> + tax</xsl:text>
      </fo:block>
  </xsl:template>
</xsl:stylesheet>
```

In this example, we're now targeting the `<OReilly:Books>` element, printing the word "Books:" before it in an 18-point font. In addition, the `<OReilly:Product>` element now applies a 12-point font to each of its children, and the `<OReilly:Price>` tag now uses a 14-point font to display its children, overriding the default 18-point font of its parent, `<OReilly:Books>`. (Of course, neither one has any children elements; they simply have text between their tags in the XML document.) The text "`Price: $`" will now precede each of `<OReilly:Price>`'s children, and the characters " `+ tax`" will now come after it, formatted accordingly.*

Here is the result after we pass it through an XSL processor:

```
<?xml version="1.0"?>
<fo:display-sequence>
  <fo:block font-size="18pt">
Books:
    <fo:block font-size="12pt">
Webmaster in a Nutshell
    </fo:block>
    <fo:block font-size="14pt">
Price $24.95 + tax
```

* You may have noticed that we are using the `<fo:display-sequence>` element instead of `<fo:block>` for the root element. This is primarily because the pattern matching our root element really doesn't do anything anymore. However, you needn't be concerned with this here.

```
    </fo:block>
  </fo:block>
</fo:display-sequence>
```

And that's it: everything needed for a simple XML document! Running it through an XML processor, you should see something similar to Figure 10-1.

Books:
Webmaster in a Nutshell
Price $24.95 + tax

Figure 10-1: Sample XML output

XML

XML Reference

Now that you have had a quick taste of working with XML, here is an overview of the more common rules and constructs of the XML language.

Well-Formed XML

These are the rules for a well-formed XML document:

- The document must either use a DTD or contain an XML declaration with the `standalone` attribute set to `"no"`. For example:

  ```
  <?xml version="1.0" standalone="no"?>
  ```

- All element attribute values must be in quotation marks.
- An element must have both an opening and closing tag, unless it is an empty element.
- If a tag is a standalone empty element, it must contain a closing slash (/) before the end of the tag.
- All opening and closing element tags must nest correctly.
- Isolated markup characters are not allowed in text: < or & must use entity references instead. In addition, the sequence `]]>` must be expressed as `]]>` when used as regular text. (Entity references are discussed in further detail below.)
- Well-formed XML documents without a corresponding DTD must have all attributes of type CDATA by default.

XML Instructions

The XML instructions in the following table are legal.

<?xml ... ?>

```
<?xml version="number" [encoding="encoding"] [standalone="yes|no"] ?>
```

Although they are not required to, XML documents typically begin with an XML declaration. An XML declaration must start with the characters `<?xml` and end with the characters `?>`.

Attributes

`version`
: The `version` attribute specifies the correct version of XML required to process the document, such as `"1.0"`. This attribute cannot be omitted.

`encoding`
: The `encoding` attribute specifies the character encoding used in the document (e.g., "US-ASCII" or "iso-8859-1"). This attribute is optional.

`standalone`
: The optional `standalone` attribute specifies whether a DTD is required to parse the document. The value must be either `yes` or `no`. If the value is no, a DTD must be declared with an XML `<!DOCTYPE>` instruction.

For example:

```
<?xml version="1.0"?>
<?xml version="1.0" encoding="US-ASCII" standalone="no"?>
```

<!DOCTYPE>

```
<!DOCTYPE root-element SYSTEM|PUBLIC [name] URI-of-DTD>
```

The `<!DOCTYPE>` instruction allows you to specify a DTD for an XML document. This instruction can currently take one of two forms:

```
<!DOCTYPE root-element SYSTEM "URI_of_DTD">
<!DOCTYPE root-element PUBLIC "name" "URI_of_DTD">
```

Keywords

`SYSTEM`
: The `SYSTEM` variant specifies the URI location of a DTD for private use in the document. The DTD is applied to all elements inside of *root-element.* For example:

```
<!DOCTYPE <Book> SYSTEM
 "http://mycompany.com/dtd/mydoctype.dtd">
```

`PUBLIC`
: The `PUBLIC` variant is used in situations where a DTD has been publicized for widespread use. In those cases, the DTD is assigned a unique name, which the XML processor may use by itself to attempt to retrieve

→

the DTD. If that fails, the URI is used:

```
<!DOCTYPE <Book> PUBLIC
  "-//O'Reilly//DTD//EN"
  "http://www.oreilly.com/dtd/nutshellbook.dtd">
```

Public DTDs follow a specific naming convention. See the XML specification for more details on naming public DTDs.

<?...?>

`<?target attribute1="value" attribute2="value" ... ?>`

A processing instruction allows developers to place information specific to an outside application within the document. Processing instructions always begin with the characters <? and end with the characters ?>. For example:

```
<?works document="hello.doc" data="hello.wks"?>
```

You can create your own processing instructions if the XML application processing the document is aware of what the data means and acts accordingly.

CDATA

`<![CDATA[ ... ]]>`

You can define special marked sections of character data, or CDATA, which the XML processor will not attempt to interpret as markup. Anything that is included inside a CDATA marked section is treated as plain text. CDATA marked sections begin with the characters `<![CDATA[` and end with the characters `]]>`.

```
<![CDATA[
  I'm now discussing the <element> tag of documents
  5 & 6: "Sales" and "Profit and Loss". Luckily, the
  XML processor won't apply rules of formatting to
  these sentences!
]]>
```

Note that you may not use entity references inside a `CDATA` marked section, as they will not be expanded.

<!-- ... -->

`<!-- comments -->`

You can place comments anywhere in an XML document, except within element tags or before the initial XML processing instructions. Comments in an XML document always start with the characters `<!--` and end with the characters `-->`. In addition, they may not include double hyphens within the comment. The contents of the comment are ignored by the XML processor:

→

```
<!-- Sales Figures Start Here -->
<Units>2000</Units>
<Cost>49.95</Cost>
```

Element and Attribute Rules

An element is either bound by its starting and ending tags, or is an empty element. Elements can contain text, other elements, or a combination of both. For example:

```
<para>Elements can contain text, other elements, or a combination. For
example, a chapter might contain a title and multiple paragraphs, and
a paragraph might contain text and <emphasis>emphasis
elements</emphasis>:</para>
```

An element name must start with a letter or underscore. It can then have any number of letters, numbers, hyphens, periods, or underscores in its name. Elements are case-sensitive: `<Para>`, `<para>`, and `<pArA>` are considered three different element types.

Element type names may not start with the string `xml`, in any variation of upper- or lowercase. Names beginning with `xml` are reserved for special uses by the W3C XML Working Group. Colons are permitted in element type names only for specifying namespaces; otherwise, colons are forbidden. For example:

`<Italic>`	Legal
`<_Budget>`	Legal
`<Punch line>`	Illegal: has a space
`<205Para>`	Illegal: starts with number
`<repair@log>`	Illegal: contains @ character
`<xml>`	Illegal: starts with `xml`

Element type names can also include accented Roman characters, letters from other alphabets (e.g., Cyrillic, Greek, Hebrew, Arabic, Thai, Hiragana, Katakana, or Devanagari), and ideograms from the Chinese, Japanese, and Korean languages. Valid element type names can therefore include `<peut-être>`, `<são>`, `<più>`, and `<niño>`, plus a number of others our publishing system isn't equipped to handle.

If you are using a DTD, the content of an element is constrained by its DTD declaration. Better XML applications inform you what elements and attributes can appear inside a specific element. Otherwise, you should check the element declaration in the DTD to determine the exact semantics.

Attributes describe additional information about an element. They always consist of a name and a value, as follows:

```
<price currency="Euro">
```

The attribute value is always quoted, using either single or double quotes. Attribute names are subject to the same restrictions as element type names.

XML Reserved Attributes

The following are reserved attributes in XML.

xml:lang

`xml:lang='iso_639_identifier'`

The `xml:lang` attribute can be used on any element. Its value indicates the language of that element. This is useful in a multilingual context. For example, you might have:

```
<para xml:lang="en">Hello</para>
<para xml:lang="fr">Bonjour</para>
```

This format allows you to display one or the other, depending on the user's language preference.

The syntax of the `xml:lang` value is defined by RFC-1766, available at *http://ds0.internic.net/rfc/rfc1766.txt.* A two-letter language code is optionally followed by a hyphen and a two-letter country code. The languages are defined by RFC-1766 and the countries are defined by ISO-3166. Traditionally, the language is given in lowercase and the country in uppercase (and for safety, this rule should be followed), but processors are expected to use the values in a case-insensitive manner.

In addition, RFC-1766 also provides extensions for nonstandardized languages or language variants. Valid `xml:lang` values include such notations as `en`, `en-US`, `en-UK`, `en-cockney`, `i-navajo`, and `x-minbari`.

xml:space

`xml:space='default|preserve'`

The `xml:space` attribute indicates whether any whitespace inside the element is significant and should not be altered by the XML processor. The attribute can take one of two enumerated values:

`preserve`
: The XML application honors all whitespace (new lines, spaces, and tabs) present within the element.

`default`
: The XML processor is free to do whatever it wishes with the whitespace inside the element.

You should set `xml:space` to `preserve` only if you have an element you wish to behave similar to the HTML `<pre>` element, such as documenting source code.

xml:link

`xml:link='link_type'`

→

The `xml:link` attribute signals an XLink processor that an element is a link element. It can take one of the following values:

`simple`
: A one-way link, pointing to the area in the target document where the referenced element occurs.

`document`
: A link that points to a member document of an extended link group.

`extended`
: An extended link, which can point to more than one target through the use of multiple locators. Extended links can also support multidirectional and out-of-line links (a listing of links stored in a separate document).

`group`
: Contains a group of document links.

The `xml:link` attribute is always used with other attributes to form an XLink. See the section "XLink and XPointer" for much more information on the `xml:link` attribute. This section also has more information on attribute remapping. (Note that this attribute may change to `xlink:form` in the future.)

xml:attribute

`xml:attribute='`*`existing-attribute replacement-attribute`*`'`

Allows you to remap attributes to prevent conflict with other potential uses of XLink attributes. For example:

```
<person title="Reverend" title-abbr="Rev." given="Kirby"
  family="Hensley" href="http://www.ulc.org/"
  link-title="Universal Life Church"
  xml:attributes="title link-title"/>
```

In this example, since the `title` attribute is already taken, the `xml:attributes` attribute remaps it to use `link-title` instead.

See the section "XLink and XPointer" for more information on attribute remapping. (Note that this attribute may change to `xlink:attribute` in the future.)

Entity References

Entity references are used as substitutions for specific characters in XML. A common use for entity references is to denote document symbols that might otherwise be mistaken for markup by an XML processor. XML predefines five entity references for you, which are substitutions for basic markup symbols. However, you can define as many entity references as you like in your own DTD. (See the next section)

Entity references always begin with an ampersand (`&`) and end with a semicolon (`;`). They cannot appear inside `CDATA` sections, but can be used anywhere else. Predefined entities defined in XML are shown in Table 10-1.

Table 10-1: Predefined Entities in XML

Entity	*Char*	*Notes*
`&`	&	Must not be used inside processing instructions
`<`	<	Use inside attribute values quoted with `"`
`>`	>	Use after `]]` in normal text and inside processing instructions
`"`	"	
`'`	'	Use inside attribute values quoted with `'`

In addition, you can provide character references for Unicode characters by using a *hexadecimal character reference*. This consists of the string `&#x` followed by hexadecimal number representing the character, and finally a semicolon (`;`). For example, to represent the copyright character, you could use the following:

```
This document is &#xA9; 1999 by O'Reilly and Associates.
```

The entity reference is replaced with the circled-C (©) copyright character when the document is formatted.

Document Type Definitions

A DTD specifies how elements inside an XML document should relate to each other. It also provides grammar rules for the document and each of its elements. A document that adheres to the specifications outlined by its DTD is considered to be *valid*. (Don't confuse this with a well-formed document, which adheres to the XML syntax rules outlined earlier.)

Element Declarations

You must declare each of the elements that appear inside your XML document within your DTD. You can do so with the `<!ELEMENT>` declaration, which uses the following format:

```
<!ELEMENT elementname rule>
```

This declares an XML element and an associated rule, which relates the element logically in the XML document. The element name should not include <> characters. An element name must start with a letter or underscore. After that, it can have any number of letters, numbers, hyphens, periods, or underscores in its name. Element names may not start with the string `xml`, in any variation of upper- or lowercase. You can use a colon in element names if you are using namespaces; otherwise it is forbidden.

ANY and PCDATA

The simplest element declaration states that between the opening and closing tags of the element, anything can appear:

```
<!ELEMENT library ANY>
```

Using the ANY keywords allows you to include both other tags and general character data between the elements. However, you may want to specify a situation where you want only general characters appearing. This type of data is better known as *parsed character data*, or PCDATA for short. You can specify that an element can have only PCDATA in it with the following declaration:

```
<!ELEMENT title (#PCDATA)>
```

Remember, this declaration means that any character data that is *not* an element can appear between the element tags. Therefore, it's legal to write the following in your XML document:

```
<title></title>
<title>Webmaster in a Nutshell</title>
<title>Java Network Programming</title>
```

However, you cannot do the following with the previous PCDATA declaration:

```
<title>Webmaster in a <emphasis>Nutshell</emphasis></title>
```

On the other hand, you may want to specify that another element *must* appear between the two tags specified. You can do this by placing the name of the element in the parentheses. The following two rules state that a <books> element must contain a <title> element and a <title> element must contain parsed character data (or null content) but not another element;

```
<!ELEMENT books (title)>
<!ELEMENT title (#PCDATA)>
```

Multiple elements

If you wish to dictate that multiple elements must appear in a specific order between the opening and closing tags of a specific element, you can use a comma (,) to separate the two instances:

```
<!ELEMENT books (title,authors)>
<!ELEMENT title (#PCDATA)>
<!ELEMENT authors (#PCDATA)>
```

In the preceding declaration, the DTD states that within the opening <books> and closing </books> tags, there must first appear a <title> element consisting of parsed character data. It must be immediately followed by an <authors> element with parsed character data. The <authors> element cannot precede the <title> element. Here is a valid XML document for the DTD excerpt defined previously:

```
<books>
  <title>Webmaster in a Nutshell, 2nd Edition</title>
  <authors>Steven Spainhour and Robert Eckstein</authors>
</books>
```

The last example showed how to specify both elements in a declaration. You can just as easily specify that one or the other appear (but not both) by using the vertical bar (|):

```
<!ELEMENT books (title|authors)>
<!ELEMENT title (#PCDATA)>
<!ELEMENT authors (#PCDATA)>
```

This DTD states that either a <title> element or an <author> element can appear inside the <books> element. Note that it must have one or the other. If you omit both elements, or include both elements, the XML document is not considered valid.

Grouping and recurrence

You can nest parentheses inside your declarations to give finer granularity on the syntax you're specifying. For example, the DTD below states that inside the <books> element, the XML document must contain either a <description> element or a <title> element immediately followed by an <author> element. All three elements must consist of parsed character data.

```
<!ELEMENT books ((title,author)|description)>
<!ELEMENT title (#PCDATA)>
<!ELEMENT author (#PCDATA)>
<!ELEMENT description (#PCDATA)>
```

Now for the fun part: you are allowed to dictate inside an element declaration whether a single element (or a grouping of elements contained inside parentheses) must appear zero or one times, one or more times, or zero or more times. The characters used for this appear immediately after the target element (or element grouping) that they refer to, and should be familiar to shell programmers. They are shown in Table 10-2.

Table 10-2: Occurrence Operators

Attribute	*Description*
?	Must appear once or not at all (0 or 1 times)
+	Must appear at least once (1 or more times)
*	May appear any number of times, or not at all (0 or more times)

For example, if you want to provide finer granularity to the <author> element, you can redefine the following in the DTD:

```
<!ELEMENT author (authorname+)>
<!ELEMENT authorname (#PCDATA)>
```

This indicates that the <author> element must have at least one <authorname> element under it. It is allowed to have more than one as well.

You can define more complex relationships with the use of parentheses:

```
<!ELEMENT reviews (rating, synopsis?, comments+)*>
<!ELEMENT rating ((tutorial|reference)*,overall)>
<!ELEMENT synopsis (#PCDATA)>
<!ELEMENT comments (#PCDATA)>
<!ELEMENT tutorial (#PCDATA)>
<!ELEMENT reference (#PCDATA)>
<!ELEMENT overall (#PCDATA)>
```

Empty elements

You must declare each of the empty elements that can be used inside a valid XML document as well. This can be done with the `EMPTY` keyword:

```
<!ELEMENT elementname EMPTY>
```

For example, the following declaration defines an element in the XML document that can be used as `<statuscode/>` or `<statuscode></statuscode>`:

```
<!ELEMENT statuscode EMPTY>
```

Entities

Inside a DTD, you can declare an *entity*, which allows you to use an *entity reference* to substitute a series of characters for another in an XML document, similar to macros.

General entities

A general entity is one that can substitute for other characters inside the XML document. The declaration for a general entity uses the following format:

```
<!ENTITY name "replacement_characters">
```

We have already seen five general entity references, one each for the characters <, >, &, ', and ". Each of these can be used inside an XML document to prevent the XML processor from interpreting the characters as markup. (Incidentally, you do not need to declare these in your DTD; they are always provided for you.)

Earlier in this chapter, we provided an entity reference for the copyright character. We could declare such an entity in the DTD with the following:

```
<!ENTITY copyright "&#xA9;">
```

Again, we have tied the `©right;` entity to Unicode value 169 (or hexadecimal 0xA9), which is the "circled-C" (©) copyright character. Then you can use the following in your XML document:

```
<copyright>&copyright; 1998 by MyCompany, Inc.</copyright>
```

There are a couple of restrictions to declaring entities:

- You cannot make circular references in the declarations. For example, the following is invalid:

  ```
  <!ENTITY entitya "&entityb; is really neat!">
  <!ENTITY entityb "&entitya; is also really neat!">
  ```

- You cannot substitute nondocument text in a DTD with a general entity reference. The general entity reference is resolved only in an XML document, not a DTD document. (If you wish to have an entity reference resolved in the DTD, you must instead use a *parameter entity reference*.)

Parameter entities

Parameter entity references appear only in DTDs and are replaced by their entity definitions in the DTD. All parameter entity references begin with a percent sign, which denotes that they cannot be used in an XML document—only the DTD they are defined in. Here is how to define a parameter entity:

```
<!ENTITY % name "replacement_characters">
```

Here are some examples using parameter entity references:

```
<!ENTITY % pcdata "(#PCDATA)">
<!ELEMENT authortitle %pcdata;>
```

As with general entity references, you cannot make circular references in declarations. In addition, parameter entity references cannot be used before they are declared.

External entities

XML allows you to declare an external entity with the following syntax:

```
<!ENTITY quotes SYSTEM "http://www.oreilly.com/stocks/quotes.xml">
```

This allows you to copy in the XML content (located at the specified URI) into the current XML document using an external entity reference. For example:

```
<document>
  <heading>Current Stock Quotes</heading>
  &quotes;
</document>
```

This copies the XML content located at the URI *http://www.oreilly.com/stocks/quotes.xml* into the document when it's run through the XML processor. As you might guess, this works quite well when dealing with dynamic data.

Unparsed entities

By the same token, you can use an *unparsed entity* to declare non-XML content in an XML document. For example, if you wanted to declare an outside image to be used inside an XML document, you could specify the following in the DTD:

```
<!ENTITY image1 SYSTEM "http://www.oreilly.com/ora.gif" NDATA GIF89a>
```

Note that we also specify the `NDATA` (notation data) keyword, which tells exactly what type of unparsed entity the XML processor is dealing with. You typically use an unparsed entity reference as the value of an element's attribute, one that is defined in the DTD with the type `ENTITY` or `ENTITIES`. Here is how you might use the unparsed entity declared previously:

```
<image src="&image1;"/>
```

Notations

Finally notations are used in conjunction with unparsed entities. A notation declaration simply matches the value of an NDATA keyword above with more specific information. The XML processor is free to use this information as it sees fit, or ignore it.

```
<!NOTATION GIF89a SYSTEM
      "-//CompuServe//NOTATION Graphics Interchange Format 89a//EN">
```

Attribute Declarations in the DTD

Attributes for various XML elements must be specified in the DTD. You can specify each of the attributes with the <!ATTLIST> declaration, which uses the following form:

```
<!ATTLIST target_element attribute_name attribute_type default>
```

The <!ATTLIST> declaration consists of the target element name, the name of the attribute, its data type, and any default value you want to give it.

Here are some examples of legal <!ATTLIST> declarations:

```
<!ATTLIST box length CDATA "0">
<!ATTLIST box width CDATA "0">
<!ATTLIST frame visible (true|false) "true">
<!ATTLIST person
     marital (single | married | divorced | widowed) #IMPLIED>
```

In these examples, the first keyword after ATTLIST declares the name of the target element (i.e., box, frame, person). This is followed by the name of the attribute (i.e., length, width, visible, marital). This is generally followed by the data type of the attribute, and its default value.

Default values

Let's look at the default value first. You can specify any default value allowed by the specified data type. In the event a default value may not be appropriate, you can alternatively specify the keywords listed in Table 10-3 in its place.

Table 10-3: Default Modifiers in DTD Attributes

Attribute	*Description*
#REQUIRED	The attribute value must be specified with the element.
#IMPLIED	The attribute value can remain unspecified.
#FIXED	The attribute value is fixed and cannot be changed by the user.

A few notes: with the #IMPLIED keyword, if the value is not specified and none is given in the XML document, the XML parser must notify the application that no value has been specified. The application can take whatever action it deems appropriate at that point. Also, with the `#FIXED` keyword, you must specify the default value immediately afterwards, as shown:

```
<!ATTLIST date year CDATA #FIXED "1999">
```

Datatypes

Table 10-4 lists legal datatypes to use in a DTD.

Table 10-4: Datatypes in DTD Attributes

Attribute	*Description*
`CDATA`	Character data
enumerated	A series of values from which only one can be chosen
`ENTITY`	An entity declared in the DTD
`ENTITIES`	Multiple whitespace-separated entities declared in the DTD
`ID`	A unique element identifier
`IDREF`	The value of a unique ID type attribute
`IDREFS`	Multiple IDREFs of elements
`NMTOKEN`	An XML name token
`NMTOKENS`	Multiple whitespace-separated XML name tokens
`NOTATION`	A notation declared in the DTD

The `CDATA` keyword simply declares that any character data can appear. Here are some examples of attribute declarations that use `CDATA`:

```
<!ATTLIST person name CDATA #REQUIRED>
<!ATTLIST person email CDATA #REQUIRED>
<!ATTLIST person company CDATA #FIXED "O'Reilly">
```

Here is an enumerated data type. In this case, there is no keyword specified. Instead, the enumeration itself is simply listed:

```
<!ATTLIST person marital (single | married | divorced | widowed) #IMPLIED>
<!ATTLIST person sex (male | female) #REQUIRED>
```

The `ID`, `IDREF`, and `IDREFS` data types allow you to define attributes as IDs and ID references. An ID is simply an attribute whose value distinguishes this element from all others in the current XML document. IDs are useful for linking to various sections of a document that contain an element with a uniquely tagged ID. IDREFs are attributes that reference other IDs. For example, consider the following XML document:

```
<?xml version="1.0" standalone="yes"?>
<!DOCTYPE sector SYSTEM sector.dtd>
<sector>
  <employee empid="e1013">Jack Russell</employee>
  <employee empid="e1014">Samuel Tessen</employee>
  <employee empid="e1015" boss="e1013">Terri White</employee>
  <employee empid="e1016" boss="e1014">Steve McAlister</employee>
</sector>
```

And its DTD:

```
<!ELEMENT sector (employee*)>
<!ELEMENT employee (#PCDATA)>
<!ATTLIST employee empid ID #REQUIRED>
<!ATTLIST employee boss IDREF #IMPLIED>
```

Here, each employee has his own identification number (e1013, e1014, etc.), which we define in the DTD with the ID keyword using the `empid` attribute. This attribute then forms an ID for each `<employee>` element; no two `<employee>` elements can have the same ID.

Attributes that only reference other elements use the IDREF data type. In this case, the `boss` attribute is an IDREF because it can use only the values of other IDs attributes as its values. IDs will come into play when we discuss XLink and XPointer.

The `NMTOKEN` and `NMTOKENS` attributes declare XML name tokens. An *XML name token* is simply a legal XML name that consists of letters, digits, underscores, hyphens, and periods. It can contain a colon if it is part of a namespace. However, an XML name token cannot contain spaces. These datatypes are useful in the event that you are enumerating tokens of languages or other keyword sets that match these restrictions in the DTD.

An `ENTITY` allows you to exploit an entity declared in the DTD. This includes unparsed entities. For example, to link to an image:

```
<!ELEMENT image EMPTY>
<!ATTLIST image src ENTITY #REQUIRED>
<!ENTITY chapterimage SYSTEM "chapimage.jpg" NDATA "jpg">
```

Which you can use as follows:

```
<image src="chapterimage">
```

The `NOTATION` keyword simply expects a notation that appears in the DTD with a `<!NOTATION>` declaration. Here, the "player" attribute of the `<media>` element can be either `mpeg` or `jpeg`.

```
<!NOTATION mpeg SYSTEM "mpegplay.exe">
<!NOTATION jpeg SYSTEM "netscape.exe">
<!ATTLIST media player NOTATION (mpeg | jpeg) #REQUIRED>
```

Note that you must enumerate each of the notations allowed in the attribute. For example, to dicate the possible values of the "player" attribute of the `<media>` element, use the following:

```
<!NOTATION mpeg SYSTEM "mpegplay.exe">
<!NOTATION jpeg SYSTEM "netscape.exe">
<!NOTATION mov SYSTEM "mplayer.exe">
<!NOTATION avi SYSTEM "mplayer.exe">
<!ATTLIST media player NOTATIONS (mpeg | jpeg | mov) #REQUIRED>
```

Note that by the rules of this DTD, the `<media>` element is not allowed to play AVI files.

Note that you can place all the declarations inside a single `ATTLIST` declaration, as long as you follow the rules of each datatype:

```
<!ATTLIST person
          name CDATA #REQUIRED
          number IDREF #REQUIRED
          company CDATA #FIXED "O'Reilly">
```

Included and Ignored Marked Sections

Within a DTD, you can bundle together a group of declarations that should be ignored using the `IGNORE` directive:

```
<![ IGNORE [
   DTD content to be ignored
]]>
```

Conversly, if you wish to ensure that declarations are included in your DTD, you can use the `INCLUDE` directive, which has a similar syntax:

```
<![ INCLUDE [
   DTD content to be included
]]>
```

Why you would want to use either of these declarations is not obvious until you consider replacing the `INCLUDE` or `IGNORE` directives with a parameter entity reference you can change easily on the spot. For example, consider the following DTD:

```
<!ENTITY % ifstrict "INCLUDE">

<![ %ifstrict; [
  <!ELEMENT reviews (rating, synopsis?, comments+)*>
  <!ELEMENT rating ((tutorial|reference)*,overall)>
  <!ELEMENT synopsis (#PCDATA)>
  <!ELEMENT comments (#PCDATA)>
  <!ELEMENT tutorial (#PCDATA)>
  <!ELEMENT reference (#PCDATA)>
  <!ELEMENT overall (#PCDATA)>
]]>
```

You can either include or remove the enclosed declarations in this DTD by simply setting the parameter entity `%ifstrict;` to either the characters "IGNORE" or "INCLUDE", instead of commenting out each one when it is not needed.

Internal Subsets

As mentioned earlier in this chapter, you can place parts of your DTD declarations inside the DOCTYPE declaration of the XML document, as shown:

```
<!DOCTYPE boilerplate SYSTEM "generic-inc.dtd" [
  <!ENTITY corpname "Acme, Inc.">
]>
```

The region between brackets is called the DTD's *internal subset*. When a parser reads the DTD, the internal subset is read first, followed by the *external subset*, which is the file referenced by the `DOCTYPE` declaration.

There are restrictions on the complexity of the internal subset, as well as processing expectations that change how you should structure it:

- First, conditional marked sections (such as `INCLUDE` or `IGNORE`) are not permitted in an internal subset.
- Second, any parameter entity reference in the internal subset must expand to zero or more declarations. For example, specifying the following parameter entity reference is legal:

  ```
  %paradecl;
  ```

  so long as `%paradecl;` expands to the following:

  ```
  <!ELEMENT para CDATA>
  ```

  However, if you simply the wrote the following in the internal subset, it would be considered illegal, as it does not expand to a whole declaration:

  ```
  <!ELEMENT para (%paracont;)>
  ```

A nonvalidating parser (one that doesn't check the external subset) is still expected to process any attribute defaults and entity declarations in the internal subset. However, a parameter entity can change the meaning of those declarations in an unresolvable way. Therefore, a parser must stop processing the internal subset when it comes to the first external parameter entity reference it does not process. If it's an internal reference, it can expand it, and if it chooses to fetch the entity, it can continue processing. If it does not process the entity's replacement, it must not process the attribute list or entity declarations in the internal subset.

Why use this? Since some entity declarations are often relevant only to a single document (for example, declarations of chapter entities or other content files), the internal subset is a good place to put them. Similarly, if a particular document needs to override or alter the DTD values it uses, you can place a new definition in the internal subset. Finally, in the event that an XML processor is nonvalidating (as we mentioned previously), the internal subset is the best place to put certain DTD-related information, such as the identification of `ID` and `IDREF` attributes, attribute defaults, and entity declarations.

The Extensible Stylesheet Language

The Extensible Stylesheet Language (XSL) is one of the most intricate parts of the XML specification. As of this printing, the XSL specification itself is undergoing many revisions; the information presented here comes from the XSL specification dated 16 December 1998, which is classified as a "work in progress." A final W3C recommendation is expected from the XSL working group by August 1999. If you wish to obtain more recent information on the standard, we encourage you to visit the W3C XSL working group home page at *http://www.w3.org/Style/XSL/*.

As we mentioned, XSL works by applying element-formatting rules that you define to each XML document it encounters. In reality, XSL simply transforms each XML document from one series of element types to another. For example, XSL can be used to apply HTML formatting to an XML document, which would transform it from:

```
<?xml version="1.0"?>
<OReilly:Book title="XML Comments">
  <OReilly:Chapter title="Working with XML">
    <OReilly:Image src="http://www.oreilly.com/xmlch1.gif"/>
    <OReilly:HeadA>Starting XML</OReilly:HeadA>
    <OReilly:Body>If you haven't used XML, then you're in...
      </OReilly:Body>
  </OReilly:Chapter>
</OReilly:Book>
```

to the following HTML:

```
<HTML>
  <HEAD>
  <TITLE>XML Comments</TITLE>
  </HEAD>
  <BODY>
    <H1>Working with XML</H1>
    <img src="http://www.oreilly.com/xmlch1.gif"/>
    <H2>Starting XML</H2>
    <P>If you haven't used XML, then you're in...</P>
  </BODY>
</HTML>
```

XML

If you look carefully, you can see a predefined hierarchy that remains from the source content to the resulting content. To venture a guess, the `<OReilly:Book>` element probably maps to the `<HTML>`, `<HEAD>`, `<TITLE>`, and `<BODY>` elements in HTML. The `<OReilly:Chapter>` element maps to the HTML `<H1>` element, the `<OReilly:Image>` element maps to the `<img>` element, and so on.

This demonstrates an essential aspect of XML: each document contains a hierarchy of elements that can be organized in a tree-like fashion. (If the document uses a DTD, that hierarchy is well-defined.) In the previous XML example the `<OReilly:Chapter>` element would be a leaf of the `<OReilly:Book>` element, while in the HTML document, the `<BODY>` and `<HEAD>` elements are leaves of the `<HTML>` element. XSL's primary purpose is to apply formatting rules to a *source tree*, rendering its results to a *result tree*, as we've previously done.

Formatting objects

One area of the XSL specification that is gaining steam is the idea of *formatting objects*. These objects serve as universal formatting tags that can be applied to virtually any arena, including both video and print. However, this (rather large) area of the specification is still in its infancy, so while we use formatting objects on occasion, we will not delve into their definitions. Where we do employ formatting objects, their meaning should be obvious.

Formatting objects do not use the `xsl` namespace, but instead employ the `fo` namespace, as shown here:

```
<fo:block font-size="10pt">
  Formatted text using 10 point font
<fo:block>
```

The `fo` namespace is mapped to the URI *http://www.w3.org/TR/WD-xsl/FO*. If you wish to learn more about formatting objects, see the W3C XSL home page at *http://www.w3.org/Style/XSL/*.

General Formatting

The general order for elements in an XSL stylesheet is as follows:

```
<?xml version="1.0"?>
<xsl:stylesheet xmlns:xsl="http://www.w3.org/TR/WD-xsl">
    <xsl:import/>
    <xsl:include/>
    <xsl:id/>
    <xsl:strip-space/>
    <xsl:preserve-space/>
    <xsl:macro/>
    <xsl:attribute-set/>
    <xsl:constant/>
    <xsl:template match="pattern">
        template action
    </xsl:template>
    <xsl:template match="pattern">
        template action
    </xsl:template>
    ...
</xsl:stylesheet>
```

Essentially, this ordering boils down to a few simple rules. First, all XSL stylesheets must be well-formed XML documents, and each XSL element must use the **xsl:** namespace. Second, all XSL stylesheets must begin with the XSL root element tag **<xsl:stylesheet>** and close with a corresponding tag **</xsl:stylesheet>**. Within the opening tag, the XSL namespace must be defined:

```
<xsl:stylesheet xmlns:xsl="http://www.w3.org/TR/WD-xsl">
```

After the root element, you can import or include other XSL data using the **<xsl:include>** and **<xsl:import>** elements. Following that, you can use any of the following optional elements: **<xsl:id>**, **<xsl:strip-space>**, **<xsl:preserve-space>**, **<xsl:macro>**, **<xsl:attribute-set>**, or **<xsl:constant>**. Each of these must be performed before defining any rules of your own using the **<xsl:template>** element.

Pattern Matching

Before going further, we should discuss the concept of pattern matching in XSL. XSL requires you to match elements in an XML document based on various characteristics. The most common of these XSL elements is the **<xsl:template>** element, which uses the **match** attribute to determine which elements to format.

With **<xsl:template>** and other elements, you can apply several pattern-matching strategies. These patterns match an element that has a relationship to the current *node*. A node defines the element that is at the current level of the hierarchy tree you are matching from. For example, consider this XML document:

```
<?xml version="1.0"?>
<book>
  <chapter>
    <image src="ch1.gif"/>
    <head>Learning XML</head>
    <body>XML is a <emphasis>wonderful</emphasis> tool</body>
```

```
  </chapter>
</book>
```

The stylesheet we wish to apply to this document is:

```
<?xml version="1.0"?>
<xsl:stylesheet xmlns:xsl="http://www.w3.org/TR/WD-xsl">
  <xsl:template match="book/chapter/head">
      <xsl:text>The heading is: </xsl:text><xsl:apply-templates/>
      <xsl:text>.</xsl:text>
  </xsl:template>
  <xsl:template match="book/chapter/body">
      <xsl:text>The body is: </xsl:text><xsl:apply-templates/>
  </xsl:template>
</xsl:stylesheet>
```

Consider the line `<xsl:template match="book/chapter/head">`. Its current node is the <book> element that has the <chapter> as its child even though the <head> element is the element that is matched.

Matching on ancestry

As we hinted, you can ensure that a template formatting rule is applied only to, say, a <body> element that has a <chapter> parent with the following syntax:

```
<xsl:template match="chapter/body">
```

This matches the <body> element in following XML fragment:

```
<chapter>
  <body>Woe as I looked upon the raging sea.</body>
</chapter>
```

However, it will not match this <body> element:

```
<book>
  <body>In this day and age, we must wonder.</body>
</book>
```

Nor will it match this <body>:

```
<chapter>
  <section>
    <body>Woe as I looked upon the raging sea.</body>
  </section>
</chapter>
```

The latter example failed to match because the <chapter> element was not the direct parent of the <body> element. If you want to expand your matching capability to include *any* ancestor of a specific element, specify the following:

```
<xsl:template match="chapter//body">
```

This allows any number of elements (including zero) to appear between the <chapter> element and the <body> element in a qualifying match. As you might expect, you can get quite specific when matching on ancestry:

```
<xsl:template match="book//chapter/section//body">
```

You can select the first ancestor of the current node using the ancestor() keyword. For example:

```
<xsl:template match="ancestor(chapter)/head">
```

This selects the <head> elements of the first <chapter> ancestor of the current node. Note that the <chapter> element doesn't have to be the immediate parent of the current node. Now let's add an interesting twist:

```
<xsl:template match="*/body">
```

As you might expect, the asterisk performs the role of a wildcard. The previous example matches instances where the <body> element is the direct child of any element. (In fact, the only case it will not match is where the <body> element is the root element.)

By the same token, consider this:

```
<xsl:template match="section/*">
```

This template will match any element that has the <section> element as its immediate parent. Note that it will not match any element that has the <section> element as its grandparent.

You can select the current node with the period (.) operator. For example, to ensure that the <section> element is a child of the current node, use:

```
<xsl:template match="./section">
```

In the same manner, you can select the parent of the current node with a double period (..):

```
<xsl:template match="../section">
```

This matches a <section> element that is a sibling (parent's child) of the current node. Now let's suppose you want to choose one of two possible elements to match upon. These will work:

```
<xsl:template match="head|body">
<xsl:template match="chapter/head|chapter/body">
```

The first example matches either the <head> element or the <body> element from the current node. The second one does the same thing, ensuring that both elements are the child of a <chapter> element. (Note that a "|" has the lowest order of precedence.)

Tests

Let's look at some other pattern-matching rules:

```
<xsl:template match="book[index]/chapter">
```

This matches a <chapter> element that has a <book> element as its immediate parent. In addition, the <book> element is tested to ensure it has an <index> element as its immediate child. (This means that the <index> and <chapter> elements are siblings.) In other words, for this template to match, the following XML document elements must be in place:

```
<book>
  <chapter>Chapter 1: The Opening of Pandora's Box</chapter>
  <index>An index element</index>
</book>
```

The square brackets ([]) indicate that a test occurs to see if a particular element matched. Here, each <chapter> element that has a <book> element as its parent is tested to see if there is an <index> sibling.

If you wish to match an element that has a specific attribute defined, you can do so with the following:

```
<xsl:template match="book[@title]">
```

This matches any book element that has a title attribute defined, such as the following:

```
<book title="Webmaster in a Nutshell">...</book>
```

However, it doesn't match the XML fragment shown here, as the book has no title attribute defined:

```
<book>
  <index>An index element</index>
</book>
```

To take this a step further, if you wish to match against an element attribute set to a known value, you can augment the rule by adding a test using the following pattern:

```
<xsl:template match="book[@title='Webmaster in a Nutshell']">
```

This matches only if the attribute for the XML element is defined and has the matching value (in this case, "Webmaster in a Nutshell").

You can negate a test using not(). For example, if you want to match every <book> element without a title attribute defined:

```
<xsl:template match="book[not(@title)]">
```

The not() keyword negates the result of any test inside its parentheses.

In addition, XSL allows you to match a pattern based on an element's position compared to other siblings, using the qualifiers shown in Table 10-5.

Table 10-5: Position Matching Qualifiers in XSL

Qualifier	*Description*
first-of-type()	Matches a single element that is the first sibling of its type
last-of-type()	Matches a single element that is the last sibling of its type
first-of-any()	Matches the first sibling element of any type
last-of-any()	Matches the last sibling element of any type

For example, if you want to place the text "First Index:" before the first <index> element in the document and "Next Index:" before the other <index> elements, you could use the following:

XML

```
<xsl:template match="index[first-of-type()]">
    <xsl:text>First Index:</xsl:text><xsl:apply-templates/>
</xsl:template>
<xsl:template match="index[not(first-of-type())]">
    <xsl:text>Next Index:</xsl:text><xsl:apply-templates/>
</xsl:template>
```

Also, you can use the and and or logical operators in tests as well:

```
<xsl:template match="chapter[first-of-type() or last-of-type()]">
<xsl:template match="chapter[first-of-any() and last-of-any()]">
```

Other matchings

To match any comment children of the current node, you can use the comment() keyword:

```
<xsl:template match="book/comment()">
```

This matches:

```
<book>
   <!--This comment will be matched-->
</book>
```

This is useful in the event that you want to style any of the comments in the XML document. We should warn you, however, that this is not always guaranteed to work, as many XML parsers throw comments away. By the same token, to match any processing instruction children of the current node, use the pi() keyword:

```
<xsl:template match="book/pi(works)">
```

This matches any processing instructions that are children of the <book> element and use the works application, such as:

```
<book>
   <?works version="4.0" document="rihol.xmp"?>
</book>
```

If you wish to match against the value of an element's ID attribute, use the following code:

```
<xsl:template match="id('definition')">
```

This matches the following XML:

```
<book code="definition">...</book>
```

where the code attribute has been defined as a special ID attribute in the DTD.

Attribute value templates

Finally, you can use the {} characters as a template to match attribute values in result-tree elements. This is a little different than what we've seen, as the expression inside the curly braces is evaluated while processing, and both the expression and the curly braces are replaced immediately by the result. For example,

```
<xsl:constant name="codebase" value="/src/code"/>

<xsl:template match="applet">
<APPLET CODE="{code/@class}" CODEBASE="{constant(codebase)}/java"/>
</xsl:template>
```

This could be evaluated on the following XML:

```
<applet>
   <code class="myapplet"/>
</applet>
```

The result after processing is:

```
<APPLET CODE="myapplet" CODEBASE="/src/code/java"/>
```

Note that the `<xsl:constant>` element is still considered to be on the result tree of the XSL processor, even though an analogous element isn't present in the output XML.

You are not allowed to use curly braces inside an attribute value template.

XML

Numbering elements

Let's assume we want to provide an autonumber for each element matched. For this, we can use the `<xsl:number>` element, which helps us assign a number based on the attributes we pass into it. For example, consider the following XML document:

```
<?xml version="1.0"?>
<book>
    <chapter>
        <title>A Mystery Unfolds</title>
        <paragraph>It was a dark and stormy...</paragraph>
    </chapter>
    <chapter>
        <title>A Sudden Visit</title>
        <paragraph>He awoke to a horrible sound...</paragraph>
    </chapter>
</book>
```

Here is how we would autonumber the `<chapter>` elements in the previous example:

```
<xsl:template match="book">
  <ol>
    <xsl:for-each select="chapter">
      <li>
      <xsl:text>Chapter </xsl:text>
      <xsl:number level="single" count="chapter" format="1"/>
      <xsl:text>:</xsl:text>
      <xsl:apply-templates select="title"/>
      </li>
    </xsl:for-each>
  </ol>
</xsl:template>
```

This creates the following:

```
<ol>
<li>Chapter 1: A Mystery Unfolds</li>
<li>Chapter 2: A Sudden Visit</li>
</ol>
```

In this case, the <xsl:number> element replaces itself with a numeral based on the number of <chapter> elements it has encountered so far.

You can use the <xsl:number> element to come up with much more extensive numbering schemes. The <xsl:number> element has three primary attributes that can be set: `count`, `level`, and `format`. In addition, there are three other attributes you can set: `letter-value`, `digit-group-sep`, and `n-digits-per-group`.

`count`
: The `count` attribute decides which elements should be counted. You can use the standard pattern matching described previously to determine which elements will be numbered, such as:

```
<xsl:number count="chapter[attribute(number)='4']">
```

This selects <chapter> elements with a number attribute of 4. The following example accepts any of three types of elements:

```
<xsl:number count="chapter|section|paragraph">
```

`level`
: Next, the `level` attribute specifies what levels of the source tree should be considered for counting. The `level` attribute always climbs the hierarchy of the source tree, searching for elements to pattern match against. Note that the <xsl:number> element never travels lower in the hierarchy than the position of the current element. The `level` attribute can take one of three string values:

`single`
: Number each of the elements matched by the `count` attribute that are siblings of the current element. This is the default value.

`multi`
: Number each of the elements matched by the `count` attribute that are children of any of the current element's ancestors, so long as they do not travel deeper than the current element.

`any` Number each of the elements matched by the `count` attribute that are anywhere in the document, so long as they do not travel deeper than the current element.

`from`
: You can set a limit to the level of ancestry that is searched using the <xsl:number> `from` attribute. For example, let's assume you wish to number all the <paragraph> elements in the following document example:

```
<book>
  <paragraph>This book is copyright 1998 by O'Reilly</paragraph>
  <chapter number="1">
```

```
        <title>A Mystery Unfolds</title>
        <paragraph>It was a dark and stormy night...</paragraph>
        <paragraph>Luckily, as Marcus downed a steaming java...</paragraph>
        <paragraph>"Are you sure that's what it was?"...</paragraph>
    </chapter>
    <chapter number="2">
        <title>A Sudden Visit</title>
        <paragraph>Marcus found himself sleeping...</paragraph>
        <paragraph>"How could you come back to me?"...</paragraph>
        <paragraph>Marcus had no idea how to answer this...</paragraph>
    </chapter>
</book>
```

However, anything not inside a <chapter> element should be ignored. The following XSL does the trick:

```
<xsl:template match="chapter">
    <xsl:number level="any" from="chapter" count="paragraph">
    <xsl:text>. </xsl:text>
</xsl:template>
```

This catches each of the <paragraph> elements inside the chapters, without picking up the copyright statement.

`format`

The `format` attribute tells XSL how you would like the numbers formatted. The default is a standard cardinal number. However, the XML specification lists several choices with <xsl:number>, including several Unicode values with numerical properties as shown in Table 10-6.

Table 10-6: <xsl:number> Format Values

Attribute	*Description*
1	Use standard numbers (1, 2, 3, 4 . . . 10, 11 . . .)
A	Use standard capital letters (A, B, C . . . AA, BB . . .)
a	Use standard lowercase leters (a, b, c . . . aa, bb . . .)
i	Use lowercase Roman numerals (i, ii, iii, iv . . .)
I	Use capital Roman numerals (I, II, III, IV . . .)
ア	Use Katakana numbering
イ	Use Katakana numbering in iroha order
๑	Use Thai digits for numbering
א	use traditional Hebrew (`letter-value="other"`)
ა	Use Gregorian (`letter-value="other"`)
α	use classical Greek (`letter-value="other"`)
а	Use Old Slavic (`letter-value="other"`)

All other characters appear as standard text. Consider, for example, the following format:

```
<xsl:number count="chapter|paragraph" format="1.1">
```

Assuming that <paragraph> elements are always contained inside of <chapter> elements, the first number corresponds to the chapter number, while the second number corresponds to the paragraph number. This yields a numbering system such as:

```
1.1
1.2
1.3
2.1
2.2
2.3
```

`letter-value`
: You can use the `letter-value` attribute of the `<number>` element to differentiate numbering schemes that order letters from those that don't when using other languages. The value `alphabetic` specifies that the ordering should take place using an increment of the character codes of the language (e.g., a, b, c, d, e, f, . . .), while `other` specifies that an alternate rule should be used (e.g., i, ii, iii, iv, v, vi, . . .). In some alphabets, there can be two or more numbering systems that start with the same letter; the `letter-value` attribute can clarify those cases.

`digit-group-sep` and `n-digits-per-group`
: Finally, the `digit-group-sep` attribute specifies the separator characters used between a succession of digits. For example, to place a comma between each of three digits in a number, use the following:

```
<xsl:number ...  digit-group-sep="," n-digits-per-group="3">
```

The `n-digits-per-group` attribute specifies the maximum amount of digits that should come between the `digit-group-sep` separator. For example, the United States uses a maximum of three digits between each comma when representing large numbers.

There are many other interesting possibilities you can use with the `<xsl:number>` element. See the W3C specification for more details.

Template matching rules

In the event that more than one template matches a given element in the XML document, the following rules apply:

- Template rules that have greater *importance* are chosen over those with lesser importance. This applies in a case where one stylesheet has been imported into another, in which case its contents are considered less important than the contents of the stylesheet containing the import statement.
- The template rule with the highest priority (if there is more than one remaining) is then chosen, as specified by the `priority` attribute of the `<xsl:template>` element.

If there is no template match, the XML processor generally performs a default format, which processes the children of elements and renders any text in the current context.

Linking in stylesheets

You can link stylesheets from your XML documents using a processor directive that points to the stylesheet:

```
<?xml-stylesheet href="http://www.oreilly.com/stylesheet1.xsl" type="text/xsl"?>
```

The directive points to the address of the XSL document, as well as the type of stylesheet used. This directive must come after the initial XML processor directive but before any DTD directives.

Although we do not cover it here, CSS is also a legitimate value for the type pseudo-attribute, indicating a cascading stylesheet:

```
<?xml-stylesheet href="http://www.oreilly.com/stylesheet2.css" type="text/css"?>
```


XSL Elements

The following list is an enumeration of XSL elements.

<xsl:apply-imports>

```
<xsl:apply-imports/>
```

Styles the current node and each of its children, using the imported stylesheet rules, ignoring those in the stylesheet that performed the import. Note that the rules aren't applied to the current node's siblings or ancestors.

<xsl:apply-templates>

```
<xsl:apply-templates [select="pattern"]/>
```

Specifies that the immediate children of the source element should be processed further. For example:

```
<xsl:template match="section"/>
  <B><xsl:apply-templates/><B>
</xsl:template>
```

This example processes the children of the selected `<section>` element after applying a bold tag. You can optionally use the `select` attribute to determine which children should be processed.

```
<xsl:template match="section"/>
  <HR>
  <xsl:apply-templates select="paragraph(indent)//sidebar"/>
  <HR>
  <xsl:apply-templates select="paragraph(indent)/quote"/>
  <HR>
</xsl:template>
```

This example processes only specific children of the selected `<section>` element. In this case, the first target is a `<sidebar>` element that is a descendant of a `<paragraph>` element that has defined an `indent` attribute. The second

→

target is a <quote> element that is the direct child of a <paragraph> element that has defined an `indent` attribute.

<xsl:arg>

`<xsl:arg name="`*`string`*`" default="`*`value`*`"/>`

Defines an argument and default value, which can be used when invoking a macro. For example:

```
<xsl:macro name="mymacro">
  <xsl:macro-arg name="format" default="A. "/>
  <xsl:number format="{arg(format)}"/>
  <xsl:contents/>
</xsl:macro>

<xsl:template match="toc/entry">
  <xsl:invoke macro="mymacro">
    <xsl:arg name="format" value="1. "/>
    <xsl:apply-templates/>
  </xsl:invoke>
</xsl:template>
```

This passes the value `"1. "` into the XSL macro `mymacro` when invoking it.

<xsl:attribute>

`<xsl:attribute name="`*`name`*`">. . .</xsl:attribute>`

Adds an attribute with the given name to an element in the result tree. There can only be one attribute with a given name added to a specific element. The contents of the `<xsl:attribute>` element form the value of the attribute:

```
<xsl:element name="book">
  <xsl:attribute name="title">Moby Dick</xsl:attribute>
  <xsl:text>This is about a whale</xsl:text>
</xsl:element>
```

This creates the following element in the result tree:

```
<book title="Moby Dick">This is about a whale</book>
```

<xsl:attribute-set>

`<xsl:attribute-set name="`*`value`*`" . . . />`

Allows the naming of a collection of formatting attributes, which can be applied using a formatting object. For example, the following will assign a bold 24-point font to the name `"heading-style"`, which can be used with the `xsl:use` attribute.

```
<xsl:attribute-set name="heading-style"
                   font-size="24pt"
                   font-weight="bold"/>

<xsl:template match="heading">
  <fo:block xsl:use="heading-style">
```

→

```
      <xsl:apply-templates/>
    </fo:block>
  </xsl:template>
```

<xsl:choose>

<xsl:choose> . . . </xsl:choose>

The <xsl:choose> element, in conjunction with the <xsl:when> and <xsl:otherwise> elements, offers the ability to perform multiple condition tests. For example:

```
<xsl:template match="chapter/title">
  <xsl:choose>
    <xsl:when test=".[first-of-type()]">
        Start Here:
    </xsl:when>
    <xsl:otherwise>
        Then Read:
    </xsl:otherwise>
  </xsl:choose>
  <xsl:apply-templates/>
</xsl:template>
```

This example matches against each of the qualifying <title> elements, but it must test each <title> element to determine how to format it. Here, the formatting used depends on whether the element is the first of its type or not. If it is, it applies the letters "Start Here:" before the first <title> element. Otherwise, the letters "Then Read: " are placed before the others.

<xsl:comment>

<xsl:comment> . . . </xsl:comment>

Inserts a comment into the XML document. For example, the following:

```
<xsl:comment>English material below</xsl:comment>
```

is translated into a comment in the XML document when it is processed:

```
<!-- English material below -->
```

<xsl:constant>

<xsl:constant name="*name*" value="*value*"/>

Allows the definition of a named constant that can be substitued in XSL documents. For example:

```
<xsl:constant name="size" value="24pt"/>
<xsl:template match="copyright">
  <fo:block font-size="{constant(size)}">
    <xsl:apply-templates/>
  </fo:block>
</xsl:template>
```

<xsl:contents>

`<xsl:contents/>`

Used inside <xsl:macro>. When the macro is invoked, the contents of the <xsl:invoke> invocation element are inserted at this point. (See <xsl:macro> for an example.)

<xsl:copy>

`<xsl:copy> . . . </xsl:copy>`

Copies all nodes matched inside the opening and closing tags.

<xsl:counter>

<xsl:counter name="*string*"/>

Provides a named counter that appears in the result tree. The counter is initialized using the <xsl:counter-reset/> element and incremented using the <xsl:counter-increment/> element. Consider the following XML document:

```
<book>
  <chapter>Introduction</chapter>
  <chapter>Learning to Fly</chapter>
  <chapter>Simple Aerobatics</chapter>
</book>
```

The following XSL numbers and lists each of the chapters in the result tree:

```
<xsl:template match="book">
  <xsl:counter-reset name="chaps"/>
  <xsl:apply-templates>
</xsl:template>

<xsl:template match="book/chapter">
  <xsl:text>Chapter </xsl:text>
  <xsl:counter name="chaps"/>
  <xsl:counter-increment name="chaps"/>
  <xsl:text>:</xsl:text>
  <xsl:apply-templates>
</xsl:template>
```

<xsl:counters>

<xsl:counters name="*string*" format="*format*"/>

Provides a named counter that appears in the result tree. The counter is formatted according to the string given using the format attribute. It can be initialized using the <xsl:counter-reset> element and incremented using the <xsl:counter-increment/> element. This differs from the <xsl:counter> element in that it maintains a counter for each level of ancestry it encounters. For example:

→

```
<xsl:template match="header">
  <fo:block>
    <xsl:counter-increment name="head"/>
    <xsl:counters name="head" format="1.1. "/>
    <xsl:apply-templates/>
  </fo:block>
  <xsl:counter-reset name="head"/>
</xsl:template>
```

Here, if we have a document as follows:

```
<header>The Long Road Home</header>
<header>Joyful Reunions</header>
```

the counter would return the following result: `(1, 2)`. However, if we had nested levels of the <header> element, such as:

```
<header>The Long Road Home
  <header>Starting the Long Road</header>
  <header>Halfway There</header>
</header>
<header>Joyful Reunions
  <header>Starting the Long Road</header>
  <header>Halfway There</header>
</header>
```

the counter returns the result (1, 1.1, 1.2, 2, 2.1, 2.2) for the <header> elements that it encounters.

XML

<xsl:counter-increment>

`<xsl:counter-increment name="`*`string`*`"/>`

Increments the named counter by a value of one.

<xsl:counter-reset>

`<xsl:counter-reset name="`*`string`*`" [value="`*`value`*`"]/>`

Resets the counter identified by the *name* attribute to the value specified, or zero (0) if none is given. If the counter is not part of the set of named counters for this element, it is added.

<xsl:counter-scope>

`<xsl:counter-scope/>`

This element marks the scope of a set of counters but otherwise does nothing.

<xsl:element>

`<xsl:element name="`*`name|URI#name`*`">. . .</xsl:element>`

Inserts the element pointed to by the attribute *name* into the result document. For example:

→

```
<xsl:element name="book">
  <xsl:element name="chapter">
    <xsl:text>The Opening of Pandora's Box</xsl:text>
  </xsl:element>
</xsl:element>
```

This creates the following in the result node:

```
<book>
  <chapter>The Opening of Pandora's Box </chapter>
</book>
```

Elements without explicit namespaces use the default namespace of their current context. Also, you can create a namespace for the element yourself:

```
<xsl:element name="http://www.oreilly.com/#book">
```

This employs the namespace associated with the URI *http://www.oreilly.com* with the element. If there are no namespaces associated with the URI, it becomes the default namespace.

<xsl:for-each>

```
<xsl:for-each select="pattern"/>
```

The `<xsl:for-each>` directive allows you to select any number of identical siblings in an XML document. For example, consider the following XML document:

```
<book>
  <chapter>
    <title>A Mystery Unfolds</title>
    <paragraph>It was a dark and stormy night...</paragraph>
  </chapter>
  <chapter>
    <title>A Sudden Visit</title>
    <paragraph>Marcus found himself sleeping...</paragraph>
  </chapter>
</book>
```

Note there are two `<chapter>` siblings in the document. Let's assume we want to provide an HTML numbered list for each `<title>` element that is the direct child of a `<chapter>` element, which in turn has a `<book>` element as a parent. The following XSL performs the task:

```
<xsl:template match="book>
  <ol>
  <xsl:for-each select="chapter">
    <li><xsl:process select="title"></li>
  </xsl:for-each>
  </ol>
</xsl:template>
```

After formatting, here is what the result looks like:

```
<ol>
<li>A Mystery Unfolds</li>
<li>A Sudden Visit</li>
</ol>
```

→

The XSL processor processes a <title> element in each <chapter> element that is the child of a <book> element. The result is a list for each chapter that could be used for a table of contents.

<xsl:id>

```
<xsl:id attribute="value" [element="element"]/>
```

Identifies a specific attribute that appears in an XML element as an XML ID attribute. This is useful in the event that an XML document without a corresponding DTD needs to be formatted. If `element` is used, only attributes localized to that element are marked as ID attributes. If `element` is omitted, the XML processor assumes that all element attributes matching the `value` specified, no matter what the element, should be treated as ID attributes:

```
<xsl:id attribute="id"/>
<xsl:id attribute="marker" element="Body"/>
```

You are allowed to use multiple <xsl:id> elements. However, remember that the same ID cannot be assigned to more than one XML element at a time. If this instruction identifies several XML attributes as ID attributes such that any of those attributes have identical values, the XML processor could generate an error.

This element may change in the future.

<xsl:if>

```
<xsl:if test="pattern">. . .</xsl:if>
```

You can use the <xsl:if> conditional to select a specific element while inside a template. The <xsl:if> element uses the `test` attribute to determine which elements should be selected. The `test` attribute takes a standard pattern matching string. For example:

```
<xsl:template match="chapter/title">
  <xsl:apply-templates/>
  <xsl:if test=".not([last-of-type()])">, </xsl:if>
</xsl:template>
```

This template matches each of the qualifying <title> elements, but inserts commas after those that are not the last <title> element. The result is a standard comma-separated list.

<xsl:import>

```
<xsl:import href="address"/>
```

Specifies the URI of an XSL stylesheet whose rules should be imported into this stylesheet. The import statement must occur before any other elements in the stylesheet. If a conflict arises between matching rules, imported stylesheets are of lesser importance to those rules in the XSL stylesheet performing the import. In addition, if more than one stylesheet is imported into

→

this document, the more recently imported stylesheet will be of greater importance than stylesheets imported before it.

```
<xsl:import href="webpage.xsl"/>
```

This example imports the stylesheet included in the file *webpage.xsl*.

<xsl:include>

`<xsl:include href="address"/>`

Specifies the name of an XSL stylesheet to be included in the document. The include process will replace the `<xsl:include>` statement with the contents of the file (moving any other `<xsl:import>` elements before it). Because the included document has been inserted in the referring stylesheet, any included rules will be of equal importance to those in the referring stylesheet. (Compare to `<xsl:import>`.)

```
<xsl:include href="chapterFormats.xsl"/>
```

<xsl:macro>

`<xsl:macro> . . . </xsl:macro>`

Creates a reusable XSL fragment thata can be inserted verbatim at given points by invoking its macro name. A macro is defined using the `<xsl:macro>` element and can be inserted into an XSL document using the `<xsl:invoke>` element, as shown:

```
<xsl:macro name="warning-header">
    <B>WARNING! </B>
    <xsl:contents/>
</xsl:macro>

<xsl:template match="warning">
  <xsl:invoke macro="warning-header">
    <xsl:apply-templates/>
  </xsl:invoke>
</xsl:template>
```

This example places the HTML bold letters "WARNING!" in front of any child elements of the `<warning>` element in the target document. When the macro is invoked, the contents of the `<xsl:macro>` element replace the `<xsl:invoke>` element. In addition, the `<xsl:contents/>` element, seen in the macro itself, are replaced with the contents of the `<xsl:invoke>` element.

XSL macros are allowed to take arguments using the `<xsl:macro-arg>` element.

<xsl:macro-arg>

`<xsl:macro-arg name="string" default="value"/>`

Used to declare an argument that should be passed to an XSL macro, as defined with the `<xsl:macro>` command. The macro argument can take a

→

default value, specified by the *default* attribute, in the event that the programmer does not specify one.

```
<xsl:macro name="function">
  <xsl:macro-arg name="x" default="0"/>
  ...
  <xsl:contents/>
</xsl:macro>
```

<xsl:number>

`<xsl:number level="`*`level`*`" count="`*`section`*`" format="`*`format`*`"/>`

This element can autonumber elements within the XML document. See the section "Numbering elements" earlier in this chapter.

<xsl:otherwise>

`<xsl:otherwise> . . . </xsl:otherwise>`

Default conditional for testing in an `<xsl:choose>` element. See `<xsl:choose>`.

<xsl:pi>

`<xsl:pi name="`*`name`*`"/> . . . </xsl:pi>`

Creates a processing instruction in the XML document. The name attribute is mandatory; it specifies the name of the application this instruction will be processed by. Any other attributes should appear between the opening and closing tags. For example:

```
<xsl:pi name="works">applevel="A" version="3.0"</xsl:pi>
```

This is translated in the output XML document as:

```
<?works applevel="A" version="3.0"?>
```

<xsl:preserve-space>

`<xsl:preserve-space element="`*`element_name`*`"/>`

Declares an XML element in which all whitespace located between its opening and closing tags is preserved; hence, the XML processor will not remove it.

```
<xsl:preserve-space element="title"/>
```

This is similar to the `xml:space=preserve` attribute.

<xsl:strip-space>

`<xsl:strip-space element="element_name"/>`

Declares an XML element in which all whitespace located between its opening and closing tags is insignificant and should be removed by the XML processor.

```
<xsl:strip-space element="title"/>
```

Note that this is not necessarily the same as the `xml:space=default` attribute, which allows the XSL processor more freedom to decide how to handle whitespace.

<xsl:value-of>

`<xsl:value-of select="pattern"/>`

Extracts a specific value from a source tree. The only attribute to the `<xsl:value>` element is a single pattern-matching expression that resolves to the value of a string, an element, or an attribute.

```
<xsl:template match="index">
   This index is <xsl:value-of select="@(type)">
   <xsl:apply-templates/>
</xsl:template>
```

The `select` attribute extracts the value of an element or attribute in the source tree and prints it verbatim in the result tree.

<xsl:template>

`<xsl:template match="pattern">. . . </xsl:template>`

The XSL template directive localizes various elements from which stylesheet rules can be applied. Each element is targeted with the `match` attribute. Formatting directives are located inside the opening and closing `<xsl:template>` tags.

```
<xsl:template match="para">
  <fo:block font-size="12pt">
    <xsl:apply-templates/>
  </fo:block>
</xsl:template>
```

See the earlier section "Pattern Matching" for more information on matching elements.

<xsl:text>

`<xsl:text>. . . </xsl:text>`

→

Inserts text verbatim into the document. For example:

```
<xsl:text>The price is $20.00.</xsl:text>
```

is inserted into the XML document as:

```
The price is $20.00.
```

<xsl:use>

```
<xsl:use attribute-set="name"/>
```

Uses a specific attribute set. See `<attribute-set>`.

<xsl:when>

```
<xsl:when test="pattern"> . . . </xsl:when>
```

Conditional for testing in an `<xsl:choose>` element. See `<xsl:choose>`.

XML

XLink and XPointer

The final piece of XML we cover is XLink and XPointer. These two creations fall under the Extensible Linking Language (XLL), a separate portion of the XML standard dedicated to working with XML links. Before we delve into this, however, we should warn you that the standard described here is subject to change at any time.

It's important to remember that an XML link is only an *assertion* of a relationship between pieces of documents; how the link is actually presented to a user depends on a number of factors, including the application processing the XML document.

Unique Identifiers

In order to create a link, we must first have a labeling scheme for XML elements. We do this by assigning an identifier to specific elements we want to reference using an ID attribute:

```
<paragraph id="attack">Suddenly the skies were filled with aircraft.
</paragraph>
```

You can think of IDs in XML documents as street addresses: they provide a unique identifier for an element within a document. However, just as there might be an identical address in a different city, an element in a different document might have the same ID. Consequently, you can tie together an IDs with the document's URI, as shown below:

```
http://www.oreilly.com/documents/story.xml#attack
```

The combination of a document's URI and an element's ID should uniquely identify that element throughout the universe. Remember that an ID attribute does not need to be named "id," as we showed in the first example. You can name it anything you want as long as you define it as an XML ID in the document's DTD. (However, using "id" is preferred in the event that the XML processor does not read the DTD.)

Should you give an ID to every element in your documents? No: the odds are that most elements will never be referred to. It's best to place IDs on items that a reader would want to refer to later, such as chapter and section divisions, as well as important items, such as term definitions.

ID References

The easiest way to refer to an ID attribute is with an ID reference, or IDREF. Consider this example:

```
<?xml version="1.0" standalone="yes"?>
<DOCTYPE document [
   <!ELEMENT document (employee*)>
   <!ELEMENT employee (#PCDATA)>
   <!ATTLIST person empnumber ID #REQUIRED>
   <!ATTLIST person boss IDREF #IMPLIED>
]>

<employee empnumber="emp123">Jay</employee>
<employee empnumber="emp124">Kay</employee>
<employee empnumber="emp125" boss="emp123">Frank</employee>
<employee empnumber="emp126" boss="emp124">Hank</employee>
```

As with ID attributes, an IDREF can be declared in the DTD. However, if you're in an environment where the processor might not read the DTD, you might want to call your ID references "idref."

The chief benefit of using an IDREF is that a validating parser can ensure that every one points to an actual element; unlike other forms of linking, an IDREF is guaranteed to refer to something within the current document.

As we mentioned before, the IDREF only asserts a relationship of some sort; the stylesheet and the browser will determine what is to be done with it. If the referring element has some content, it might become a link to the target. But if the referring element is empty, the stylesheet might instruct the browser to perform some other action.

As for the linking behavior, remember that in HTML a link can point to an entire document (which the browser will download and display, positioned at the top), or it can point to a specific location in a document (which the browser will display, usually positioned with that point at the top of the screen). However, linking changes drastically in XML. What does it mean to have a link to an entire element, which might be a paragraph (or smaller), or might be an entire group of chapters? The XML application will attempt some kind of guess, but the display is best controlled by the stylesheet. For now, it's best to simply make a link as meaningful as you can.

XPointers

ID references provide a convenient and efficient way to refer to elements within the same document. However, what if you want to refer to a point (or even a range) in a different document, especially if the point doesn't have a convenient ID to anchor to and you don't have permission to change the document? Luckily, XPointer can help.

XPointer uses the URI-augmented addressing scheme we introduced above. A typical XPointer looks like this:

```
http://www.oreilly.com/documents/webmaster/chapter1.xml#XPointer
```

There are two parts, separated by a hash mark (#). The first portion locates a resource (usually a document); the other forms the XPointer that locates something within that resource. The behavior and syntax of the XPointer portion is defined by the kind of document to which it is applied; in HTML, it finds an <a> element with a name attribute equal to the specified string. In XML, the syntax is defined by XPointer.

XML

ID references with XPointer

The easiest way to use an XPointer is to place an ID on the element you wish to point to. A simple string after the hash mark with no other qualifiers is assumed to refer to the element with that ID. For example, to find the element with an ID equal to "chapter01" in a document *book.xml*, the partial URL would look like this:

```
book.xml#chapter01
```

This would locate an element in a file *book.xml* such as:

```
<chapter id="chapter01"> ... </chapter>
```

With XPointers, it's best to use references to IDs whenever possible. That way, if the document is edited and your target section is moved, XPointer will still find the correct location so long as you refer directly to an element's ID. On the other hand, if the element is deleted, the XPointer will break. This is better than being taken to the approximate place where the information was and having to search fruitlessly for it.

Absolute location terms

The XPointer ID reference we saw previously is actually shorthand for a slightly more verbose syntax. The same element as above could be identified as:

```
sample.xml#id(chapter01)
```

The syntax of a keyword followed by parentheses is common to all the pieces of XPointer. Some location terms, such as `id()`, locate a specific element anywhere in a document without help from anything else. These terms are called *absolute location terms.* When used, they immediately follow the pound sign. You can use only one absolute location term per XPointer.

Besides `id()`, there are three other absolute location terms we should discuss: `root()`, `html()`, and `origin()`.

`root()`
: `root()` locates the root element of the document to which the base URI points. For instance, this chapter's Examples have a root element of `<OReilly:Books>`. Thus, if we name that document `simpledoc.xml`, `simpledoc.xml#root()` points to the `<OReilly:Books>` element.

`html()`
: `html()` is intended as a transitional term for use with XML documents that are primarily HTML. The `html()` term finds the element `<a>` whose name attribute has the value given between parentheses. For example:

```
http://www.oreilly.com/documents/webmaster.xml#html(authors)
```

points to the following HTML:

```
<A NAME="authors">Steve Spainhour and Valerie Quercia</A>
```

The `html()` term works the same way that the fragment locator does when pointing to an HTML document, with one difference: the `html()` term always finds the first match, unlike the HTML fragment locator, whose behavior varies depending on the browser in use.

`origin()`
: The `origin()` keyword is similar to `root()`, but it points to the document element from which the user began the link. `origin()` is useful only when used in association with a relative location term, which we discuss next.

Relative location terms

Relative location terms locate an element relative to the position given by another. The preceding terms (often an absolute location term) provide a *location source* for the relative term to work from. Relative location terms are concatenated onto the end of other location terms with a period (`.`) character.

There are seven relative location terms: `child()`, `ancestor()`, `descendant()`, `preceding()`, `following()`, `psibling()`, and `fsibling()`. Each term can take up to four arguments. The arguments of a relative location term hold the same meaning from one keyword to the next. The first argument can be either a number or the word `all`. The second argument is the type of object being located, and the third and fourth arguments filter the results based on attributes and their values.

Here are some examples using relative location terms:

```
root().child(6, para)
root().descendant(3, emphasis)
root().child(1, employee, boss, #IMPLIED)
```

Arguments

Let's start with the arguments and cover each one by one.

The first term selects the number, or instance, of the match from a set of candidates. For example, `child(all, para)` selects all the <para> elements that are children of the location source. Alternatively, `child(2, para)` selects the second <para> element. The word `all` simply selects all the eligible elements. A positive integer selects an element by counting forward in the list of candidates, while a negative integer selects an element by counting backward in the list.

The second argument is the *node type*. For most purposes, this will be the name of an element type. For instance, as you've probably already guessed, `child(all, para)` will locate all of the <para> elements that are children of the current location source. In addition, you can use the keywords `#element` and `#text` as the second argument. For example, `child(all, #element)` finds all of the elements (of any type) that are children of the location source. If the second argument is omitted, it is the same as if `#element` had been specified. On the other hand, the `#text` keyword finds chunks of text that are directly contained within the location source; that is, they're not in any other element besides the current one. For example, given this XML:

```
<para>This is a <literal>#text</literal> example.</para>
```

the XPointer term `child(all,#text)` would locate two text chunks: the one containing "This is a " and the one containing " example." (including the spaces after "a" and before "example"). The other chunk of text could be found with the term `child(1,literal).(all,#text)`.

The third argument forms the name of an attribute, and the fourth is its value. These can be used to locate elements with specific attribute values. The location term `child(all,#element,type,"zarknab")` will find any and all child elements of the location source that have `type="zarknab"` given as an attribute. The attribute name can also be given as `*`, meaning that any attribute with the value is acceptable: `child(all,#element,*,"zarknab")` will find any child element with any attribute with a value of `"zarknab"`.

The fourth argument, instead of a value, can also be `*` or `#IMPLIED`. The first requires that some value was specified for the attribute, but its exact value doesn't matter. The value might have been given in the document directly, or it might have been provided as a default value in the DTD. `#IMPLIED` means the opposite, that no value at all was specified, nor was any default given. So `child(all,#element,type,*)` finds all the children who specified any value at all for the `type` attribute, while `child(all,#element,type,#IMPLIED)` finds all of the other children, the ones that did not specify any value for `type`.

You can chain together keywords of the same type by placing periods between the sets of arguments and omitting the keywords. For example:

```
child(1,para).(1,emph)
```

is equivalent to:

```
child(1,para).child(1,emph)
```

Terms

Here is an example of the relative location terms. For the following, consider this simple XML document:

```
<?xml version="1.0"?>
<!DOCTYPE simpledoc [
  <!ELEMENT simpledoc (title, para+)>
  <!ELEMENT title (#PCDATA)>
  <!ELEMENT para (#PCDATA | emph)*>
  <!ATTLIST para
          type CDATA #IMPLIED>
  <!ELEMENT emph (#PCDATA)>
]>

<simpledoc>
<title>A Simple Document</title>
<para>This is a <emph>very</emph> simple document.</para>
<para type="sarcastic">Yeah, like there's <emph>so</emph> much going
on here.</para>
</simpledoc>
```

`child()`
: The `child()` keyword locates elements that are immediate children of the location source. For example, `root().child(1,para)` finds the first `<para>` in the previous example, while `root().child(1,*,type,"sarcastic")` finds the second. Both `root().child(all,title)` and `#root().child(1,*)` finds the `<title>`.

  Negative numbers for `child()` simply count backward from the end of the list of candidates. In this example, `root().child(2,para)` and `root().child(-1,para)` find the second `<para>` and the last `<para>`, respectively—which are the same element.

`descendant()`
: The `descendant()` keyword works like the `child()` keyword, except that it is not limited to the immediate children. In the example above, both `<emph>` elements are descendants of `<simpledoc>`. For example:

```
root().descendant(2,emph)
root().descendant(-1,emph)
root().descendant(2,para).(1,emph)
root().child(2,para).(1,emph)
root().descendant(all,*,type,"sarcastic").child(-1,emph)
```

  These XPointers all locate the same element, the final `<emph>` in the document.

  Negative numbers are more complicated for descendants than for children. Since an element's descendants can contain other descendants, it matters whether you count the beginnings or the ends of the elements. The XPointer specification states that it is the ends that matter when using negative numbers, not the beginnings (which count with positive numbers). In the example, the first `<para>` starts before its child `<emph>`, but it ends after the `<emph>`. Table 10-7 shows a set of positive-numbered descendants and the elements they locate.

Table 10-7: Negative XPointers with descendant()

Positive XPointer	*Element*	*Negative XPointer*
`root().descendant(1,*)`	<title>	`root().descendant(-5,*)`
`root().descendant(2,*)`	the first <para>	`root().descendant(-3,*)`
`root().descendant(3,*)`	the first <emph>	`root().descendant(-4,*)`
`root().descendant(4,*)`	the second <para>	`root().descendant(-1,*)`
`root().descendant(5,*)`	the second <emph>	`root().descendant(-2,*)`

Note that this isn't a strict reversal. The <emph> elements always come after their containing <para> elements, whether you count forward or backward.

You may be wondering, since every child is a descendant, why have the `child()` keyword at all? The first reason is that `child()` is slightly more robust; a change in the document's structure is more likely to change the descendants of an element than its children, as there are (usually) more descendants than children. The second reason is that it is faster for a computer program to look through the children than through the descendants, so you may get better performance from your XPointers using `child()`.

`ancestor()`
: The `ancestor()` keyword works up the tree to locate an element that contains the location source. For example, `root().descendant(2,emph).ancestor(1,simpledoc)` finds the root element in the previous example. So do `root().descendant(2,emph).ancestor(2,*)` and `root().descendant(2,emph).ancestor(-1,*)`.

Negative numbers are simple once again; positive numbers count upward from the location source towards the root; negative numbers count downward along the same path, with the root element (<simpledoc> in this case) being -1.

`preceding()`
: The `preceding()` keyword finds elements that start before the location source. From the second <emph>, everything is a preceding element; from the <title>, only the <simpledoc> precedes it.

Positive and negative numbers work in a way that might seem backward at first for preceding elements. Positive numbers count backward in the document; that is, from the second <emph>, `preceding(1,*)` locates the <para> that contains it. Negative numbers count forward from the root element: from that same <emph>, `preceding(-1,*)` finds the <simpledoc>, and `preceding(-2,*)` finds the <title>.

`following()`
: The `following()` keyword picks from among the elements that end after the current one; the second <para> follows the second <emph>, as does <simpledoc>.

Positive numbers count forward for the `following()`. Beware, however, that anything that ends after the current element is considered to follow it. So, from the second <emph>, `following(1,*)` and `following(-2,*)` both find the second <para> element, while following(2,*) and following(-1,*) both find the <simpledoc> element.

psibling()
: The psibling() keyword is to preceding() as child() is to descendant(). It can locate only those elements that both precede it and have the same parent. In other words, the second <para> element has two previous siblings, the first <para> has one, and the <title> has none at all.

  Counting works the same way as it does with preceding(). From the second <para>, psibling(2,*) and psibling(-1,*) both find the <title> element.

fsibling()
: This keyword is like psibling(), only it locates elements after it instead of before it that share the same parent. From the <title>, both fsibling(1,*) and fsibling(-2,*) find the first <para>.

Now let's take a peek at how these might be used in an actual XML link:

```
<?xml version="1.0"?>
<linkdoc>
<link xml:link="extended" inline="false" title="origin() link">

  <start xml:link="locator" role="start" actuate="user"
    href="simpledoc.xml#id(target-section).child(1,para)"/>

  <end xml:link="locator" role="end" actuate="none"
    href="#origin().fsibling(1,*)"/>
</link>
</linkdoc>
```

The xml:link attribute helps us form the appropriate link (<link>, <linkdoc>, <start>, and <end> are our own elements). When the XML link is activated, it links to the following element of any type, from wherever the link was activated. (In this case, that simply means the following paragraph.) In the previous example, id(target-section) found the element that has an ID of target-section; then child(1,para) finds the first <para> element that is its child.

Note that the origin() location term in the end link does not follow a filename; an error will occur if a filename is given that differs from the one in which the link traversal actually began. Also, note that neither root() nor origin() have anything between their parentheses. They are not permitted to; in reality, the parentheses are there for consistency with other location terms, and to avoid a potential clash with an ID called root or origin.

Strings

Once you've found an element, you may not want the whole thing. You may only want the third word in the paragraph, or the first sentence, or the last three letters. XPointer provides the string() location term to select specific text within an element. Like the relative location term keywords, string() takes up to four arguments. But don't let that fool you; the arguments have little to do with those of the other keywords.

The simplest form of string() takes two arguments. The first argument is the keyword all or a number, the second is a string to look for: string(2,"fnord") finds the second occurrence of the string "fnord" within the location source. (Note that there is no restriction on matching only words; this example finds a part of "Medfnord" as well as the whole word "fnord.") Also, the match is case-sensitive.

To simply count characters, you can give an empty string for the second argument: string(23,"") will find the point immediately before the 23rd character in the location source.

Having found the string, you're not necessarily done. You may want to move relative to the string you found; for example, you may want to find the string "Medfnord", and then move relative to its location. To do that, use the following:

```
string(all,Medfnord,3,5)
```

The first two arguments locate all occurrences of the string "Medfnord," and the next two select the string beginning three characters from the beginning of the targeted string (just before the "f" and continuing for five characters (ending just after the "d").

The offsets don't have to locate something within the string you found; for example, string(1,Medfnord,8,0) locates the point immediately after the word. Also, the located object doesn't need to actually contain any characters; it can just be a point. That may be a difficult link for a user to click on with a mouse, but is a perfectly acceptable destination for a link, or an insertion point for a block text from another page.

When counting text within an element, all of the text of that element and its descendants are counted. So for the paragraph:

```
<para id="somnolence">Some sought <emph>so</emph> sonorous sounds
<emph>south</emph>ward.</para>
```

The XPointer id(somnolence).string(all,"so") locates five occurrences (remember, the match is case-sensitive. "So" doesn't count.); id(somnolence).string(1,"southward") would locate the last word, even though it is partly in one element and partly outside of it.

Spans

Not everything you want to locate is going to lend itself to neat packaging as an element or a bit of text entirely within one element. For this reason, XPointer gives you a way to locate two objects and everything in between using the *span* keyword:

The syntax is very simple:

```
span(XPointer,XPointer)
```

For instance, in our <simpledoc> example above you could locate the range from the emphasized word "very" to the emphasized word "so" with root().span (descendant(1,emph),descendant(2,emph)).

Arcana

XPointers can actually do a bit more. These things aren't really of interest to someone reading a document in a browser or preparing a document for viewing in a browser. They're mostly of interest to programmers who are processing XML documents. However, we have included them here for completeness.

Additional node types

XPointers can locate more than elements and text. For example, everywhere `#element` is allowed, you can also use these keywords:

`#pi`
: Finds processing instructions; for example, `id(foo).child(5,#pi)` finds the fifth processing instruction in the element with ID "foo."

`#comment`
: This finds comments; `id(fnord).child(1,#comment)` locates the first comment in the element with ID "fnord".

`#all`
: Finds all children. In the example at the beginning of the previous section "Terms," the XPointer `root().child(1,para).child(all,#all)` finds the first text chunk (`"This is a "`), the `<emph>` element, and the last text chunk (`"simple document."`).

Locating attributes

You can locate elements with specific attributes using `attr()`. As with the special node types above, this is really only of interest to programmers processing XML documents. Since attributes aren't displayed (though they can be used as the source for text created by a stylesheet), there's really nothing for a browser to link to. This is more of a programmer's abstraction, providing a uniform interface to all of the pieces of a document.

The `attr()` keyword doesn't have a number like `child()` because attributes aren't ordered; `<para type="sarcastic" clearance="low">` is the same as `<para clearance="low" type="sarcastic">`.

When XPointers fail

There are two uses for XPointers: finding where a link can begin and finding where it can end. In both cases, we would expect a link-checking program to tell you that it can't find the end of the XPointer you provided. However, for a browser, things can fail silently. If the XPointer is supposed to find where a link can begin and doesn't find any matching objects in a document, the browser simply won't create any linking points. The user may never know that the link was intended to exist, although a browser might provide an option to tell the user.

If the beginning of a link was successfully located, but the end is broken, the browser may not notice until the user requests that the browser follow the link. In that case, it would be much like if you linked to an HTML page that no longer existed; the browser would return an error message stating that it simply couldn't find the end of the link.

This is largely speculation, since the XPointer draft is not final and does not describe behavior in the face of error. Moreover, as of this writing, there are only a few small test implementations of XPointer.

XLink

Now that we know about XPointers, let's take a look at some inline links:

```
<?xml version="1.0"?>
<simpledoc>
<title>An XLink Demonstration</title>

<section id="target-section">

<para>This is a paragraph in the first section.</para>

<para>More information about XLink can be found at
   <reference xml:link="simple" href="http://www.w3.org/">
     the W3C
   </reference>.
</para>

</section>
<section id="origin-section">

<para>This is a paragraph in the second section.</para>
<para>You should go read
   <reference xml:link="simple" href="#target-section">
     the first section
   </reference>
first.
</para>

</section>
</simpledoc>
```

The first link states that the text "the W3C" is linked to the URL *http://www.w3.org/*. How does the browser know? Simple. An HTML browser knows that every <a> element is a link because the browser has to handle only one document type. In XML, you can make up your own element type names, so the browser needs some way of identifying links.

XLink provides the `xml:link` attribute for link identification. A browser knows that it has found a simple link when any element sets the `xml:link` attribute to a value of "simple." A simple link is like the links in HTML: one-way, beginning at the point in the document where it occurs. (In fact, HTML links can be recast as XLinks with minimal effort.) In other words, the content of the link element can be selected for traversal at the other end. Returning to the source document is left to the browser.

Once an XLink processor has found a simple link, it looks for other attributes that it knows:

`href`
: This attribute is deliberately named to be familiar to anyone who's used the Web before. Its value is the URI of the other end of the link; it can refer to an entire document, or to a point or element within that document. If the target is in an XML document, the fragment part of the URI is an XPointer.

  This attribute must be specified, since without it, the link is meaningless. It is an error not to include it.

`role`
: This is the nature of the object at the other end of the link. XLink doesn't predefine any roles; you might use a small set to distinguish different types of links in your documents, such as cross-references, additional reading, and contact information. The stylesheet might take a different action (such as presenting the link in a different color) based on the role, but the application won't do anything automatically. It is possible that a set of roles will be standardized, similar to the `rel` and `rev` attributes in HTML, and that a browser would automatically recognize those values, but primarily this attribute is for your own use.

`title`
: A title for the resource at the other end of the link can be provided, identical to HTML's title attribute for the <a> element. A GUI browser might display the title as a tool tip; an aural browser might read the title when the user pauses at the link before selecting it. A stylesheet might also make use of the information, perhaps to build a list of references for a document.

`show`
: This attribute is a bit anachronistic. In a world without stylesheets, there's no need for information like this in a link, but since XLink will be complete before XSL, it includes some hints for a user agent on what to do with the link. This attribute suggests what to do when the link is traversed. It can take three values:

  `embed`
  : The content at the other end of the link should be retrieved and displayed where the link is. An example of this behavior in HTML is the `<img>` element, whose target is usually displayed within the document.

  `replace`
  : When the link is activated, the browser should replace the current view with a view of the resource targeted by the link. This is what happens with the <a> element in HTML: the new page replaces the current one.

  `new`
  : The browser should somehow create a new context, if possible. This is similar to the hackery done in HTML to convince Netscape to open a new window.

  You do not need to give a value for this attribute. Remember that a link primarily *asserts* a relationship between data; behavior is best left to a stylesheet. So unless the behavior is paramount (as it might be in some cases of `wmbed`), it is best not to use this attribute.

actuate

The second of the behavioral attributes specifies when the link should be activated. It can take the following values:

user

Wait until the user requests that the link be followed, as the <a> element in HTML does.

auto

The link should be followed immediately by the program; this is what most HTML browsers do with <img> elements, unless the user has turned off image loading.

behavior

The last of the behavioral attributes is a free-form one. If you are writing documents for an intranet and can make certain assumptions about the software used to process your documents, you can put instructions in this attribute specific to that software. Similarly, your stylesheet can take advantage of this information; you might use this as a place to hide special scripts that only apply to this one link and aren't sufficiently general to live in a stylesheet. Do not expect any browser to automatically understand the value you specify for this attribute, if any.

content-role

This is similar to the role attribute above; it specifies the role the content of the link plays. For instance, a link containing a name might specify that the role is "bibliography," and the content-role is "author," indicating that this is a link to the works of the author named in the link.

content-title

Analogously, this is the title of the content of the link. It might be used by a browser displaying a navigational diagram of a web, or as a "tool tip" on the "Back" button of a browser.

XML

Attribute remapping

As if that weren't complicated enough, XLink provides a way to call all of those attributes something else. For instance, you may have existing data that uses the "title" attribute for something else; perhaps the honorific for a person, or the name of a book. But you still want the function provided by XLink's title; what do you do?

The xml:attributes attribute lets you rename, or remap, the attributes used. Its value is a series of pairs, all separated by spaces. The first item in each pair is the name of an attribute that an XLink processor expects to find, such as "title" or "role"; the second is the name of the attribute that you actually used.

In this example, since "title" is already taken, you might want to use the attribute "link-title" instead. Your element might look like this:

```
<person title="Reverend" title-abbr="Rev." given="Kirby"
  family="Hensley" href="http://www.ulc.org/"
  link-title="Universal Life Church"
  xml:attributes="title link-title"/>
```

In this case, the `xml:attributes` attribute says that the title of the link is in the "link-title" attribute; the browser might display "Universal Life Church" when the mouse hovers over the link, instead of "Reverend" (which wouldn't be helpful).

The remapping attribute can take more than one pair of attribute names; this is a more degenerate example:

```
<job title="Managerial Analyst" role="counting beans"
  show="Dog and Pony" actuate="self" behavior="bland"
  href="http://www.oreilly.com/oreilly/jobs/"
  href-role="job description" href-title="Full Description"
  link-show="replace" link-actuate="user"
  xml:attributes="title href-title role href-role show link-show
    actuate link-actuate behavior link-behavior"/>
```

Notice that there doesn't need to be any system to the new names, and that even unused attributes (link-behavior, in this case) can be referred to.

Building Extended Links

XLink has much more to offer, including links similar to simple ones but that can travel to multiple destinations, and links that aren't even in the same document as any of the information that they link to.

Inline multiended links

Consider the following:

```
<para>More information about XLink can be found at these sites
<references xml:link="extended" inline="true">
<resource xml:link="locator" href="http://www.w3.org/" title="W3C"/>
<resource xml:link="locator" href="http://www.ucc.ie/xml/" title="The XML FAQ"/>
<resource xml:link="locator" href="http://www.xml.com/" title="XML.com"/>
</reference>.</para>
```

This somewhat complicated example creates a link with four ends:

- The text "these sites"
- *http://www.w3.org/*
- *http://www.ucc.ie/xml/*
- *http://www.xml.com/*

The text is part of the link because `inline="true"`. The other ends of the link are identified by a locator; in this case, the `<resource>` elements (identified as locators by its `xml:link` attributes).

An extended link is an element that might contain text and also contains locators. Each locator identifies one end of the link; the content of the element itself might also be part of the link. The extended link element is identified to an XLink processor by the `xml:link` attribute having a value of `extended`, similar to how simple links are identified.

Extended links also share a number of attributes with simple links, but now those attributes are split between the extended link and the locators themselves. Links on the extended link element itself are:

`inline`
: This states whether or not (`true` or `false`) the content of the extended link is one end of the link. In the previous example, this attribute is set to `ftrue`, so the text (or other content) of the link element acts as one end, selectable by the user.

`role`
: In slight contrast to the same attribute on a simple link, the role is a free-form attribute describing the nature of the whole link. You need not specify this attribute, but it can be used by your stylesheet to distinguish between different kinds of links that you might use, or by future browsers or specialized applications to understand certain predefined kinds of links.

`content-role`
: This is identical to the `content-role` of the simple link; it identifies the role of the content, as a link end, if inline is true.

`content-title`
: Like `content-role`, this is the title for the content as a link end, if indeed it is one.

Note that link group itself does not have an `href` attribute; rather, each locator child identifies a separate end of the link, with the content of the link group perhaps acting as one end.

Each link locator can have attributes that further describe it. For any of these, a value can be specified on the extended link, which will act as a default for any links contained therein that don't specify an explicit value of their own.

`href`
: As with a simple link, this is the URI of one of the other ends of the link. Each link end locator can have a different `href`.

`role`
: This is also like the role of the simple link but different from the role of the extended link itself. This role is the role of the information at the other end of the link. There are no prescribed values; use whatever seems appropriate, and take advantage of the information in a stylesheet.

`title`
: The same as the simple link's title, this is a descriptive string that might be shown by a browser before the link is activated; for instance, in a pop-up menu of link destinations.

`show`
: This is the same as in a simple link. It is a hint to a browser in the absence of a stylesheet, to suggest behavior for the browser to take regarding the link.

`actuate`
: This is the same as in a simple link.

`behavior`
: This is the same as in a simple link.

Out-of-line links

A multiended link already links multiple resources. That means that the link could choose not to participate, and the link would still make sense. In other words, one document can create a link between two or more completely separate documents. The creator of the link doesn't even need to be able to change those other documents!

Out-of-line links are just as easy as inline multiended ones. Just use `inline="false"` and add locators for the portions of the other documents that you want to link. You'll probably want to use `role` attributes to denote which end of the link should be the beginning point for a user to activate, and which should be the end. Right now, there's no formalized mechanism for specifying this, but we expect that there will be shortly, as the Working Group is aware of the need.

Naturally, a browser won't know about the link you've added to a document unless it's also seen the document containing the link itself. XLink provides a feature called *extended link groups* (not to be confused with the similarly named extended links). A group contains links to multiple documents. When encountering a group, a browser is expected to read all the referenced documents; for the following political commentary, the hub document would direct the browser to the opponent's web site, and would either contain links to be applied to it or direct the browser to the document that did.

```
<critique xml:link="group">
  <hogwash xml:link="document" href="http://www.bobroberts.org/"/>
  <sanity xml:link="document" href="http://www.ourside.org/hooray.xml"/>
</critique>
```

A group takes one attribute: `steps`, which is a sort of sanity check an author can apply. Its value is a number; if a linked document contains a group that in turn links to other documents, there is a potential for a browser to get caught in a perfidious descent. The steps attribute says how far to go. Its value is not binding on a processor; one would hope that any XLink-enabled browser would have some reasonable error detection and recovery behavior built-in, rendering this attribute unnecessary.

The document only takes an `href` attribute that points to the document, or part thereof, in question. Obviously, on both the document and the group, any other attributes can be applied as you see necessary for your particular use, and a document with a group in it can have other things as well.

PART IV

JavaScript

CHAPTER 11

JavaScript

JavaScript

JavaScript is a lightweight, object-based scripting language. The general-purpose core of the language has been embedded in Netscape Navigator, Microsoft Internet Explorer, and other web browsers and embellished for web programming with the addition of objects that represent the web browser window and its contents. This client-side version of JavaScript allows executable content to be included in web pages. With JavaScript, you can move beyond static HTML to write web pages that include programs that interact with the user, control the browser, and dynamically create HTML content. JavaScript is the most popular scripting language for client-side web development.

This chapter provides a complete overview of the core JavaScript language and contains summaries of both core and client-side objects, methods, and properties. The material covers JavaScript 1.2, the version of the language supported by Netscape Navigator 4 and Microsoft Internet Explorer 4. For complete coverage of JavaScript, we recommend *JavaScript: The Definitive Guide, 3rd Edition,* by David Flanagan (O'Reilly).

Versions of JavaScript

The name JavaScript is owned by Netscape. Microsoft's implementation of the language is officially known as JScript, but very few people actually make a distinction between JavaScript and JScript. Versions of JScript are more or less compatible with the equivalent versions of JavaScript, although JScript skipped a version and went directly from JavaScript 1.0 compatibility to JavaScript 1.2 compatibility.

JavaScript has been standardized by ECMA (the organization formerly known as the European Computer Manufacturers Association) and is on the fast track for standardization by the International Standards Organization (ISO). The relevant standards are ECMA-262 and, when standardized by ISO, ISO-16262. These standards define a language officially known as ECMAScript, which is approximately equivalent to JavaScript 1.1, although not all implementations of JavaScript currently conform to all details of the ECMA standard. The name ECMAScript is universally regarded as ugly and cumbersome and was chosen precisely for this reason: it favors neither Netscape's JavaScript nor Microsoft's JScript.

In this material, we universally use the term JavaScript to refer to the scripting language. Where certain functionality is implemented only by either Navigator or Internet Explorer, we've noted that fact. When necessary, we use the term ECMA-262 to refer to the standardized version of the language.

JavaScript Reference

The following table specifies what versions of client-side JavaScript are supported by various versions of Netscape Navigator and Microsoft Internet Explorer.

Version	Navigator	Internet Explorer
2	JavaScript 1.0	
3	JavaScript 1.1	JavaScript 1.0
4	JavaScript 1.2; not fully ECMA-262-compliant prior to Version 4.5	JavaScript 1.2; ECMA-262-compliant

JavaScript Syntax

JavaScript syntax is modeled on Java syntax; Java syntax, in turn, is modeled on C and C++ syntax. Therefore, C, C++, and Java programmers should find that JavaScript syntax is comfortably familiar.

Case sensitivity

JavaScript is a case-sensitive language. All keywords are in lowercase. All variables, function names, and other identifiers must be typed with a consistent capitalization.

Whitespace

JavaScript ignores whitespace between tokens. You may use spaces, tabs, and newlines to format and indent your code in a readable fashion.

Semicolons

JavaScript statements are terminated by semicolons. When a statement is followed by a newline, however, the terminating semicolon may be omitted. Note that this places a restriction on where you may legally break lines in your JavaScript programs: you may not break a statement across two lines if the first line can be a complete legal statement on its own.

Comments

JavaScript supports both C and C++ comments. Any amount of text, on one or more lines, between /* and */ is a comment and is ignored by JavaScript. Also, any text between // and the end of the current line is a comment and is ignored. Examples:

```
// This is a single-line, C++-style comment.
/*
* This is a multiline, C-style comment.
* Here is the second line.
*/
/* Another comment. */
// This too.
```

Identifiers

Variable, function, and label names are JavaScript identifiers. Identifiers are composed of any number of ASCII letters and digits, and the underscore (_) and dollar sign ($) characters. The first character of an identifier must not be a digit, however, and the $ character is not allowed in identifiers in JavaScript 1.0. The following are legal identifiers:

```
i
my_variable_name
v13
$str
```

Keywords

The following keywords are part of the JavaScript language and have special meaning to the JavaScript interpreter. Therefore, they may not be used as identifiers:

```
break      export     new     var
case       false      null    void
continue   for        return  while
default    function   switch  with
delete     if         this
do         import     true
else       in         typeof
```

In addition, JavaScript reserves the following words for possible future extensions. You may not use any of these words as identifiers either:

```
catch      enum      throw
class      extends   try
const      finally
debugger   super
```

Variables

Variables are declared, and optionally initialized, with the `var` statement:

```
var i;
var j = 1+2+3;
var k,l,m,n;
var x = 3, message = 'hello world';
```

Variable declarations in top-level JavaScript code may be omitted, but they are required to declare local variables within the body of a function.

JavaScript variables are *untyped:* they can contain values of any data type.

Global variables in JavaScript are implemented as properties of a special global object. Local variables within functions are implemented as properties of the Argument object for that function.

Data Types

JavaScript supports three primitive data types: numbers, boolean values, and strings. In addition, it supports two compound data types: object and arrays. Functions are also a first-class data type in JavaScript, and JavaScript 1.2 adds support for regular expressions (described later) as a specialized type of object.

Numbers

Numbers in JavaScript are represented in 64-bit floating-point format. JavaScript makes no distinction between integers and floating-point numbers. Numeric literals appear in JavaScript programs using the usual syntax: a sequence of digits, with an optional decimal point and an optional exponent. For example:

```
1
3.14
.0001
6.02e23
```

Integers may also appear in octal or hexadecimal notation. An octal literal begins with 0, and a hexadecimal literal begins with 0x:

```
0377 // The number 255 in octal
0xFF // The number 255 in hexadecimal
```

When a numeric operation overflows, it returns a special value that represents positive or negative infinity. When an operation underflows, it returns zero. When an operation such as taking the square root of a negative number yields an error or meaningless result, it returns the special value NaN, which represents a value that is not-a-number. Use the global function *isNaN()* to test for this value. The Number object defines useful numeric constants. The Math object defines various mathematical operations.

Booleans

The boolean type has two possible values, represented by the JavaScript keywords `true` and `false`. These values represent truth or falsehood, on or off, yes or no, or anything else that can be represented with one bit of information.

Strings

A JavaScript string is a sequence of arbitrary letters, digits, and other characters. The ECMA-262 standard requires JavaScript to support the full 16-bit Unicode character set. Internet Explorer 4 supports Unicode, but Navigator 4 supports only the Latin-1 character set. String literals appear in JavaScript programs between single or double quotes. One style of quotes may be nested within the other:

```
'testing'
"3.14"
'name="myform"'
"Wouldn't you prefer O'Reilly's book?"
```

When the backslash character (\) appears within a string literal, it changes or "escapes" the meaning of the character that follows it. The following table lists these special escape sequences:

Escape	*Represents*
\b	Backspace
\f	Form feed
\n	Newline
\r	Carriage return
\t	Tab
\'	Apostrophe or single quote that does not terminate the string
\"	Double quote that does not terminate the string
\\	Single backslash character
\ddd	Character with Latin-1 encoding specified by three octal digits ddd
\xdd	Character with Latin-1 encoding specified by two hexadecimal digits dd
\udddd	Character with Unicode encoding specified by four hexadecimal digits dddd
n	*n*, where *n* is any character other than those shown above

The String class defines many methods you can use to operate on strings. It also defines the length property, which specifies the number of characters in a string. The addition (+) operator concatenates strings. The equality (==) operator compares two strings to see if they contain exactly the same sequences of characters. (This is compare-by-value, not compare-by-reference, as C, C++, or Java programmers might expect.) The inequality operator (!=) does the reverse. The relational operators (<, <=, >, and >=) compare strings using alphabetical order. JavaScript strings are *immutable*, which means there is no way to change the contents of a string. Methods that operate on strings typically return a modified copy of the string.

Objects

An *object* is a compound data type that contains any number of properties. Each property has a name and a value. The . operator is used to access a named property of an object. For example, you can read and write property values of an object o as follows:

```
o.x = 1;
o.y = 2;
o.total = o.x + o.y;
```

Object properties are not defined in advance as they are in C, C++, or Java; any object can be assigned any property. JavaScript objects are associative arrays: they associate arbitrary data values with arbitrary names. Because of this fact, object properties can also be accessed using array notation:

```
o["x"] = 1;
o["y"] = 2;
```

Objects are created with the new operator. You can create a new object with no properties as follows:

```
var o = new Object();
```

Typically, however, you use predefined constructors to create objects that are members of a class of objects and have suitable properties and methods automatically defined. For example, you can create a Date object that represents the current time with:

```
var now = new Date();
```

You can also define your own object classes and corresponding constructors.

In JavaScript 1.2, you can use object literal syntax to include objects literally in a program. An object literal is a comma-separated list of name/value pairs, contained within curly braces. For example:

```
var o = {x:1, y:2, total:3};
```

Arrays

An array is a type of object that contains numbered values rather than named values. The `[]` operator is used to access the numbered values of an array:

```
a[0] = 1;
a[1] = a[0] + a[0];
```

The first element of a JavaScript array is element 0. Every array has a length property that specifies the number of elements in the array. The last element of an array is element `length-1`.

You create an array with the `Array()` constructor:

```
var a = new Array();         // Empty array
var b = new Array(10);       // 10 elements
var c = new Array(1,2,3);    // Elements 1,2,3
```

In JavaScript 1.2, you can use array literal syntax to include arrays directly in a program. An array literal is a comma-separated list of values enclosed within square brackets. For example:

```
var a = [1,2,3];
var b = [1, true, [1,2], {x:1, y:2}, "Hello"];
```

The Array class defines a number of useful methods for working with arrays.

Functions and methods

A function is a piece of JavaScript code that is defined once and can be executed multiple times by a program. A function definition looks like this:

```
function sum(x, y) {
  return x + y;
}
```

Functions are invoked using the () operator and passing a list of argument values:

```
var total = sum(1,2);  // Total is now 3
```

In JavaScript 1.1, you can create functions using the Function() constructor:

```
var sum = new Function("x", "y", "return x+y;");
```

In JavaScript 1.2, you can define functions using function literal syntax:

```
var sum = function(x,y) { return x+y; }
```

When a function is assigned to a property of an object, it is called a *method* of that object. Within the body of the function, the keyword this refers to is the object for which the function is a property.

Within the body of a function, the *arguments[]* array contains the complete set of arguments passed to the function. The Function and Arguments classes represent functions and their arguments.

`null` *and undefined*

The JavaScript keyword `null` is a special value that indicates "no value". If a variable contains `null`, you know that it does not contain a valid value of any type. There is one other special value in JavaScript: the undefined value. This is the value returned when you use an undeclared or uninitialized variable or when you use a nonexistent object property. There is no JavaScript keyword for this value.

JavaScript

Expressions and Operators

JavaScript expressions are formed by combining literal values and variables with JavaScript operators. Parentheses can be used in an expression to group subexpressions and alter the default order of the evaluation of the expression. Here's an example:

```
1+2
total/n
sum(o.x, a[3])++
(1+2)*3
```

JavaScript defines a complete set of operators, most of which should be familiar to all C, C++, and Java programmers. In Table 11-1, the P column specifies operator precedence and the A column specifies operator associativity: L means left-to-right associativity, and R means right-to-left associativity.

Table 11-1: Expressions and Operators

<table>
<tr><th>P</th><th>A</th><th>Operator</th><th>Operation Performed</th></tr>
<tr><td>15</td><td>L</td><td><code>.</code></td><td>Access an object property</td></tr>
<tr><td></td><td>L</td><td><code>[]</code></td><td>Access an array element</td></tr>
<tr><td></td><td>L</td><td><code>()</code></td><td>Invoke a function</td></tr>
<tr><td>14</td><td>R</td><td><code>++</code></td><td>Unary pre- or post-increment</td></tr>
<tr><td></td><td>R</td><td><code>--</code></td><td>Unary pre- or post-decrement</td></tr>
<tr><td></td><td>R</td><td><code>-</code></td><td>Unary minus (negation)</td></tr>
<tr><td></td><td>R</td><td><code>~</code></td><td>Numeric bitwise complement</td></tr>
<tr><td></td><td>R</td><td><code>!</code></td><td>Unary boolean complement</td></tr>
<tr><td></td><td>R</td><td><code>delete</code></td><td>Undefine a property (1.2)</td></tr>
<tr><td></td><td>R</td><td><code>new</code></td><td>Create a new object</td></tr>
<tr><td></td><td>R</td><td><code>typeof</code></td><td>Return type of operand (1.1)</td></tr>
<tr><td></td><td>R</td><td><code>void</code></td><td>Return undefined value (1.1)</td></tr>
<tr><td>13</td><td>L</td><td><code>*, /, %</code></td><td>Multiplication, division, modulo</td></tr>
<tr><td>12</td><td>L</td><td><code>+, -</code></td><td>Addition, subtraction</td></tr>
<tr><td></td><td>L</td><td><code>+</code></td><td>String concatenation</td></tr>
<tr><td>11</td><td>L</td><td><code><<</code></td><td>Integer shift left</td></tr>
<tr><td></td><td>L</td><td><code>>></code></td><td>Shift right, sign extension</td></tr>
<tr><td></td><td>L</td><td><code>>>></code></td><td>Shift right, zero extension</td></tr>
<tr><td>10</td><td>L</td><td><code><, <=</code></td><td>Less than, less than or equal</td></tr>
<tr><td></td><td>L</td><td><code>>, >=</code></td><td>Greater than, greater than or equal</td></tr>
<tr><td>9</td><td>L</td><td><code>==, !=</code></td><td>Test for equality or inequality</td></tr>
<tr><td></td><td>L</td><td><code>===, !==</code></td><td>Test for identity or nonidentity (no type conversion)</td></tr>
<tr><td>8</td><td>L</td><td><code>&</code></td><td>Integer bitwise AND</td></tr>
<tr><td>7</td><td>L</td><td><code>^</code></td><td>Integer bitwise XOR</td></tr>
<tr><td>6</td><td>L</td><td><code>|</code></td><td>Integer bitwise OR</td></tr>
<tr><td>5</td><td>L</td><td><code>&&</code></td><td>Logical AND; evaluate 2nd operand only if 1st is true</td></tr>
<tr><td>4</td><td>L</td><td><code>||</code></td><td>Logical OR; evaluate 2nd operand only if 1st is false</td></tr>
<tr><td>3</td><td>R</td><td><code>?:</code></td><td>Conditional: <code>if?then:else</code></td></tr>
<tr><td>2</td><td>R</td><td><code>=</code></td><td>Assignment</td></tr>
<tr><td></td><td>R</td><td><code>*=, +=,
-=, etc.</code></td><td>Assignment with operation</td></tr>
<tr><td>1</td><td>L</td><td><code>,</code></td><td>Multiple evaluation</td></tr>
</table>

Statements

A JavaScript program is a sequence of JavaScript statements. Most JavaScript statements have the same syntax as the corresponding C, C++, and Java statements:

Expression statements
Every JavaScript expression can stand alone as a statement. Assignments, method calls, increments, and decrements are expression statements. For example:

```
s = "hello world";
x = Math.sqrt(4);
x++
```

Compound statements

When a sequence of JavaScript statements is enclosed within curly braces, it counts as a single compound statement. For example, the body of a `while` loop consists of a single statement. If you want the loop to execute more than one statement, use a compound statement. This is a common technique with if, for, and other statements described later.

Empty statements

The empty statement is simply a semicolon by itself. It does nothing and is occasionally useful for coding empty loop bodies.

Labeled statements

In JavaScript 1.2, any statement can be labeled with a name. Labeled loops can then be used with the labeled versions of the `break` and `continue` statements:

```
label: statement
```

`break`

The `break` statement terminates execution of the innermost enclosing loop or, in JavaScript 1.2, the named loop:

```
break ;
break label ;  // JavaScript 1.2
```

`case`

`case` is not a true statement. Instead it is a keyword used to label statements within a JavaScript 1.2 `switch` statement:

```
case constant-expression:
  statements
  [ break ; ]
```

Because of the nature of the `switch` statement, a group of statements labeled by case should usually end with a break statement.

`continue`

The `continue` statement restarts the innermost enclosing loop or, in JavaScript 1.2, restarts the named loop:

```
continue ;
continue label ;  //JavaScript 1.2
```

`default`

Like `case`, `default` is not a true statement but is instead a label that may appear within a JavaScript 1.2 switch statement:

```
default:
  statements
  [ break ; ]
```

`do/while`

The `do/while` loop repeatedly executes a statement while an expression is true. It is like the `while` loop, except that the loop condition appears (and is tested) at the bottom of the loop. This means that the body of the loop is executed at least once:

```
do
  statement
while ( expression) ;
```

This statement is new in JavaScript 1.2. In Navigator 4, the continue statement does not work correctly within do/while loops.

export
: The export statement was introduced in Navigator 4. It makes the specified functions and properties accessible to other windows or execution contexts:

```
export expression [, expression... ];
```

for
: The for statement is an easy-to-use loop that combines the initialization and increment expressions with the loop condition expression:

```
for (initialize ; test ; increment)
   statement
```

The for loop repeatedly executes a statement as long as its test expression is true. It evaluates the initialization expression once before starting the loop and evaluates the increment expression at the end of each iteration.

for/in
: The for/in statement loops through the properties of a specified object:

```
for (variable in object)
   statement
```

The for/in loop executes a statement once for each property of an object. Each time through the loop, it assigns the name of the current property to the specified variable. Some properties of predefined JavaScript objects are not enumerated by the for/in loop. User-defined properties are, however, always enumerated.

function
: The function statement defines a function in a JavaScript program:

```
function funcname(args) {
  statements
}
```

This statement defines a function named *funcname*, with a body that consists of the specified statement and arguments as specified by *args*. *args* is a comma-separated list of zero or more argument names. These arguments can be used in the body of the function to refer to the parameter values passed to the function.

if/else
: The if statement executes a statement if an expression is true:

```
if ( expression )
  statement
```

When an `else` clause is added, the statement executes a different statement if the expression is false:

```
if ( expression )
  statement
else
  statement2
```

Any `else` clause may be combined with a nested `if/else` statement to produce an `else if` statement:

```
if ( expression )
  statement
else if ( expression2 )
  statement2
else
  statement3
```

`import`

The `import` statement was introduced in Navigator 4 along with export. It makes the named functions and variables available in the current window or execution context or, in the second form of the statement, makes all properties and methods of the specified object available within the current context:

```
import expression [, expression];
import expression.* ;
```

`return`

The `return` statement causes the currently executing function to stop executing and return to its caller. If followed by an expression, the value of that expression is used as the function return value:

```
return ;
return expression ;
```

`switch`

The `switch` statement is a multiway branch. It evaluates an expression and then jumps to a statement that is labeled with a `case` clause that matches the value of the expression. If no matching `case` label is found, the `switch` statement jumps to the statement, if any, labeled with `default`:

```
switch ( expression ) {
  case constant-expression: statements
  [ case constant-expression: statements ]
  [ . . . ]
  default: statements
}
```

`var`

The `var` statement declares and optionally initializes one or more variables. Variable declaration is optional in top-level code but is required to declare local variables within function bodies:

```
var name [ = value ] [ , name2 [ = value2 ]  . . . ] ;
```

`while`

The `while` statement is a basic loop. It repeatedly executes a statement while an expression is true:

```
while ( expression )
    statement ;
```

`with`

The `with` statement adds an object to the scope chain, so that a statement is interpreted in the context of the object:

```
with ( object )
    statement ;
```

The use of `with` statements is discouraged.

Regular Expressions

JavaScript 1.2 supports regular expressions, using the same syntax as Perl 4. A regular expression is specified literally as a sequence of characters within forward slashes (/), or as a JavaScript string passed to the *RegExp()* constructor. The optional `g` (global search) and `i` (case-insensitive search) modifiers may follow the second / character, or may be passed to *RegExp()*.

The following table summarizes regular expression syntax:

Character	*Meaning*
\n, \r, \t	Match literal newline, carriage return, tab
\\, \/, *, \+, \?, etc.	Match a special character literally, ignoring or escaping its special meaning
[. . .]	Match any one character between brackets
[^ . . .]	Match any one character not between brackets
.	Match any character other than newline
\w, \W	Match any word/nonword character
\s, \S	Match any whitespace/nonwhitespace
\d, \D	Match any digit/nondigit
^, $	Require match at beginning/end of a string, or in multiline mode, beginning/end of a line
\b, \B	Require match at a word boundary nonboundary
?	Optional term; match zero or one time
+	Match previous term one or more times
*	Match term zero or more times
{*n*}	Match previous term exactly *n* times
{*n*,}	Match previous term *n* or more times
{*n*,*m*}	Match at least *n* but no more than *m* times
a | *b*	Match either a or b
(*sub*)	Group subexpression *sub* into a single term, and remember the text that it matched
n	Match exactly the same characters that were matched by subexpression number *n*
$*n*	In replacement strings, substitute the text that matched the *n*th subexpression

JavaScript in HTML

Client-side JavaScript code may be embedded in HTML files in several ways:

<SCRIPT> tag
: Most JavaScript code appears in HTML files between a <SCRIPT> tag and a </SCRIPT> tag. The <SCRIPT> tag can also be used to include an external file of JavaScript code into an HTML document. The <SCRIPT> tag supports a number of attributes, including these three important ones:

  LANGUAGE
  : Specifies the scripting language in which the script is written. In most browsers, this attribute defaults to "JavaScript." You must set it if you are mixing scripting languages, such as JavaScript and VBScript. Set this attribute to "JavaScript1.1" to specify that the code uses JavaScript 1.1 features, and that it should not be interpreted by JavaScript 1.0 browsers. Set this attribute to "JavaScript1.2" to specify that only JavaScript 1.2 browsers should interpret the code. (Note, however, that Navigator 4 has some nonstandard behaviors when "JavaScript1.2" is specified.)

  SRC
  : Specifies the URL of an external script to be loaded and executed. Files of JavaScript code typically have a *.js* extension. Note that the </SCRIPT> tag is still required when this attribute is used. Supported in JavaScript 1.1 and later.

  ARCHIVE
  : Specifies the URL of a JAR file that contains the script specified by the SRC attribute. Supported in JavaScript 1.2 and later. Archives are required to use Navigator 4 signed scripts.

Event handlers
: JavaScript code may also appear as the value of event handler attributes of HTML tags. Event handler attributes always begin with "on." The code specified by one of these attributes is executed when the named event occurs. For example, the following HTML specifies a button that displays a dialog box when clicked:

```
<INPUT TYPE=button VALUE="Press Me"
    onClick="alert('hello world!');">
```

JavaScript URLs
: JavaScript code may appear in a URL that uses the special `javascript:` pseudo-protocol. The JavaScript code is evaluated, and the resulting value (converted to a string, if necessary) is used as the contents of the URL. Use the void operator if you want a JavaScript URL that executes JavaScript statements without overwriting the current document:

```
<FORM ACTION="javascript:void validate()">
```

JavaScript entities
: In JavaScript 1.1, HTML attribute values may contain JavaScript code in the form of JavaScript entities. An HTML entity is a string like `<` that represents

some other character or string. A JavaScript entity is JavaScript code contained within `&{` and `};`. Its value is the value of the JavaScript expression within:

```
<BODY BGCOLOR="&{getFavoriteColor()};">
```

Client-Side Object Hierarchy

Client-side JavaScript has access to a suite of client-side objects that represent the browser, browser windows and frames, HTML documents, and elements within HTML documents. These objects are structured in a hierarchy as shown in Figure 11-1.

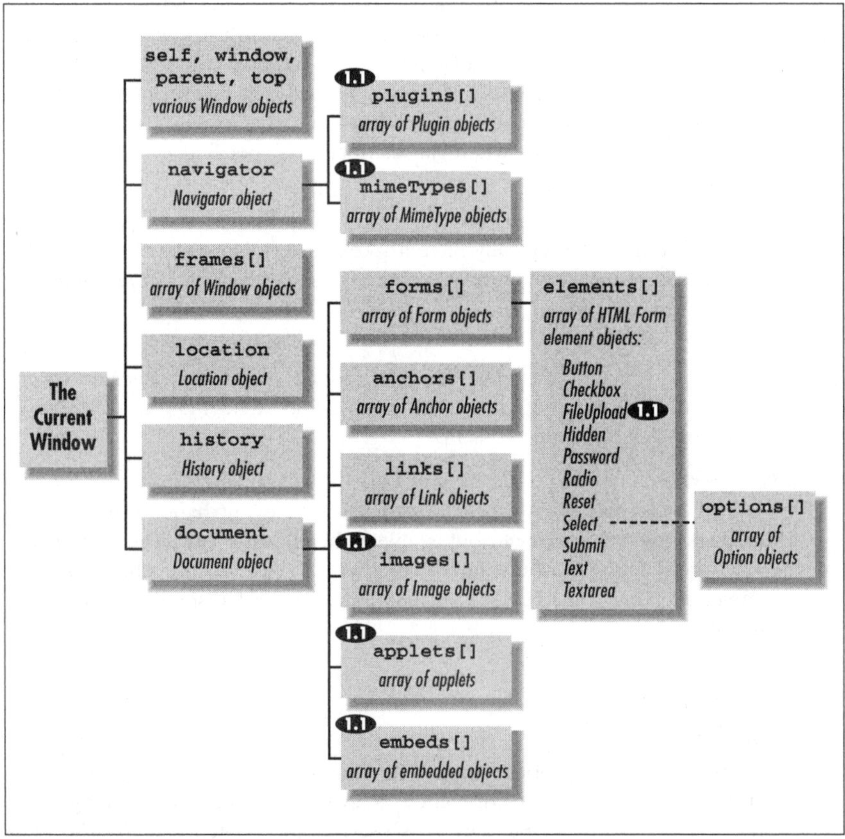

Figure 11-1: The client-side object hierarchy

Windows and Frames

The Window object represents a browser window or frame in client-side JavaScript. Each Window object has properties that refer to its nested frames, if any, and its containing window or frame, if any. Figure 11-2 illustrates these properties.

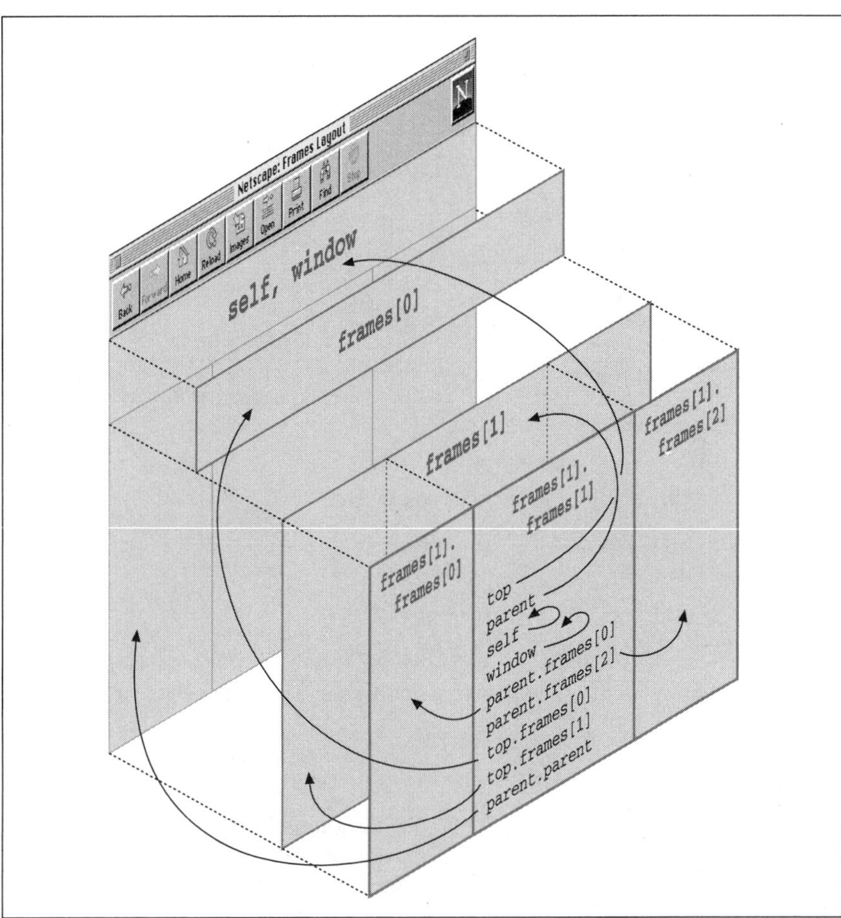

Figure 11-2: Windows and frames

Forms

One of the powerful features of JavaScript is its ability to manipulate HTML forms. HTML defines the following form elements:

Button (`<INPUT TYPE=button>`)
: A graphical push button; `onClick` events

Checkbox (`<INPUT TYPE=checkbox>`)
A toggle button without mutually exclusive behavior; `onClick` events

FileUpload (`<INPUT TYPE=file>`)
A file entry field and file browser; `onChange` events

Hidden (`<INPUT TYPE=hidden>`)
A nonvisual data field; no event handlers

Option (`<OPTION>`)
An item within a Select list; event handlers are on the Select object, not Option objects

Password (`<INPUT TYPE=password>`)
An input field for sensitive data; `onChange` events

Radio (`<INPUT TYPE=radio>`)
A toggle button with mutually exclusive "radio" behavior; `onClick` events

Reset (`<INPUT TYPE=reset>`)
A button that resets a form; `onClick` events

Select (`<SELECT[MULTIPLE]> . . . </SELECT>`)
A list or drop-down menu from which one or more Option items may be selected; `onChange` events

Submit (`<INPUT TYPE=submit>`)
A button that submits a form; `onClick` events

Text (`<INPUT TYPE=text>`)
A single-line text entry field; `onChange` events

TextArea (`<TEXTAREA> . . . </TEXTAREA>`)
A multiline text entry field; `onChange` events

Figure 11-3 shows a web page that contains each type of form element.

Events

Client-side JavaScript supports a number of event types. Table 11-2 lists the event handlers and the client-side objects that support the handlers. Note that some events, such as `onDblClick`, are not reliably generated on all platforms.

Table 11-2: Event Handlers

Event Handler	*Supported By*
`onAbort`	Image (JavaScript 1.1)
`onBlur,onFocus`	Text elements; Window and all other form elements (1.1)
`onChange`	Select, text input elements
`onClick`	Button elements, Link; return `false` to cancel default action
`onDblClick`	Document, Link, Image, Button elements (1.2)

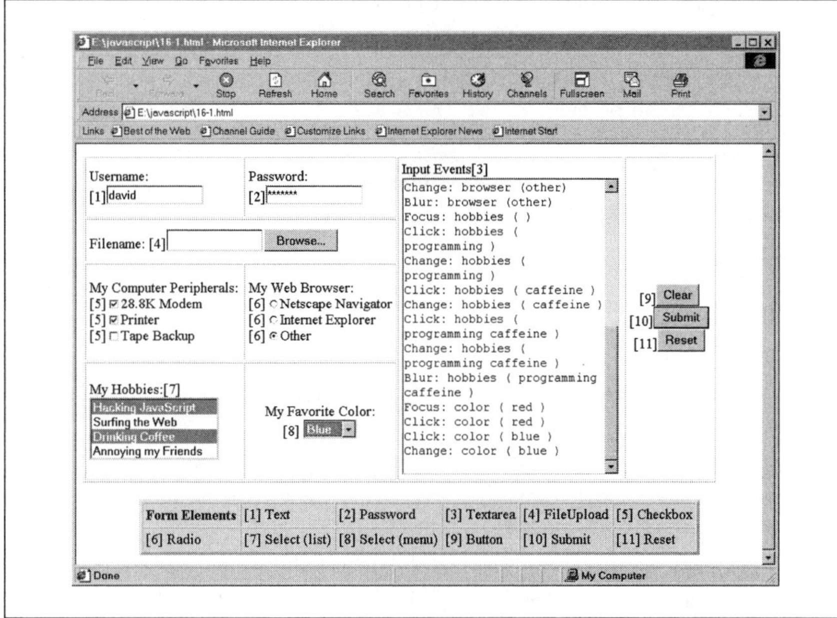

Figure 11-3: Form elements

Table 11-2: Event Handlers (continued)

Event Handler	*Supported By*
`onError`	Image, Window (1.1)
`onKeyDown` `onKeyPress`, `onKeyUp`	Document, Image, Link, text elements (1.2); return `false` to cancel
`onLoad`, `onUnload`	Window; Image in 1.1
`onMouseDown`, `onMouseUp`	Document, Link, Image, Button elements (1.2); return `false` to cancel
`onMouseOver`, `onMouseOut`	Link; Image and Layer (1.2); return `true` to prevent URL display
`onReset`, `onSubmit`	Form (1.1); return `false` to prevent reset or submission

JavaScript Security Restrictions

For security reasons, there are restrictions on the tasks that untrusted JavaScript code can perform. In Navigator 4, signed scripts can circumvent these restrictions by requesting certain privileges:

Same origin policy
: Scripts can read only properties of windows and documents that were loaded from the same web server unless they have UniversalBrowserRead.

User's browsing history
: Scripts cannot read the array of URLs from the History object without UniversalBrowserRead.

File uploads
: Scripts cannot set the value property of the FileUpload form element without UniversalBrowserRead.

Sending email and posting news
: Scripts cannot submit forms to a `mailto:` or news: URL without user confirmation or UniversalSendMail.

Closing windows
: A script can close only browser windows that it created, unless it gets user confirmation or has UniversalBrowserWrite.

Snooping in the cache
: A script cannot load any `about:` URLs, such as *about:cache*, without UniversalBrowserRead.

Hidden windows and window decorations
: A script cannot create small or offscreen windows or windows without a titlebar, and cannot show or hide window decorations without UniversalBrowserWrite.

Intercepting or spoofing events
: A script cannot capture events from windows or documents from a different server and cannot set the fields of an Event object without UniversalBrowserWrite.

Reading and setting preferences
: A script cannot read or write user preferences using *Navigator.preference()* without UniversalPreferencesRead or UniversalPreferencesWrite.

Global Properties

Core JavaScript defines two global constants:

`Infinity`
: A numeric constant that represents infinity. Internet Explorer 4; ECMA-262; not supported by Navigator 4.

`NaN`
: The not-a-number constant. Internet Explorer 4; ECMA-262; not supported by Navigator 4.

In addition to these core global properties, the Window object defines a number of client-side global properties.

Global Functions

Core JavaScript defines a handful of global functions:

`escape(s)`
: Encode a string for transmission. JavaScript 1.0; ECMA-262; Unicode support in Internet Explorer 4.

`eval(code)`
: Execute JavaScript code from a string.

`getClass(javaobj)`
: Return the JavaClass of a JavaObject. Navigator 3.

`isFinite(n)`
: Determine whether a number is finite. JavaScript 1.2; ECMA-262.

`isNaN(x)`
: Check for not-a-number. JavaScript 1.1; ECMA-262.

`parseFloat(s)`
: Convert a string to a number. JavaScript 1.0; enhanced in JavaScript 1.1; ECMA-262.

`parseInt(s, radix)`
: Convert a string to an integer. JavaScript 1.0; enhanced in JavaScript 1.1; ECMA-262.

`unescape(s)`
: Decode an escaped string. JavaScript 1.0; ECMA-262; Unicode support in Internet Explorer 4.

In addition to these core global functions, the Window object defines a number of client-side global methods.

Alphabetical Object Reference

Anchor — the target of a hypertext link

Availability

Client-side JavaScript 1.2

Inherits From

HTMLElement

Synopsis

```
document.anchors[i]
document.anchors.length
```

Properties

Anchor inherits properties from HTMLElement, and also defines or overrides the following:

name
: The name of an anchor.

text
: The text of an anchor. Navigator 4.

x
: The X coordinate of an anchor. Navigator 4.

y
: The Y coordinate of an anchor. Navigator 4.

Applet — an applet embedded in a web page

Availability

Client-side JavaScript 1.1

Synopsis

```
document.applets[i]
document.appletName
```

Properties

The properties of an Applet object are the same as the public fields of the Java applet it represents.

Methods

The methods of an Applet object are the same as the public methods of the Java applet it represents.

Area — see Link

Arguments — arguments and other properties of a function

Availability

Core JavaScript 1.1; ECMA-262; only defined within a function body

Synopsis

```
arguments
```

Properties

callee
The function that is currently running. JavaScript 1.2; ECMA-262.

caller
The calling context. Navigator 4.

length
The number of arguments passed to a function.

Array built-in support for arrays

Availability

Core JavaScript 1.1; enhanced by ECMA-262; enhanced in Navigator 4. Array functionality is available in JavaScript 1.0, but the Array object itself is not supported by Navigator 2.

Constructor

```
new Array()
new Array(size)
new Array(element0, element1, . . . , elementn)
```

Properties

length
The size of an array. JavaScript 1.1, Internet Explorer 3; ECMA-262.

Methods

concat(value, . . .)
Concatenate arrays. JavaScript 1.2.

join(separator)
Concatenate array elements to form a string. JavaScript 1.1; ECMA-262.

pop()
Remove and return the last element of an array. Navigator 4.

push(value, . . .)
Append elements to an array. Navigator 4.

reverse()
Reverse the elements of an array. JavaScript 1.1; ECMA-262.

shift()
Shift array elements down. Navigator 4.

slice(start, end)
Return a portion of an array. JavaScript 1.2.

sort(orderfunc)
Sort the elements of an array. JavaScript 1.1; ECMA-262.

splice(start, deleteCount, value, . . .)
Insert, remove, or replace array elements. Navigator 4.

toString()
Convert an array to a string. JavaScript 1.1; ECMA-262.

unshift(value, . . .)
Insert elements at the beginning of an array. Navigator 4.

Boolean — support for boolean values

Availability

Core JavaScript 1.1; ECMA-262

Constructor

```
// Constructor function
new Boolean(value)
// Conversion function
Boolean(value)
```

Methods

toString()
Convert a boolean value to a string.

Button — a graphical pushbutton

Availability

Client-side JavaScript 1.0; enhanced in JavaScript 1.1

Inherits From

Input, HTMLElement

Synopsis

```
form.name
form.elements[i]
```

Properties

Button inherits properties from Input and HTMLElement and also defines or overrides the following:

value
The text that appears in a Button.

Methods

Button inherits methods from Input and HTMLElement.

Event Handlers

Button inherits event handlers from Input and HTMLElement and also defines or overrides the following:

onclick
The handler invoked when a Button is clicked.

Checkbox — a graphical checkbox

Availability

Client-side JavaScript 1.0; enhanced in JavaScript 1.1

Inherits From

Input, HTMLElement

Synopsis

```
// A single checkbox with a unique name
form.name
form.elements[i]
// A group of checkboxes with the same name
form.name[i]
```

Properties

Checkbox inherits properties from Input and HTMLElement and also defines or overrides the following:

checked
Whether a Checkbox is checked.

defaultChecked
The initial state of a Checkbox.

value
The value returned when a form is submitted.

Methods

Checkbox inherits the methods of Input and HTMLElement.

Event Handlers

Checkbox inherits event handlers from Input and HTMLElement and also defines or overrides the following:

onclick
The handler invoked when a Checkbox is selected.

Crypto — cryptography-related resources

Availability

Client-side Navigator 4.04 and later

Synopsis

```
crypto
```

Functions

crypto.random(numbytes)
Generate random byte strings.

crypto.signText(text, CASelection, allowedCA . . .)
Ask the user to digitally sign text.

Date — manipulate dates and times

Availability

Core JavaScript 1.0; enhanced by ECMA-262

Constructor

```
new Date();
new Date(milliseconds)
new Date(datestring);
new Date(year, month, day, hours, minutes,
new Date(seconds, ms)
```

Methods

Note that unlike most JavaScript objects, the Date object has no properties that can be read and written directly; instead, all access to date and time fields is done through methods:

getDate()
Return the day of the month. JavaScript 1.0; ECMA-262.

getDay()
Return the day of the week. JavaScript 1.0; ECMA-262.

getFullYear()
Return the year (local time). JavaScript 1.2; ECMA-262.

getHours()
Return the hours field of a Date. JavaScript 1.0; ECMA-262.

getMilliseconds()
Return the milliseconds field of a Date (local time). JavaScript 1.2; ECMA-262.

getMinutes()
Return the minutes field of a Date. JavaScript 1.0; ECMA-262.

getMonth()
Return the month of a Date. JavaScript 1.0; ECMA-262.

getSeconds()
Return the seconds field of a Date. JavaScript 1.0; ECMA-262.

getTime()
Return a Date in milliseconds. JavaScript 1.0; ECMA-262.

getTimezoneOffset()
Determine the offset from GMT. JavaScript 1.0; ECMA-262.

getUTCDate()
Return the day of the month (universal time). JavaScript 1.2; ECMA-262.

getUTCDay()
Return the day of the week (universal time). JavaScript 1.2; ECMA-262.

getUTCFullYear()
Return the year (universal time). JavaScript 1.2; ECMA-262.

getUTCHours()
Return the hours field of a Date (universal time). JavaScript 1.2; ECMA-262.

getUTCMilliseconds()
Return the milliseconds field of a Date (universal time). JavaScript 1.2; ECMA-262.

getUTCMinutes()
Return the minutes field of a Date (universal time). JavaScript 1.2; ECMA-262.

getUTCMonth()
Return the month of the year (universal time). JavaScript 1.2; ECMA-262.

getUTCSeconds()
Return the seconds field of a Date (universal time). JavaScript 1.2; ECMA-262.

getYear()
Return the year field of a Date. JavaScript 1.0; ECMA-262; deprecated in JavaScript 1.2 in favor of *getFullYear ()*.

setDate(day_of_month)
Set the day of the month. JavaScript 1.0; ECMA-262.

setFullYear(year)
Set the year (local time). JavaScript 1.2; ECMA-262.

setHours(hours)
Set the hours field of a Date. JavaScript 1.0; ECMA-262.

setMilliseconds(millis)
Set the milliseconds field of a Date (local time). JavaScript 1.2; ECMA-262.

setMinutes(minutes)
Set the minutes field of a Date. JavaScript 1.0; ECMA-262.

setMonth(month)
Set the month field of a Date. JavaScript 1.0; ECMA-262.

setSeconds(seconds)
Set the seconds field of a Date. JavaScript 1.0; ECMA-262.

setTime(milliseconds)
Set a Date in milliseconds. JavaScript 1.0; ECMA-262.

setUTCDate(day_of_month)
Set the day of the month (universal time). JavaScript 1.2; ECMA-262.

setUTCFullYear(year)
Set the year (universal time). JavaScript 1.2; ECMA-262.

setUTCHours(hours)
Set the hours field of a Date (universal time). JavaScript 1.2; ECMA-262.

setUTCMilliseconds(millis)
Set the milliseconds field of a Date (universal time). JavaScript 1.2; ECMA-262.

setUTCMinutes(minutes)
Set the minutes field of a Date (universal time). JavaScript 1.2; ECMA-262.

setUTCMonth(month)
Set the month (universal time). JavaScript 1.2; ECMA-262.

setUTCSeconds(seconds)
Set the seconds field of a Date (universal time). JavaScript 1.2; ECMA-262.

setYear(year)
Set the year field of a Date. JavaScript 1.0; ECMA-262; deprecated in JavaScript 1.2 in favor of *setFullYear()*.

toGMTString()
Convert a date to a universal time string. JavaScript 1.0; ECMA-262; deprecated in JavaScript 1.2 in favor of *toUTCString()*.

toLocaleString()
Convert a Date to a string. JavaScript 1.0; ECMA-262.

toString()
Convert a Date to a string. JavaScript 1.0; ECMA-262.

toUTCString()
Convert a Date to a string (universal time). JavaScript 1.2; ECMA-262.

valueOf()
Convert a Date to a number. JavaScript 1.1; ECMA-262.

Static Methods

Date.parse(date)
Parse a Date/time string. JavaScript 1.0; ECMA-262.

Date.UTC(year, month, day, hours, minutes,Date.UTC(seconds, ms)
Convert a Date specification to milliseconds. JavaScript 1.0; ECMA-262.

Document represents an HTML document

Availability

Client-side JavaScript 1.0; enhanced in JavaScript 1.1 and in Navigator 4 and Internet Explorer 4

Inherits From

HTMLElement

Synopsis

```
window.document
document
```

Properties

Document inherits properties from HTMLElement and also defines numerous properties. Navigator 4 and Internet Explorer 4 both define a number of incompatible Document properties, used mostly for DHTML; they are listed separately after the generic properties:

alinkColor
: The color of activated links.

anchors[]
: The Anchors in a document. JavaScript 1.0; array elements are null prior to JavaScript 1.2.

applets[]
: The applets in a document. JavaScript 1.1.

bgColor
: The document background color.

cookie
: The cookie(s) of the document.

domain
: The security domain of a document. JavaScript 1.1.

embeds[]
: The objects embedded in a document. JavaScript 1.1.

fgColor
: The default text color.

forms[]
: The forms in a document.

images[]
: The images embedded in a document. JavaScript 1.1.

lastModified
: The modification date of a document.

linkColor
The color of unfollowed links.

links[]
The Link objects in a document.

location
The URL of the current document. JavaScript 1.0; deprecated in JavaScript 1.1 in favor of *Document.URL.*

plugins[]
The objects embedded in a document. JavaScript 1.1.

referrer
The URL of the linked-from document. JavaScript 1.0; nonfunctional in Internet Explorer 3.

title
The title of a document.

URL
The URL of the current document. JavaScript 1.1.

vlinkColor
The color of visited links.

Navigator 4 Properties

classes
Define style classes.

height
The height of a document.

ids Define styles for individual tags.

layers[]
The layers contained in a document.

tags
Define styles for HTML tags.

width
The width of a document.

Internet Explorer 4 Properties

activeElement
Which input element has the focus.

all[]
All HTML elements in a document.

charset
The character set in use.

children[]
The child elements of the document.

defaultCharset
The default character set of a document.

expando
Disallow new property creation.

parentWindow
The window of a document.

readyState
The loading status of a document.

Methods

Document inherits methods from HTMLElement and also defines some methods. Navigator 4 and IE 4 both define a number of incompatible Document methods, used mostly for DHTML; they are listed separately after the generic methods:

clear()
Clear a document. JavaScript 1.0; deprecated.

close()
Close an output stream.

open(mimetype)
Begin a new document.

write(value, . . .)
Append data to a document.

writeln(value, . . .)
Append data and a newline to a document.

Navigator 4 Methods

captureEvents(eventmask)
Specify event types to be captured.

contextual(style1, style2, . . .)
Define a contextual style.

getSelection()
Return the selected text.

releaseEvents(eventmask)
Stop capturing events.

routeEvent(event)
Pass a captured event to the next handler.

Internet Explorer 4 Methods

elementFromPoint(x, y)
Determine which HTML element is at a given point.

Event Handlers

The <BODY> tag has `onLoad` and `onUnload` attributes. Technically, however, the onload and onunload event handlers belong to the Window object, rather than the Document object.

Event — details about an event

Availability

Client-side JavaScript; incompatible versions are supported by Navigator 4 and Internet Explorer 4

Synopsis

```
// Event handler argument in Navigator 4
function handler (event) { . . . }
// Window property in IE 4
window.event
```

Navigator 4 Properties

data
: Data from a DragDrop event. Requires UniversalBrowserWrite privilege to set; requires UniversalBrowserRead privilege to read.

height
: The new height of a resized window or frame.

layerX
: The X coordinate, within a layer, of the event.

layerY
: The Y coordinate, within a layer, of the event.

modifiers
: Which modifier keys are held down.

pageX
: The X coordinate, within a page, of the event.

pageY
: The Y coordinate, within a page, of the event.

screenX
: The screen X coordinate of the event. JavaScript 1.2.

screenY
: The screen Y coordinate of the event. JavaScript 1.2.

target
: The object on which the event occurred.

type
: The type of the event. JavaScript 1.2.

TYPE
Static event type constants for bitmasks.

which
Which key or mouse button was clicked.

width
The new width of a resized window or frame.

x The X coordinate of the event within a positioned element. JavaScript 1.2.

y The Y coordinate of the event within a positioned element. JavaScript 1.2.

Internet Explorer 4 Properties

altKey
Whether the ALT key was pressed during an event.

button
Which mouse button was pressed.

cancelBubble
Stop event propagation.

clientX
The X coordinate, within a page, of the event.

clientY
The Y coordinate, within a page, of the event.

ctrlKey
Whether the CTRL key was pressed during an event.

fromElement
The object the mouse is moving from.

keyCode
The Unicode encoding of the key typed.

offsetX
The X coordinate of the event, relative to the container.

offsetY
The Y coordinate of the event, relative to the container.

reason
Data transfer status.

returnValue
Specify a return value for the event handler.

screenX
The screen X coordinate of the event. JavaScript 1.2.

screenY
The screen Y coordinate of the event. JavaScript 1.2.

shiftKey
Whether the Shift key was pressed during an event.

srcElement
The object on which the event occurred.

srcFilter
The filter that changed.

toElement
The object to which the mouse is moving.

type
The type of the event. JavaScript 1.2.

x The X coordinate of the event within a positioned element. JavaScript 1.2.

y The Y coordinate of the event within a positioned element. JavaScript 1.2.

FileUpload — a file upload field for form input

Availability

Client-side JavaScript 1.0

Inherits From

Input, HTMLElement

Synopsis

```
form.name
form.elements[i]
```

Properties

FileUpload inherits properties from Input and HTMLElement and defines or overrides the following:

value
The filename selected by the user. JavaScript 1.1.

Methods

FileUpload inherits methods from Input and HTMLElement.

Event Handlers

FileUpload inherits event handlers from Input and HTMLElement and defines or overrides the following:

onchange
The handler invoked when input value changes.

Form — an HTML input form

Availability

Client-side JavaScript 1.0

Inherits From

HTMLElement

Synopsis

```
document.form_name
document.forms[form_number]
```

Properties

Form inherits properties from HTMLElement and also defines or overrides the following:

action
: The URL for form submission. JavaScript 1.0; read-only in Internet Explorer 3.

elements[]
: The input elements of the form.

elements.length
: The number of elements in a form.

encoding
: The encoding of form data. JavaScript 1.0; read-only in Internet Explorer 3.

length
: The number of elements in a form.

method
: The submission method for the form. JavaScript 1.0; read-only in Internet Explorer 3.

name
: The name of a form.

target
: The window for form results. JavaScript 1.0; read-only in Internet Explorer 3.

Methods

Form inherits methods from HTMLElement and also defines the following:

reset()
: Reset the elements of a form. JavaScript 1.1.

submit()
: Submit a form.

Event Handlers

Form inherits event handlers from HTMLElement and also defines the following:

onreset
: The handler invoked when a form is reset. JavaScript 1.1.

onsubmit
: Invoked when a form is submitted.

Frame

a type of Window object; see Window

Availability

Client-side JavaScript 1.0

Synopsis

```
window.frames[i]
window.frames.length
frames[i]
frames.length
```

Function

a JavaScript function

Availability

Core JavaScript 1.0; enhanced in JavaScript 1.1 and 1.2

Synopsis

```
// Function definition statement
function functionname(argument_name_list)
{
   body
}
// Unnamed function literal; JavaScript 1.2
function (argument_name_list ) { body}
// Function invocation
functionname(argument _value_list)
```

Constructor

```
// JavaScript 1.1 and later
new Function(argument_names, body)
```

Properties

arguments[]
: Arguments passed to a function. JavaScript 1.0; ECMA-262; deprecated in favor of the Arguments object.

arity
: The number of declared arguments. Navigator 4, with `LANGUAGE="JavaScript1.2"`.

caller
: The function that called this one.

length
: The number of declared arguments. JavaScript 1.1; ECMA-262.

prototype
: The prototype for a class of objects. JavaScript 1.1.

Methods

apply(thisobj, args)
Invoke a function as a method of an object. Navigator 4.

toString()
Convert a function to a string. JavaScript 1.0; ECMA-262.

Hidden — hidden data for client/server communication

Availability

Client-side JavaScript 1.0; enhanced in JavaScript 1.1

Inherits From

Input, HTMLElement

Synopsis

```
form.name
form.elements[i]
```

Properties

Hidden inherits properties from Input and HTMLElement and defines or overrides the following:

value
Arbitrary data submitted with a form.

History — the URL history of the browser

Availability

Client-side JavaScript 1.0; additional features available in Navigator 4 with the UniversalBrowserRead privilege

Synopsis

```
window.history
frame.history
history
```

Properties

current
The URL of the currently displayed document. Navigator 4; requires UniversalBrowserRead.

length
The number of elements in the history array. Navigator 2, Internet Explorer 4.

next
The URL of the next document in the history array. Navigator 4; requires UniversalBrowserRead.

JavaScript

previous
The URL of the previous document in the history array. Navigator 4; requires UniversalBrowserRead.

Methods

back()
Return to the previous URL. JavaScript 1.0.

forward()
Visit the next URL. JavaScript 1.0.

go(relative_position, target_string)
Revisit a URL. JavaScript 1.0; enhanced in JavaScript 1.1.

toString()
Return browsing history, formatted in HTML. Navigator 4; requires UniversalBrowserRead.

HTMLElement — the superclass of all HTML elements

Availability

Client-side JavaScript 1.2

Internet Explorer 4 Properties

all[]
All elements contained within an element.

children[]
The direct children of an element.

className
The value of the `CLASS` attribute.

document
The Document object that contains an element.

id The value of the `ID` attribute.

innerHTML
The HTML text contained within the element.

innerText
The text within the element.

lang
The value of the `LANG` attribute.

offsetHeight
The height of the element.

offsetLeft
The X coordinate of the element.

offsetParent
Defines the coordinate system of the element.

offsetTop
The Y coordinate of the element.

offsetWidth
The width of the element.

outerHTML
The HTML of an element.

outerText
The text of an element.

parentElement
The container of an element.

sourceIndex
The index of the element in `Document.all[]`.

style
The inline CSS style of the element.

tagName
The tag type of an element.

title
Tool tip for an element.

Navigator 4 Methods

handleEvent(event)
Pass an event to an appropriate handler.

Internet Explorer 4 Methods

contains(target)
Whether one element is contained in another.

getAttribute(name)
Get an attribute value.

insertAdjacentHTML(where, text)
Insert HTML text before or after an element.

insertAdjacentText(where, text)
Insert plain text before or after an element.

removeAttribute(name)
Delete an attribute.

scrollIntoView(top)
Make an element visible.

setAttribute(name, value)
Set the value of an attribute.

Event Handlers

onclick
The handler invoked when the user clicks on an element. JavaScript 1.2; HTML 4.0.

ondblclick
The handler invoked when the user double-clicks on an element. JavaScript 1.2; HTML 4.0.

onhelp
The handler invoked when the user presses F1. Internet Explorer 4.

onkeydown
The handler invoked when the user presses a key. JavaScript 1.2; HTML 4.0.

onkeypress
The handler invoked when the user presses a key. JavaScript 1.2; HTML 4.0.

onkeyup
The handler invoked when the user releases a key. JavaScript 1.2; HTML 4.0.

onmousedown
The handler invoked when the user presses a mouse button. JavaScript 1.2; HTML 4.0.

onmousemove
The handler invoked when the mouse moves within an element. JavaScript 1.2; HTML 4.0.

onmouseout
The handler invoked when the mouse moves out of an element. JavaScript 1.2; HTML 4.0.

onmouseover
The handler invoked when the mouse moves over an element. JavaScript 1.2; HTML 4.0.

onmouseup
The handler invoked when the user releases a mouse button. JavaScript 1.2; HTML 4.0.

Image — an image embedded in an HTML document

Availability

Client-side JavaScript 1.1

Inherits From

HTMLElement

Synopsis

```
document.images[i]
document.images.length
document.image-name
```

Constructor

```
new Image(width, height)
```

Properties

Image inherits properties from HTMLElement and defines or overrides the following:

border
: The border width of an image.

complete
: Whether an image load is complete.

height
: The height of an image.

hspace
: The horizontal padding for an image.

lowsrc
: An alternate image for low-resolution displays.

name
: The name of an image.

src The URL of the embedded image.

vspace
: The vertical padding for an image.

width
: The width of an image.

Event Handlers

Image inherits event handlers from HTMLElement and also defines the following:

onabort
: The handler invoked when user aborts image loading.

onerror
: The handler invoked when an error occurs during image loading.

onload
: The handler invoked when an image finishes loading.

Input — an input element in an HTML form

Availability

Client-side JavaScript 1.0; enhanced in JavaScript 1.1

Inherits From

HTMLElement

Synopsis

```
form.elements[i]
form.name
```

Properties

Input inherits properties from HTMLElement and defines or overrides the following:

checked
: Whether a Checkbox or Radio element is checked.

defaultChecked
: A Checkbox or Radio element's default status.

defaultValue
: The default text displayed in an element.

form
: The Form containing the element.

name
: The name of a form element.

type
: The type of a form element. JavaScript 1.1.

value
: The value displayed or submitted by a form element. Navigator 2; buggy in Internet Explorer 3.

Methods

Input inherits methods from HTMLElement and defines or overrides the following:

blur()
: Remove keyboard focus from a form element.

click()
: Simulate a mouseclick on a form element.

focus()
: Give keyboard focus to a form element.

select()
: Select the text in a form element.

Event Handlers

Input inherits event handlers from HTMLElement and defines or overrides the following:

onblur
: The handler invoked when a form element loses focus.

onchange
: The handler invoked when a form element's value changes.

onclick
: The handler invoked when a form element is clicked. JavaScript 1.0; enhanced in JavaScript 1.1.

onfocus
: The handler invoked when a form element gains focus.

JavaArray — JavaScript representation of a Java array

Availability

Client-side Navigator 3

Synopsis

```
// The length of the array
javaarray.length
// Read or write an array element
javaarray[index]
```

Properties

length
: The number of elements in a Java array.

JavaClass — JavaScript representation of a Java class

Availability

Client-side Navigator 3

Synopsis

```
// Read or write a static Java field or method
javaclass.static_member
// Create a new Java object
new javaclass( . . . )
```

Properties

Each JavaClass object contains properties that have the same names as the public static fields and methods of the Java class it represents. These properties allow you to read and write the static fields of the class. The properties that represent Java methods refer to JavaMethod objects, which are JavaScript objects that allow you

JavaScript

to invoke Java methods. Each JavaClass object has different properties; you can use a `for/in` loop to enumerate them for any given JavaClass object.

JavaObject — JavaScript representation of a Java object

Availability

Client-side Navigator 3

Synopsis

```
// Read or write an instance field or method
javaobject.member
```

Properties

Each JavaObject object contains properties that have the same names as the public instance fields and methods (but not the static or class fields and methods) of the Java object it represents. These properties allow you to read and write the value of public fields. The properties of a given JavaObject object obviously depend on the type of Java object it represents. You can use the `for/in` loop to enumerate the properties of any given JavaObject.

JavaPackage — JavaScript representation of a Java package

Availability

Client-side Navigator 3

Synopsis

```
// Refers to another JavaPackage
package.package_name
// Refers to a JavaClass object
package.class_name
```

Properties

The properties of a JavaPackage object are the names of the JavaPackage objects and JavaClass objects that it contains. These properties are different for each individual JavaPackage. Note that it is not possible to use the JavaScript `for/in` loop to iterate over the list of property names of a Package object. Consult a Java reference manual to determine the packages and classes contained within any given package.

JSObject — Java representation of a JavaScript object

Availability

A Java class in the *netscape.javascript* package included with Navigator 3 and later

Synopsis

```
public final class netscape.javascript.JSObject
```

Methods

call(methodName, args[])
Invoke a method of a JavaScript object.

eval(s)
Evaluate a string of JavaScript code.

getMember(name)
Read a property of a JavaScript object.

getSlot(index)
Read an array element of a JavaScript object.

getWindow(applet)
Return initial JSObject for browser window.

removeMember(name)
Delete a property of a JavaScript object.

setMember(name, value)
Set a property of a JavaScript object.

setSlot(index, value)
Set an array element of a JavaScript object.

toString()
Return the string value of a JavaScript object.

Layer an independent layer in a DHTML document

Availability

Client-side Navigator 4

Synopsis

```
document.layers[i]
```

Constructor

```
new Layer(width, parent)
```

Properties

above
The layer above this one.

background
The background image of a layer.

below
The layer below this one.

bgColor
The background color of a layer.

clip.bottom
The bottom of the layer's clipping region.

clip.height
The height of the layer's clipping region.

clip.left
The left edge of the layer's clipping region.

clip.right
The right edge of the layer's clipping region.

clip.top
The top of the layer's clipping region.

clip.width
The width of the layer's clipping region.

document
The Document object of a layer.

hidden
Whether a layer is hidden. Navigator 4; deprecated; use *Layer.visibility* instead.

layers[]
The layers contained within a layer. Navigator 4; deprecated; use *Layer.document.layers* instead.

left The X coordinate of a layer.

name
The name of a layer. Client-side Navigator 4.

pageX
The X coordinate of a layer, relative to the page.

pageY
The Y coordinate of a layer, relative to the page.

parentLayer
The parent of the layer.

siblingAbove
The sibling layer above this one.

siblingBelow
The sibling layer below this one.

src The source URL of a layer's content.

top The Y coordinate of a layer.

visibility
Whether a layer is visible.

window
The window that contains a layer.

x The X coordinate of a layer.

y The Y coordinate of a layer.

zIndex
Stacking order of a layer.

Methods

captureEvents(eventmask)
Specify event types to be captured.

handleEvent(event)
Pass an event to the appropriate handler.

load(src, width)
Change layer contents and width.

moveAbove(target)
Move one layer above another.

moveBelow(target)
Move one layer below another.

moveBy(dx, dy)
Move a layer to a relative position.

moveTo(x, y)
Move a layer.

moveToAbsolute(x, y)
Move a layer to page coordinates.

offset(dx, dy)
Move a layer to a relative position; deprecated; use *Layer.moveBy()* instead.

releaseEvents(eventmask)
Stop capturing events.

resizeBy(dw, dh)
Resize a layer by a relative amount.

resizeTo(width, height)
Resize a layer.

routeEvent(event)
Pass a captured event to the next handler.

Link — a hypertext link

Availability

Client-side JavaScript 1.0; enhanced in JavaScript 1.1

Inherits From

HTMLElement

Synopsis

```
document.links[]
document.links.length
```

Properties

Link inherits properties from HTMLElement and also defines or overrides the following properties:

hash
: The anchor specification of a link.

host
: The hostname and port portions of a link.

hostname
: The hostname portion of a link.

href
: The complete URL of a link.

pathname
: The path portion of a link.

port
: The port portion of a link.

protocol
: The protocol portion of a link.

search
: The query portion of a link.

target
: The target window of a hypertext link.

text
: The text of a link. Navigator 4.

x The X coordinate of a link. Navigator 4.

y The Y coordinate of a link. Navigator 4.

Methods

Link inherits the methods of HTMLElement.

Event Handlers

Link inherits the event handlers of HTMLElement and defines special behavior for the following three:

onclick
: The handler invoked when a link is clicked. JavaScript 1.0; enhanced in JavaScript 1.1.

onmouseout
: The handler invoked when the mouse leaves a link. JavaScript 1.1.

onmouseover
: The handler invoked when the mouse goes over a link.

Location — represents and controls browser location

Availability

Client-side JavaScript 1.0; enhanced in JavaScript 1.1

Synopsis

```
location
window.location
```

Properties

The properties of a Location object refer to the various portions of a URL.

hash
: The anchor specification of the current URL.

host
: The hostname and port portions of the current URL.

hostname
: The hostname portion of the current URL.

href
: The complete currently displayed URL.

pathname
: The path portion of the current URL.

port
: The port portion of the current URL.

protocol
: The protocol portion of the current URL.

search
: The query portion of the current URL.

Methods

reload(force)
: Reload the current document. JavaScript 1.1.

replace(url)
: Replace one displayed document with another. JavaScript 1.1.

Math a placeholder for mathematical functions and constants

Availability

Core JavaScript 1.0; ECMA-262

Synopsis

```
Math.constant
Math.function()
```

Constants

Math.E
The mathematical constant *e*.

Math.LN10
The mathematical constant $log_e 10$.

Math.LN2
The mathematical constant $log_e 2$.

Math.LOG10E
The mathematical constant $log_{10} e$.

Math.LOG2E
The mathematical constant $log_2 e$.

Math.PI
The mathematical constant π.

Math.SQRT1_2
The mathematical constant $1/\sqrt{2}$.

Math.SQRT2
The mathematical constant $\sqrt{2}$.

Static Functions

Math.abs(x)
Compute an absolute value.

Math.acos(x)
Compute an arc cosine.

Math.asin(x)
Compute an arc sine.

Math.atan(x)
Compute an arc tangent.

Math.atan2(x, y)
Compute the angle from the X axis to a point.

Math.ceil(x)
Round up a number.

Math.cos(x)
: Compute a cosine.

Math.exp(x)
: Compute e^x.

Math.floor(x)
: Round down a number.

Math.log(x)
: Compute a natural logarithm.

Math.max(a, b)
: Return the larger of two values.

Math.min(a, b)
: Return the smaller of two values.

Math.pow(x, y)
: Compute x^y.

Math.random()
: Return a pseudo-random number. JavaScript 1.1; ECMA-262.

Math.round(x)
: Round to the nearest integer.

Math.sin(x)
: Compute a sine.

Math.sqrt(x)
: Compute a square root.

Math.tan(x)
: Compute a tangent.

JavaScript

MimeType — represents a MIME data type

Availability

Client-side Navigator 3

Synopsis

```
navigator.mimeTypes[i]
navigator.mimeTypes["type"]
navigator.mimeTypes.length
```

Properties

description
: A description of a MIME type.

enabledPlugin
: The plugin that handles the MIME type.

suffixes
: Common file suffixes for a MIME type.

type
The name of a MIME type.

Navigator information about the browser in use

Availability

Client-side JavaScript 1.0; enhanced in JavaScript 1.1 and 1.2

Synopsis

```
navigator
```

Properties

navigator.appCodeName
The code name of the browser.

navigator.appName
The application name of the browser.

navigator.appVersion
The platform and version of the browser.

navigator.language
The default language of the browser. Navigator 4.

navigator.mimeTypes[]
An array of supported MIME types. JavaScript 1.1; empty in Internet Explorer 4.

navigator.platform
The operating system the browser is running under. JavaScript 1.2.

navigator.plugins[]
An array of installed plugins. JavaScript 1.1; empty in Internet Explorer 4.

navigator.systemLanguage
The default language of the underlying system. Internet Explorer 4.

navigator.userAgent
The HTTP user-agent value.

navigator.userLanguage
The language of the current user. Internet Explorer 4.

Functions

navigator.javaEnabled()
Test whether Java is available. JavaScript 1.1.

navigator.plugins.refresh()
Make newly installed plugins available. Navigator 3.

navigator.preference(prefname, value)
Set or retrieve user preferences. Navigator 4; requires UniversalPreferencesRead privilege to query preferences; requires UniversalPreferencesWrite privilege to set preference values.

navigator.savePreferences()
Save the user's preferences. Navigator 4; requires UniversalPreferencesWrite privilege.

navigator.taintEnabled()
Test whether data tainting is enabled. JavaScript 1.1; deprecated.

Number — support for numbers

Availability

Core JavaScript 1.1; ECMA-262

Synopsis

```
Number.constant
```

Constructor

```
new Number(value)
Number(value)
```

Constants

Number.MAX_VALUE
The maximum numeric value.

Number.MIN_VALUE
The minimum numeric value.

Number.NaN
The special not-a-number value.

Number.NEGATIVE_INFINITY
Negative infinity.

Number.POSITIVE_INFINITY
Infinity.

Methods

toString(radix)
Convert a number to a string.

Object — a superclass that contains features of all JavaScript objects

Availability

Core JavaScript 1.0; ECMA-262; enhanced in JavaScript 1.1 and Navigator 4

Constructor

```
new Object()
new Object(value)
```

Properties

constructor
An object's constructor function. JavaScript 1.1; ECMA-262.

Methods

assign(value)
Overload the assignment operator. Navigator 3; deprecated in favor of *Object.watch()*.

eval(code)
Evaluate JavaScript code in a string. Navigator 3; deprecated in favor of global *eval()* function in Navigator 4.

toString()
Define an object's string representation.

unwatch(propname)
Remove a watchpoint. Navigator 4.

valueOf(typehint)
The primitive value of the specified object. JavaScript 1.1; ECMA-262.

watch(propname, handler)
Set a watchpoint. Navigator 4.

Option — an option in a Select box

Availability

Client-side JavaScript 1.0; enhanced in JavaScript 1.1

Inherits From

HTMLElement

Synopsis

```
select.options[i]
```

Properties

Option inherits the properties of HTMLElement and also defines the following:

defaultSelected
Whether an object is selected by default.

index
The position of the option.

selected
Whether the option is selected.

text
: The label for an option. JavaScript 1.0; read/write in JavaScript 1.1.

value
: The value returned when the form is submitted.

Password — a text input field for sensitive data

Availability

Client-side JavaScript 1.0; enhanced in JavaScript 1.1

Inherits From

Input, HTMLElement

Synopsis

```
form.name
form.elements[i]
```

Properties

Password inherits properties from Input and HTMLElement and defines or overrides the following:

value
: User input to the Password object. JavaScript 1.0; modified in JavaScript 1.2.

Methods

Password inherits methods from Input and HTMLElement.

Event Handlers

Password inherits methods from Input and HTMLElement.

Plugin — describes an installed plugin

Availability

Client-side Navigator 3

Synopsis

```
navigator.plugins[i]
navigator.plugins['name']
```

Properties

description
: English description of a plugin.

filename
: The filename of the plugin program.

length
The number of MIME types supported.

name
The name of a plugin.

PrivilegeManager — Java class used by signed scripts

Availability

Client-side Navigator 4

Synopsis

```
netscape.security.PrivilegeManager
```

Methods

disablePrivilege(privilege)
Disable a privilege.

enablePrivilege(privilege)
Enable a privilege.

Radio — a graphical radio button

Availability

Client-side JavaScript 1.0; enhanced in JavaScript 1.1

Inherits From

Input, HTMLElement

Synopsis

```
// A group of radio buttons with the same name
form.name[i]
```

Properties

Radio inherits properties from Input and HTMLElement and defines or overrides the following:

checked
Whether a Radio button is selected.

defaultChecked
Initial state of a Radio button.

value
Value returned when form is submitted.

Methods

Radio inherits methods from Input and HTMLElement.

Event Handlers

Radio inherits event handlers from Input and HTMLElement and defines or overrides the following:

onclick
The handler invoked when a Radio button is selected.

RegExp regular expressions for pattern matching

Availability

Core JavaScript 1.2

Constructor

```
new RegExp(pattern, attributes)
```

Instance Properties

global
Whether a regular expression matches globally. Not implemented in Internet Explorer 4.

ignoreCase
Whether a regular expression is case-insensitive. Not implemented in Internet Explorer 4.

lastIndex
The character position after the last match. Not implemented in Internet Explorer 4.

source
The text of the regular expression.

Static Properties

RegExp.$n
The text that matched the *n*th subexpression.

RegExp.input or RegExp.$_
The input buffer for pattern matching. Nonfunctional in Internet Explorer 4.

RegExp.lastMatch or RegExp["$&"]
The text of the last successful pattern match. Not implemented in Internet Explorer 4.

RegExp.lastParen or RegExp["$+"]
The text that matched the last subexpression. Not implemented in Internet Explorer 4.

RegExp.leftContext or RegExp["$`"]
The text before the last match. Not implemented in Internet Explorer 4.

RegExp.multiline or RegExp["$"]*
Whether matches are performed in multiline mode. Not implemented in Internet Explorer 4.

JavaScript

RegExp.rightContext or RegExp["$'"]
The text after the last match. Not implemented in Internet Explorer 4.

Methods

compile(newpattern, attributes)
Change a regular expression.

exec(string)
General-purpose pattern matching. Buggy in Internet Explorer 4.

test(string)
Test whether a string contains a match.

Reset — a button to reset a form's values

Availability

Client-side JavaScript 1.0; enhanced in JavaScript 1.1

Inherits From

Input, HTMLElement

Synopsis

```
form.name
form.elements[i]
```

Properties

Reset inherits properties from Input and HTMLElement and defines or overrides the following:

value
The label of a Reset button.

Methods

Reset inherits the methods of Input and HTMLElement.

Event Handlers

Reset inherits the event handlers of Input and HTMLElement and defines or overrides the following:

onclick
The handler invoked when a Reset button is clicked. JavaScript 1.0; enhanced in JavaScript 1.1.

Screen — provides information about the display

Availability

Client-side JavaScript 1.2

Synopsis

```
screen
```

Properties

screen.availHeight
The available height of the screen.

screen.availLeft
The first available horizontal pixel. Navigator 4.

screen.availTop
The first available vertical pixel. Navigator 4.

screen.availWidth
The available width of the screen.

screen.colorDepth
The depth of the web browser's color palette.

screen.height
The height of the screen.

screen.pixelDepth
The color depth of the screen. Navigator 4.

screen.width
The width of the screen.

Select — a graphical selection list

Availability

Client-side JavaScript 1.0; enhanced in JavaScript 1.1

Inherits From

Input, HTMLElement

Synopsis

```
form.element_name
form.elements[i]
```

Properties

Select inherits properties from Input and HTMLElement and defines or overrides the following:

length
The number of options in a Select object.

options[]
The choices in a Select object. JavaScript 1.0; enhanced in JavaScript 1.1.

selectedIndex
The selected option. JavaScript 1.0; writeable in JavaScript 1.1.

type
Type of form element. JavaScript 1.1.

Methods

Select inherits the methods of Input and HTMLElement.

Event Handlers

Select inherits event handlers from Input and HTMLElement and defines or overrides the following:

onchange
The handler invoked when the selection changes.

String support for strings

Availability

Core JavaScript 1.0; enhanced in Navigator 3

Constructor

```
new String(value)    // JavaScript 1.1
```

Properties

length
The length of a string. JavaScript 1.0; ECMA-262.

Methods

anchor(name)
Add an HTML anchor to a string.

big()
Make a string <BIG>.

blink()
Make a string <BLINK>.

bold()
Make a string bold with <B>.

charAt(n)
Get the *n*th character from a string. JavaScript 1.0; ECMA-262.

charCodeAt(n)
Get the *n*th character code from a string. JavaScript 1.2; ECMA-262.

concat(value, . . .)
Concatenate strings. JavaScript 1.2.

fixed()
Make a string fixed-width with <TT>.

fontcolor(color)
Set a string's color with <FONT>.

fontsize(size)
Set a string's font size with <FONT>.

indexOf(substring, start)
Search a string. JavaScript 1.0; ECMA-262.

italics()
Make a string italic with <I>.

lastIndexOf(substring, start)
Search a string backward. JavaScript 1.0; ECMA-262.

link(href)
Add a hypertext link to a string.

match(regexp)
Find one or more regular expression matches. JavaScript 1.2.

replaceregexp (replacement)
Replace substring(s) matching a regular expression. JavaScript 1.2.

search(regexp)
Search for a regular expression. JavaScript 1.2.

slice(start, end)
Extract a substring. JavaScript 1.2.

small()
Make a string <SMALL>.

split(delimiter)
Break a string into an array of strings. JavaScript 1.1; ECMA-262.

strike()
Strike out a string with <STRIKE>.

sub()
Make a string a subscript with <SUB>.

substring(from, to)
Return a substring of a string. JavaScript 1.0; ECMA-262.

substr(start, length)
Extract a substring. JavaScript 1.2.

sup()
Make a string a superscript with <SUP>.

toLowerCase()
Convert a string to lowercase. JavaScript 1.0; ECMA-262.

toUpperCase()
Convert a string to uppercase. JavaScript 1.0; ECMA-262.

Static Methods

String.fromCharCode(c1, c2, . . .)
Create a string from character encodings. JavaScript 1.2; ECMA-262.

Style

cascading style sheet attributes

Availability

Client-side JavaScript 1.2

Synopsis

```
// Navigator
document.classes.className.tagName
document.ids.elementName
document.tags.tagName
document.contextual(...)
// Internet Explorer
htmlElement.style
```

Properties

The Style object has properties corresponding to each of the CSS attributes supported by the browser.

Methods

borderWidths(top, right, bottom, left)
Set all border width properties. Navigator 4.

margins(top, right, bottom, left)
Set all margin properties. Navigator 4.

paddings(top, right, bottom, left)
Set all padding properties. Navigator 4.

Submit

a button to submit a form

Availability

Client-side JavaScript 1.0; enhanced in JavaScript 1.1

Inherits From

Input, HTMLElement

Synopsis

```
form.name
form.elements[i]
```

Properties

Submit inherits properties from Input and HTMLElement and defines or overrides the following:

value
The label of a Submit button.

Methods

Submit inherits the methods from Input and HTMLElement.

Event Handlers

Submit inherits event handlers from Input and HTMLElement and defines or overrides the following:

onclick
: Invoked when a Submit button is clicked. JavaScript 1.0; enhanced in JavaScript 1.1.

Text — a graphical text input field

Availability

Client-side JavaScript 1.0; enhanced in JavaScript 1.1

Inherits From

Input, HTMLElement

Synopsis

```
form.name
form.elements[i]
```

Properties

Text inherits properties from Input and HTMLElement and defines or overrides the following:

value
: User input to the Text object.

Methods

Text inherits the methods of Input and HTMLElement.

Event Handlers

Text inherits the event handlers of Input and HTMLElement and defines or overrides the following:

onchange
: The handler invoked when input value changes.

Textarea — a multiline text input area

Availability

Client-side JavaScript 1.0; enhanced in JavaScript 1.1

Inherits From

Input, HTMLElement

Synopsis

```
form.name
form.elements[i]
```

Properties

Textarea inherits the properties of Input and HTMLElement and defines or overrides the following:

value
: User input to the Textarea object.

Methods

Textarea inherits the methods of Input and HTMLElement.

Event Handlers

Textarea inherits the event handlers of Input and HTMLElement and defines or overrides the following:

onchange
: The handler invoked when input value changes.

URL — see Link, Location, or Document.URL

Window — a web browser window or frame

Availability

Client-side JavaScript 1.0; enhanced in JavaScript 1.1 and 1.2

Synopsis

```
self
window
window.frames[i]
```

Properties

The Window object defines the following properties. Nonportable, browser-specific properties are listed separately after this list:

closed
: Whether a window has been closed. JavaScript 1.1.

defaultStatus
: The default status line text.

document
: The Document of the window.

frames[]
: List of frames within a window.

history
The history of the window.

length
The number of frames in the window.

location
The URL of the window.

name
The name of a window. JavaScript 1.0; read/write in JavaScript 1.1.

navigator
A reference to the Navigator object.

offscreenBuffering
Whether window updates are buffered. JavaScript 1.2.

opener
The window that opened this one. JavaScript 1.1.

parent
The parent of a frame.

screen
Information about the screen. JavaScript 1.2.

self The window itself.

status
Specify a transient status-line message.

top The window of a frame.

window
The window itself.

Navigator Properties

crypto
Reference to the Crypto object. Navigator 4.04 and later.

innerHeight
The height of the document display area. Navigator 4; UniversalBrowserWrite privilege required to set to less than 100 pixels.

innerWidth
The width of the document display area. Navigator 4; UniversalBrowserWrite privilege required to set to less than 100 pixels.

java
The *java.** LiveConnect package. Navigator 3.

locationbar
The visibility of the browser's location bar. Navigator 4; UniversalBrowser-Write privilege required to change visibility.

menubar
The visibility of the browser's menubar. Navigator 4; UniversalBrowserWrite privilege required to change visibility.

netscape
The *netscape.** LiveConnect Java package. Navigator 3.

outerHeight
The height of the window area. Navigator 4; UniversalBrowserWrite privilege required to set to less than 100 pixels.

outerWidth
The width of the window. Navigator 4; UniversalBrowserWrite privilege required to set to less than 100 pixels.

Packages
LiveConnect packages of Java classes. Navigator 3.

pageXOffset
The current horizontal scroll position. Navigator 4.

pageYOffset
The current vertical scroll position. Navigator 4.

personalbar
The visibility of the browser's personal bar. Navigator 4; UniversalBrowserWrite privilege required to change visibility.

screenX
The X coordinate of a window on the screen. Navigator 4.

screenY
The Y coordinate of a window on the screen. Navigator 4.

scrollbars
The visibility of the browser's scroll bars. Navigator 4; UniversalBrowserWrite privilege required to change visibility.

statusbar
The visibility of the browser's status line. Navigator 4; UniversalBrowserWrite privilege required to change visibility.

sun
The *sun.** LiveConnect Java package. Navigator 3.

toolbar
The visibility of the browser's toolbar. Navigator 4; UniversalBrowserWrite privilege required to change visibility.

Internet Explorer Properties

clientInformation
Synonym for `Window.navigator`. Internet Explorer 4.

event
Describes the most recent event. Internet Explorer 4.

Methods

The Window object has the following portable methods. Non-portable, browser-specific methods are listed after this list.

alert(message)
: Display a message in a dialog box.

blur()
: Remove keyboard focus from a top-level window. JavaScript 1.1.

clearInterval(intervalId)
: Stop periodically executing code. JavaScript 1.2.

clearTimeout(timeoutId)
: Cancel deferred execution.

close()
: Close a browser window.

confirm(question)
: Ask a yes-or-no question.

focus()
: Give keyboard focus to a top-level window. JavaScript 1.1.

moveBy(dx, dy)
: Move a window to a relative position. JavaScript 1.2; Navigator 4 requires UniversalBrowserWrite privilege to move the window off-screen.

moveTo(x, y)
: Move a window to an absolute position. JavaScript 1.2; Navigator 4 requires UniversalBrowserWrite privilege to move the window off-screen.

open(url, name, features, replace)
: Open a new browser window or locate a named window. JavaScript 1.0; enhanced in JavaScript 1.1.

prompt(message, default)
: Get string input in a dialog.

resizeBy(dw, dh)
: Resize a window by a relative amount. JavaScript 1.2; Navigator 4 requires UniversalBrowserWrite privilege to set either width or height to less than 100 pixels.

resizeTo(width, height)
: Resize a window. JavaScript 1.2; Navigator 4 requires UniversalBrowserWrite privilege to set either width or height to less than 100 pixels.

scroll(x, y)
: Scroll a document in a window. JavaScript 1.1; deprecated in JavaScript 1.2 in favor of *scrollTo()*.

scrollBy(dx, dy)
: Scroll the document by a relative amount. JavaScript 1.2.

scrollTo(x, y)
Scroll the document. JavaScript 1.2.

setInterval(code, interval)

setInterval(func, interval, args . . .)
Periodically execute specified code. JavaScript 1.2; Internet Explorer 4 supports only the first form of this method.

setTimeout(code, delay)
Defer execution of code.

Navigator 4 Methods

atob(str64)
Decode base-64 encoded data.

back()
Go back to previous document.

btoa(data)
Encode binary data using base-64 ASCII encoding.

captureEvents(eventmask)
Specify event types to be captured.

disableExternalCapture()
Disable cross-server event capturing. Requires UniversalBrowserWrite privilege.

enableExternalCapture()
Enable cross-server event capturing. Requires UniversalBrowserWrite privilege.

find(target, caseSensitive, backwards)
Search the document.

forward()
Go forward to next document.

handleEvent(event)
Pass an event to the appropriate handler.

home()
Display the home page.

print()
Print the document.

releaseEvents(eventmask)
Stop capturing events.

routeEvent(event)
Pass a captured event to the next handler.

setHotkeys(enabled)
Allow/disallow keyboard shortcuts. Requires UniversalBrowserWrite privilege.

setResizable(resizable)
Allow or disallow window resizing. Requires UniversalBrowserWrite privilege.

setZOptions(option)
Control window stacking. Requires UniversalBrowserWrite privilege.

stop()
Stop loading the document.

Internet Explorer Methods

navigate(url)
Load a new URL. Internet Explorer 3.

Event Handlers

onblur
The handler invoked when the window loses keyboard focus. JavaScript 1.1.

ondragdrop
The handler invoked when the user drops items in the window. Navigator 4.

onerror
The handler invoked when a JavaScript error occurs. JavaScript 1.1.

onfocus
The handler invoked when window is given focus. JavaScript 1.1.

onload
The handler invoked when a document finishes loading.

onmove
The handler invoked when a window is moved. Navigator 4; not supported on Navigator 4 Unix platforms.

onresize
The handler invoked when a window is resized. JavaScript 1.2.

onunload
The handler invoked when the browser leaves a page.

PART V

CGI and Perl

CHAPTER 12

CGI Overview

The Common Gateway Interface (CGI) is an essential tool for creating and managing comprehensive web sites. With CGI, you can write scripts that create interactive, user-driven applications.

CGI allows the web server to communicate with other programs that are running on the server. For example, with CGI, the web server can invoke an external program, while passing user-specific data to the program (such as what host the user is connecting from, or input the user has supplied through an HTML form). The program then processes that data, and the server passes the program's response back to the web browser.

Rather than limiting the Web to documents written ahead of time, CGI enables web pages to be created on the fly, based upon the input of users. You can use CGI scripts to create a wide range of applications, from surveys to search tools, from Internet service gateways to quizzes and games. You can count the number of users who access a document or let them sign an electronic guestbook. You can provide users with all types of information, collect their comments, and respond.

Teaching CGI programming from scratch is beyond the scope of this book—for that, we recommend O'Reilly's upcoming *CGI Programming with Perl*, by Scott Guelich, Shishir Gundavaram and Gunther Birznieks.

This chapter through Chapter 15, summarize the essential components of CGI:

- This chapter gives a quick introduction to the mechanism of CGI and lists the environment variables commonly defined by servers for CGI programs.
- Chapter 13, covers Server Side Includes, which are used with many CGI applications.
- Chapter 14, *The CGI.pm Module*, is a reference for the popular Perl module CGI.pm. CGI.pm defines one of the most widely used interfaces for creating CGI programs.

- Chapter 15 describes *mod_perl*, which embeds Perl into the Apache web server. *mod_perl* can greatly enhance the performance of CGI and also provides an interface to the Apache API for Perl programmers.

In addition, CGI programmers will probably also be interested in Chapter 6, *Forms*, and Chapter 17, *HTTP*.

A Typical CGI Interaction

For an example of a CGI application, suppose you create a guestbook for your web site. The guestbook page asks users to submit their first name and last name using a fill-in form composed of two input text fields. Figure 12-1 shows the form you might see in your browser window.

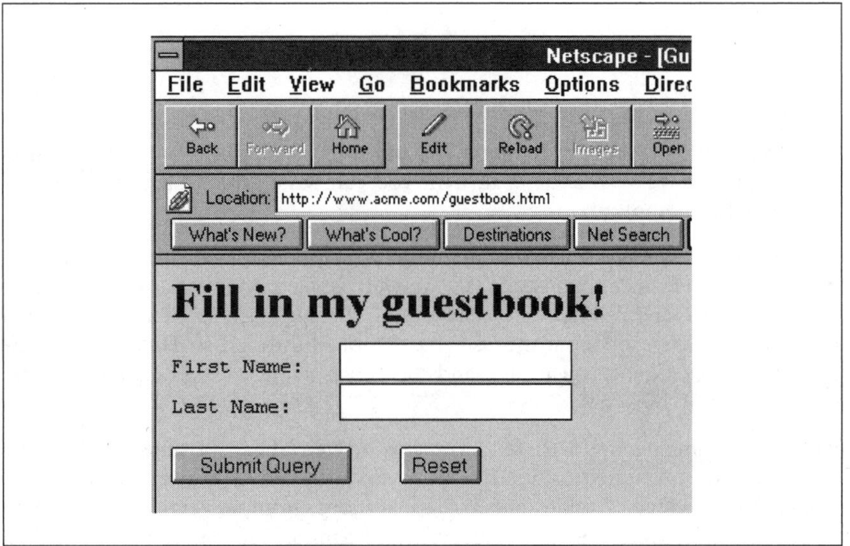

Figure 12-1: HTML form

The HTML that produces this form might read as follows:

```
<HTML><HEAD><TITLE>Guestbook</TITLE></HEAD>
<BODY>
<H1>Fill in my guestbook!</H1>
<FORM METHOD="GET" ACTION="/cgi-bin/guestbook.pl">
<PRE>
First Name:    <INPUT TYPE="TEXT" NAME="firstname">
Last Name:     <INPUT TYPE="TEXT" NAME="lastname">

<INPUT TYPE="SUBMIT">    <INPUT TYPE="RESET">
</FORM>
```

The form is written using special "form" tags (discussed in detail in Chapter 6):

- The <form> tag defines the *method* used for the form (either GET or POST) and the *action* to take when the form is submitted—that is, the URL of the CGI program to pass the parameters to.
- The <input> tag can be used in many different ways. In its first two invocations, it creates a text input field and defines the variable name to associate with the field's contents when the form is submitted. The first field is given the variable name "firstname," and the second field is given the name "lastname."
- In its last two invocations, the <input> tag creates a Submit button and a Reset button.
- The </form> tag indicates the end of the form.

When the user presses the Submit button, data entered into the <input> text fields is passed to the CGI program specified by the action attribute of the <form> tag (in this case, the */cgi-bin/guestbook.pl* program).

Transferring the Form Data

Parameters to a CGI program are transferred either in the URL or in the body text of the request. The method used to pass parameters is determined by the method attribute to the <form> tag. The GET method says to transfer the data within the URL itself; for example, under the GET method, the browser might initiate the HTTP transaction as follows:

```
GET /cgi-bin/guestbook.pl?firstname=Joe&lastname=Schmoe HTTP/1.0
```

See Chapter 17, for more information on HTTP transactions.

The POST method says to use the body portion of the HTTP request to pass parameters. The same transaction with the POST method would read as follows:

```
POST /cgi-bin/guestbook.pl HTTP/1.0
        ... [More headers here]

firstname=Joe&lastname=Schmoe
```

In both examples, you should recognize the firstname and lastname variable names that were defined in the HTML form, coupled with the values entered by the user. An ampersand (&) is used to separate the variable=value pairs.

The server now passes the variable=value pairs to the CGI program. It does this either through Unix environment variables or in standard input (STDIN). If the CGI program is called with the GET method parameters are expected to be embedded in the URL of the request, and the server transfers them to the program by assigning them to the QUERY_STRING environment variable. The CGI program can then retrieve the parameters from QUERY_STRING as it would read any environment variable (for example, from the *%ENV* associative array in Perl). If the CGI program is called with the POST method, parameters are expected to be embedded into the body of the request, and the server passes the body text to the program as standard input.

(Other environment variables defined by the server for CGI programs are listed later in this chapter. These variables store such information as the format and length of the input, the remote host, the user, and various client information. They also store the server name, the communication protocol, and the name of the software running the server.)

The CGI program needs to retrieve the information as appropriate and then process it. The sky's the limit on what the CGI program actually does with the information it retrieves. It might return an anagram of the user's name, or tell them how many times their name uses the letter "t," or it might just compile the name into a list that the programmer regularly sells to telemarketers. Only the programmer knows for sure.

Creating Virtual Documents

Regardless of what the CGI program does with its input, it's responsible for giving the browser something to display when it's done. It must either create a new document to be served to the browser or point to an existing document. On Unix, programs send their output to standard output (STDOUT) as a data stream that consists of two parts. The first part is either a full or partial HTTP header that (at minimum) describes the format of the returned data (e.g., HTML, ASCII text, GIF, etc.). A blank line signifies the end of the header section. The second part is the body of the output, which contains the data conforming to the format type reflected in the header. For example:

```
Content-type: text/html

<HTML>
<HEAD><TITLE>Thanks!</TITLE></HEAD>
<BODY><H1>Thanks for signing my guest book!</H1>
        ...
</BODY></HTML>
```

In this case, the only header line generated is `Content-type`, which gives the media format of the output as HTML (`text/html`). This line is essential for every CGI program, since it tells the browser what kind of format to expect. The blank line separates the header from the body text (which, in this case, is in HTML format as advertised). See Chapter 17 for a listing of other media formats that are commonly recognized on the Web.

(Notice that it does not matter to the web server what language the CGI program is written in. On Unix platforms, the most popular language for CGI programming is Perl. Other languages used on Unix are C, C++, Tcl, and Python. On Macintosh computers, programmers use Applescript and C/C++, and on Microsoft Windows, programmers use Visual Basic, Perl, and C/C++. As long as there's a way in a programming language to get data from the server and send data back, you can use it for CGI.)

The server transfers the results of the CGI program back to the browser. The body text is not modified or interpreted by the server in any way, but the server generally supplies additional headers with information such as the date, the name and version of the server, etc. See Chapter 17 for a list of valid HTTP response headers.

CGI programs can also supply a complete HTTP header itself, in which case the server does not add any additional headers but instead transfers the response verbatim as returned by the CGI program. (The server may need to be configured to allow this behavior.)

Here is the sample output of a program generating an HTML virtual document, with a complete HTTP header:

```
HTTP/1.0 200 OK
Date:  Thursday, 28-June-96 11:12:21 GMT
Server: NCSA/1.4.2
Content-type: text/html
Content-length: 2041

<HTML>
<HEAD><TITLE>Thanks!</TITLE></HEAD>
<BODY>
<H1>Thanks for signing my guestbook!</H1>
         ...
</BODY>
</HTML>
```

The header contains the communication protocol, the date and time of the response, and the server name and version. (The `200 OK` is a *status code* generated by the HTTP protocol to communicate the status of a request, in this case successful. See Chapter 17 for a list of valid HTTP status codes.) Most importantly, it also contains the content type and the number of characters (equivalent to the number of bytes) of the enclosed data.

As seen in Figure 12-2, the result is that after users click the Submit button, they see the message contained in the HTML section of the response thanking them for signing the guestbook.

CGI and Perl

URL Encoding

Before data supplied on a form can be sent to a CGI program, each form element's name (specified by the `name` attribute) is equated with the value entered by the user to create a key-value pair. For example, if the user entered "30" when asked for his or her age, the key-value pair would be "age=30". In the transferred data, key-value pairs are separated by the ampersand (&) character.

Since under the GET method the form information is sent as part of the URL, form information can't include any spaces or other special characters that are not allowed in URLs, and also can't include characters that have other meanings in URLs, like slashes (/). (For the sake of consistency, this constraint also exists when the POST method is being used.) Therefore, the web browser performs some special encoding on user-supplied information.

Encoding involves replacing spaces and other special characters in the query strings with their hexadecimal equivalents. (Thus, URL encoding is also sometimes

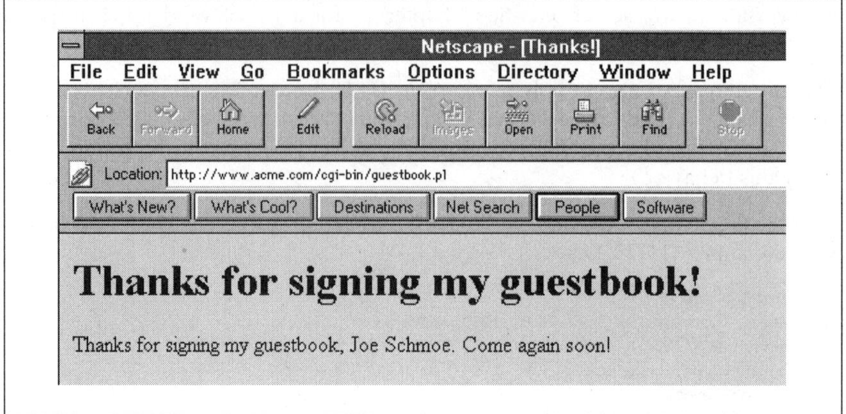

Figure 12-2: Guestbook acknowledgment

called *hexadecimal encoding*.) Suppose a user fills out and submits a form containing his or her birthday in the syntax mm/dd/yy (e.g., 11/05/73). The forward slashes in the birthday are among the special characters that can't appear in the client's request for the CGI program. Thus, when the browser issues the request, it encodes the data. The following sample request shows the resulting encoding:

```
POST /cgi-bin/birthday.pl HTTP/1.0
Content-length: 21

birthday=11%2F05%2F73
```

The sequence `%2F` is actually the hexadecimal equivalent of the slash character.

CGI scripts have to provide some way to "decode" form data the client has encoded. The best way to do this is to use CGI.pm (covered in Chapter 14) and let it do the work for you.

Extra Path Information

In addition to passing query strings, you can pass additional data, known as *extra path information*, as part of the URL. The server gauges where the CGI program name ends; anything following is deemed "extra" and is stored in the environment variable PATH_INFO. The following line calls a script with extra path information:

```
http://some.machine/cgi-bin/display.pl/cgi/cgi_doc.txt
```

In this example, we use a script with a *.pl* suffix to make it clear where the CGI program's path ends and the extra path information begins. Everything after *display.pl* is the extra path. The PATH_TRANSLATED variable is also set, mapping the PATH_INFO to the document root (DOCUMENT_ROOT) directory (e.g., */usr/local/etc/httpd/public/cgi/cgi_doc.txt*).

CGI Environment Variables

Much of the information needed by CGI programs is made available via Unix environment variables. Programs can access this information as they would any environment variable (e.g., via the *%ENV* associative array in Perl). Table 12-1 lists the environment variables commonly available through CGI. However, since servers occasionally vary on the names of environment variables they assign, check with your own server documentation for more information.

Table 12-1: CGI Environment Variables

Environment Variable	*Content Returned*
AUTH_TYPE	The authentication method used to validate a user. See REMOTE_IDENT and REMOTE_USER.
CONTENT_LENGTH	The length of the query data (in bytes or the number of characters) passed to the CGI program through standard input.
CONTENT_TYPE	The media type of the query data, such as `text/html`. See Chapter 17, for a listing of commonly used content types.
DOCUMENT_ROOT	The directory from which web documents are served.
GATEWAY_INTERFACE	The revision of the Common Gateway Interface the server uses.
HTTP_ACCEPT	A list of the media types the client can accept.
HTTP_COOKIE	A list of cookies defined for that URL. (See Chapter 17, for more information.)
HTTP_FROM	The email address of the user making the query (many browsers do not support this variable).
HTTP_REFERER	The URL of the document the client points to before accessing the CGI program.
PATH_INFO	Extra path information passed to a CGI program.
PATH_TRANSLATED	The translated version of the path given by the variable PATH_INFO.
QUERY_STRING	The query information passed to the program. It is appended to the URL following a question mark (?).
REMOTE_ADDR	The remote IP address from which the user is making the request.
REMOTE_HOST	The remote hostname from which the user is making the request.
REMOTE_IDENT	The user making the request.
REMOTE_USER	The authenticated name of the user making the query.

CGI and Perl

Table 12-1: CGI Environment Variables (continued)

Environment Variable	*Content Returned*
REQUEST_METHOD	The method with which the information request was issued (e.g., GET, POST, HEAD). See Chapter 17, for more information on request methods.
SCRIPT_NAME	The virtual path (e.g., */cgi-bin/program.pl*) of the script being executed.
SERVER_NAME	The server's hostname or IP address.
SERVER_PORT	The port number of the host on which the server is running.
SERVER_PROTOCOL	The name and revision of the information protocol the request came in with.
SERVER_SOFTWARE	The name and version of the server software that is answering the client request.

Here's a simple Perl CGI script that uses environment variables to display various information about the server:

```
#!/usr/local/bin/perl

print "Content-type: text/html", "\n\n";

print "<HTML>", "\n";
print "<HEAD><TITLE>About this Server</TITLE></HEAD>", "\n";
print "<BODY><H1>About this Server</H1>", "\n";
print "<HR><PRE>";
print "Server Name:        ", $ENV{'SERVER_NAME'}, "<BR>", "\n";
print "Running on Port:    ", $ENV{'SERVER_PORT'}, "<BR>", "\n";
print "Server Software:    ", $ENV{'SERVER_SOFTWARE'}, "<BR>", "\n";
print "Server Protocol:    ", $ENV{'SERVER_PROTOCOL'}, "<BR>", "\n";
print "CGI Revision:       ", $ENV{'GATEWAY_INTERFACE'}, "<BR>", "\n";
print "<HR></PRE>", "\n";
print "</BODY></HTML>", "\n";

exit (0);
```

The preceding program outputs the contents of five environment variables into an HTML document. In Perl, you can access the environment variables using the *%ENV* associative array. Here's a typical output of the program:

```
<HTML>
<HEAD><TITLE>About this Server</TITLE></HEAD>
<BODY><H1>About this Server</H1>
<HR><PRE>
Server Name:        oreilly.com
Running on Port:    80
Server Software:    NCSA/1.4.2
Server Protocol:    HTTP/1.0
CGI Revision:       CGI/1.1
<HR></PRE>
</BODY></HTML>
```

CHAPTER 13

Server Side Includes

Server Side Includes (SSI) are directives you can place into an HTML document to execute other programs or to output data, such as file statistics or the contents of environment variables. SSI directives can save you the trouble of writing complete CGI programs to output documents containing a small amount of dynamic information. While Server Side Includes are not technically CGI, they can become an important tool for incorporating CGI-like information as well as output from CGI programs.

Keep in mind, however, that not all servers support these directives. In addition, some servers allows the setting of server-side variables, which can be used in Extended Server Side Includes (XSSI) conditional expressions. These expressions determine which portion of a server document should be displayed.

When a client requests a document from an SSI-enabled server and the document is coded appropriately, the server parses the specified document looking for SSI directives. We've already considered the advantages to this system; there are also a couple of liabilities. First, parsing documents before sending them to the client represents additional server overhead. Second, enabling SSI can create a security risk. For example, an unwise user might embed directives to execute system commands that output confidential information. In short, SSI can be very handy, but it must be used cautiously and efficiently.

This chapter summarizes the Server Side Includes, as well as the Extended Server Side Includes from Apache. There aren't many, but they perform some useful CGI-like operations and can spare you quite a bit of coding.

Configuring the Apache Server for SSI and XSSI

In order to tell the Apache servers which files to parse, you must modify two server configuration files, *srm.conf* and *access.conf*, as follows:

1. In the server configuration file *srm.conf*, specify the extension(s) of the files the server should parse and assign them to the "server-parsed" handler. For example, the following two lines specify that the server should handle documents with the *.shtml* suffix as HTML documents, and should assign the document to the "server-parsing" handler (*mod_include*), which handles all SSI:

   ```
   AddType text/html .shtml
   AddHandler server-parsed .shtml
   ```

   Alternatively, specifying the suffix *.html* would make the server parse all HTML documents; however, keep in mind that parsing every HTML file could present a noticeable server drain.

2. In the access configuration file *access.conf*, include the following directive, possibly for each directory (`<Directory>`) that contains documents with server-side includes:

   ```
   Options+ Includes
   ```

See Chapter 19, *Apache Modules*, for more on configuring the Apache server.

Basic SSI Directives

All SSI directives have the format:

```
<!--#command parameter(s)="argument" -->
```

Each of the symbols is important; be careful not to forget the pound sign (#) or the dual dashes (--). Also, it is recommended that you place whitespace between the final arguments and the closing dashes to prevent it from being interpreted as part of an SSI argument.

Following is a list of the primary server-side directives, the parameters they take, and their function.

---

config

`config errmsg|sizefmt|timefmt="string"`

Modifies various aspects of SSI.

Arguments

`errmsg`
: Default error message.

```
<!--#config errmsg="Error: File not found"-->
```

`sizefmt`
: Format for the size of the file (returned by the `fsize` directive). Acceptable values are `bytes`, or `abbrev`, which rounds the file size to the nearest kilobyte. For example:

```
<!--#config sizefmt="abbrev"-->
```

→

`timefmt`
: Format for times and dates. SSI offers a wide range of formats. See the section "Configurable Time Formats for SSI Output" later in this chapter for more information.

---

echo

`echo var="`*`environment_variable`*`"`

Inserts value of special SSI variables, as well as other CGI environment variables. For example:

```
<H1>Welcome to my server at <!--#echo var="SERVER_NAME"-->...</H1>
```

See also Chapter 12, *CGI Overview*, and the next section.

---

exec

`exec cmd|cgi="`*`string`*`"`

Executes external programs and inserts output in the current document.

Arguments

`cmd` Any application on the host.

`cgi` The URI of a CGI program.

For example:

```
<!--#exec cmd="/bin/finger $REMOTE_USER@$REMOTE_HOST"-->
This page has been accessed
<!--#exec cgi="/cgi-bin/counter.pl"-->
times.
```

CGI and Perl

---

flastmod

`flastmod file="`*`path`*`"`

Inserts the last modification date and time for a specified file.

```
The file was last modified on
<!--#flastmod file="/mybook.ps"-->.
```

You can specify the format of the date and time returned using the `config` directive with the `timefmt` argument; `timefmt` takes a wide range of values described in the section "Configurable Time Formats for SSI Output" later in this chapter.

---

fsize

`fsize file|virtual="`*`path`*`"`

Inserts the size of a specified file.

→

Arguments

`file` Pathname relative to a document on the server.

`virtual`
Virtual path to a document on the server.

For example:

```
The size of the file is
<!--#fsize file="/mybook.ps"--> bytes.
<!--#fsize virtual="/personal/mydata.txt"-->
```

---

include

`include file|virtual="`*`path`*`"`

Inserts text of document into current file.

Arguments

`file` Pathname relative to a document on the server.

`virtual`
Virtual path to a document on the server.

For example:

```
<!--#include file="stuff.html"-->
<!--#include virtual="/personal/stuff.html"-->
```

---

printenv

`printenv`

Prints all environment variables on the server.

For example:

```
<!--#printenv-->
```

---

set

`set var="`*`name`*`" value="`*`value`*`"`

Sets a server-side variable to a given value.

Arguments

`var` The name of the variable.

`value` The value to be assigned to the variable.

For example:

```
<!--#set var="myvar" value="activated"-->
```

SSI Environment Variables

You can use SSI directives to output the values of environment variables in an otherwise static HTML document. These might be standard CGI variables (listed in Chapter 12); or they might be:

DOCUMENT_NAME
: The current file:

```
You are reading a document called:
<!--#echo var="DOCUMENT_NAME"-->
```

DOCUMENT_URI
: Virtual path to the file:

```
You can access this document again by pointing to the URI:
<!--#echo var="DOCUMENT_URI"-->
```

DATE_LOCAL
: Current date and time in the local time zone:

```
The time is now <!--#echo var="DATE_LOCAL"-->
```

DATE_GMT
: Current date and time in Greenwich Mean Time:

```
The Greenwich Mean Time is <!--#echo var="DATE_GMT"-->
```

LAST_MODIFIED
: Last modification date and time for current file:

```
The current document was last modified on:
<!--#echo var="LAST_MODIFIED"-->
```

CGI and Perl

Configurable Time Formats for SSI Output

Among its functions, the `config` SSI command allows you to specify the way the time and date are displayed with the `timefmt` argument. It takes a number of special values that are summarized in Table 13-1.

Table 13-1: SSI Time Formats

Status Code	*Meaning*	*Example*
%a	Day of the week abbreviation	Sun
%A	Day of the week	Sunday
%b	Month name abbreviation (also %h)	Jan
%B	Month name	January
%d	Date	01
%D	Date as %m/%d/%y	06/23/95
%e	Date	1 (*not* 01)
%H	24-hour clock hour	13
%I	12-hour clock hour	01

Table 13-1: SSI Time Formats (continued)

Status Code	*Meaning*	*Example*
%j	Decimal day of the year	360
%m	Month number	11
%M	Minutes	08
%p	AM | PM	AM
%r	Time as %I:%M:%S %p	09:21:13 PM
%S	Seconds	09
%T	24-hour time as %H:%M:%S	12:22:40
%U	Week of the year (also %W)	37
%w	Day of the week number (starting with Sunday=0)	2
%y	Year of the century	96
%Y	Year	1996
%Z	Time zone	EST

The config command in the following example makes use of two of those special time values:

```
<!--#config timefmt="%D %r"-->
The file address.html was last modified on:
        <!--#flastmod file="address.html"-->.
```

where %D specifies that the date appear in "mm/dd/yy" format, and %r specifies that the time appear as "hh/mm/ss AM|PM."

Thus the previous example produces output such as:

```
The file address.html was last modified on: 12/23/95 07:17:39 PM
```

Conditional Statements

Apache allows you to include only select portions of a server document using conditional statements. These conditional statements are based on the value of server-side variables initialized earlier using the SSI set command. The Apache flow-control statements allow you to effectively customize a document without adding more complex CGI programs to perform the same task.

There are four Apache flow-control statements:

```
<!--#if expr="expression"-->
<!--#elif expr="expression"-->
<!--#else-->
<!--#endif-->
```

Each works as you would expect from an ordinary scripting language. Note that each if must have a closing endif server-side statement. For example:

```
<!--#if expr="$myvar=activated"-->
<B>The variable appears to be activated</B>
<!--#elif expr="$myvar=inactive"-->
<B>The variable appears to be inactive</B>
<!--#else-->
<B>The variable has an unknown value</B>
<!--#endif-->
```

Table 13-2 shows the allowed expressions, where the order of operations is as expected in a traditional programming language. Note that in some cases, *var2* is allowed to be an **egrep**-based regular expression if it is surrounded by slashes (/) on both sides.

Table 13-2: XSSI Conditional Expressions

Expression	*Meaning*
var	True if the variable is not empty
var1=var2	True if the variables match
var1!=var2	True if the variables do not match
var1<var2	True if the first variable is less than the second
var1<=var2	True if the first variable is less than or equal to the second
var1>var2	True if the first variable is greater than the second
var1>=var2	True if the first variable is greater than or equal to the second
(*expr*)	True if the enclosed condition is true
! *expr*	True if the condition is false
expr1&&expr2	True if both expressions evaluate to true
expr1 || *expr2*	True if either expressions evaluates to true

Finally, you can place regular strings inside single quotes to preserve any whitespaces. If a string is not quoted, extra whitespaces are ignored. Take for example:

```
this    is    too   much     space
```

This string does not have quotes and will be collapsed to:

```
this is too much space
```

However, if you place the string in single quotes, the whitespace is preserved:

```
'this    is    too   much     space'
```

You can also place strings in double quotes, but you will have to escape each one while inside the **expr=""** expression, as shown here:

```
<!--#if expr="\"$HTTP_REFERER\" != " -->
```

CGI and Perl

CHAPTER 14

The CGI.pm Module

CGI.pm is a Perl module for creating and parsing CGI forms. It is distributed with core Perl as of Perl 5.004, but you can also retrieve CGI.pm from CPAN, and you can get the very latest version at any time from *ftp://ftp-genome.wi.mit.edu/pub/software/WWW/*. Due to space constraints, this book doesn't include a complete reference for the Perl language itself. But if you already use Perl for CGI, you know how essential CGI.pm can be, so we include this chapter on CGI.pm as a convenience for Perl-savvy readers.

CGI is an object-oriented module. Don't let the object-oriented nature scare you, though; CGI.pm is very easy to use, as evidenced by its overwhelming popularity among all levels of Perl programmers. To give you an idea of how easy it is to use CGI.pm, let's take a scenario in which a user fills out and submits a form containing her birthday. Without CGI.pm, the script would have to translate the URL-encoded input by hand (probably using a series of regular expressions) and assign it to a variable. For example, you might try something like this:

```
#!/usr/bin/perl
# cgi script without CGI.pm
$size_of_form_info = $ENV{'CONTENT_LENGTH'};
read ($STDIN, $form_info, $size_of_form_info);
# Split up each pair of key=value pairs
foreach $pair (split (/&/, $form_info)) {

          # For each pair, split into $key and $value variables
          ($key, $value) = split (/=/, $pair);
        # Get rid of the pesky %xx encodings
          $key =~ s/%([\dA-Fa-f][\dA-Fa-f])/pack ("C", hex ($1))/eg;
          $value =~ s/%([\dA-Fa-f][\dA-Fa-f])/pack ("C", hex ($1))/eg;
        # Use $key as index for %parameters hash, $value as value
          $parameters{$key} = $value;
}
# Print out the obligatory content-ytype line
print "Content-type: text/plain\n\n";
```

```
# Tell the user what they said
print "Your birthday is on " . $parameters{birthday} . ".\n";
```

Regardless of whether this code actually works, you must admit it's ugly. With CGI.pm, the script could be written:

```
#!/usr/bin/perl -w
# cgi script with CGI.pm

use CGI;

$query = CGI::new();
$bday = $query->param("birthday");
print $query->header();
print $query->p("Your birthday is $bday.");
```

Even for this tiny program, you can see that CGI.pm can alleviate many of the headaches associated with CGI programming.

As with any Perl module, the first thing you do is call the module with `use`. You then call the constructor (`new()`), creating a new CGI object called `$query`. Next, get the value of the `birthday` parameter from the CGI program using the `param` method. Note that CGI.pm does all the work of determining whether the CGI program is being called by the GET or POST methods, and it also does all the URL decoding for you. To generate output, use the `header` method to return the content type header, and the `p` method to generate a paragraph marker `<P>` tag.

However, this is only the tip of the iceberg as far as what CGI.pm can do for you. There are three basic categories of CGI.pm methods: CGI handling, creating forms, and retrieving environment variables. (A fourth category is creating HTML tags, but we don't cover those in detail.) Table 14-1 lists most of these methods. They are also covered in more detail later in this chapter.

Table 14-1: CGI.pm Methods

CGI Handling

`keywords`	Get keywords from an `<ISINDEX>` search
`param`	Get (or set) the value of parameters
`append`	Append to a parameter
`import_names`	Import variables into a namespace
`delete`	Delete a parameter
`delete_all`	Delete all parameters
`save`	Save all parameters to a file
`self_url`	Create self-referencing URL
`url`	Get URL of current script without query information
`header`	Create HTTP header
`redirect`	Create redirection header
`cookie`	Get (or sets) a cookie
`nph`	Declare this to be a NPH script
`dump`	Print all name/value pairs

Table 14-1: CGI.pm Methods (continued)

Form Generation

start_html	Generate an <HTML> tag
end_html	Generate an </HTML> tag
autoEscape	Set whether to use automatic escaping
isindex	Generate an <ISINDEX> tag
startform	Generate a <FORM> tag
start_multipart_form	Generate a <FORM> tag for multipart/form-data encoding
textfield	Generate an <INPUT TYPE=TEXT> tag
textarea	Generate an <TEXTAREA> tag
password_field	Generate an <INPUT TYPE=PASSWORD> tag
filefield	Generate an <INPUT TYPE=FILE> tag
popup_menu	Generate a pop-up menu via <SELECT SIZE=1> and <OPTION> tags
scrolling_list	Generate a scrolling list via <SELECT> and <OPTION> tags
checkbox_group	Generate a group of checkboxes via multiple <INPUT TYPE=CHECKBOX> tags
checkbox	Generate a single checkbox via a <INPUT TYPE=CHECKBOX> tag
radio_group	Generate a group of radio buttons via <INPUT TYPE=RADIO> tags
submit	Generate a <SUBMIT> tag
reset	Generate a <RESET> tag.
defaults	Generate a <DEFAULTS> tag
hidden	Generate an <INPUT TYPE=HIDDEN> tag
image_button	Generate a clickable image button via a <SELECT> tag
button	Generate a JavaScript button

Handling Environment Variables

accept	Get accept types from ACCEPT header
user_agent	Get value of USER_AGENT header
path_info	Get value of EXTRA_PATH_INFO header
path_translated	Get value of PATH_TRANSLATED header
remote_host	Get value of REMOTE_HOST header
raw_cookie	Get value of HTTP_COOKIE header
script_name	Get value of SCRIPT_NAME header
referer	Get value of REFERER header
auth_type	Get value of AUTH_TYPE header
remote_user	Get value of REMOTE_USER header

Table 14-1: CGI.pm Methods (continued)

Handling Environment Variables

user_name	Get user name (not via headers)
request_method	Get value of REQUEST_METHOD header

Each of these methods is covered later in this chapter, in alphabetical order.

HTML Tag Generation

In addition to the form-generation methods, CGI.pm also includes a group of methods for creating HTML tags. The names of the HTML tag methods generally follow the HTML tag name (e.g., `p` for `<P>`) and take named parameters that are assumed to be valid attributes for the tag (e.g., `img(src=>'camel.gif')` becomes `<IMG SRC="camel.gif">`). We do not list all tags in this book; see the CGI.pm manpage for more information, or the book *Official Guide to Programming with CGI.pm* by Lincoln Stein (John Wiley & Sons, 1998).

Importing Method Groups

The syntax for calling CGI methods can be unwieldy. However, you can import individual methods and then call the methods without explicit object calls. The "birthday" example shown earlier could be written even more simply as follows:

```
#!/usr/bin/perl

use CGI param,header,p;

$bday = param("birthday");
print header();
print p("Your birthday is $bday.");
```

By importing the `param`, `header`, and `p` methods into your namespace, you no longer have to use the `new` constructor (since it is called automatically now), and you don't need to specify a CGI object with every method call.

CGI.pm also lets you import groups of methods, which can make your programs much simpler and more elegant. For example, to import all form-creation methods and all CGI-handling methods:

```
use CGI qw/:form :cgi/;
```

The method groups supported by CGI.pm are:

`:cgi`
All CGI-handling methods

`:cgi-lib`
All methods supplied for backwards compatibility with *cgi-lib*

`:form`
All form-generation methods

`:html`
: All HTML methods

`:html2`
: All HTML 2.0 methods

`:html3`
: All HTML 3.0 methods

`:netscape`
: All methods generating Netscape extensions

`:ssl`
: All SSL methods

`:standard`
: All HTML 2.0, form-generation, and CGI methods

`:all`
: All available methods

You can also define new methods for HTML tag generation by simply listing them on the import line and letting CGI.pm make some educated guesses. For example:

```
use CGI shortcuts,smell;

print smell {type=>'garlic',
            intensity=>'strong'}, "Scratch here!";
```

This causes the following tag to be generated:

```
<SMELL TYPE="garlic" INTENSITY="strong">Scratch here!</SMELL>
```

Maintaining State

One of the first complications for any nontrivial CGI script is how to "maintain state." Since HTTP is a stateless protocol, there's no built-in mechanism for keeping track of requests from the server end. A CGI transaction involving multiple forms, therefore, needs to find a way to remember information supplied on previous forms. One way to deal with this issue is to use *cookies*, which allow the CGI program to save information on the browser's end; but not all browsers support cookies, and some users are uncomfortable with the perceived privacy infringement associated with cookies.

CGI.pm simplifies maintaining state without cookies. When a CGI.pm script is called multiple times, the input fields are given default values from the previous invocation.

Named Parameters

For most CGI.pm methods, there are two syntax styles. In the "standard" style, the position of the parameters determines how they will be interpreted; for example, parameter 1 is the name the script should assign, parameter 2 is the initial value, etc. For example:

```
print $query=textfield('username', 'anonymous');
```

In the "named parameters" style, the parameters can be assigned like a hash, and the order doesn't matter. For example:

```
print $query->textfield(-name=>'name',
                        -default=>'value');
```

If you want to use named parameters, just call the `use_named_parameters` method early in the script.

Which syntax style should you use? It depends on how lazy you are and much control you need. Generally, "standard" syntax is faster to type. However, it is also harder to read, and there are many features that are simply not available using standard syntax (such as JavaScript support). In general, we recommend using the "named parameters" syntax for all but the most trivial scripts.

Using JavaScript Features

CGI.pm supports JavaScript scripting by allowing you to embed a JavaScript script in the HTML form within `<SCRIPT>` tags, and then calling the script using the `-script` parameter to the `start_html` method. You can then call the JavaScript functions as appropriate to the form elements.

Debugging

A complication of writing CGI scripts is that when debugging the script, you have to wrestle with the web server environment. CGI.pm provides support for debugging the script on the command line.

If you run the script on the command line without arguments, you will be placed into an "offline" mode, in which name-value pairs can be entered one-by-one. When you press CTRL-D, the script runs. For example:

```
% birthday
(offline mode: enter name=value pairs on standard input)
birthday=6/4/65
^D
Content-type: text/html

<P>Your birthday is 6/4/65.</P>
```

You can also supply the name/value parameters directly on the command line. For example:

```
% test birthday=6/4/65
Content-type: text/html

<P>Your birthday is 6/4/65.</P>
```

Multiple values can be separated by spaces (as separate arguments on the command line) or by ampersands (as in URL-encoded syntax). In fact, you can use URL-encoded syntax on the command line. This makes it easy to supply raw CGI input to the script for testing purposes. Just remember to protect the ampersand from the shell. For example:

```
% test 'birthday=6%2f4%2f65&name=Fred%20Flintstone'
Content-type: text/html

<P>Fred Flintstone, your birthday is 6/4/65.</P>
```

CGI.pm Reference

The following methods are supported by CGI.pm.

---

accept

`$query->accept(['content_type'])`

Returns a list of media types that the browser accepts.

content_type
: If specified, returns instead the browser's preference for the specified content type, between 0.0 and 1.0.

---

append

`$query->append(-name=>'name',-values=>'value')`

Appends a value or list of values to the named parameter.

–name=>'*name*'
: The parameter to be appended.

–values=>'*value*'
: The value to append. Multiple values can be specified as a reference to an anonymous array.

---

auth_type

`auth_type()`

Returns the authorization method.

---

autoEscape

`$query->autoEscape(undef)`

Turns off autoescaping of form elements.

---

button

`print $query->button('name','function')`

Generates a JavaScript button.

→

name
  The name of the button.

function
  The function to execute when the button is clicked.

Using named parameters, the syntax is:

```
print $query->button(-name=>'name',
                     -value=>'label',
                     -onClick=>"function");
```

-value=>'*label*'
  The label to display for the button.

checkbox

print *$query*->checkbox('*name*' [,'*checked*','*value*','*label*'])

Generates a single checkbox.

name
  The name to assign the input to (required).

checked
  Checkbox should be checked initially.

value
  The value to return when checked (default is on).

label
  The label to use for the checkbox (default is the name of the checkbox).

Using named parameters, the syntax is:

```
print $query->checkbox(-name=>'name',
                       -checked=>'checked',
                       -value=>'value',
                       -label=>'label',
                       -onClick=>function);
```

-onClick=>*function*
  Browser should execute *function* when the user clicks on any checkbox in the group.

checkbox_group

print *$query*->checkbox_group('*name*', \@*list* [,*selected* true',\%*labelhash*])

Generates a list of checkbox elements.

name
  The name to assign the input to (required).

→

\@*list*

An array reference with the list items. You can also use an anonymous array reference.

selected

The menu item(s) to be initially selected (default is that nothing is selected). This can be a single value or a reference to an array of values.

true

Insert newlines between the checkboxes.

\%*labelhash*

A hash reference listing labels for each list item. Default is the list text itself. See popup_menu for an example.

Using named parameters, the syntax is:

```
print $query->checkbox_group(-name=>'name',
                             -values=>\@list,
                             -default=>selected,
                             -linebreak=>'true',
                             -labels=>\%labelhash,
                             -columns=>n,
                             -columnheader=>'string',
                             -rows=>m,
                             -rowheader=>'string',
                             -onClick=>function);
```

`-columns=>`*n*

The number of columns to use.

`-columnheader=>'`*string*`'`

A header for the column.

`-rows=`*m*

The number of rows to use. If omitted and `-columns` is specified, the rows are calculated for you.

`-rowheader=>'`*string*`'`

A header for the row.

`-onClick=>`*function*

Browser should execute *function* when the user clicks on any checkbox in the group.

cookie

$cookie=$query->`cookie('`*name*`')`

Defines or retrieves a cookie. See also header.

name

Name of the cookie (required).

Using named parameters, the syntax is:

```
$cookie = $query->cookie(-name=>'name',
                         -value=>'value',
                         -expires=>'expcode',
```

→

```
                           -path=>'partial_url',
                           -domain=>'domain_name',
                           -secure=>1);
print $query->header(-cookie=>$cookie);
```

-value=>'*value*'
: A value to assign to the cookie. You can supply a scalar value, or a reference to an array or hash. If omitted, a cookie is retrieved rather than defined.

-expires=>*expcode*
: Specify an expiration timestamp (such as `+3d` for 3 days). Values for *expcode* are:

  *n*s *n* seconds

  *n*m *n* minutes

  *n*h *n* hours

  *n*d *n* days

  *n*M *n* months

  *n*Y *n* years

  day_of_week, dd-MMM-YY hh:mm:ss GMT
  : At the specified time

  now
  : Expire immediately.

-path=>'*partial_url*'
: The partial URL for which the cookie is valid. Default is the current URL.

-domain=>'*domain_name*'
: The domain for which the cookie is valid.

-secure=>1
: Only use this cookie for a secure session.

defaults

`print $query->defaults('label')`

Generates a button that resets the form to its defaults. See also `reset`.

label
: The label to use for the button. If omitted, the label is "Defaults."

delete

`$query->delete('parameter')`

Deletes a parameter.

parameter
: The parameter to delete.

CGI and Perl

delete_all

$query->delete_all()

Deletes the entire CGI object.

dump

print *$query->dump*([true])

Dumps all name/value pairs as an HTML list.

true
: If specified, print as plain text.

end_html

print $query->end_html()

Ends an HTML document.

filefield

print *$query*->filefield(*'name'*
[,*'default'*,*size*,*maxlength*])

Generates a file upload field for Netscape browsers.

name
: The filename to assign the supplied file contents to (required).

default
: The initial value (filename) to place in the text field.

size
: The size of the text field (in characters).

maxlength
: The maximum length of the text field (in characters).

Using named parameters, the syntax is:

```
print $query->textfield(-name=>'name',
                        -default=>'value',
                        -size=>size,
                        -maxlength=>maxlength,
                        -override=>1,
                        -onChange=>function,
                        -onFocus=>function,
                        -onBlur=>function,
                        -onSelect=>function);
```

-override=>1
: Text field should not inherit its value from a previous invocation of the script.

→

-onChange=>*function*

Browser should execute *function* when the user changes the text field.

-onFocus=>*function*

Browser should execute *function* when the focus is on the text field.

-onBlur=>*function*

Browser should execute *function* when the focus leaves the text field.

-onSelect=>*function*

Browser should execute *function* when the user changes a selected portion of the text field.

header

print *$query*->header([*content_type*, *status*, *headers*])

Generates the HTTP header for the document.

content_type

The content type to return. Default is text/html.

status

The HTTP status code and description to return. Default is 200 OK.

headers

Additional headers to include, such as Content-Length: 123.

Using named parameters, the syntax is:

```
print $query->header(-type=>'content_type',
                     -nph=>1,
                     -status=>'status_code',
                     -expires=>'expcode',
                     -cookie=>'cookie',
                     -target=>'frame',
                     -header=>'value');
```

-type=>*content_type*

Specify the content type.

-nph=>1

Use headers for a no-parse-header script.

-status=>*status_code*

Specify the status code.

-expires=>*expcode*

Specify an expiration timestamp (such as +3d for 3 days). Values for *expcode* are:

*n*s   *n* seconds

*n*m   *n* minutes

→

*n*h *n* hours

*n*d *n* days

*n*M *n* months

*n*Y *n* years

day_of_week, dd-MMM-YY hh:mm:ss GMT
    At the specified time

now
    Expire immediately.

-cookie=>*cookie*
    Specify a cookie. The cookie may be a scalar value or an array reference.

-header=>*value*
    Specify any HTTP header.

-target=>*frame*
    Write to specified frame.

---

hidden

`print $query->hidden('name', 'value' [,'value'... ])`

Generates a hidden text field.

name
    The name to give the value (required).

value
    The value to assign to *name*. Multiple values can be specified.

Using named parameters, the syntax is:

```
print $query->hidden(-name=>'name',
                     -default=>'value');
```

With named parameters, the value can also be represented as a reference to an array, such as:

```
print $query->hidden(-name=>'name',
                     -default=>['value1', 'value2', ... ]);
```

---

image_button

`print $query->image_button('name','url' [,'align'])`

Generates a clickable image map.

name
    The name to use. When clicked, the *x,y* position is returned as *name.x* and *name.y*, respectively.

url The URL of the image for the image map.

→

align
The alignment type. May be TOP, BOTTOM, or MIDDLE.

Using named parameters, the syntax is:

```
print $query->image_button(-name=>'name',
                           -src=>'url',
                           -align=>'align',
                           -onClick=>function);
```

-onClick=>*function*
Browser should execute *function* when the user clicks on the image.

import_names

`$query->import_names('package')`

Creates variables in the specified package. Called `import` in older versions of CGI.pm.

package
The package to import names into.

isindex

`print $query->isindex([action])`

Generates an <ISINDEX> tag.

action
The URL of the index script. Default is the current URL.

Using named parameters, the syntax is:

```
print $query->isindex(-action=>$action);
```

keywords

`@keyarray = $query->keywords()`

Retrieves keywords from an <ISINDEX> search.

@keyarray
The array to contain the retrieved keywords.

nph

`nph(1)`

Treats a CGI script as a no-parsed-header (NPH) script.

→

param

@name = *$query*->param([*parameter*[*newvalue1*, *newvalue2*, . . .]])

Gets or sets parameter names.

@name
: The array to contain the parameter names.

parameter
: An optional single parameter to fetch. When used with no arguments, param returns a list of all known parameter names.

newvalue1, newvalue2, ...
: The optional new values to assign to the parameter.

Using named parameters, the syntax is:

```
$query->param(-name=>'parameter',
              -value=>'newvalue');
```

or:

```
$query->param(-name=>'parameter',
              -values=>'newvalue1', 'newvalue2', ...);
```

password_field

print *$query*->password_field('*name*' [,'*value*',*size*,*maxlength*])

Generates a password input field.

name
: The name to assign the input to (required).

value
: The default password to place in the password field.

size
: The size of the password field (in characters).

maxlength
: The maximum length of the password field (in characters).

Using named parameters, the syntax is:

```
print $query->password_field(-name=>'name',
                             -default=>'value',
                             -size=>size,
                             -maxlength=>maxlength,
                             -override=>1,
                             -onChange=>function,
                             -onFocus=>function,
                             -onBlur=>function,
                             -onSelect=>function);
```

→

-override=>1
: Text field should not inherit its value from a previous invocation of the script.

-onChange=>*function*
: Browser should execute *function* when the user changes the text field.

-onFocus=>*function*
: Browser should execute *function* when the focus is on on the text field.

-onBlur=>*function*
: Browser should execute *function* when the focus leaves the text field.

-onSelect=>*function*
: Browser should execute *function* when the user changes a selected portion of the text field.

path_info

`path_info()`

Returns extra path information.

path_translated

`path_translated()`

Returns translated extra path information.

popup_menu

print *$query*->popup_menu(*'name'*, \@*array* [,*'selected'*, \%*labelhash*])

Generates a popup menu.

name
: The name to assign the input to (required).

\@*array*
: An array reference listing the menu items. You can also use an anonymous array reference (see the second example).

selected
: The menu item to be initially selected (default is first menu item or the item selected in previous queries).

\%*labelhash*
: A hash reference listing labels for each menu item. Default is menu item text. For example:

```
%labels = ('UPS'=>'United Parcel Service (UPS)',
           'FedExO'=>'Federal Express Overnight - 10AM delivery',
```

→

CGI and Perl

```
                'FedExS'=>'Federal Express Standard - 2PM delivery',
                'FedEx2'=>'Federal Express 2nd Day Delivery');

    print $query->popup_menu('delivery_method',
                             ['UPS', 'FedExO', 'FedExS', 'FedEx2'],
                             'FedExO',
                             \%labels);
```

Using named parameters, the syntax is:

```
print $query->popup_menu(-name=>'name',
                         -values=>\@array,
                         -default=>'selected',
                         -labels=>\%labelhash,
                         -onChange=>function,
                         -onFocus=>function,
                         -onBlur=>function);
```

-onChange=>*function*
: Browser should execute *function* when the user changes the text field.

-onFocus=>*function*
: Browser should execute *function* when the focus is on the text field.

-onBlur=>*function*
: Browser should execute *function* when the focus leaves the text field.

radio_group

print *$query*->radio_group(*'name'*, \\@*list* [, *selected*, 'true', \\%*label*])

Generates a set of radio buttons.

name
: The name to assign the input to (required).

\@*list*
: An array reference with the list items. You can also use an anonymous array reference.

selected
: The menu item to be initially selected.

true
: Insert newlines between radio buttons.

\%*label*
: A hash reference listing labels for each list item. Default is the list text itself. See popup_menu for an example.

Using named parameters, the syntax is:

```
print $query->radio_group(-name=>'name',
                          -values=>\@list,
                          -default=>'selected',
```

→

```
                              -linebreak=>'true',
                              -labels=>\%labelhash,
                              -columns=>n,
                              -columnheader=>'string',
                              -rows=>m,
                              -rowheader=>'string');
```

`-columns=>n`
: The number of columns to use.

`-columnheader=>'string'`
: A header for the column.

`-rows=m`
: The number of rows to use. If omitted and `-columns` is specified, the rows are calculated for you.

`-rowheader=>'string'`
: A header for the row.

raw_cookie

`raw_cookie()`

Returns the value of the HTTP_COOKIE header.

ReadParse

`ReadParse()`

Creates a hash named `%in` containing query information. Used for backward compatibility with the Perl4 *cgi-lib.pl.*

redirect

`print $query->redirect('url')`

Generates a header for redirecting the browser.

url The absolute URL to redirect to.

Using named parameters, the syntax is:

```
print $query->redirect(-uri=>'url',
                       -nph=>1);
```

referer

`referer()`

Returns the referring URL.

remote_host

```
remote_host()
```

Returns the remote hostname or IP address, depending on the configuration of the server.

remote_user

```
remote_user()
```

Returns the username supplied for authorization.

request_method

```
request_method()
```

Returns the request method.

reset

```
print $query->reset
```

Generates a button that resets the form to its initial values. See also `defaults`.

save

```
$query->save(filehandle)
```

Saves the form to the specified filehandle, to be read back with the `new` constructor.

filehandle
: The filehandle to save the file to.

script_name

```
script_name()
```

Returns the current partial URL.

scrolling_list

```
print $query->scrolling_list('name',\@list
[,selected,size,'true',\%labelhash])
```

Generates a scrolling list.

name
: The name to assign the input to (required).

\@list
: An array reference with the list items. You can also use an anonymous array reference.

→

selected

The menu item(s) to be initially selected (default is that nothing is selected). This can be a single value or a reference to a list of values.

size

The number of elements to display in the list box.

true

Allow multiple selections.

\%*labelhash*

A hash reference listing labels for each list item. Default is the list text itself. See popup_menu for an example.

Using named parameters, the syntax is:

```
print $query->scrolling_list(-name=>'name',
                             -values=>\@listarray,
                             -default=>selected,
                             -size=>size,
                             -multiple=>'true',
                             -labels=>\%labelhash,
                             -onChange=>function,
                             -onFocus=>function,
                             -onBlur=>function);
```

-onChange=>*function*

Browser should execute *function* when the user changes the text field.

-onFocus=>*function*

Browser should execute *function* when the focus is on the text field.

-onBlur=>*function*

Browser should execute *function* when the focus leaves the text field.

CGI and Perl

self_url

`$url = $query->self_url`

Returns the URL of the current script with all its state information intact.

start_html

`print $query->start_html(['title', 'email', 'base', 'attribute='value'])`

Generates <HTML> and <BODY> tags.

title

The title of the page.

email

The author's email address.

→

base
Whether to use a <BASE> tag in the header.

attribute='value'
Specifies an attribute to the <BODY> tag.

Using named parameters, the syntax is:

```
print $query->start_html(-title=>'title',
                         -author=>'email_address',
                         -base=>'true',
                         -xbase=>'url',
                         -meta=>{'metatag1'=>'value1',
                                 'metatag2'=>'value2'},
                         -script=>'$script',
                         -onLoad=>'$function',
                         -onUnload=>'$function',
                         -attribute=>'value');
```

`-title=>'title'`
Specifies the title of the page.

`-author=>'email_address'`
Specifies the author's email address.

`-xbase=>'url'`
Provides an HREF for the <BASE> tag. Default is the current location.

`-meta=>{'metatag1'=>'value1', . . . }`
Adds arbitrary meta information to the header as a reference to a hash. Valid tags are:

`keywords`
Keywords for this document.

`copyright`
Description for this document.

`attribute=>'value'`
Specify an attribute to the <BODY> tag.

`-script=>'$script'`
Specify a JavaScript script to be embedded within a <SCRIPT> block.

`-onLoad=>'$function'`
Browser should execute the specified function upon entering the page.

`-onUnload=>'$function'`
Browser should execute the specified function upon leaving the page.

startform

`print $query->startform([method, action, encoding])`

Generates a <FORM> tag.

→

method

The request method for the form. Values are:

POST

Use the POST method (default).

GET

Use the GET method.

action

The URL of the CGI script. Default is the current URL.

encoding

The encoding scheme. Possible values are `application/x-www-form-urlencoded` and `multipart/form-data`.

Using named parameters, the syntax is:

```
print $query->startform(-method=>$method,
                        -action=>$action,
                        -encoding=>$encoding,
                        -name=>$name,
                        -target=>frame,
                        -onSubmit=>function);
```

`-name=>`*name*

Names the form for identification by JavaScript functions.

`-target=>`*frame*

Writes to the specified frame.

`-onSubmit=>`*function*

A JavaScript function that the browser should execute upon submitting the form.

start_multipart_form

`print $query->start_multipart_form([method, action])`

Generates <HTML> and <BODY> tags. Same as `startform` but assumes `multipart/form-data` encoding as the default.

submit

`print $query->submit([ 'label','value' ])`

Generates a submit button.

label

The label to use for the button.

value

The value to return when the form is submitted.

Using named parameters, the syntax is:

```
print $query->submit(-name=>'name',
                     -value=>'value',
                     -onClick=>function);
```

→

-onClick=>*function*

Browser should execute *function* when the user clicks the Submit button.

textarea

```
print $query->textarea('name' [,'value',rows,columns ])
```

Generates a large multiline text input box.

name

The name to assign the input to (required).

value

The initial value to place into the text input box.

rows

The number of rows to display.

columns

The number of columns to display.

Using named parameters, the syntax is:

```
print $query->textarea(-name=>'name',
                       -default=>'value',
                       -rows=>rows,
                       -columns=>columns,
                       -override=>1,
                       -onChange=>function,
                       -onFocus=>function,
                       -onBlur=>function,
                       -onSelect=>function);
```

-override=>1

Text field should not inherit its value from a previous invocation of the script.

-onChange=>*function*

Browser should execute *function* when the user changes the text field.

-onFocus=>*function*

Browser should execute *function* when the focus is on on the text field.

-onBlur=>*function*

Browser should execute *function* when the focus leaves the text field.

-onSelect=>*function*

Browser should execute *function* when the user changes a selected portion of the text field.

textfield

`print $query->textfield('name' [,'value', size, maxlength])`

Generates a text input field.

name
: The name to assign the input to (required).

value
: The initial value to place in the text field.

size
: The size of the text field (in characters).

maxlength
: The maximum length of the text field (in characters).

Using named parameters, the syntax is:

```
print $query->textfield(-name=>'name',
                        -default=>'value',
                        -size=>size,
                        -maxlength=>maxlength,
                        -override=>1,
                        -onChange=>function,
                        -onFocus=>function,
                        -onBlur=>function,
                        -onSelect=>function);
```

`-override=>1`
: Text field should not inherit its value from a previous invocation of the script.

`-onChange=>function`
: Browser should execute *function* when the user changes the text field.

`-onFocus=>function`
: Browser should execute *function* when the focus is on the text field.

`-onBlur=>function`
: Browser should execute *function* when the focus leaves the text field.

`-onSelect=>function`
: Browser should execute *function* when the user changes a selected portion of the text field.

url

`$url = $query->url`

Returns a URL of the current script without query information.

use_named_parameters

`use_named_parameters()`

Specifies that functions should take named parameters.

user_agent

`$query->user_agent( [string] )`

Returns the value of the HTTP_USER_AGENT header.

string
: If specified, only returns headers matching the specified string.

user_name

`user_name()`

Returns the remote user's login name; unreliable.

CHAPTER 15

Web Server Programming with mod_perl

A common criticism of CGI is that it requires forking extra processes each time a script is executed. If you have only a few hits an hour, or even a few hits a minute, this isn't a big deal. But for a high-traffic site, lots of CGI scripts repeatedly spawning can have an unfortunate effect on the machine running the web server. The CGI scripts will be slow, the web server will be slow, and other processes on the machine will come to a crawl.

One solution to this problem is *mod_perl. mod_perl*, written by Doug MacEachern and distributed under CPAN, embeds the Perl interpreter directly into the web server. The effect is that your CGI scripts are precompiled by the server and executed without forking, thus running much more quickly and efficiently. Furthermore, CGI efficiency is only one facet of *mod_perl*. Since *mod_perl* is a complete Apache/Perl hybrid, other benefits to *mod_perl* include:

- Writing server side includes in Perl
- Embedding Perl code into the Apache configuration files
- Writing complete Apache modules in Perl

Design of mod_perl

mod_perl is not a Perl module. It is a module of the Apache server, which is currently the most commonly used web server. With *mod_perl*, you can use Apache configuration directives not only to process CGI scripts much more efficiently, but also to handle all stages in processing a server request.

mod_perl embeds a copy of the Perl interpreter into the Apache *httpd* executable, providing complete access to Perl functionality within Apache. This enables a set of *mod_perl*-specific configuration directives, all of which start with the string `Perl*`. Most of these directives are used to specify handlers for various stages of the request, but not all. In addition, *mod_perl* lets you embed Perl code into your

Apache configuration files (within `<Perl> ... </Perl>` directives) and allows you to use Perl for server side includes.

It may be obvious that sticking a large program into another large program makes a very, very large program. *mod_perl* certainly makes *httpd* significantly bigger. If you have limited memory capacity, *mod_perl* may not be for you. There are several ways to minimize the size of Apache with *mod_perl* (which you can find in the *mod_perl* manpage or the FAQs), ranging from fiddling with Apache configuration directives to building Perl with reduced memory consumption.

Installing mod_perl

If you already have Apache installed on your machine, you will have to rebuild it with *mod_perl*. You can get the source for both Apache and *mod_perl* from *http://www.apache.org/*. (You can also get *mod_perl* from CPAN.) If there isn't already an Apache *httpd* in the Apache source tree, you must build one. Then build *mod_perl* as directed in the *INSTALL* file for the *mod_perl* distribution.

As we've mentioned, *mod_perl* allows you to hook in Perl modules as handlers for various stages of a request. By default, however, the only callback hook that is enabled is `PerlHandler`, which is the one that processes content (i.e., a CGI document). If you want to use other hooks—for example, to extend Apache's logging facilities via the `PerlLogHandler` directive; you need to specify it at build time as directed in the *INSTALL* file. For example:

```
% perl Makefile.PL PERL_LOG=1
```

The *mod_perl* Makefile replaces the *httpd* in the Apache source tree with a Perl-enabled one. When you install *mod_perl*, it installs not only the new *httpd* in your system area, but also several Perl modules, including Apache::Registry.

At the time of this writing, both Apache and *mod_perl* are being ported to Win32. However, *mod_perl* runs only with the standard Perl Win32 port (not with ActiveState's). The *INSTALL.win32* file contains the instructions for installing *mod_perl* under Win32.

mod_perl Handlers

To understand *mod_perl*, you should understand how the Apache server works. When Apache receives a request, it processes it in several stages. First, it translates the URL to the associated resource (i.e., filename, CGI script, etc.) on the server machine. Then it checks to see if the user is authorized to access that resource, perhaps by requesting and checking an ID and password. Once the user has passed inspection, the server figures out what kind of data it's sending back (e.g., it decides a file ending in *.html* is probably a `text/html` file), creates some headers, and sends those headers back to the client with the resource itself. When all is said and done, the server makes a log entry.

At each stage of this process, Apache looks for routines to "handle" the request. Apache supplies its own handlers; for example, one of the default handlers is `cgi-script`, often seen applied to */cgi-bin*:

```
<Location /cgi-bin>
  ...
SetHandler cgi-script
  ...
</Location>
```

mod_perl allows you to write your own handlers in Perl, by embedding the Perl runtime library directly into the Apache *httpd* server executable. To use *mod_perl* for CGI (which is all that most people want to do with it), assign the **SetHandler** directive to **perl-script**, and then assign the *mod_perl*-specific **PerlHandler** directive to a special Perl module called Apache::Registry:

```
SetHandler perl-script
PerlHandler Apache::Registry
```

PerlHandler is the *mod_perl* handler for the content retrieval stage of the transaction. To use other handlers, you don't need to reassign **SetHandler**. For example, to identify a handler for the logging stage of the request:

```
<Location /snoop/>
PerlLogHandler Apache::DumpHeaders
</Location>
```

In order for this to work, *mod_perl* must be built with the logging hooks enabled (as described in the previous section), and the Apache::DumpHeaders module must be installed. *mod_perl* looks in Apache::DumpHeaders for a routine called **handler()** and executes it as the logging handler for that resource.

The following is a list of each of the handler directives that can be enabled by *mod_perl* and the stages that each is used for. Only **PerlHandler** is enabled by default.

Handler	*Purpose*
PerlAccessHandler	Access stage
PerlAuthenHandler	Authentication stage
PerlAuthzHandler	Authorization stage
PerlChildInitHandler	Child initialization stage
PerlChildExitHandler	Child termination stage
PerlCleanupHandler	Cleanup stage
PerlFixupHandler	Fixup stage
PerlHandler	Response stage
PerlHeaderParserHandler	Header-parsing stage
PerlInitHandler	Initialization
PerlLogHandler	Logging stage
PerlPostReadRequestHandler	Post-request stage
PerlTransHandler	Translation stage
PerlTypeHandler	Type-handling stage

You can write your own handlers for each of these stages. But there are also dozens of modules you can download from CPAN, some of which are listed at the end of this chapter.

Running CGI Scripts with mod_perl

What most people want to do with *mod_perl* is improve CGI performance. The *mod_perl* installation assumes this request by enabling the `PerlHandler` callback hook by default and by installing the Apache::Registry module. `PerlHandler` is the handler used for the content retrieval stage of the server transaction. Apache::Registry is the Perl module that emulates the CGI environment so you can use "standard" Perl CGI scripts with *mod_perl* without having to rewrite them (much). This is by far the cheapest way to get improved CGI performance.

With Apache::Registry, each individual CGI program is compiled and cached the first time it is called (or whenever it is changed) and remains available for all subsequent instances of that CGI script. This process avoids the costs of startup time.

Whereas most CGI scripts are kept in */cgi-bin/*, scripts that use Apache::Registry are placed in a separate directory, e.g., */perl-bin/*. The *access.conf* Apache configuration file needs to point to this directory by setting an alias and defining a handler for this new location:

```
Alias /perl-bin/ /usr/local/apache/perl-bin/

<Location /perl-bin>
SetHandler perl-script
PerlHandler Apache::Registry
PerlSendHeader On
Options ExecCGI
</Location>
```

Instead of the `cgi-script` handler, use the `perl-script` handler to give control to *mod_perl*. Next, the `PerlHandler` directive tells *mod_perl* that the Apache::Registry module should be used for serving all files in that directory. `PerlSendHeader` is another *mod_perl*-specific directive; in this case, it tells *mod_perl* to send response lines and common headers; by default, none are sent. (For NPH scripts, you'll want to turn this feature off again.) `Options ExecCGI` is a standard Apache header needed to tell Apache to treat the script as a CGI script.

If you want to load Perl modules in addition to Apache::Registry, use the PerlModule directive:

```
PerlModule CGI
```

If you include this line, you shouldn't need to explicitly `use CGI` in each Perl CGI script anymore, as CGI.pm is loaded directly from the Apache server. Up to 10 modules can be listed with the `PerlModule` directive.

CGI scripts in the new directory should work now. However, if you have problems, the *mod_perl* manpage offers some words of wisdom:

Always `use strict`
: "Standard" CGI scripts start with a clean slate every time. When switching to *mod_perl*, CGI programmers are often surprised to learn how often they take advantage of this fact. `use strict` tells you when your variables haven't been properly declared and might inherit values from previous invocations of the script.

Don't call exit()

Calling exit() at the end of every program is a habit of many programmers. While often totally unnecessary, it usually doesn't hurt... except with *mod_perl*. If you're using *mod_perl* without Apache::Registry, exit() kills the server process. If exit() is the last function call, just remove it. If the structure of your program is such that it is called from the middle of the script, you can put a label at the end of the script and use goto(). There's also an Apache->exit() call you can use if you're really attached to exit().

If you're using Apache::Registry, you don't have to worry about this problem. Apache::Registry is smart enough to override all exit() calls with Apache->exit().

In addition, you should use recent versions of Perl and CGI.pm. You can scan the *mod_perl* documentation for the very latest compatibility news.

Server Side Includes with mod_perl

server side includes (SSI) are tags embedded directly into an HTML file that perform special functions. They are most commonly used for running CGI scripts and displaying the result; most web page counters are performed using SSI.

If you use *mod_perl* with *mod_include* (another Apache server module), you can embed Perl subroutines into SSI directives. For example:

```
<!--#perl sub="sub {print ++Count}" -->
```

The Apache::Include module lets you include entire Apache::Registry scripts:

```
<!--#perl sub="Apache::Include" arg="/perl-bin/counter.pl" -->
```

You could have used standard SSI to include a CGI script for the same purpose, but this way is faster. To use *mod_include* with *mod_perl*, you need to configure *mod_perl* to do so at compile-time.

<Perl> Sections

With *mod_perl*, you can use Perl in Apache configuration files. What this means is that you can make your Apache configuration much more flexible by using conditionals.

Any Perl code in Apache configuration files should be placed between <Perl> and </Perl> directives. This code can define variables and lists used by *mod_perl* to assign the associated Apache configuration directives; for example, assigning the $ServerAdmin variable redefines the ServerAdmin Apache configuration directive.

Suppose you share the same Apache configuration files across multiple servers, and you only want to allow personal directories on one of them. You can use Perl directives like this:

```
<Perl>
if (`hostname` =~ /public/) {
        $UserDir = "public.html";
```

```
} else {
        $UserDir = "DISABLED";
}
1;
</Perl>
```

Directive blocks (such as `<Location> . . . </Location>`) can be represented as a hash. For example:

```
<Perl>
$Location{"/design_dept/"} = {
        DefaultType   => 'image/gif',
        FancyIndexing => 'On'
}
</Perl>
```

Apache:: Modules

Apache::Registry is the most commonly used *mod_perl* module. But there are many more, all available on CPAN. Table 15-1 lists the Apache::* modules and which handler they're designed to be used with, but you should also check the *apache-modlist.html* file on CPAN for the very latest listing.

Table 15-1: Apache::Modules

PerlHandler

Apache::CallHandler	Map filenames to subroutine calls
Apache::Dir	Control directory indexing
Apache::Embperl	Embed Perl code in HTML files
Apache::ePerl	Embedded Perl (ePerl) emulation
Apache::FTP	Emulate an FTP proxy
Apache::GzipChain	Compresse output from another handler
Apache::JavaScript	Generate JavaScript code
Apache::OutputChain	Chain multiple handlers via "filter" modules
Apache::PassFile	Send files via OutputChain
Apache::Registry	Run unaltered CGI scripts
Apache::RobotRules	Enforce *robots.txt* rules
Apache::Sandwich	Add per-directory headers and footers
Apache::VhostSandwich	Add headers and footers for virtual hosts
Apache::SSI	Implement server side includes in Perl
Apache::Stage	Manage a document staging directory
Apache::WDB	Query databases via DBI

PerlHeaderParserHandler

Apache::AgentDeny	Deny abusive clients

Table 15-1: Apache::Modules (continued)

PerlAuthenHandler

Apache::Authen	Authenticate users
Apache::AuthCookie	Authenticate and authorize users via cookies
Apache::AuthenDBI	Authenticate via Perl's DBI
Apache::AuthExpire	Expire authentication credentials
Apache::AuthenGSS	Authenticate users with Generic Security Service
Apache::AuthenLDAP	Authenticate users with LDAP
Apache::AuthNIS	Authenticate users with NIS
Apache::BasicCookieAuth	Accept cookie or basic authentication credentials
Apache::DBILogin	Authenticate using a backend database
Apache::DCELogin	Authenticate within a DCE login context
Apache::AuthAny	Authenticate with any username/password

PerlAuthzHandler

Apache::AuthCookie	Authenticate and authorize via cookies
Apache::AuthzAge	Authorize based on age
Apache::AuthzDCE	Authorize based on DFS/DCE ACL
Apache::AuthzDBI	Authorize groups via DBI
Apache::AuthNIS	Authenticate and authorize via NIS
Apache::RoleAuthz	Role-based authorization

PerlAccessHandler

Apache::AccessLimitNum	Limit user access by the number of requests
Apache::DayLimit	Limit access based on the day of the week
Apache::RobotLimit	Limit access of robots

PerlTypeHandler

Apache::AcceptLanguage	Send file types based on user's language preference

PerlTransHandler

Apache::DynaRPC	Translate URIs into RPCs
Apache::Junction	Mount remote web-server namespace
Apache::LowerCaseGETs	Translate to lowercase URIs as needed
Apache::MsqlProxy	Translate URIs into mSQL queries
Apache::ProxyPassThru	Skeleton for vanilla proxy
Apache::ProxyCache	Caching proxy

Table 15-1: Apache::Modules (continued)

PerlFixupHandler

Apache::HttpEquiv	Convert HTML HTTP-EQUIV tags to HTTP headers
Apache::Timeit	Benchmark Perl handlers

PerlLogHandler

Apache::DumpHeaders	Display HTTP transaction headers
Apache::Traffic	Log the number of bytes transferred on a per-user basis
Apache::WatchDog	Look for problematic URIs

PerlChildInitHandler

Apache::Resource	Limit resources used by *httpd* children

Server Configuration

Apache::ConfigLDAP	Configure server via LDAP and `<Perl>` sections
Apache::ConfigDBI	Configure server via DBI and `<Perl>` sections
Apache::ModuleConfig	Interface to configuration API
Apache::PerlSections	Utilities for `<Perl>` sections
Apache::httpd_conf	Methods to configure and run an *httpd*
Apache::src	Methods for finding and reading bits of source

Database

Apache::DBI	Manage persistent DBI connections
Apache::Sybase	Manage persistent DBlib connections
Apache::Mysql	Manage persistent mysql connections

Interfaces and Integration with Various Apache C Modules

Apache::Constants	Constants defined in *httpd.h*
Apache::Include	Enable use of Apache::Registry scripts within SSI with *mod_include*
Apache::Global	Give access to server global variables
Apache::LogError	Give an interface to *aplog_error*
Apache::LogFile	Give an interface to Apache's piped logs, etc.
Apache::Mime	Give an interface to *mod_mime* functionality
Apache::Module	Give an interface to Apache C module structures
Apache::Options	Import Apache::Constants "options"
Apache::Scoreboard	Give an interface to scoreboard API
Apache::Servlet	Give an interface to the Java Servlet engine
Apache::Sfio	Give an interface to `r->connection->client->sf*`

Table 15-1: Apache::Modules (continued)

Development and Debug Tools

Apache::Debug	Provide debugging utilities to *mod_perl*
Apache::DProf	Hook Devel::DProf into *mod_perl*
Apache::FakeRequest	Implement Apache methods offline
Apache::Peek	Emulate Devel::Peek for *mod_perl*
Apache::SawAmpersand	Make sure no one is using `$&`, `$'`, or `` $` ``
Apache::StatINC	Reloads `used` or `required` files when updated
Apache::Status	Get information about loaded modules
Apache::Symbol	Support symbols
Apache::test	Define handy routines for *make test* scripts

Miscellaneous

Apache::Byterun	Run Perl bytecode modules
Apache::Mmap	Share data via Mmap module
Apache::Persistent	Store data via IPC::, DBI, or disk
Apache::PUT	Handler for the HTTP PUT method
Apache::RegistryLoader	Apache::Registry startup script loader
Apache::Safe	Adaptation of *safecgiperl*
Apache::Session	Maintain client <-> *httpd* session/state
Apache::SIG	Signal handlers for *mod_perl*
Apache::State	Powerful state engine

PART VI

PHP

CHAPTER 16

PHP

PHP is a server-side, HTML-embedded, cross-platform scripting language—quite a mouthful. In simpler terms, PHP provides a way for you to put instructions in your HTML files to create dynamic content. These instructions are read and parsed by the web server; they never actually make it to the browser that is displaying the page. The web server replaces your PHP code with the content that the code was written to produce.

PHP can be configured to run either as a server module or as a standalone CGI script. At the time of this writing, the server-module version is production-ready for the Apache web server only on Unix systems. The CGI version runs with all web servers on both Unix and Windows 95/98/NT. On the Windows platform, the server module is being developed to work with ISAPI, NSAPI, and WSAPI, which means the server module will eventually work with Microsoft's IIS, Netscape's Enterprise Server, and O'Reilly & Associates's WebSite. See *http://www.php.net* for availability details.

The PHP language itself borrows concepts from other common languages, such as C and Perl. If you have some experience with one of these languages, you should feel right at home with PHP. In addition to the core language, PHP provides a wide variety of functions that support everything from array manipulation to regular-expression support.

Database connectivity is one popular use for PHP. PHP supports a large number of databases natively, and many others are accessible through PHP's ODBC functions. Through this database connectivity, it is possible, for example, to take a company's database of products and write a web interface to it using PHP.

This chapter provides an overview of the core PHP language and contains summaries of all the functions available in PHP. The material covers PHP 3.0.

Configuration

When you use PHP as an Apache module, PHP processing is triggered by a special MIME type. This is defined in the Apache configuration file with the line:

```
AddType application/x-httpd-php3 .php3
```

This tells Apache to treat all files that end with that *.php3* extension as PHP files, which means that any file with that extension is parsed for PHP tags. The actual extension is completely arbitrary, and you are free to change it to whatever you wish to use.

When you run PHP as a CGI script (with any web server), PHP processing is still triggered by this special MIME type, but a bit more work is needed. The web server needs to know that it has to redirect the request for the PHP MIME type to the CGI version of PHP. With ApacheNT, for example, this redirect is done with a set of configuration lines like the following:

```
ScriptAlias /php3/ "/path-to-php-dir/php.exe"
AddType application/x-httpd-php3 .php3
Action application/x-httpd-php3 "/php3/php.exe"
```

For IIS, this redirect is set up through the Windows registry. Refer to the PHP installation instructions for full details.

PHP has a number of compile-time configuration options. The various major modules, such as the Oracle database connectivity module, have to be enabled at this time. In PHP 3.1, the various major modules can be compiled as dynamic modules and optionally loaded at runtime.

At runtime, most aspects of PHP can be controlled with the *php3.ini* file. For the Apache module version of PHP, this file is read only when the server is started or reinitialized. Changes to this file should be treated the same as changes to Apache's own configuration files. In other words, if you make a change, you need to send your Apache server an HUP or a USR1 signal before the change will take effect.

Many aspects of PHP can also be controlled on a per-directory level (or even per-location or per-request) when using the Apache module version. Most of the directives available in the *php3.ini* file are also available as native Apache directives. The name of a particular directive is the *php3.ini* name with *php3_* prepended. For a list of all available Apache directives, run your Apache *httpd* binary with the *-h* switch.

Embedding PHP in HTML

You embed PHP code into a standard HTML page. For example, here's how you can dynamically generate the title of an HTML document:

```
<HTML><HEAD><TITLE><?echo $title?></TITLE></HEAD>-..
```

The `<?echo $title?>` portion of the document is replaced by the contents of the `$title` PHP variable. `echo` is a basic language statement you can use to output data.

There are a few different ways to embed your PHP code. As you just saw, you can put PHP code between <? and ?> tags:

```
<? echo "Hello World"; ?>
```

This style is the most common way to embed PHP, but it is a problem if your PHP code needs to coexist with XML, as XML may use that tagging style itself. If this is the case, you can turn off this style in the *php3.ini* file with the `short_open_tag` directive. Another way to embed PHP code is within <?php and ?> tags:

```
<?php echo "Hello World"; ?>
```

This style is always available and is recommended when your PHP code needs to be portable to many different systems. Embedding PHP within `<SCRIPT>` tags is another style that is always available:

```
<SCRIPT LANGUAGE="php"> echo "Hello World"; </SCRIPT>
```

One final style, where the code is between `<%` and `%>` tags, is disabled by default:

```
<% echo "Hello World"; %>
```

You can turn on this style with the `asp_tags` directive in your *php3.ini* file. The style is most useful when you are using Microsoft FrontPage or another HTML authoring tool that prefers that tag style for HTML-embedded scripts.

You can embed multiple statements by separating them with semicolons:

```
<?
echo "Hello World";
echo "A second statement";
?>
```

It is legal to switch back and forth between HTML and PHP at any time. For example, if you want to output 100 `<BR>` tags for some reason, do it this way:

```
<? for($i=0; $i<100; $i++) { ?>
<BR>
<? } ?>
```

When you embed PHP code in an HTML file, you need to use the *.php3* file extension for that file, so that your web server knows to send the file to PHP for processing. Or, if you have configured your web server to use a different extension for PHP files, use that extension instead.

When you have PHP code embedded in an HTML page, you can think of that page as being a PHP program. The bits and pieces of HTML and PHP combine to provide the functionality of the program. A collection of pages that contain programs can be thought of as a web application.

Including Files

A very important feature of PHP is its ability to include files. These files may contain additional PHP tags. When you are designing a web application, it can be useful to break out some common components and place them in a single file. This makes it much easier to later change certain aspects in one place and have it take effect across the entire application. To include a file, use the `include` keyword:

```
<?
$title="My Cool Web Application";
include "header.inc";
?>
```

The *header.inc* file might look as follows:

```
<HTML><HEAD>
<TITLE><?echo $title?></TITLE>
</HEAD>
```

This example illustrates two important concepts of included files in PHP. First, variables set in the including file are automatically available in the included file. Second, each included file starts out in HTML mode. In other words, if you want to include a file that has PHP code in it, you have to embed that code just as you would any PHP code.

Language Syntax

Variable names in PHP are case-sensitive. That means that `$A` and `$a` are two distinct variables. However, function names in PHP are not case-sensitive. This applies to both built-in functions and user-defined functions.

PHP ignores whitespace between tokens. You can use spaces, tabs, and newlines to format and indent your code to make it more readable. PHP statements are terminated by semicolons.

There are three types of comments in PHP:

```
/* C style comments */
// C++ style comments
# Bourne shell-style comments
```

The C++ and Bourne shell-style comments can be inserted anywhere in your code. Everything from the comment characters to the end of the line is ignored. The C-style comment tells PHP to ignore everything from the start of the comment until the end-comment characters are seen. This means that this style of comment can span multiple lines.

Variables

In PHP, all variable names begin with a dollar sign (`$`). The `$` is followed by an alphabetic character or an underscore, optionally followed by a sequence of alphanumeric characters and underscores. Variable names in PHP are case-sensitive. Here are some examples:

```
$i
$counter
$first_name
$_TMP
```

In PHP, unlike in many other languages, you do not have to explicitly declare variables. PHP automatically declares a variable the first time a value is assigned to it. PHP variables are untyped; you can assign a value of any type to a variable.

Dynamic Variables

Sometimes it is useful to set and use variables dynamically. Normally, you assign a variable like this:

```
$var = "hello";
```

Now let's say you want a variable whose name is the value of the `$var` variable. You can do that like this:

```
$$var = "World";
```

PHP parses `$$var` by first dereferencing the innermost variable, meaning that `$var` becomes "hello." The expression that is left is then `$"hello"`, which is just `$hello`. In other words, we have just created a new variable named `hello` and assigned it the value "World." You can nest dynamic variables to an infinite level in PHP, although once you get beyond two levels, it can be very confusing for someone trying to read your code.

There is a special syntax for using dynamic variables inside quoted strings in PHP:

```
echo "Hello ${$var}";
```

This syntax can resolve an ambiguity that occurs when variable arrays are used. Something like `$$var[1]` is ambiguous because it is impossible for PHP to know which level to apply the array index to. `${$var[1]}` tells PHP to dereference the inner level first and apply the array index to the result before dereferencing the outer level. `${$var}[1]`, on the other hand, tells PHP to apply the index to the outer level.

Dynamic variables may not initially seem that useful, but there are times when they can shorten the amount of code you need to write to perform certain tasks. For example, say you have an associative array that looks like this:

```
$array["abc"] = "Hello";
$array["def"] = "World";
```

Associative arrays like this are returned by various functions in the PHP modules. *mysql_fetch_array()* is one example. The indexes in the array usually refer to fields or entity names within the context of the module you are working with. It can be handy to turn these entity names into real PHP variables, so you can refer to them as simply `$abc` and `$def`. This can be done as follows:

```
while(list($index,$value) = each($array)) {
    $$index = $value;
}
```

Data Types

PHP provides three primitive data types: integers, floating-point numbers, and strings. In addition, there are two compound data types: arrays and objects.

Integers

Integers are whole numbers. The range of integers in PHP is equivalent to the range of the long data type in C. On 32-bit platforms, integer values can range from -2,147,483,648 to +2,147,483,647. PHP automatically converts larger values to floating-point numbers if you happen to overflow the range. An integer can be expressed in decimal (base-10), hexadecimal (base-16), or octal (base-8). For example:

```
$decimal=16;
$hex=0x10;
$octal=020;
```

Floating-Point Numbers

Floating-point numbers represent decimal values. The range of floating-point numbers in PHP is equivalent to the range of the double type in C. On most platforms a double can range from 1.7E-308 to 1.7E+308. A double may be expressed either as a regular number with a decimal point or in scientific notation. For example:

```
$var=0.017;
$var=17.0E-3
```

Note that PHP also has a set of functions known as the binary calculator (BC) functions. These functions can manipulate arbitrary precision numbers. You should use these functions when dealing with very large numbers or numbers that require a high degree of precision,

Strings

A string is a sequence of characters. A string can be delimited by single quotes or double quotes:

```
"Hello, World!"
```

Double-quoted strings are subject to variable substitution and escape sequence handling, while single-quoted strings are not. For example:

```
$a="World";
echo "Hello\t$a\n";
```

This displays "Hello" followed by a tab and then "World" followed by a newline. In other words, variable substitution is performed on the variable `$a`, and the escape sequences are converted to their corresponding characters. Contrast that with:

```
echo 'Hello\t$a\n';
```

In this case, the output is exactly `Hello\t$a\n`. There is no variable substitution or handling of escape sequences.

Table 16–1 shows the escape sequences understood by PHP.

Table 16-1: Escape Sequences

Escape Sequence	*Meaning*
`\n`	Newline
`\t`	Tab
`\r`	Carriage return
`\\`	Backslash
`\$`	Dollar sign

Arrays

An array is a compound data type that can contain multiple data values, indexed either numerically or with strings. For example, an array of strings can be written like this:

```
$var[0]="Hello";
$var[1]="World";
```

Note that when you assign array elements like this, you do not have to use consecutive numbers to index the elements.

As a shortcut, PHP allows you to add an element onto the end of an array without specifying an index. For example:

```
$var[] ="Test";
```

PHP picks the next logical numerical index. In this case, the "Test" element is given the index 2 in our `$var` array: if the array has nonconsecutive elements, PHP selects the index value that is one greater than the current highest index value. This auto-indexing feature is most useful when dealing with multiple-choice HTML `<SELECT>` form elements, as we'll see in a later example.

Although we have called strings a primitive data type, it is actually possible to treat a string as a compound data type, where each character in the string can be accessed separately. In other words, you can think of a string as an array of characters, where the first character is at index 0. Thus, you can pick the third character out of a string with:

```
$string[2]
```

Arrays can also be indexed using strings; these kinds of arrays are called *associative arrays*:

```
$var["January"]=1;
$var["February"]=2;
```

In fact, you can use a mix of numerical and string indexes with a single array. That is because internally PHP treats all arrays as hash tables, and the hash, or index, can be whatever you want.

All arrays in PHP can be traversed safely with the following mechanism:

```
while(list($key,$value)=each($array)) {
  echo "array[$key]=$value<br>\n";
}
```

This is the most common way to loop through each element of an array, whether it is a linear or an associative array. PHP provides a number of array manipulation functions; these are detailed in the section "Function Reference."

Objects

An object is a compound data type that can contain any number of variables and functions. PHP's support for objects is very basic; it's designed to make it easy to encapsulate data structures and functions in order to package them into reusable classes. Here's a simple example:

```
class test {
  var $str = "Hello World";
  function init($str) {
    $this->str = $str;
  }
}

$class = new test;
print $class->str;
$class->init("Hello");
print $class->str;
```

This code creates a `test` object using the new operator. Then it sets a variable called `str` within the object. In object-speak, a variable in an object is known as a *property* of that object. The test object also defines a function, known as a *method*, called *init()*. This method uses the special-purpose `$this` variable to change the value of the `str` property within that object.

If you are familiar with object-oriented programming, you should recognize that PHP's implementation is minimal. It should improve somewhat in future versions, however. Right now, PHP does not support multiple inheritance, data protection (or encapsulation), and destructors. PHP does have inheritance and constructors, though.

Boolean Values

Every value in PHP has a boolean truth value (`true` or `false`) associated with it. This value is typically used in control structures, like `if/else` and `for`. The boolean value associated with a data value is determined as follows:

- For an integer or floating-point value, the boolean value is `false` if the value is 0; otherwise the boolean value is `true`.
- For a string value, the boolean value is `false` if the string is empty; otherwise the boolean value is `true`.

- For an array, the boolean value is `false` if the array has no elements; otherwise the boolean value is `true`.
- For an object, the boolean value is `false` if the object has no defined variables or functions; otherwise the boolean value is `true`.

PHP has two built-in keywords, `true` and `false`, where `true` represents the integer value 1, and `false` represents the empty string.

Type Casting

Variables in PHP do not need to be explicitly typed. PHP sets the type when a variable is first used in a script. You can explicitly specify a type using C-style casting. For example:

```
$var = (int) "123abc";
```

Without the `(int)` in this example, PHP creates a string variable. With the explicit cast, however, we have created an integer variable with a value of 123. The following table shows the available casting operators in PHP.

Operators	*Function*
`(int)`, `(integer)`	Cast to an integer
`(real)`, `(double)`, `(float)`	Cast to a floating-point number
`(string)`	Cast to a string
`(array)`	Cast to an array
`(object)`	Cast to an object

Although they are not usually needed, PHP does provide the following built-in functions to check variable types in your program: *gettype()*, *is_long()*, *is_double()*, *is_string()*, *is_array()*, and *is_object()*.

Expressions

An expression is the basic building block of the language. Anything with a value can be thought of as an expression. Examples include:

```
5
5+5
$a
$a==5
sqrt(9)
```

By combining many of these basic expressions, you can build larger and more complex expressions.

Note that the echo statement we've used in numerous examples cannot be part of a complex expression because it does not have a return value. The `print` statement, on the other hand, can be used as part of a complex expression, as it does have a return value. In all other respects, echo and `print` are identical: they output data.

PHP

Operators

Expressions are combined and manipulated using operators. Table 16-2 shows the operators available in PHP, along with their precedence and associativity. The table lists the operators from highest to lowest precedence. These operators should be familiar to you if you have any C, Java, or Perl experience.

Table 16-2: PHP Operators

<table>
<tr><th>Operators</th><th>Precedence</th><th>Associativity</th></tr>
<tr><td>!, ~, ++, --, @ (the casting operators)</td><td>16</td><td>Right</td></tr>
<tr><td>*, /, %</td><td>15</td><td>Left</td></tr>
<tr><td>+, -, .</td><td>14</td><td>Left</td></tr>
<tr><td><<, >></td><td>13</td><td>Left</td></tr>
<tr><td><, <=, >=, ></td><td>12</td><td>Nonassociative</td></tr>
<tr><td>==, !=</td><td>11</td><td>Nonassociative</td></tr>
<tr><td>&</td><td>10</td><td>Left</td></tr>
<tr><td>^</td><td>9</td><td>Left</td></tr>
<tr><td>|</td><td>8</td><td>Left</td></tr>
<tr><td>&&</td><td>7</td><td>Left</td></tr>
<tr><td>||</td><td>6</td><td>Left</td></tr>
<tr><td>? : (conditional operator)</td><td>5</td><td>Left</td></tr>
<tr><td>=, +=, -=, *=, /=, %=, ^=, .=, &=, |=</td><td>4</td><td>Left</td></tr>
<tr><td>And</td><td>3</td><td>Left</td></tr>
<tr><td>Xor</td><td>2</td><td>Left</td></tr>
<tr><td>Or</td><td>1</td><td>Left</td></tr>
</table>

Control Structures

The control structures in PHP are very similar to those used by the C language. Control structures are used to control the logical flow through a PHP script. PHP's control structures have two syntaxes that can be used interchangeably. The first form uses C-style curly braces to enclose statement blocks, while the second style uses a more verbose syntax that includes explicit ending statements. The first style is preferable when the control structure is completely within a PHP code block. The second style is useful when the construct spans a large section of intermixed code and HTML. The two styles are completely interchangeable, however, so it is really a matter of personal preference which one you use.

if

The `if` statement is a standard conditional found in most languages. Here are the two syntaxes for the `if` statement:

```
if(expr) {
  statements
}
elseif(expr) {
  statements
}
else {
  statements
}
```

```
if(expr):
  statements
elseif(expr):
  statements
else:
  statements
endif;
```

The `if` statement causes particular code to be executed if the expression it acts on is `true`. With the first form, you can omit the braces if you need to execute only a single statement.

switch

The `switch` statement can be used in place of a lengthy `if` statement. Here are the two syntaxes for `switch`:

```
switch(expr) {
  case expr:
    statements
    break;
  default:
    statements
    break;
}
```

```
switch(expr):
  case expr:
    statements
    break;
  default:
    statements
    break;
endswitch;
```

The expression for each `case` statement is compared against the `switch` expression, and if they match, the code following that particular case is executed. The `break` keyword signals the end of a particular case; it may be omitted, which causes control to flow into the next case. If none of the `case` expressions matches the switch expression, the default case is executed.

while

The `while` statement is a looping construct that repeatedly executes some code while a particular expression is `true`:

```
while(expr) {
  statements
}
```

```
while(expr):
  statements
endwhile;
```

The `while` expression is checked before the start of each iteration. If the expression evaluates to `true`, the code within the loop is executed. If the expression evaluates to `false`, however, execution skips to the code immediately following the `while` loop. Note that you can omit the curly braces with the first form of the `while` statement if you need to execute only a single statement.

PHP

It is possible to break out of a running loop at any time using the **break** keyword. This stops the current loop, and if control is within a nested set of loops, the next outer loop continues. It is also possible to break out of many levels of nested loops by passing a numerical argument to the **break** statement (**break n**) that specifies the number of nested loops it should break out of. You can skip the rest of a given loop and go onto the next iteration using the **continue** keyword. With **continue n**, you can skip the current iterations of the **n** innermost loops.

do/while

The **do/while** statement is similar to the **while** statement, except that conditional expression is checked at the end of each iteration instead of before it:

```
do {
  statements
} while(expr);
```

Note that due to the order of the parts of this statement, there is only one valid syntax. If you need to execute only a single statement, you can omit the curly braces from the syntax. The **break** and **continue** statements work with this statement in the same way that they do with the **while** statement.

for

A **for** loop is a more complex looping construct than the simple **while** loop:

```
for(start_expr; cond_expr; iter_expr) {
  statements
}

for(start_expr; cond_expr; iter_expr):
  statements
endfor;
```

A **for** loop takes three expressions. The first is the start expression; it is evaluated once when the loop begins. This is generally used for initializing a loop counter. The second expression is a conditional expression that controls the iteration of the loop. This expression is checked prior to each iteration. The third expression, the iterative expression, is evaluated at the end of each iteration and is typically used to increment the loop counter. With the first form of the **for** statement, you can omit the braces if you need to execute only a single statement.

The **break** and **continue** statements work with a **for** loop as they do with a **while** loop, except that **continue** causes the iterative expression to be evaluated before the loop conditional expression is checked.

Functions

A function is a named sequence of code statements that can optionally accept parameters and return a value. A function call is an expression that has a value; its value is the returned value from the function. PHP provides a large number of internal functions. The section "Function Reference" lists all commonly available functions. PHP also supports user-definable functions. To define a function, use the function keyword. For example:

```
function soundcheck($a, $b, $c) {
  return "Testing, $a, $b, $c";
}
```

When you define a function, you need to be careful what name you give it. In particular, you need to make sure that the name does not conflict with any of the internal PHP functions. If you do use a function name that conflicts with an internal function, you get the following error:

```
Fatal error: Can't redeclare already declared function in e on line X
```

After you define a function, you call it by passing in the appropriate arguments. For example:

```
echo soundcheck(4, 5, 6);
```

You can also create functions with optional parameters. To do so, set a default value for each optional parameter in the definition, using C++ style. For example, here's how to make all the parameters to the *soundcheck()* function optional:

```
function soundcheck($a=1, $b=2, $c=3) {
  return "Testing, $a, $b, $c";
}
```

Variable Scope

The scope of a variable refers to where in a program the variable is available. If a variable is defined in the main part of a PHP script (i.e., not inside a function or a class), it is in the global scope. Note that global variables are available only during the current request. The only way to make variables in one page available to subsequent requests to another page is to pass them to that page via cookies, GET method data, or PUT method data. To access a global variable from inside a function, use the global keyword. For example:

```
function test() {
  global $var;
  echo $var;
}
$var="Hello World";
test();
```

The $GLOBALS array is an alternative mechanism for accessing variables in the global scope. This is an associative array of all the variables currently defined in the global scope.

```
function test() {
  echo $GLOBALS["var"];
}
$var="Hello World";
test();
```

Every function has its own scope. When you create a variable inside a function, that variable has *local scope*. In other words, it is available only within the function. In addition, if there is a global variable with the same name as a variable within a function, any changes to the function variable do not affect the value of the global variable.

When you call a function, the arguments passed to the function (if any) are defined as variables within the function, using the parameter names as variable names. Just as with variables created within a function, these parameters are available only within the scope of the function.

Passing Arguments

There are two ways you can pass arguments to a function: by value and by reference. To pass an argument by value, you pass in any valid expression. That expression is evaluated, and the value is assigned to the corresponding parameter defined within the function. Any changes you make to the parameter within the function have no effect on the argument passed to the function. For example:

```
function triple($x) {
  $x=$x*3;
  return $x;
}
$var=10;
$triplevar=triple($var);
```

In this case, `$var` evaluates to 10 when `triple()` is called, so `$x` is set to 10 inside the function. When `$x` is tripled, that change does not affect the value of `$var` outside the function.

In contrast, when you pass an argument by reference, changes to the parameter within the function do affect the value of the argument outside the scope of the function. That's because when you pass an argument by reference, you must pass a variable to the function. Now the parameter in the function refers directly to the value of the variable, meaning that any changes within the function are also visible outside the function. For example:

```
function triple($x) {
  $x=$x*3;
  return $x;
}
$var=10;
triple(&$var);
```

The `&` that precedes `$var` in the call to `triple()` causes the argument to be passed by reference, so the end result is that `$var` ends up with a value of 30.

Static Variables

PHP supports declaring local function variables as `static`. A static variable retains its value between function calls but is still accessible only from within the function it is declared in. Static variables can be initialized, and this initialization takes place only the first time the static declaration is executed. Static variables are often used as counters, as in this example:

```
function hitcount() {
  static $count = 0;
```

```
    if ($count== 0) {
      print "This is the first time this page has been accessed";
    }
    else {
      print "This page has been accessed $count times";
    }
    $count++;
  }
```

Web-Related Variables

PHP automatically creates global variables for all the data it receives in an HTTP request. This can include GET data, POST data, cookie data, and environment variables. Say you have an HTML form that looks as follows:

```
<FORM ACTION="test.php3" METHOD="POST">
<INPUT TYPE=text NAME=var>
</FORM>
```

When the form is submitted to the *test.php3* file, the **$var** variable within that file is set to whatever the user entered in the text field.

A variable can also be set in a URL like this:

```
http://your.server/test.php3?var=Hello+World
```

When the request for this URL is processed, the **$var** variable is set for the *test.php3* page.

Any environment variables present in your web server's configuration are also made available, along with any CGI-style variables your web server might set. The actual set of variables varies between different web servers. The best way to get a list of these variables is to use PHP's special information tag. Put the following code in a page and load the page in your browser:

```
<? phpinfo() ?>
```

You should see a page with quite a bit of information about PHP and the machine it is running on. There is a table that describes each of the extensions currently enabled in PHP. Another table shows the current values of all the various configuration directives from your *php3.ini* file. Following those two tables are more tables showing the regular environment variables, the special PHP internal variables, and the special environment variables that your web server has added. Finally, the HTTP request and response headers for the current request are shown.

Sometimes it is convenient to create a generic form handler, where you don't necessarily know all the form element names. To support this, PHP provides GET, POST, and cookie associative arrays that contain all of the data passed to the page using the different techniques. These arrays are named **$HTTP_GET_VARS**, **$HTTP_POST_VARS**, and **$HTTP_COOKIE_VARS**, respectively. For example, here's another way to access the value of the text field in our form:

```
echo $HTTP_POST_VARS["var"];
```

PHP sets global variables in a particular order. By default, global variables are set first from GET data, then from POST data, and then finally from cookie data. This means that if you have a form with a field named `var` that uses the GET method and a cookie with a `var` value, there will be one global variable named `$var` that has the value of the cookie data. Of course, you can still access the GET data through the `$HTTP_GET_DATA` array. The default order can be defined with the *gpc_order* directive in the *php3.ini file*.

Examples

The best way to understand the power of PHP is to examine some real examples of PHP in action, so we'll look at some common uses of PHP in this section.

Showing the Browser and IP Address

Here is a simple page that prints out the browser string and the IP address of the HTTP request. Create a file with the following content in your web directory, name it something like *example.php3*, and load it in your browser:

```
<HTML><HEAD><TITLE>PHP Example</TITLE></HEAD>
<BODY>
You are using <? echo $HTTP_USER_AGENT ?><BR>
and coming from <? echo $REMOTE_ADDR ?>
</BODY></HTML>
```

You should see something like the following in your browser window:

```
You are using Mozilla/4.0 (compatible; MSIE 4.01; Windows 98)
and coming from 207.164.141.23
```

Intelligent Form Handling

Here is a slightly more complex example. We are going to create an HTML form that asks the user to enter a name and select one or more interests from a selection box. We could do this in two files, where we separate the actual form from the data-handling code, but instead, this example shows how it can be done in a single file:

```
<HTML><HEAD><TITLE>Form Example</TITLE></HEAD>
<BODY>
<H1>Form Example</H1>
<?
function show_form($first="",$last="",$interests="") {
  $options = array("Sports","Business","Travel","Shopping","Computers");
  if(empty($interests)) $interests=array(-1);
?>
<FORM ACTION="form.php3" METHOD="POST">
First Name:
<INPUT TYPE=text NAME=first VALUE="<?echo $first?>"><BR>
Last Name:
<INPUT TYPE=text NAME=last VALUE="<?echo $last?>"><BR>
Interests:
<SELECT MULTIPLE NAME="interests[]">
<?
  for($i=0, reset($interests); $i<count($options); $i++) {
    echo "<OPTION";
```

```
      if(current($interests)==$options[$i]) {
        echo " SELECTED ";
        next($interests);
      }
      echo "> $options[$i]\n";
    }
  ?>
  </SELECT><BR>
  <INPUT TYPE=submit>
  </FORM>
  <? }

  if(!isset($first)) {
    show_form();
  }
  else {
    if(empty($first) || empty($last) || count($interests)==0)  {
      echo "You did not fill in all the fields, please try again<P>\n";
      show_form($first,$last,$interests);
    }
    else {
      echo "Thank you, $first $last, you selected ". join($interests, " and ");
      echo " as your interests.<P>\n";
    }
  }
  ?>
  </BODY></HTML>
```

There are a few things you should study carefully in this example. First, we have isolated the display of the actual form to a PHP function called *show_form()*. This function is intelligent in that it can take the default value for each of the form elements as an optional argument. If the user does not fill in all the form elements, we use this feature to redisplay the form with whatever values the user has already entered. This means that the user has to fill only the fields he missed, which is much better than asking the user to hit the Back button or force him to reenter all the fields.

Notice how the file switches back and forth between PHP code and HTML. Right in the middle of defining our *show_form()* function, we switch back to HTML to avoid having numerous echo statements that just echo normal HTML. Then, when we need a PHP variable, we switch back to PHP code temporarily just to print the variable.

We've given the multiple-choice <SELECT> element the name `interests[]`. The `[]` tells PHP that the data coming from this form element should be treated as an auto-indexed array. This means that PHP automatically gives each element the next sequential index, starting with 0 (assuming the array is empty to begin with).

The final thing to note is the way we determine what to display. We check if `$first` is set. If it isn't, we know that the user has not submitted the form yet, so we call *show_form()* without any arguments. This displays the empty form. If `$first` is set, however, we check to make sure that the `$first` and `$last` text fields are not empty, and that the user has selected at least one interest.

Web Database Integration

To illustrate a complete database-driven application, we are going to build a little web application that lets people make suggestions and vote on what you should name your new baby. The example uses MySQL, but it can be changed to run on any of the databases that PHP supports.

The schema for our baby-name database looks like this:

```
CREATE TABLE baby_names (
  name varchar(30) NOT NULL,
  votes int(4),
  PRIMARY KEY (name)
);
```

This is in MySQL's query format and can be used directly to create the actual table. It simply defines a text field and an integer field. The text field is for the suggested baby name, and the integer field is for the vote count associated with that name. We are making the name field a primary key, which means uniqueness is enforced, so that the same name cannot appear twice in the database.

We want this application to do a number of things. First, it should have a minimal check that prevents someone from voting many times in a row. We do this using a session cookie. Second, we want to show a fancy little barchart that depicts the relative share of the votes that each name has received. The barchart is created using a one-pixel-by-one-pixel blue-dot GIF image and scaling the image using the height and width settings of the HTML `<IMG>` tag. We could also use PHP's built-in image functions to create a fancier-looking bar.

Everything else is relatively straightforward form and database work. We use a couple of shortcuts as well. For example, instead of reading all the entries from the database and adding up all the votes in order to get a sum (which we need to calculate the percentages), we ask MySQL to do it for us with its built-in `SUM` function. The part of the code that displays all the names and their votes, along with the percentage bar, gets a little ugly, but you should be able to follow it. We are simply sending the correct HTML table tags before and after the various data we have fetched from the database.

Here's the full example:

```
<? if($vote && !$already_voted) SetCookie("already_voted","1");?>
<HTML><HEAD><TITLE>Name the Baby</TITLE></HEAD>
<H3>Name the Baby</H3>
<FORM ACTION="baby.php3" METHOD="POST">
Suggestion: <INPUT TYPE=text NAME=new_name><P>
<INPUT TYPE=submit VALUE="Submit suggestion and/or vote">
<?
  mysql_pconnect("localhost","","");
  $db = "test";
  $table = "baby_names";

  if($new_name) {
    if(!mysql_db_query($db,"insert into $table values ('$new_name',0)")) {
      echo mysql_errno().": ".mysql_error()."<BR>";
    }
  }
```

```
if($vote && $already_voted) {
  echo "<FONT COLOR=#ff0000>Hey, you voted already! Vote ignored.</FONT><P>\n";
}
else if($vote) {
  if(!mysql_db_query($db,
                       "update $table set votes=votes+1 where name='$vote'")) {
    echo mysql_errno().": ".mysql_error()."<BR>";
  }
}
$result=mysql_db_query($db,"select sum(votes) as sum from $table");
if($result) {
  $sum = (int) mysql_result($result,0,"sum");
  mysql_free_result($result);
}

$result=mysql_db_query($db,"select * from $table order by votes DESC");
echo "<TABLE BORDER=0><TR><TH>Vote</TH>";
echo "<TH>Suggestion</TH><TH COLSPAN=2>Votes</TH></TR>\n";
while($row=mysql_fetch_row($result)) {
  echo "<TR><TD ALIGN=center>";
  echo "<INPUT TYPE=radio NAME=vote VALUE=
  echo $row[0]."</TD><TD ALIGN=right>".$row[1]."</TD><TD>";
  if($sum && (int)$row[1]) {
    $per = (int)(100 * $row[1]/$sum);
    echo "<IMG SRC=bline.gif HEIGHT=12 WIDTH=$per> $per %</TD>";
  }
  echo "</TR>\n";
}
echo "</TABLE>\n";
mysql_free_result($result);
?>
<INPUT TYPE=submit VALUE="Submit suggestion and/or vote">
<INPUT TYPE=reset>
</FORM>
</BODY></HTML>
```

Function Reference

The remaining sections summarize the internal functions that are available in PHP. The synopsis for each function lists the expected argument types for the function and its return type. The possible types are `int`, `double`, `string`, `array`, `void`, and `mixed`. `mixed` means that the argument or return type can be of any type. Optional arguments are shown in square brackets.

Array Functions

PHP supports arrays that are indexed both by integers and by arbitrary strings—known as associative arrays. Internally, PHP does not distinguish between associative arrays and integer-indexed arrays, as arrays are implemented as hash tables. Here are the array functions supported by PHP:

array array(. . .)
    Create an array that contains all of the specified arguments

int array_walk(array array_arg, string function)
    Apply a function to every member of an array

int arsort(array array_arg)
Sort an array in reverse order and maintain index association

int asort(array array_arg)
Sort an array and maintain index association

int count(mixed var)
Count the number of elements in a variable (usually an array)

mixed current(array array_arg)
Return the element currently pointed to by the internal array pointer

mixed each(array array_arg)
Return the next key/value pair from an array

mixed end(array array_arg)
Advance the array's internal pointer to the last element and return the value of that element

mixed key(array array_arg)
Return the key of the element currently pointed to by the internal array pointer

int ksort(array array_arg)
Sort an array by key

mixed max(mixed arg1 [, mixed arg2 [, ...]])
Return the highest value in an array or a series of arguments

mixed min(mixed arg1 [, mixed arg2 [, ...]])
Return the lowest value in an array or a series of arguments

mixed next(array array_arg)
Move the array's internal pointer to the next element and return the value of that element

mixed pos(array array_arg)
An alias for `current`

mixed prev(array array_arg)
Move the array's internal pointer to the previous element and return the value of that element

mixed reset(array array_arg)
Set the array's internal pointer to the first element and return the value of that element

int rsort(array array_arg)
Sort an array in reverse order

int sort(array array_arg)
Sort an array

int uasort(array array_arg, string cmp_function)
Sort an array with a user-defined comparison function and maintain index association

int uksort(array array_arg, string cmp_function)
Sort an array by keys using a user-defined comparison function

int usort(array array_arg, string cmp_function)
Sort an array using a user-defined comparison function

Configuration and Logging Functions

Here are functions for getting and setting PHP configuration options at runtime, as well as logging and other functions that are useful during debugging:

int debugger_off(void)
Disable the internal PHP debugger

int debugger_on(string ip_address)
Enable the internal PHP debugger

int error_log(string message, int message_type [, string destination] [, string extra_headers])
Send an error message somewhere

int error_reporting([int level])
Set/get the current error reporting level

string get_cfg_var(string option_name)
Get the value of a PHP configuration option

int get_magic_quotes_gpc(void)
Get the current active configuration setting of *magic_quotes_gpc*

int get_magic_quotes_runtime(void)
Get the current active configuration setting of *magic_quotes_runtime*

void phpinfo(void)
Output a page of useful information about PHP and the current request

string phpversion(void)
Return the current PHP version

int set_magic_quotes_runtime(int new_setting)
Set the current active configuration setting of *magic_quotes_runtime* and return the previous value

void set_time_limit(int seconds)
Sets the execution time limit for the current script

int short_tags(int state)
Turn the short tags option on or off and return the previous state

Syslog Functions

The *syslog* functions provide an interface to the Unix *syslog* facility. On NT, these functions have been abstracted to use NT's Event Log mechanism instead:

PHP

int closelog(void)
Close the connection to the system logger

void define_syslog_variables(void)
Initialize all *syslog*-related variables

int openlog(string ident, int option, int facility)
Open a connection to the system logger

int syslog(int priority, string message)
Generate a system log message

Database Functions

PHP supports a number of databases directly through the databases' own native APIs. Each of the databases is covered in a separate section. Many of the databases can also be accessed through ODBC if appropriate ODBC drivers are available for that particular database. Adabas-D, Solid, Empress, and Velocis have native APIs that are so similar to the ODBC API that having a separate set of functions for each one was redundant. So, for these three databases, use the ODBC set of functions. It is important to understand, however, that for those four databases, the actual communication is direct and native and does not go through any sort of intermediary ODBC layer.

dBase Functions

PHP allows you to access records stored in dBase-format (dbf) databases. dBase files are simple sequential files of fixed length records. Records are appended to the end of the file and delete records are kept until you call *dbase_pack()*. Unlike with SQL databases, once a dBase file is created, the database definition is fixed. There are no indexes that speed searching or otherwise organize your data. Because of these limitations, we don't recommend using dBase files as your production database. Choose a real SQL server, such as MySQL or Postgres, instead. PHP provides dBase support to allow you to import and export data to and from your web database, as the format is understood by Windows spreadsheets and organizers. In other words, the import and export of data is about all that dBase support is good for.

Here are the dBase functions supported by PHP:

bool dbase_add_record(int identifier, array data)
Add a record to the database

bool dbase_close(int identifier)
Close an open dBase-format database file

bool dbase_create(string filename, array fields)
Create a new dBase-format database file

bool dbase_delete_record(int identifier, int record)
Mark a record to be deleted

array dbase_get_record(int identifier, int record)
Return an array representing a record from the database

array dbase_get_record_with_names(int identifier, int record)
Return an associative array representing a record from the database

int dbase_numfields(int identifier)
Return the number of fields (columns) in the database

int dbase_numrecords(int identifier)
Return the number of records in the database

int dbase_open(string name, int mode)
Open a dBase-format database file

bool dbase_pack(int identifier)
Pack the database (i.e., delete records marked for deletion)

DBM Functions

PHP supports DBM-style databases. This type of database stores key/value pairs, as opposed to the full-blown records supported by relational databases). Here are the DBM functions:

string dblist(void)
Describe the DBM-compatible library being used

bool dbmclose(int dbm_identifier)
Close a DBM database

int dbmdelete(int dbm_identifier, string key)
Delete the value for a key from a DBM database

int dbmexists(int dbm_identifier, string key)
Tell if a value exists for a key in a DBM database

string dbmfetch(int dbm_identifier, string key)
Fetch a value for a key from a DBM database

string dbmfirstkey(int dbm_identifier)
Retrieve the first key from a DBM database

int dbminsert(int dbm_identifier, string key, string value)
Insert a value for a key in a DBM database

string dbmnextkey(int dbm_identifier, string key)
Retrieve the next key from a DBM database

int dbmopen(string filename, string mode)
Open a DBM database

int dbmreplace(int dbm_identifier, string key, string value)
Replace the value for a key in a DBM database

FilePro Functions

PHP supports read-only access to data stored in filePro databases. You can find more information about filePro at *http://www.fptechnologies.com/*. Here are the filePro functions:

bool filepro(string directory)
Read and verify the map file

int filepro_fieldcount(void)
Find out how many fields are in a filePro database

string filepro_fieldname(int fieldnumber)
Get the name of a field

string filepro_fieldtype(int field_number)
Get the type of a field

int filepro_fieldwidth(int field_number)
Get the width of a field

string filepro_retrieve(int row_number, int field_number)
Retrieve data from a filePro database

int filepro_rowcount(void)
Find out how many rows are in a filePro database

Hyperwave Functions

Hyperwave Information Server (*http://www.hyperwave.com*) is an information system similar to a database that focuses on the storage and management of documents. PHP supports Hyperwave with the following functions:

string hw_array2objrec(array objarr)
Return the object record of an object array

void hw_changeobject(int link, int objid, array attributes)
Change attributes of an object

array hw_children(int link, int objid)
Return an array of children object IDs

array hw_childrenobj(int link, int objid)
Return an array of children object records

void hw_close(int link)
Close a connection to a Hyperwave server

int hw_connect(string host, int port [string username [, string password]])
Connect to a Hyperwave server

void hw_connection_info(int link)
Print information about the connection to a Hyperwave server

void hw_cp(int link, array objrec, int dest)
Copy an object

void hw_deleteobject(int link, int objid)
Delete an object

int hw_docbyanchor(int link, int anchorid)
Return an object ID of a document belonging to anchor ID

array hw_docbyanchorobj(int link, int anchorid)
Return the object record of a document belonging to anchor ID

string hw_document_attributes(hwdoc doc)
Return the object record of a document

string hw_document_bodytag(hwdoc doc [, string prefix])
Return the body tag for the document with the specified prefix

string hw_document_content(hwdoc doc)
Return the contents of a document

int hw_document_size(hwdoc doc)
Return the size of a document

string hw_documentattributes(hwdoc doc)
An alias for *hw_document_attributes*

string hw_documentbodytag(hwdoc doc [, string prefix])
An alias for *hw_document_bodytag*

int hw_documentsize(hwdoc doc)
An alias for *hw_document_size*

void hw_edittext(int link, hwdoc doc)
Modify the text in a document

int hw_error(int link)
Return the last error number

string hw_errormsg(int link)
Return the last error message

void hw_free_document(hwdoc doc)
Free the memory for a document

array hw_getanchors(int link, int objid)
Return all the anchors of an object

array hw_getanchorsobj(int link, int objid)
Return all the object records for the anchors of an object

string hw_getandlock(int link, int objid)
Return an object record and lock the object

hwdoc hw_getcgi(int link, int objid)
Return the output of a CGI script

array hw_getchildcoll(int link, int objid)
Return an array of child collection object IDs

array hw_getchildcollobj(int link, int objid)
    Return an array of child collection object records

array hw_getchilddoccoll(int link, int objid)
    Return all the children IDs that are documents

array hw_getchilddoccollobj(int link, int objid)
    Return all the children object records that are documents

string hw_getobject(int link, int objid)
    Return an object record

array hw_getobjectbyquery(int link, string query, int maxhits)
    Search for `query` and return `maxhits` object IDs

array hw_getobjectbyquerycoll(int link, int collid, string query, int maxhits)
    Search for `query` in a collection and return `maxhits` object IDs

array hw_getobjectbyquerycollobj(int link, int collid, string query, int maxhits)
    Search for `query` in a collection and return `maxhits` object records

array hw_getobjectbyqueryobj(int link, string query, int maxhits)
    Search for `query` and return `maxhits object records`

array hw_getparents(int link, int objid)
    Return an array of parent object IDs

array hw_getparentsobj(int link, int objid)
    Return an array of parent object records

string hw_getrellink(int link, int rootid, int sourceid, int destid)
    Return the link from source to destination relative to root ID

hwdoc hw_getremote(int link, int objid)
    Return the output of a remote document

[array | hwdoc] hw_getremotechildren(int link, int objid)
    Return the remote document if there is only one or an array of object records if more than one

int hw_getsrcbydestobj(int link, int destid)
    Return the object ID of the source document by destination anchor

hwdoc hw_gettext(int link, int objid[, int rootid])
    Return a text document; links are relative to root ID if specified

string hw_getusername(int link)
    Return the current username

void hw_identify(int link, string username, string password)
    Identify a Hyperwave server

array hw_incollections(int link, array objids, array collids, int para)
    Return object IDs that are in collections

void hw_info(int link)
    Output an informational string

void hw_inscoll(int link, int parentid, array objarr)
Insert a collection

void hw_insdoc(int link, int parentid, array objarr [, string text])
Insert a document

void hw_insertdocument(int link, int parentid, hwdoc doc)
Insert a new document

int hw_insertobject(int link, string objrec, string parms)
Insert an object

void hw_mv(int link, array objrec, int from, int dest)
Move an object

hwdoc hw_new_document(int link, string data, string objrec, int size)
Create a new document

array hw_objrec2array(string objrec)
Return an object array of the object record

void hw_output_document(hwdoc doc)
Print a document

void hw_outputdocument(hwdoc doc)
An alias for *hw_output_document*

int hw_pconnect(string host, int port [string username [, string password]])
Create a persistent connection to the Hyperwave server

hwdoc hw_pipecgi(int link, int objid)
Return the output of a CGI script

hwdoc hw_pipedocument(int link, int objid)
Return a document

int hw_root(void)
Return the object ID of the root collection

void hw_setlinkroot(int link, int rootid)
Sets the ID to which links are calculated

string hw_stat(int link)
Return a status string

void hw_unlock(int link, int objid)
Unlock an object

array hw_who(int link)
Return the names of users who are logged in and information about them

Informix Functions

PHP supports Informix databases with the following functions:

int ifx_affected_rows(int resultid)
Return the number of rows affected by the query identified by `resultid`

void ifx_blobinfile_mode(int mode)
Set the default blob-mode for all select queries

void ifx_byteasvarchar(int mode)
Set the default byte-mode for all select queries

int ifx_close(int connid)
Close the Informix connection

int ifx_connect([string database[, string userid[, string password]]])
Connect to the database using user ID and password, if provided, and return a connection ID

int ifx_copy_blob(int bid)
Duplicate the given blob-object

int ifx_create_blob(int type, int mode, string param)
Create a blob-object

int ifx_create_char(string param)
Create a char-object

int ifx_do(int resultid)
Execute a previously prepared query or opens a cursor for it

string ifx_error();
Return the Informix error codes (`SQLSTATE` and `SQLCODE`)

string ifx_errormsg([int errorcode])
Return the Informix error message associated with the error code

array ifx_fetch_row(int resultid, [mixed position])
Fetch the next row or the `position` row if using a scroll cursor

array ifx_fieldproperties(int resultid)
Return an associative array for the `resultid` query, using field names as keys

array ifx_fieldtypes(int resultid)
Return an associative array with field names as keys for the query `resultid`

int ifx_free_blob(int bid)
Delete the blob-object

int ifx_free_char(int bid)
Delete the char-object

int ifx_free_result(int resultid)
Release resources for the query associated with `resultid`

string ifx_get_blob(int bid)
Return the content of the blob-object

string ifx_get_char(int bid)
Return the content of the char-object

int ifx_htmltbl_result(int resultid, [string htmltableoptions])
Format all rows of the `resultid` query into an HTML table

void ifx_nullformat(int mode)
Set the default return value of a NULL value on a fetch-row

int ifx_num_fields(int resultid)
Return the number of columns in the query `resultid`

int ifx_num_rows(int resultid)
Return the number of rows already fetched for the query identified by `resultid`

int ifx_pconnect([string database[, string userid[, string password]]])
Create a persistent connection to the database using user ID and password, if specified, and returns a connection ID

int ifx_prepare(string query, int connid, [int cursortype], [array idarray])
Prepare a query on a given connection

int ifx_query(string query, int connid, [int cursortype], [array idarray])
Perform a query on a given connection

void ifx_textasvarchar(int mode)
Set the default text-mode for all select queries

int ifx_update_blob(int bid, string content)
Update the content of the blob-object

int ifx_update_char(int bid, string content)
Update the content of the char-object

int ifxus_close_slob(int bid)
Delete the slob-object

int ifxus_create_slob(int mode)
Create a slob-object and open it

int ifxus_free_slob(int bid)
Delete the slob-object

int ifxus_open_slob(long bid, int mode)
Open a slob-object

int ifxus_read_slob(long bid, long nbytes)
Read `nbytes` of the slob-object

int ifxus_seek_slob(long bid, int mode, long offset)
Set the current file or seek position of an open slob-object

int ifxus_tell_slob(long bid)
Return the current file or seek position of an open slob-object

int ifxus_write_slob(long bid, string content)
Write a string into the slob-object

PHP

InterBase Functions

PHP supports InterBase databases with the following functions:

int ibase_bind (int query)
Bind parameter placeholders in a previously prepared query (still nonfunctional)

int ibase_close([int link_identifier])
Close an InterBase connection

int ibase_connect(string database [, string username] [, string password])
Open a connection to an InterBase database

int ibase_execute(int query)
Execute a previously prepared (and possibly binded) query

int ibase_fetch_row(int result)
Fetch a row from the results of a query

int ibase_free_query(int query)
Free memory used by a query

int ibase_free_result(int result)
Free the memory used by a result

int ibase_pconnect(string database [, string username] [, string password])
Open a persistent connection to an InterBase database

int ibase_prepare([int link_identifier,]string query)
Prepare a query for later binding of parameter placeholders and execution

int ibase_query([int link_identifier,]string query)
Execute a query (without parameter placeholders)

int ibase_timefmt(string format)
Set the format of date/time columns returned from queries (still nonfunctional)

mSQL Functions

PHP supports mSQL databases with the following functions:

int msql_affected_rows(int query)
Return the number of affected rows

int msql_close([int link_identifier])
Close an mSQL connection

int msql_connect([string hostname[:port]] [, string username] [, string password])
Open a connection to an mSQL server

int msql_create_db(string database_name [, int link_identifier])
Create an mSQL database

int msql_data_seek(int query, int row_number)
Move the internal result pointer

int msql_db_query(string database_name, string query [, int link_identifier])
Send an SQL query to mSQL

int msql_drop_db(string database_name [, int link_identifier])
Drop (delete) an mSQL database

string msql_error([int link_identifier])
Return the text of the error message from the previous mSQL operation

array msql_fetch_array(int query)
Fetch a result row as an associative array

object msql_fetch_field(int query [, int field_offset])
Get column information from a result and return it as an object

object msql_fetch_object(int query)
Fetch a result row as an object

array msql_fetch_row(int query)
Get a result row as an enumerated array

string msql_field_flags(int query, int field_offset)
Get the flags associated with the specified field in a result

int msql_field_len(int query, int field_offet)
Return the length of the specified field

string msql_field_name(int query, int field_index)
Get the name of the specified field in a result

int msql_field_seek(int query, int field_offset)
Set the result pointer to a specific field offset

string msql_field_table(int query, int field_offset)
Get the name of the table the specified field is in

string msql_field_type(int query, int field_offset)
Get the type of the specified field in a result

int msql_free_result(int query)
Free result memory

int msql_list_dbs([int link_identifier])
List databases available on an mSQL server

int msql_list_fields(string database_name, string table_name [, int link_identifier])
List mSQL result fields

int msql_list_tables(string database_name [, int link_identifier])
List tables in an mSQL database

int msql_num_fields(int query)
Get the number of fields in a result

int msql_num_rows(int query)
Get the number of rows in a result

int msql_pconnect([string hostname[:port]] [, string username] [, string password])
Open a persistent connection to an mSQL server

int msql_query(string query [, int link_identifier])
Send an SQL query to mSQL

int msql_result(int query, int row [, mixed field])
Get result data

int msql_select_db(string database_name [, int link_identifier])
Select an mSQL database

MySQL Functions

PHP supports MySQL databases (*http://www.mysql.com/*) with the following functions:

int mysql_affected_rows([int link_identifier])
Get the number of affected rows in the previous MySQL operation

int mysql_close([int link_identifier])
Close a MySQL connection

int mysql_connect([string hostname[:port]] [, string username] [, string password])
Open a connection to a MySQL server

int mysql_create_db(string database_name [, int link_identifier])
Create a MySQL database

int mysql_data_seek(int result, int row_number)
Move the internal result pointer

int mysql_db_query(string database_name, string query [, int link_identifier])
Send an SQL query to MySQL

int mysql_drop_db(string database_name [, int link_identifier])
Drop (delete) a MySQL database

int mysql_errno([int link_identifier])
Return the number of the error message from the previous MySQL operation

string mysql_error([int link_identifier])
Return the text of the error message from the previous MySQL operation

array mysql_fetch_array(int result)
Fetch a result row as an associative array

object mysql_fetch_field(int result [, int field_offset])
Get column information from a result and return it as an object

array mysql_fetch_lengths(int result)
Get the maximum data size of each column in a result

object mysql_fetch_object(int result)
Fetch a result row as an object

array mysql_fetch_row(int result)
Get a result row as an enumerated array

string mysql_field_flags(int result, int field_offset)
Get the flags associated with the specified field in a result

int mysql_field_len(int result, int field_offet)
Return the length of the specified field

string mysql_field_name(int result, int field_index)
Get the name of the specified field in a result

int mysql_field_seek(int result, int field_offset)
Set the result pointer to a specific field offset

string mysql_field_table(int result, int field_offset)
Get the name of the table the specified field is in

string mysql_field_type(int result, int field_offset)
Get the type of the specified field in a result

int mysql_free_result(int result)
Free result memory

int mysql_insert_id([int link_identifier])
Get the ID generated from the previous `INSERT` operation

int mysql_list_dbs([int link_identifier])
List the databases available on a MySQL server

int mysql_list_fields(string database_name, string table_name [, int link_identifier])
List MySQL result fields

int mysql_list_tables(string database_name [, int link_identifier])
List the tables in a MySQL database

int mysql_num_fields(int result)
Get the number of fields in a result

int mysql_num_rows(int result)
Get the number of rows in a result

int mysql_pconnect([string hostname[:port]] [, string username] [, string password])
Open a persistent connection to a MySQL server

int mysql_query(string query [, int link_identifier])
Send an SQL query to MySQL

int mysql_result(int result, int row [, mixed field])
Get result data

int mysql_select_db(string database_name [, int link_identifier])
Select a MySQL database

ODBC Functions

PHP supports ODBC databases with the following functions. Remember that these functions double as native API functions for Adabas-D, Solid, Velocis, and Empress databases:

int odbc_autocommit(int connection_id, int OnOff)
Toggle autocommit mode

int odbc_binmode(int result_id, int mode)
Handle binary column data

void odbc_close(int connection_id)
Close an ODBC connection

void odbc_close_all(void)
Close all ODBC connections

int odbc_commit(int connection_id)
Commit an ODBC transaction

int odbc_connect(string DSN, string user, string password [, int cursor_option])
Connect to a data source

string odbc_cursor(int result_id)
Get the cursor name

int odbc_exec(int connection_id, string query)
Prepare and execute an SQL statement

int odbc_execute(int result_id [, array parameters_array])
Execute a prepared statement

int odbc_fetch_into(int result_id [, int rownumber], array result_array)
Fetch one result row into an array

int odbc_fetch_row(int result_id [, int row_number])
Fetch a row

int odbc_field_len(int result_id, int field_number)
Get the length of a column

string odbc_field_name(int result_id, int field_number)
Get a column name

int odbc_field_num(int result_id, string field_name)
Return the column number

string odbc_field_type(int result_id, int field_number)
Get the data type of a column

int odbc_free_result(int result_id)
Free resources associated with a result

int odbc_longreadlen(int result_id, int length)
Handle LONG columns

int odbc_num_fields(int result_id)
Get the number of columns in a result

int odbc_num_rows(int result_id)
Get the number of rows in a result

int odbc_pconnect(string DSN, string user, string password [, int cursor_option])
Establish a persistent connection to a data source

int odbc_prepare(int connection_id, string query)
Prepare a statement for execution

mixed odbc_result(int result_id, mixed field)
Get result data

int odbc_result_all(int result_id [, string format])
Print results as an HTML table

int odbc_rollback(int connection_id)
Rollback a transaction

int odbc_setoption(int id, int function, int option, int param)
Adjust ODBC settings.

Oracle Functions

PHP supports Oracle databases with the following functions:

int ora_bind(int cursor, string php_variable_name, string sql_parameter_name, int length [, int type])
Bind a PHP variable to an Oracle parameter

int ora_close(int cursor)
Close an Oracle cursor

string ora_columnname(int cursor, int column)
Get the name of an Oracle result column

int ora_columnsize(int cursor, int column)
Return the size of the column

string ora_columntype(int cursor, int column)
Get the type of an Oracle result column

int ora_commit(int connection)
Commit an Oracle transaction

int ora_commitoff(int connection)
Disable automatic commit

int ora_commiton(int connection)
Enable automatic commit

int ora_do(int connection, int cursor)
Parse and execute a statement and fetch the first result row

string ora_error(int cursor_or_connection)
Get an Oracle error message

int ora_errorcode(int cursor_or_connection)
Get an Oracle error code

int ora_exec(int cursor)
Execute a parsed statement

int ora_fetch(int cursor)
Fetch a row of result data from a cursor

int ora_fetch_into(int cursor, array result)
Fetch a row into the specified result array

mixed ora_getcolumn(int cursor, int column)
Get data from a fetched row

int ora_logoff(int connection)
Close an Oracle connection

int ora_logon(string user, string password)
Open an Oracle connection

int ora_numcols(int cursor)
Return the number of columns in a result

int ora_numrows(int cursor)
Return the number of rows in a result

int ora_open(int connection)
Open an Oracle cursor

int ora_parse(int cursor, string sql_statement [, int defer])
Parse an Oracle SQL statement

int ora_plogon(string user, string password)
Open a persistent Oracle connection

int ora_rollback(int connection)
Roll back an Oracle transaction

int OCIBindByName(int stmt, string name, mixed & var)
Bind a PHP variable to an Oracle placeholder by name

int OCIColumnIsNULL(int stmt, int col)
Tell whether a column is `NULL`

int OCIColumnSize(int stmt, int col)
Tell the maximum data size of a column

int OCIExecute(int stmt)
Execute a parsed statement

int OCIFetch(int stmt)
Prepare a new row of data for reading

int OCIFetchInto(int stmt, array &output)
Fetch a row of result data into an array

int OCIFreeStatement(int stmt)
Free all resources associated with a statement

int OCILogoff(int conn)
Disconnect from database

int OCILogon(string user, string pass[, string db])
Connect to an Oracle database and log on

int OCINumCols(int stmt)
Return the number of result columns in a statement

int OCIParse(int conn, string query)
Parse a query and return a statement

int OCIStatementType(int stmt)
Return the query type of an OCI statement

void OCIDebug(int onoff)
Toggle internal debugging output for the OCI extension

mixed OCIColumnType(int stmt, int col)
Tell the data type of a column

string OCIColumnName(int stmt, int col)
Tell the name of a column

string OCIResult(int stmt, mixed column)
Return a single column of result data

string OCIServerVersion(int conn)
Return a string that contains server version information

PostgreSQL Functions

PostgreSQL is an open source database available at *http://www.postgreSQL.org*. PHP supports PostgreSQL databases with the following functions:

bool pg_close([int connection])
Close a PostgreSQL connection

int pg_cmdtuples(int result)
Return the number of affected tuples

int pg_connect([string connection_string] | [string host, string port, [string options, [string tty,]] string database)
Open a PostgreSQL connection

string pg_dbname([int connection])
Get the database name

string pg_errormessage([int connection])
Get the error message string

int pg_exec([int connection,] string query)
Execute a query

array pg_fetch_array(int result, int row)
Fetch a row as an array

object pg_fetch_object(int result, int row)
Fetch a row as an object

array pg_fetch_row(int result, int row)
Get a row as an enumerated array

int pg_fieldisnull(int result, int row, mixed field_name_or_number)
Test if a field is `NULL`

string pg_fieldname(int result, int field_number)
Return the name of the field

int pg_fieldnum(int result, string field_name)
Return the field number of the named field

int pg_fieldprtlen(int result, int row, mixed field_name_or_number)
Return the printed length

string pg_fieldtype(int result, int field_number)
Return the type name for the given field

int pg_freeresult(int result)
Free result memory

int pg_getlastoid(int result)
Return the last object identifier

string pg_host([int connection])
Return the hostname associated with the connection

void pg_loclose(int fd)
Close a large object

int pg_locreate(int connection)
Create a large object

int pg_loopen([int connection,] int objoid, string mode)
Open a large object and return the file descriptor

string pg_loread(int fd, int len)
Read a large object

void pg_loreadall(int fd)
Read a large object and send it straight to the browser

void pg_lounlink([int connection,] int large_obj_id)
Delete a large object

int pg_lowrite(int fd, string buf)
Write a large object

int pg_numfields(int result)
Return the number of fields in the result

int pg_numrows(int result)
Return the number of rows in the result

string pg_options([int connection])
Get the options associated with the connection

int pg_pconnect([string connection_string] | [string host, string port, [string options, [string tty,]] string database)
Open a persistent PostgreSQL connection

int pg_port([int connection])
Return the port number associated with the connection

mixed pg_result(int result, int row_number, mixed field_name)
Return values from a result identifier

string pg_tty([int connection])
Return the `tty` name associated with the connection

pg_fieldsize(int result, int field_number)
Return the internal size of the field

Sybase Functions

PHP supports Sybase databases with the following functions:

int sybase_affected_rows([int link_id])
Get the number of affected rows in the last query

bool sybase_close([int link_id])
Close a Sybase connection

int sybase_connect([string host[, string user[, string password]]])
Open a Sybase server connection

bool sybase_data_seek(int result, int offset)
Move the internal row pointer

array sybase_fetch_array(int result)
Fetch a row as an array

object sybase_fetch_field(int result[, int offset])
Get field information

object sybase_fetch_object(int result)
Fetch a row as an object

array sybase_fetch_row(int result)
Get a row as an enumerated array

bool sybase_field_seek(int result, int offset)
Set the field offset

PHP

bool sybase_free_result(int result)
Free result memory

string sybase_get_last_message(void)
Return the last message from the server

int sybase_num_fields(int result)
Get the number of fields in `result`

int sybase_num_rows(int result)
Get the number of rows in `result`

int sybase_pconnect([string host[, string user[, string password]]])
Open a persistent Sybase connection

int sybase_query(string query[, int link_id])
Send a Sybase query

string sybase_result(int result, int row, mixed field)
Get `result` data

bool sybase_select_db(string database[, int link_id])
Select a Sybase database

Date/Time Functions

PHP provides the following functions for working with dates and times:

bool checkdate(int month, int day, int year)
Validate a date/time

string date(string format[, int timestamp])
Format a local date/time

array getdate([int timestamp])
Get date/time information

array gettimeofday(void)
Return the current time as array

string gmdate(string format[, int timestamp])
Format a GMT/CUT date/time

int gmmktime(int hour, int min, int sec, int mon, int mday, int year)
Get Unix timestamp for a GMT date

string microtime(void)
Return a string containing the current time in seconds and microseconds

int mktime(int hour, int min, int sec, int mon, int mday, int year)
Get Unix timestamp for a date

void sleep(int seconds)
Delay for a given number of seconds

string strftime(string format[, int timestamp])
Format a local time/date according to locale settings

int time(void)
: Return current Unix timestamp

void usleep(int micro_seconds)
: Delay for a given number of microseconds

Directory Functions

The following functions are used to manipulate directories. For example, to open the current directory and read in all the entries, you can do something like this:

```
$handle = opendir('.');
while($entry = readdir($handle)) {
echo "$entry<br>\n";
}
closedir($handle);
```

PHP supports a `dir` class that represents a directory:

```
class dir(string directory)
```

This class has properties for the directory handle and class and methods for reading, rewinding, and closing the directory.

Here are the directory functions supported by PHP:

int chdir(string directory)
: Change the current directory

void closedir(int dir_handle)
: Close the directory connection identified by the `dir_handle`

int opendir(string directory)
: Open a directory and return a `dir_handle`

string readdir(int dir_handle)
: Read a directory entry from `dir_handle`

void rewinddir(int dir_handle)
: Rewind `dir_handle` back to the start

PHP

File Functions

The following functions manipulate the local filesystem in some manner:

string basename(string path)
: Return the filename component of the path

int chgrp(string filename, mixed group)
: Change the file group

int chmod(string filename, int mode)
: Change the file mode

int chown(string filename, mixed user)
: Change the file owner

void clearstatcache(void)
Clear the file stat cache

int copy(string source_file, string destination_file)
Copy a file

string dirname(string path)
Return the directory name component of the path

int fclose(int fp)
Close an open file pointer

int feof(int fp)
Test for end-of-file on a file pointer

string fgetc(int fp)
Get a character from the file pointer

string fgets(int fp, int length)
Get a line from the file pointer

string fgetss(int fp, int length)
Get a line from the file pointer and strip HTML tags

array file(string filename)
Read an entire file into an array

int file_exists(string filename)
Check whether a file exists or not

int fileatime(string filename)
Get the last access time for a file

int filectime(string filename)
Get the last inode status change for a file

int filegroup(string filename)
Return the group ID of the file

int fileinode(string filename)
Return the inode number of the file

int filemtime(string filename)
Return the time the file was last modified

int fileowner(string filename)
Return the user ID of the owner of the file

int fileperms(string filename)
Return the file permission bits of the file

int filesize(string filename)
Return the size of the file

string filetype(string filename)
Return the type of the file (`fifo`, `char`, `block`, `link`, `file`, or `unknown`)

int fopen(string filename, string mode)
Open a file or a URL and return a file pointer

int fpassthru(int fp)
Output all remaining data from a file pointer

int fputs(int fp, string str [, int length])
Write to a file pointer

int fread(int fp, int length)
Binary-safe file read

int fseek(int fp, int offset)
Seek on a file pointer

int ftell(int fp)
Get the file pointer's read/write position

int fwrite(int fp, string str [, int length])
Binary-safe file write

array get_meta_tags(string filename [, int use_include_path])
Extract all meta tag content attributes from a file and return an array

bool is_dir(string pathname)
Return `true` if the pathname is a directory

bool is_executable(string filename)
Return `true` if filename is executable

bool is_file(string filename)
Return `true` if filename is a regular file

bool is_link(string filename)
Return `true` if filename is a symbolic link

bool is_readable(string filename)
Return `true` if filename exists and is readable

bool is_writable(string filename)
Return `true` if filename exists and is writable

int link(string target, string link)
Create a hard link

int linkinfo(string filename)
Return the `st_dev` field of the Unix C `stat` structure describing the link

array lstat(string filename)
Return an array that contains information about the file; follows symbolic links

int mkdir(string pathname, int mode)
Create a directory

int pclose(int fp)
Close a file pointer opened by *popen()*

int popen(string command, string mode)
Execute a command and open either a read or a write pipe to it

int readfile(string filename)
Output a file or a URL

int readlink(string filename)
Return the target of a symbolic link

int rename(string old_name, string new_name)
Rename a file

int rewind(int fp)
Rewind the position of a file pointer

int rmdir(string dirname)
Remove a directory

array stat(string filename)
Return an array that contains information about the file; does not follow symbolic links

int symlink(string target, string link)
Create a symbolic link

string tempnam(string dir, string prefix)
Create a unique filename in a directory

int touch(string filename[, int time])
Create an empty file or set modification time of an existing one

int umask(int mask)
Changes the current umask

int unlink(string filename)
Delete a file

GZIP File Functions

int gzclose(int zp)
Close an open GZIP file pointer

int gzeof(int zp)
Test for end-of-file on a GZIP file pointer

array gzfile(string filename)
Read and uncompress an entire GZIP file into an array

string gzgetc(int zp)
Get a character from a GZIP file pointer

string gzgets(int zp, int length)
Get a line from a GZIP file pointer

string gzgetss(int zp, int length)
Get a line from a GZIP file pointer and strip HTML tags

int gzopen(string filename, string mode [, int use_include_path])
  Open a GZIP file and return a GZIP file pointer

int gzpassthru(int zp)
  Output all remaining data from a GZIP file pointer

int gzread(int zp, int length)
  Binary-safe GZIP file read

int gzrewind(int zp)
  Rewind the position of a GZIP file pointer

int gzseek(int zp, int offset)
  Seek on a GZIP file pointer

int gztell(int zp)
  Get a GZIP file pointer's read/write position

int gzwrite(int zp, string str [, int length])
  Binary-safe GZIP file write

int readgzfile(string filename [, int use_include_path])
  Output a GZIP file

Graphics Functions

The graphics functions in PHP can dynamically create a GIF image stream. This stream can either be sent directly to the browser or saved in a standard GIF file. The following example illustrates a number of these image functions:

```
Header("Content-type: image/gif");
if(!isset($s)) $s=11;
$size = imagettfbbox($s,0,"/fonts/TIMES.TTF",$text);
$dx = abs($size[2]-$size[0]);
$dy = abs($size[5]-$size[3]);
$xpad=9; $ypad=9;
$im = imagecreate($dx+$xpad,$dy+$ypad);
$blue = ImageColorAllocate($im, 0x2c,0x6D,0xAF);
$black = ImageColorAllocate($im, 0,0,0);
$white = ImageColorAllocate($im, 255,255,255);
ImageRectangle($im,0,0,$dx+$xpad-1,$dy+$ypad-1,$black);
ImageRectangle($im,0,0,$dx+$xpad,$dy+$ypad,$white);
ImageTTFText($im, $s, 0, (int)($xpad/2)+1, $dy+(int)($ypad/2),
            $black, "/fonts/TIMES.TTF", $text);
ImageTTFText($im, $s, 0, (int)($xpad/2), $dy+(int)($ypad/2)-1,
            $white, "/fonts/TIMES.TTF", $text);
ImageGif($im);
ImageDestroy($im);
```

This example should be saved as a file named *button.php3*, for example, and then called as part of an HTML <IMG> tag like this:

```
<IMG SRC="button.php3?s=13&text=Help">
```

This produces a blue-shaded button with white-shadowed text using a 13-point Times font.

Here are the graphics functions provided by PHP.

array getimagesize(string filename)
Get the size of a GIF, JPG, or PNG image

int imagearc(int im, int cx, int cy, int w, int h, int s, int e, int col)
Draw a partial ellipse

int imagechar(int im, int font, int x, int y, string c, int col)
Draw a character

int imagecharup(int im, int font, int x, int y, string c, int col)
Draw a character rotated 90 degrees counterclockwise

int imagecolorallocate(int im, int red, int green, int blue)
Allocate a color for an image

int imagecolorat(int im, int x, int y)
Get the index of the color of a pixel

int imagecolorclosest(int im, int red, int green, int blue)
Get the index of the closest color to the specified color

int imagecolordeallocate(int im, int index)
Deallocate a color for an image

int imagecolorexact(int im, int red, int green, int blue)
Get the index of the specified color

int imagecolorresolve(int im, int red, int green, int blue)
Get the index of the specified color or its closest possible alternative

int imagecolorset(int im, int col, int red, int green, int blue)
Set the color for the specified palette index

array imagecolorsforindex(int im, int col)
Get the colors for an index

int imagecolorstotal(int im)
Find out the number of colors in an image's palette

int imagecolortransparent(int im, int col)
Define a color as transparent

int imagecopy(int dst_im, int src_im, int dstX, int dstY, int srcX, int srcY, int srcW, int srcH)
Copy part of an image

int imagecopyresized(int dst_im, int src_im, int dstX, int dstY, int srcX, int srcY, int dstW, int dstH, int srcW, int srcH)
Copy and resize part of an image

int imagecreate(int x_size, int y_size)
Create a new image

int imagecreatefromgif(string filename)
Create a new image from file or URL

int imagedashedline(int im, int x1, int y1, int x2, int y2, int col)
Draw a dashed line

int imagedestroy(int im)
Destroy an image

int imagefill(int im, int x, int y, int col)
Flood-fill

int imagefilledpolygon(int im, array point, int num_points, int col)
Draw a filled polygon

int imagefilledrectangle(int im, int x1, int y1, int x2, int y2, int col)
Draw a filled rectangle

int imagefilltoborder(int im, int x, int y, int border, int col)
Flood-fill to specific color

int imagefontheight(int font)
Get the font height

int imagefontwidth(int font)
Get the font width

int imagegif(int im, string filename)
Output the image to a browser or file

int imageinterlace(int im, int interlace)
Enable or disable interlacing

int imageline(int im, int x1, int y1, int x2, int y2, int col)
Draw a line

int imageloadfont(string filename)
Load a new font

int imagepolygon(int im, array point, int num_points, int col)
Draw a polygon

int imagerectangle(int im, int x1, int y1, int x2, int y2, int col)
Draw a rectangle

int imagesetpixel(int im, int x, int y, int col)
Set a single pixel

int imagestring(int im, int font, int x, int y, string str, int col)
Draw a string horizontally

int imagestringup(int im, int font, int x, int y, string str, int col)
Draw a string vertically, rotated 90 degrees counterclockwise

int imagesx(int im)
Get the image width

int imagesy(int im)
Get the image height

array imagettfbbox(int size, int angle, string font_file, string text)
Give the bounding box of a text using TrueType fonts

array imagettftext(int im, int size, int angle, int x, int y, int col, string font_file, string text)
Write text to the image using a TrueType font

array iptcparse(string jpeg_image)
Read the IPTC header from a JPEG image file

HTTP Functions

These functions assist you in dealing with the HTTP protocol. The encoding and decoding functions are not normally needed, as PHP takes care of these actions automatically. But there are cases where the actions need to be done manually, so these functions are provided. The header and cookie functions are very useful for sending either custom HTTP headers or cookies.

Here are the HTTP functions in PHP:

int header(string str)
Send a raw HTTP header

array parse_url(string url)
Parse a URL and return its components in an array

string rawurldecode(string str)
Decode a URL-encoded string

string rawurlencode(string str)
URL-encode a string

void setcookie(string name, string value, int expire, string path, string domain, int secure)
Send a cookie

string urldecode(string str)
Decode a URL-encoded string

string urlencode(string str)
URL-encode a string

Apache-Specific Functions

The following HTTP functions are available only if PHP is running as an Apache module.

class apache_lookup_uri(string URI)
Perform a partial request of the given URI to obtain information about it

string apache_note(string note_name [, string note_value])
Get and set Apache request notes

array getallheaders(void)
Fetch all HTTP request headers

int virtual(string filename)
Perform an Apache subrequest

IMAP Functions

These functions are used to communicate with mail and news servers via the IMAP4, POP3, or NNTP protocols. For these functions to work, you have to compile PHP with `map`. That requires the C-client library to be installed. You can get the latest version from *ftp://ftp.cac.washington.edu/imap/* and compile it.

string imap_8bit(string text)
Convert an 8-bit string to a quoted-printable string

int imap_append(int stream_id, string folder, string message [, string flags])
Append a string message to a specified mailbox

string imap_base64(string text)
Decode base-64-encoded text

string imap_binary(string text)
Convert an 8-bit string to a base-64-encoded string

string imap_body(int stream_id, int msg_no [, int options])
Read the message body

object imap_bodystruct(int stream_id, int msg_no, int section)
Read the structure of a specified body section of a specific message

object imap_check(int stream_id)
Get mailbox properties

void imap_clearflag_full(int stream_id, string sequence, string flag [, int options])
Clear flags on messages

int imap_close(int stream_id [, int options])
Close an IMAP stream

int imap_create(int stream_id, string mailbox)
An alias for *imap_createmailbox*

int imap_createmailbox(int stream_id, string mailbox)
Create a new mailbox

int imap_delete(int stream_id, int msg_no)
Mark a message for deletion

bool imap_deletemailbox(int stream_id, string mailbox)
Delete a mailbox

int imap_expunge(int stream_id)
Delete all messages marked for deletion

array imap_fetch_overview(int stream_id, int msg_no)
Read an overview of the information in the headers of the given message

string imap_fetchbody(int stream_id, int msg_no, int section [, int options])
Get a specific body section

string imap_fetchheader(int stream_id, int msg_no [, int options])
Get the full, unfiltered header for a message

object imap_fetchstructure(int stream_id, int msg_no [, int options])
Read the full structure of a message

string imap_fetchtext(int stream_id, int msg_no [, int options])
An alias for *imap_body*

object imap_header(int stream_id, int msg_no [, int from_length [, int subject_length [, string default_host]]])
Read the header of the message

object imap_headerinfo(int stream_id, int msg_no [, int from_length [, int subject_length [, string default_host]]])
An alias for *imap_header*

array imap_headers(int stream_id)
Return headers for all messages in a mailbox

array imap_list(int stream_id, string ref, string pattern)
Read the list of mailboxes

array imap_listmailbox(int stream_id, string ref, string pattern)
An alias for *imap_list*

array imap_listsubscribed(int stream_id, string ref, string pattern)
An alias for *imap_lsub*

array imap_lsub(int stream_id, string ref, string pattern)
Return a list of subscribed mailboxes

string imap_mail_compose(array envelope, array body)
Create a MIME message based on given envelope and body sections

int imap_mail_copy(int stream_id, int msg_no, string mailbox [, int options])
Copy specified message to a mailbox

bool imap_mail_move(int stream_id, int msg_no, string mailbox)
Move specified message to a mailbox

array imap_mailboxmsginfo(int stream_id)
Return information about the current mailbox in an associative array

int imap_msgno(int stream_id, int unique_msg_id)
Get the sequence number associated with a user ID

int imap_num_msg(int stream_id)
Give the number of messages in the current mailbox

int imap_num_recent(int stream_id)
Give the number of recent messages in the current mailbox

int imap_open(string mailbox, string user, string password [, int options])
Open an IMAP stream to a mailbox

int imap_ping(int stream_id)
: Check if the IMAP stream is still active

string imap_qprint(string text)
: Convert a quoted-printable string to an 8-bit string

int imap_rename(int stream_id, string old_name, string new_name)
: An alias for *imap_renamemailbox*

int imap_renamemailbox(int stream_id, string old_name, string new_name)
: Rename a mailbox

int imap_reopen(int stream_id, string mailbox [, int options])
: Reopen IMAP stream to new mailbox

array imap_rfc822_parse_adrlist(string address_string, string default_host)
: Parse an address string

string imap_rfc822_write_address(string mailbox, string host, string personal)
: Return a properly formatted email address given the mailbox, host, and personal info

array imap_scan(int stream_id, string ref, string pattern, string content)
: Read list of mailboxes containing a certain string

array imap_scanmailbox(int stream_id, string ref, string pattern, string content)
: An alias for *imap_scan*

int imap_setflag_full(int stream_id, string sequence, string flag [, int options])
: Sets flags on messages

array imap_sort(int stream_id, int criteria, int reverse [, int options])
: Sort an array of message headers

object imap_status(int stream_id, string mailbox, int options)
: Get status info from a mailbox

int imap_subscribe(int stream_id, string mailbox)
: Subscribe to a mailbox

int imap_uid(int stream_id, int msg_no)
: Get the unique message ID associated with a standard sequential message number

int imap_undelete(int stream_id, int msg_no)
: Remove the delete flag from a message

int imap_unsubscribe(int stream_id, string mailbox)
: Unsubscribe from a mailbox

LDAP Functions

The following functions are used to communicate with a Lightweight Directory Access Protocol (LDAP) server.

int ldap_add(int link, string dn, array entry)
Add entries to an LDAP directory

int ldap_bind(int link [, string dn, string password])
Bind to an LDAP directory

int ldap_close(int link)
Alias for *ldap_unbind*

int ldap_connect([string host [, int port]])
Connect to an LDAP server

int ldap_count_entries(int link, int result)
Count the number of entries in a search result

int ldap_delete(int link, string dn)
Delete an entry from a directory

string ldap_dn2ufn(string dn)
Convert a distinguished name to a user-friendly naming format

array ldap_explode_dn(string dn, int with_attrib)
Split a distinguished name into its component parts

string ldap_first_attribute(int link, int result, int ber)
Return the first attribute

int ldap_first_entry(int link, int result)
Return the first result ID

int ldap_free_result(int result)
Free result memory

array ldap_get_attributes(int link, int result)
Get attributes from a search result entry

string ldap_get_dn(int link, int result)
Get the distinguished name of a result entry

array ldap_get_entries(int link, int result)
Get all result entries

array ldap_get_values(int link, int result, string attribute)
Get all values from a result entry

int ldap_list(int link, string base_dn, string filter [, string attributes])
Single-level search

int ldap_modify(int link, string dn, array entry)
Modify an LDAP entry

string ldap_next_attribute(int link, int result, int ber)
Get the next attribute in result

int ldap_next_entry(int link, int entry)
Get the next result entry

int ldap_read(int link, string base_dn, string filter [, string attributes])
Read an entry

int ldap_search(int link, string base_dn, string filter [, string attributes])
Search LDAP tree under *base_dn*

int ldap_unbind(int link)
Unbind from an LDAP directory

Math Functions

There are two types of math functions in PHP. The first type is the standard functions that operate on regular numbers. The scope and precision of these functions are limited by the operating system.

int abs(int number)
Return the absolute value of the number

double acos(double number)
Return the arc cosine of the number in radians

double asin(double number)
Return the arc sine of the number in radians

double atan(double number)
Return the arc tangent of the number in radians

double atan2(double y, double x)
Return the arc tangent of `y/x`, with the resulting quadrant determined by the signs of `y` and `x`

string base_convert(string number, int frombase, int tobase)
Convert a number in a string from any base to any other base (where both bases are less than or equal to 36)

int bindec(string binary_number)
Return the decimal equivalent of the binary number

int ceil(double number)
Return the next higher integer value of the number

double cos(double number)
Return the cosine of the number in radians

string decbin(int decimal_number)
Return a string containing a binary representation of the number

string dechex(int decimal_number)
Return a string containing a hexadecimal representation of the given number

string decoct(int octal_number)
Return a string containing an octal representation of the given number

double deg2rad(double degrees)
Convert the number in degrees to the radian equivalent

double exp(double number)
Return *e* raised to the power of the number

int floor(double number)
Return the next lower integer value from the number

int hexdec(string hexadecimal_number)
Return the decimal equivalent of the hexadecimal number

double log(double number)
Return the natural logarithm of the number

double log10(double number)
Return the base-10 logarithm of the number

string number_format(double number [,int num_decimal_places [,string dec_separator, string thousands_separator)]])
Formats a number with grouped thousands

int octdec(string octal_number)
Return the decimal equivalent of an octal string

double pi(void)
Return an approximation of *pi*

double pow(double base, double exponent)
Return `base` raised to the power of `exponent`

double rad2deg(double radians)
Convert the radian number to the equivalent number in degrees

double round(double number)
Return the rounded value of the number

double sin(double number)
Return the sine of the number in radians

double sqrt(double number)
Return the square root of the number

double tan(double number)
Return the tangent of the number in radians

BC Arbitrary Precision Math Functions

The second type of math functions is the BC set of functions. These are arbitrary precision functions where the numbers themselves are stored as strings. The BC functions act on these strings. The benefit of using these functions is that there is no limit to the size or precision of the numbers you are working with.

string bcadd(string left_operand, string right_operand [, int scale])
Return the sum of two arbitrary precision numbers

string bccomp(string left_operand, string right_operand [, int scale])
Compare two arbitrary precision numbers

string bcdiv(string left_operand, string right_operand [, int scale])
Return the result of dividing two arbitrary precision numbers

string bcmod(string left_operand, string modulus)
Return the modulus of an arbitrary precision number

string bcmul(string left_operand, string right_operand [, int scale])
Return the product of two arbitrary precision numbers

string bcpow(string x, string y [, int scale])
Return the value of one arbitrary precision number raised to the power of another

string bcscale(int scale)
Set the default scale parameter for all BC math functions

string bcsqrt(string operand [, int scale])
Return the square root of an arbitrary precision number

string bcsub(string left_operand, string right_operand [, int scale])
Return the result of subtracting one arbitrary precision number from another

PDF Functions

PHP provides functions that can create Adobe Portable Document Format (PDF) and Forms Data Format (FDF) content on the fly.

PDF

pdf_set_info_author(int info, string author)
Fill the author field of the info structure

pdf_set_info_creator(int info, string creator)
Fill the creator field of the info structure

pdf_set_info_keywords(int info, string keywords)
Fill the keywords field of the info structure

pdf_set_info_subject(int info, string subject)
Fill the subject field of the info structure

pdf_set_info_title(int info, string title)
Fill the title field of the info structure

void pdf_add_outline(int pdfdoc, string text)
Add bookmark for current page

void pdf_arc(int pdfdoc, double x, double y, double radius, double start, double end)
Draw an arc

void pdf_begin_page(int pdfdoc, double height, double width)
Start page

void pdf_circle(int pdfdoc, double x, double y, double radius)
Draw a circle

void pdf_clip(int pdfdoc)
Clip to current path

void pdf_close(int pdfdoc)
Close the PDF document

void pdf_closepath(int pdfdoc)
Close path

void pdf_closepath_fill_stroke(int pdfdoc)
Close, fill, and stroke current path

void pdf_closepath_stroke(int pdfdoc)
Closes path and draw line along path

void pdf_continue_text(int pdfdoc, string text)
Output text in next line

void pdf_curveto(int pdfdoc, double x1, double y1, double x2, double y2, double x3, double y3)
Draw a curve

void pdf_end_page(int pdfdoc)
End page

void pdf_endpath(int pdfdoc)
End current path

void pdf_fill(int pdfdoc)
Fill current path

void pdf_fill_stroke(int pdfdoc)
Fill and strokes current path

int pdf_get_info(void)
Return a default info structure for a PDF document

void pdf_lineto(int pdfdoc, double x, double y)
Draw a line

void pdf_moveto(int pdfdoc, double x, double y)
Set current point

int pdf_open(int filedesc, int info)
Open a new PDF document

void pdf_rect(int pdfdoc, double x, double y, double width, double height)
Draw a rectangle

void pdf_restore(int pdfdoc)
Restore formerly saved environment

void pdf_rotate(int pdfdoc, double angle)
Set rotation

void pdf_save(int pdfdoc)
Save current environment

void pdf_scale(int pdfdoc, double x-scale, double y-scale)
Set scaling

void pdf_set_char_spacing(int pdfdoc, double space)
Set character spacing

void pdf_set_duration(int pdfdoc, double duration)
Set duration between pages

void pdf_set_font(int pdfdoc, string font, double size, string encoding)
Select the current font face and size

void pdf_set_horiz_scaling(int pdfdoc, double scale)
Set horizontal scaling of text

void pdf_set_leading(int pdfdoc, double distance)
Set distance between text lines

void pdf_set_text_matrix(int pdfdoc, arry matrix)
Set the text matrix

void pdf_set_text_pos(int pdfdoc, double x, double y)
Set text position

void pdf_set_text_rendering(int pdfdoc, int mode)
Determine how text is rendered

void pdf_set_text_rise(int pdfdoc, double value)
Set the text rise

void pdf_set_transition(int pdfdoc, int transition)
Set transition between pages

void pdf_set_word_spacing(int pdfdoc, double space)
Set spacing between words

void pdf_setdash(int pdfdoc, double white, double black)
Set dash pattern

void pdf_setflat(int pdfdoc, double value)
Set flatness

void pdf_setgray(int pdfdoc, double value)
Set drawing and filling color to gray value

void pdf_setgray_fill(int pdfdoc, double value)
Set filling color to gray value

void pdf_setgray_stroke(int pdfdoc, double value)
Set drawing color to gray value

void pdf_setlinecap(int pdfdoc, int value)
Set linecap parameter

void pdf_setlinejoin(int pdfdoc, int value)
Set linejoin parameter

void pdf_setlinewidth(int pdfdoc, double width)
Set line width

void pdf_setmiterlimit(int pdfdoc, double value)
Set miter limit

void pdf_setrgbcolor(int pdfdoc, double red, double green, double blue)
Set drawing and filling color to RGB color value

void pdf_setrgbcolor_fill(int pdfdoc, double red, double green, double blue)
Set filling color to RGB color value

void pdf_setrgbcolor_stroke(int pdfdoc, double red, double green, double blue)
Set drawing color to RGB color value

void pdf_show(int pdfdoc, string text)
Output text at current position

void pdf_show_xy(int pdfdoc, string text)
Output text at position

double pdf_stringwidth(int pdfdoc, string text)
Return width of text in current font

void pdf_stroke(int pdfdoc)
Draw line along path

void pdf_translate(int pdfdoc, double x, double y)
Set origin of coordinate system

FDF

void fdf_close(int fdfdoc)
Close the FDF document

void fdf_create(void)
Create a new FDF document

void fdf_get_file(int fdfdoc)
Get the value in the /F key.

void fdf_get_status(int fdfdoc)
Get the value in the /Status key.

void fdf_get_value(int fdfdoc, string fieldname)
Get the value of a field as string

void fdf_next_field_name(int fdfdoc [, string fieldname])
Get the name of the next field name or the first field name

int fdf_open(string filename)
Open a new FDF document

void fdf_save(int fdfdoc, string filename)
Write out an FDF file.

void fdf_set_ap(int fdfdoc, string fieldname, int face, string filename, int pagenr)
Set the value of a field

void fdf_set_file(int fdfdoc, string filename)
Set the value of the FDF's /F key

void fdf_set_status(int fdfdoc, string status)
Set the value in the /Status key.

void fdf_set_value(int fdfdoc, string fieldname, string value, int isName)
Set the value of a field

String Functions

These are the basic string manipulation functions supported by PHP. They are all 8-bit clean, which means that the data they act on does not necessarily have to be straight text. In other words, a string may include any character in the ASCII table including 0. Here are the string functions:

string addslashes(string str)
Escape single quotes, double quotes, and backslash characters in a string with backslashes

string base64_decode(string str)
Decode a string with MIME base-64

string base64_encode(string str)
Encode a string with MIME base-64

string chop(string str)
Remove trailing whitespace

string chr(int ascii)
Convert an ASCII code to a character

string chunk_split(string str [, int chunklen [, string ending]])
Return split line

string convert_cyr_string(string str, string from, string to)
Convert from one Cyrillic character set to another

string crypt(string str [, string salt])
DES-encrypt a string

int ereg(string pattern, string string [, array registers])
Regular expression match

string ereg_replace(string pattern, string string [, array registers])
Replace regular expression

int eregi(string pattern, string string [, array registers])
Case-insensitive regular expression match

PHP

string eregi_replace(string pattern, string string [, array registers])
Replace case-insensitive regular expression

string escapeshellcmd(string str)
Escape shell metacharacters

array explode(string separator, string str)
Split a string on the specified string separator

string hebrev(string str, int max_chars_per_line)
Convert logical Hebrew text to visual text

string hebrevc(string str, int max_chars_per_line)
Convert logical Hebrew text to visual text with newline conversion

string htmlentities(string str)
Convert all applicable characters to HTML entities

string htmlspecialchars(string str)
Convert special characters to HTML entities

string implode(array src, string glue)
Join array elements into a string

string join(array src, string glue)
Join array elements into a string

string ltrim(string str)
Strip whitespace from the beginning of a string

string md5(string str)
Calculate the *md5* hash of a string

string nl2br(string str)
Convert newlines to HTML line breaks

int ord(string character)
Return the ASCII value of character

void parse_str(string str)
Parse the string into variables

void print(string str)
Output a string

int printf(string format, mixed args, . . .)
Output a formatted string

string quoted_printable_decode(string str)
Convert a quoted-printable string to an 8-bit string

string quotemeta(string str)
Quote metacharacters

string rawurldecode(string str)
Decode URL-encoded strings

string rawurlencode(string str)
URL-encode according to RFC-1738

string rtrim(string str)
Remove trailing whitespace (alias for `chop()` function)

string setlocale(string category, string locale)
Set locale information

int similar_text(string str1, string str2 [, double percent])
Calculate the similarity between two strings

string soundex(string str)
Calculate the soundex key of a string

array split(string pattern, string string [, int limit])
Split string into array by regular expression

string sprintf(string format, mixed args, -)
Return a formatted string

string sql_regcase(string string)
Make regular expression for case-insensitive match

string str_replace(string needle, string str, string haystack)
Replace all occurrences of `needle` in haystack with `str`

int strcasecmp(string str1, string str2)
Binary-safe, case-insensitive string comparison

string strchr(string haystack, string needle)
Find the last occurrence of a character in a string

int strcmp(string str1, string str2)
Binary safe string comparison

int strcspn(string str1, string str2)
Find length of initial segment not matching mask

string stripslashes(string str)
Unquote string quoted with `addslashes()`

string stristr(string haystack, string needle)
Find first occurrence of a string within another, case-insensitive

int strlen(string str)
Get string length

int strpos(string haystack, string needle)
Find position of first occurrence of a string

string strrchr(string haystack, string needle)
Find last occurrence of a character in a string

string strrev(string str)
Reverse a string

int strrpos(string haystack, string needle)
Find position of last occurrence of a character in a string

int strspn(string str1, string str2)
Find length of initial segment-matching mask

string strstr(string haystack, string needle)
Find first occurrence of a string

string strtok(string str, string token)
Tokenize string

string strtolower(string str)
Make a string lowercase

string strtoupper(string str)
Make a string uppercase

string strtr(string str, string from, string to)
Translate certain characters

string substr(string str, int start, int length)
Return part of a string

string trim(string str)
Strip whitespace from the beginning and end of a string

string ucfirst(string str)
Make a string's first character uppercase

string ucwords(string str)
Uppercase the first character of every word in a string

string uniqid(string prefix)
Generate a unique ID

string urldecode(string str)
Decode URL-encoded string

string urlencode(string str)
URL-encode a string

Variable Manipulation Functions

The following functions operate on PHP variables. There are functions for getting and setting the type of a variable, as well as various ways to encode and decode variables for storage.

bool define(string var_name, mixed value[, int case_sensitive])
Define a constant value

int defined(string constant_name)
Test if a constant is defined

double doubleval(mixed var)
Get the double-precision value of a variable

string getenv(string varname)
Get the value of an environment variable

string gettype(mixed var)
Return the type of the variable

int intval(mixed var [, int base])
Get the integer value of a variable using the optional base for the conversion

bool is_array(mixed var)
Return `true` if variable is an array

bool is_double(mixed var)
Return `true` if variable is a double

bool is_float(mixed var)
An alias for `is_double`

bool is_int(mixed var)
An alias for `is_long`

bool is_integer(mixed var)
An alias for `is_long`

bool is_long(mixed var)
Return `true` if variable is a long (integer)

bool is_object(mixed var)
Return `true` if variable is an object

string pack(string format, mixed arg1, mixed arg2, ...)
Take one or more arguments and pack them into a binary string according to the format argument

bool is_real(mixed var)
An alias for `is_double`

bool is_string(mixed var)
Return `true` if variable is a string

void putenv(string setting)
Set the value of an environment variable

string serialize(mixed variable)
Return a string representation of variable (which can later be unserialized)

int settype(string var, string type)
Set the type of the variable

string strval(mixed var)
Get the string value of a variable

array unpack(string format, string input)
Unpack binary string into named array elements according to format argument

mixed unserialize(string variable_representation)
Take a string representation of variable and recreate it

void var_dump(mixed var)
Dump a string representation of variable to output

XML Functions

As of Version 3.0.6, PHP has XML support built on top of James Clark's *expat* library (see *http://www.guardian.no/~ssb/phpxml.html*).

XML Event Handlers

PHP's XML support is event-driven. This means you can set up functions that can handle different types of data from the parser. Here are the different types of handlers.

Element handlers
Called when the parser encounters start and end elements (tags)

Character data handler
Called when nonmarkup character data is found

Processing instruction (PI) handler
Called for processing instruction information; PHP code, among other things, can be embedded into such markup

Notation declaration handler
Called for notation definitions (notations are a way of declaring data formats)

External entity reference handler and unparsed entity declaration handler
Called for entity references and declarations

Default handler
Called for data that is not covered by any other handler

Character Encoding

The XML extension supports three character sets: US-ASCII, ISO-8859-1, and UTF-8 encoded Unicode. Input (source) and output (target) encoding can be controlled separately. UTF-16 is not supported.

Function Reference

Here are the XML functions provided by PHP:

string utf8_decode(string data)
Convert a UTF-8 encoded string to ISO-8859-1

string utf8_encode(string data)
Encode an ISO-8859-1 string to UTF-8

string xml_error_string(int code)
Get XML parser error string

int xml_get_current_byte_index(int parser)
Get the current byte index for the XML parser

int xml_get_current_column_number(int parser)
Get the current column number for the XML parser

int xml_get_current_line_number(int parser)
Get the current line number for the XML parser

int xml_get_error_code(int parser)
Get the XML parser error code

int xml_parse(int parser, string data[, int final])
Start parsing an XML document

int xml_parser_create([string encoding])
Create an XML parser and return a handle for use by other XML functions

string xml_parser_free(int parser)
Free the XML parser

mixed xml_parser_get_option(int parser, int option)
Get options from the XML parser

int xml_parser_set_option(int parser, int option, mixed value)
Set options in the XML parser

int xml_set_character_data_handler(int parser, string handler)
Set the character data handler function for the XML parser

int xml_set_default_handler(int parser, string handler)
Set the default handler function for the XML parser

int xml_set_element_handler(int parser, string shandler, string handler)
Set the element handler functions for the XML parser

int xml_set_external_entity_ref_handler(int parser, string handler)
Set the notation declaration handler function for the XML parser

int xml_set_notation_decl_handler(int parser, string handler)
Set the notation declaration handler function for the XML parser

int xml_set_processing_instruction_handler(int parser, string handler)
Set the processing instruction (PI) handler function for the XML parser

int xml_set_unparsed_entity_decl_handler(int parser, string handler)
Set the unparsed entity declaration handler function for the XML parser

PHP

Miscellaneous Functions

DNS/Networking Functions

int checkdnsrr(string host [, string type])
Check DNS records corresponding to a given Internet hostname or IP address

int fsockopen(string hostname, int port [, int errno [, string errstr]])
Open Internet or Unix domain socket connection

string gethostbyaddr(string ip_address)
Get the Internet hostname corresponding to a given IP address

string gethostbyname(string hostname)
Get the IP address corresponding to a given Internet hostname

array gethostbynamel(string hostname)
Return a list of IP addresses that a given hostname resolves to

int getmxrr(string hostname, array mxhosts [, array weight])
Get MX records corresponding to a given Internet hostname

set_socket_blocking(int socket descriptor, int mode)
Set blocking/non-blocking mode on a socket

Program Execution Functions

escapeshellcmd(string command)
Escape shell metacharacters

int exec(string command [, array output [, int return_value]])
Execute an external program

int passthru(string command [, int return_value])
Execute an external program and display raw output

int system(string command [, int return_value])
Execute an external program and display output

Random Number Functions

int getrandmax(void)
Return the maximum value a random number can have

int mt_getrandmax(void)
Return the maximum value a random number from Mersenne Twister can have

int mt_rand([int min, int max])
Return a random number from Mersenne Twister

void mt_srand(int seed)
Seed Mersenne Twister random number generator

int rand([int min, int max])
Return a random number

void srand(int seed)
Seed random number generator

Semaphore Functions

int sem_acquire(int id)
Acquire the semaphore with the given ID, blocking if necessary

int sem_get(int key [, int max_acquire [, int perm]])
Return an ID for the semaphore with the given key and allow `max_acquire` (default 1) processes to acquire it simultaneously

int sem_release(int id)
Release the semaphore with the given ID

Shared Memory Functions

int shm_attach(int key, int memsize, int perm)
Create or open a shared memory segment

int shm_detach(int shm_id)
Disconnect from shared memory segment

mixed shm_get_var(int id, int variable_key)
Return a variable from shared memory

int shm_put_var(int shm_id, int variable_key, mixed variable)
Insert or update a variable in shared memory

int shm_remove(int key)
Remove a shared memory segment

int shm_remove_var(int id, int variable_key)
Remove a variable from shared memory.

SNMP Functions

Two simple functions mimic the Unix command-line SNMP tools by the same names:

string snmpget(string host, string community, string object_id [, int timeout [, int retries]])
Fetch an SNMP object

string snmpwalk(string host, string community, string object_id [, int timeout [, int retries]])
Return all objects under the specified object ID

Miscellaneous Functions

int dl(string extension_filename)
Load a PHP extension at runtime

void flush(void)
Flush the output buffer

object get_browser([string browser_name])
Get information about the capabilities of a browser

string get_current_user(void)
Get the name of the owner of the current PHP script

int getlastmod(void)
Get time of last page modification

int getmyinode(void)
Get the inode of the current script being parsed

int getmypid(void)
Get current process ID

int getmyuid(void)
Get PHP script owner's user ID

array getrusage([int who])
Return an array of usage statistics

int mail(string to, string subject, string message [, string additional_headers])
Send an email message

void register_shutdown_function(string function_name)
Register a user-level function to be called on request termination

PART VII

HTTP

CHAPTER 17

HTTP

The Hypertext Transfer Protocol (HTTP) is the language web clients and servers use to communicate with each other. It is essentially the backbone of the World Wide Web. While HTTP is largely the realm of server and client programming, a firm understanding of HTTP is also important for CGI programming. In addition, sometimes HTTP filters back to the users—for example, when server error codes are reported in a browser window.

All HTTP transactions follow the same general format. Each client request and server response has three parts: the request or response line, a header section, and the entity body. The client initiates a transaction as follows:

1. The client contacts the server at a designated port number (by default, 80). It then sends a document request by specifying an HTTP command called a *method*, followed by a document address, and an HTTP version number.

   For example:

   ```
   GET /index.html HTTP/1.1
   ```

   This uses the `GET` method to request the document *index.html* using Version 1.1 of HTTP. HTTP methods are discussed in more detail later in this chapter.

2. Next, the client sends optional header information to inform the server of its configuration and the document formats it will accept. All header information is given line by line, each with a header name and value. For example, this header information sent by the client indicates its name and version number and specifies several document preferences:

   ```
   User-Agent: Mozilla/4.05(WinNT; I)
   Accept: image/gif, image/x-xbitmap, image/jpeg, image/pjpeg, */*
   ```

   The client sends a blank line to end the header.

3. After sending the request and headers, the client may send additional data. This data is mostly used by CGI programs that use the POST method. It may also be used by clients like Netscape Navigator Professional Edition to publish an edited page back onto the web server.

The server responds in the following way to the client's request:

1. The server replies with a status line containing three fields: HTTP version, status code, and description. The HTTP version indicates the version of HTTP the server is using to respond. The status code is a three-digit number that indicates the server's result of the client's request. The description following the status code is simply human-readable text that describes the status code. For example:

   ```
   HTTP/1.1 200 OK
   ```

   This status line indicates that the server uses Version 1.1 of HTTP in its response. A status code of 200 means that the client's request was successful, and the requested data will be supplied after the headers.

2. After the status line, the server sends header information to the client about itself and the requested document. For example:

   ```
   Date: Fri, 20 Sep 1998 08:17:58 GMT
   Server: NCSA/1.5.2
   Last-modified: Mon, 17 Jun 1998 21:53:08 GMT
   Content-type: text/html
   Content-length: 2482
   ```

   A blank line ends the header.

3. If the client's request is successful, the requested data is sent. This data may be a copy of a file or the response from a CGI program. If the client's request could not be fulfilled, the additional data may be a human-readable explanation of why the server could not fulfill the request.

In HTTP 1.0, after the server has finished sending the requested data, it disconnects from the client, and the transaction is over unless a `Connection: Keep Alive` header is sent. Beginning with HTTP 1.1, however, the default is for the server to maintain the connection and allow the client to make additional requests. Since many documents embed other documents (inline images, frames, applets, etc.), this saves the overhead of the client having to repeatedly connect to the same server just to draw a single page. Under HTTP 1.1, therefore, the transaction might cycle back to the beginning, until either the client or server explicitly closes the connection.

Being a stateless protocol, HTTP does not maintain any information from one transaction to the next, so the next transaction needs to start all over again. The advantage is that an HTTP server can serve a lot more clients in a given period of time, since there's no additional overhead for tracking sessions from one connection to the next. The disadvantage is that more elaborate CGI programs need to use hidden input fields (as described in Chapter 6, *Forms*), or external tools such as cookies (described later in this chapter) to maintain information from one transaction to the next.

Client Requests

Client requests are broken into three sections. The first line of a message always contains an HTTP command called a *method*, a URI that identifies the file or resource the client is querying, and the HTTP version number. The second section of a client request contains header information, which provides information about the client and the data entity it is sending the server. The third part of a client request is the *entity body*, the data being sent to the server.

A Uniform Resource Identifier (URI) is a general term for all valid formats of addressing schemes supported on the World Wide Web. The one in common use now is the Uniform Resource Locator (URL) addressing scheme. See Chapter 1, *Introduction*, for more information on URLs.

Methods

A method is an HTTP command that begins the first line of a client request. The method tells the server the purpose of the client request. There are three methods defined for HTTP: GET, HEAD, and POST. Other methods are also defined but not as widely supported by servers (although the other methods will be used more often in the future, not less). Methods are case-sensitive, so a "GET" is different from a "get."

The GET method

The GET method is a request for information located at a specified URI on the server. It is the most commonly used method by browsers to retrieve information. The result of a GET request can be generated in many different ways; it can be a file accessible by the server, the output of a program or CGI script, the output from a hardware device, etc.

When a client uses the GET method in its request, the server responds with a status line, headers, and the requested data. If the server cannot process the request due to an error or lack of authorization, the server usually sends a textual explanation in the data portion of the response.

The entity-body portion of a GET request is always empty. GET is basically used to say "Give me this file." The file or program the client requests is usually identified by its full pathname on the server.

Here is an example of a successful GET request to retrieve a file. The client sends:

```
GET /index.html HTTP/1.0
Connection: Keep-Alive
User-Agent: Mozilla/2.02Gold (WinNT; I)
Host: www.oreilly.com
Accept: image/gif, image/x-xbitmap, image/jpeg, image/pjpeg, */*
```

The server responds with:

```
HTTP/1.0 200 Document follows
Date: Fri, 20 Sep 1998 08:17:58 GMT
Server: NCSA/1.5.2
Last-modified: Mon, 17 Jun 1998 21:53:08 GMT
```

```
Content-type: text/html
Content-length: 2482

(body of document here)
```

The GET method is also used to send input to programs like CGI through form tags. Since GET requests have empty entity-bodies, the input data is appended to the URL in the GET line of the request. When a `<form>` tag specifies the `method="GET"` attribute value, key-value pairs representing the input from the form are appended to the URL following a question mark (?). Pairs are separated by an ampersand (&). For example:

```
GET /cgi-bin/birthday.pl?month=august&date=24 HTTP/1.0
```

This causes the server to send the *birthday.pl* CGI program the `month` and `date` values specified in a form on the client. The input data at the end of the URL is encoded to CGI specifications. For literal use of special characters, the client uses hexadecimal notation. The character encoding is described in Chapter 12, *CGI Overview*.

The GET method can also supply *extra-path information* in the same manner. This is achieved by adding the extra path after the URL, i.e., */cgi-bin/display.pl/cgi/cgi_doc.txt*. The server gauges where the program's name ends (`display.pl`); everything after that is read as the extra path.

The HEAD method

The HEAD method is functionally like GET except that the server will not send anything in the data portion of the reply. The HEAD method requests only the header information on a file or resource. The header information from a HEAD request should be the same as that from a GET request.

This method is used when the client wants to find out information about the document and not retrieve it. Many applications exist for the HEAD method. For example, the client may desire the following information:

- The modification time of a document, useful for cache-related queries
- The size of a document, useful for page layout, estimating arrival time, or determining whether to request a smaller version of the document
- The type of the document, to allow the client to examine only documents of a certain type
- The type of server, to allow customized server queries

It is important to note that most of the header information provided by a server is optional and may not be given by all servers. A good design for web clients is to allow flexibility in the server response and take default actions when desired header information is not given by the server.

The following is an example HTTP transaction using the HEAD request. The client sends:

```
HEAD /index.html HTTP/1.1
Connection: Keep-Alive
User-Agent: Mozilla/2.02Gold (WinNT; I)
Host: www.oreilly.com
Accept: image/gif, image/x-xbitmap, image/jpeg, image/pjpeg, */*
```

The server responds with:

```
HTTP/1.1 200 Document follows
Date: Fri, 20 Sep 1998 08:17:58 GMT
Server: NCSA/1.5.2
Last-modified: Mon, 17 Jun 1998 21:53:08 GMT
Content-type: text/html
Content-length: 2482
```

(No entity body is sent in response to a HEAD request.)

The POST method

The POST method allows data to be sent to the server in a client request. The data is directed to a data-handling program that the server has access to (e.g., a CGI script). The POST method can be used for many applications, such as:

- Network services, such as newsgroup postings
- Command-line interface programs
- Annotation of documents on the server
- Database operations

The data sent to the server is in the entity-body section of the client's request. After the server processes the POST request and headers, it passes the entity-body to the program specified by the URI. The encoding scheme most commonly used with POST is URL-encoding, which allows form data to be translated into a list of variables and values for CGI processing. Chapter 12, provides details on CGI and URL-encoded data.

Here is a quick example of a client request using the POST method to send birth-date data from a form:

```
POST /cgi-bin/birthday.pl HTTP/1.0
User-Agent: Mozilla/2.02Gold (WinNT; I)
Accept: image/gif, image/x-xbitmap, image/jpeg, image/pjpeg, */*
Host: www.oreilly.com
Content-type: application/x-www-form-urlencoded
Content-length: 20

month=august&date=24
```


Other methods

The following methods are also defined, although not as frequently used:

LINK
Requests that header information is associated with a document on the server.

UNLINK

Requests dissociation of header information from a document on the server.

PUT

Requests that the entity-body of the request be stored at the specified URI.

DELETE

Requests the removal of data at a URI on the server.

OPTIONS

Requests information about communications options available on the server. The request URI can be substituted with an asterisk (*) to indicate the server as a whole.

TRACE

Requests the request entity body be returned intact. Used for debugging.

CONNECT

A reserved method used specifically for Secure Sockets Layer (SSL) tunneling.

Server Responses and Status Codes

The server's response to a client request is grouped into three parts. The first line is the server response line, which contains the HTTP version number, a three-digit number indicating the status of the request (called a *server response code* or *status code*), and a short phrase describing the status. The response line is followed by the header information and an entity body if there is one.

Status codes are typically generated by web servers. However, they can also be generated by CGI scripts that bypass the server's precooked headers and supply their own. Status codes are grouped as follows:

Code Range	*Response Meaning*
100–199	Informational
200–299	Client request successful
300–399	Client request redirected, further action necessary
400–499	Client request incomplete
500–599	Server errors

HTTP defines only a few specific codes in each range, although servers may define their own as needed. If a client receives a code it does not recognize, it should understand its basic meaning from its numerical range. While most web browsers handle codes in the 100-, 200-, and 300-range silently, some error codes in the 400- and 500-range are commonly reported back to the user (e.g., "404 Not Found").

Informational

A response in the range of 100–199 is informational, indicating that the client's request was received and is being processed.

`100 Continue`
: The initial part of the request has been received and the client may continue with its request.

`101 Switching Protocols`
: The server is complying with a client request to switch protocols to the one specified in the `Upgrade` header field.

Client Request Successful

A response in the range of 200–299 means that the client's request was successful.

`200 OK`
: The client's request was successful, and the server's response contains the requested data.

`201 Created`
: This status code is used whenever a new URI is created. With this result code, the `Location` header is given by the server to specify where the new data was placed.

`202 Accepted`
: The request was accepted but not immediately acted upon. More information about the transaction may be given in the entity body of the server's response. Note that there is no guarantee that the server will actually honor the request, even though it may seem like a legitimate request at the time of acceptance.

`203 Non-Authoritative Information`
: The information in the entity header is from a local or third-party copy and not from the original server.

`204 No Content`
: A status code and header are given in the response, but there is no entity body in the reply. On receiving this response, browsers should not update their document view. This is a useful code for an imagemap handler to return when the user clicks on useless or blank areas of an image.

`205 Reset Content`
: The browser should clear the form used for this transaction for additional input. Appropriate for data-entry CGI applications.

`206 Partial Content`
: The server is returning partial data of the size requested. Used in response to a request specifying a `Range` header. The server must specify the range included in the response with the `Content-Range` header.

Redirection

A response code in the 300–399 range indicates that the request was not performed, and the client needs to take further action for a successful request.

300 `Multiple Choices`
The requested URI refers to more than one resource. For example, the URI could refer to a document that has been translated into many languages. The entity body returned by the server could have a list of more specific data about how to choose the correct resource.

301 `Moved Permanently`
The requested URI is no longer used by the server, and the operation specified in the request was not performed. The new location for the requested document is specified in the `Location` header. All future requests for the document should use the new URI.

302 `Found`
The requested URI temporarily has a new URI. The `Location` header points to the new location. If this is in response to a GET or a HEAD, the client should use the new URI to resolve the request immediately after receiving the response.

303 `See Other`
The requested URI can be found at a different URI (specified in the `Location` header) and should be retrieved by a GET on that resource.

304 `Not Modified`
This is the response code to an `If-Modified-Since` header, where the URI has not been modified since the specified date. The entity body is not sent, and the client should use its own local copy.

305 `Use Proxy`
The requested URI must be accessed through the proxy in the `Location` header.

307 `Temporary Redirect`
The requested URI has moved temporarily. The `Location` header points to the new location. Immediately after receiving this status code, the client should use the new URI to resolve the request, but the old URI should be used for all future requests.

Client Request Incomplete

A response code in the range of 400–499 means that the client's request was incomplete and may indicate further information is required from the client.

400 `Bad Request`
This response code indicates that the server detected a syntax error in the client's request.

401 `Unauthorized`
The result code is given along with the `WWW-Authenticate` header to indicate that the request lacked proper authorization, and the client should supply proper authorization when requesting this URI again.

402 `Payment Required`
This code is not yet implemented in HTTP. However, it may, one day, indicate that a payment is required to receive the document on the server.

403 `Forbidden`
The request was denied for a reason the server does not want to (or has no means to) indicate to the client.

404 `Not Found`
The document at the specified URI does not exist.

405 `Method Not Allowed`
This code is given with the `Allow` header and indicates that the method used by the client is not supported for this URI.

406 `Not Acceptable`
The URI specified by the client exists, but not in a format preferred by the client. Along with this code, the server provides the `Content-Language`, `Content-Encoding`, and `Content-Type` headers.

407 `Proxy Authentication Required`
The proxy server needs to authorize the request before forwarding it. Used with the `Proxy-Authenticate` header.

408 `Request Time-out`
This response code means the client did not produce a full request within some predetermined time (usually specified in the server's configuration), and the server is disconnecting the network connection.

409 `Conflict`
This code indicates that the request conflicts with another request or with the server's configuration. Information about the conflict should be returned in the data portion of the reply.

410 `Gone`
This code indicates that the requested URI no longer exists and has been permanently removed from the server.

411 `Length Required`
The server will not accept the request without a `Content-Length` header supplied in the request.

412 `Precondition Failed`
The condition specified by one or more `If . . .` headers in the request evaluated to `false`.

413 `Request Entity Too Large`
The server will not process the request because its entity body is too large.

414 `Request-URI Too Long`
The server will not process the request because its requested URI is too large.

415 `Unsupported Media Type`
The server will not process the request because its entity body is in an unsupported format.

416 `Requested Range Not Satisfiable`
: The server detected a `Range` header that contained no valid values for the target. In addition, an `If-Range` header was omitted.

417 `Expectation Failed`
: The condition specified in an `Expect` header could not be satisfied.

Server Errors

Response codes in the range of 500–599 indicate that the server encountered an error and may be unable to perform the client's request.

500 `Internal Server Error`
: This code indicates that a part of the server (for example, a CGI program) has crashed or encountered a configuration error.

501 `Not Implemented`
: This code indicates that the client requested an action that cannot be performed by the server.

502 `Bad Gateway`
: This code indicates that the server (or proxy) encountered invalid responses from another server (or proxy).

503 `Service Unavailable`
: This code means that the service is temporarily unavailable but should be restored in the future. If the server knows when it will be available again, a `Retry-After` header may also be supplied.

504 `Gateway Time-out`
: This response is like 408 (`Request Time-out`) except that a gateway or proxy has timed out.

505 `HTTP Version not supported`
: The server will not support the HTTP protocol version used in the request.

HTTP Headers

HTTP headers are used to transfer all sorts of information between client and server. There are four categories of headers:

General
: Information not related to the client, server, or HTTP

Request
: Preferred document formats and server parameters

Response
: Information about the server sending the response

Entity
: Information on the data being sent between the client and server

General headers and entity headers are the same for both the server and client.

All headers in HTTP messages contain the header name followed by a colon (:), then a space, and the value of the header. Header names are case-insensitive (thus, `Content-Type` is the same as `Content-type`). The value of a header can extend over multiple lines by preceding each extra line with at least one space or tab character.

General Headers

General headers are used in both client requests and server responses. Some may be more specific to either a client or server message.

Cache-Control

`Cache-Control:` *`directives`*

Specifies caching directives in a comma-separated list.

Cache request directives

`no-cache`
: Do not cache.

`no-store`
: Remove information promptly after forwarding.

`max-age` = *seconds*
: Do not send responses older than *seconds*.

`max-stale [` = *seconds* `]`
: Send expired data. If *seconds* are specified, only send data expired by less than the specified number of seconds.

`min-fresh` = *seconds*
: Send data only if still fresh after the specified number of seconds.

`only-if-cached`
: Do not retrieve new data. Only return data already in the cache. Useful unless the network connection is down.

Cache response directives

`public`
: Cachable by any cache.

`private`
: Not cachable by a shared cache.

`no-cache`
: Do not cache.

`no-store`
: Remove information promptly after forwarding.

`no-transform`
: Do not convert data.

→

HTTP

`must-revalidate`
: Client must revalidate the data.

`proxy-revalidate`
: Client must revalidate data except for private client caches.

`max-age=`*seconds*
: The document should be considered stale in the specified number of seconds.

Connection

`Connection:` *`options`*

Specifies options desired for this connection but not for further connections by proxies. The `close` connection option signifies that either the client or server wishes to end the connection (i.e., this is the last transaction).

Date

`Date:` *`dateformat`*

Indicates the current date and time. The preferred date format is described by RFC-1123. For example:

```
Mon, 06 May 1999 04:57:00 GMT
```

For backward compatibility, however, the RFC-850 and ANSI C *asctime()* formats are also acceptable:

```
Monday, 06-May-99 04:57:00 GMT
Mon May 6 04:57:00 1999
```

Use a two-digit year specification at your own risk.

MIME-Version

`MIME-Version:` *`version`*

Specifies the version of MIME (RFC-2045[7]) used in the HTTP transaction. If a message's entity-body does not conform to MIME, this header can be omitted. If the transaction involves MIME-encoded data, but this header is omitted, the default value is assumed to be 1.0.

Pragma

`Pragma: no-cache`

Specifies directives to a proxy system. This header is ignored by the target server. HTTP defines one directive for this header: `no-cache`. In HTTP 1.0, this tells the proxy to request the document from the server instead of the local cache. HTTP 1.1 prefers using `Cache Control: no-cache` instead.

Transfer-Encoding

`Transfer-Encoding: encoding_type`

Indicates what type of transformation has been applied to the message body for safe transfer. Currently only the `chunked` encoding type is defined by HTTP.

Upgrade

`Upgrade: protocol/version`

Specifies the preferred communication protocols. Used in conjunction with response code `101 Switching Protocols`. For example:

```
Upgrade: HTTP/1.2
```

Via

`Via: protocol host [comment] ...`

Used by gateways and proxies to indicate the protocols and hosts that processed the transaction between client and server.

Client Request Headers

Client header data communicates the client's configuration and preferred document formats to the server. Request headers are used in a client message to provide information about the client.

Accept

`Accept: type/subtype [; q=qvalue]`

Specifies media types that the client prefers to accept. Multiple media types can be listed, separated by commas. The optional *qvalue* represents on a scale of 0 to 1 an acceptable quality level for accept types. Media types are listed at the end of this chapter.

Accept-Charset

`Accept-Charset: character_set [; q=qvalue]`

Specifies the character sets the client prefers. Multiple character sets can be listed separated by commas. The optional *qvalue* represents on a scale of 0 to 1 an acceptable quality level for nonpreferred character sets.

Accept-Encoding

`Accept-Encoding: encoding_types`

Specifies the encoding schemes the client can accept, such as `compress` or `gzip`. Multiple encoding schemes can be listed, separated by commas. If no encoding types are listed, none are acceptable to the client.

Accept-Language

`Accept-Language: language [; q=qvalue]`

Specifies the languages the client prefers. Multiple languages can be listed, separated by commas. The optional *qvalue* represents on a scale of 0 to 1 an acceptable quality level for nonpreferred languages. Languages are written with their two-letter abbreviations (e.g., *en* for English, *de* for German, *fr* for French, etc.).

Authorization

`Authorization: scheme credentials`

Provides the client's authorization to access data at a URI. When a requested document requires authorization, the server returns a `WWW-Authenticate` header describing the type of authorization required. The client then repeats the request with the proper authorization information.

The authorization scheme generally used in HTTP is BASIC, and under the BASIC scheme the credentials follow the format *username:password* encoded in base64. For example, for the username "webmaster" and a password "zrma4v," the authorization header would look like this:

```
Authorization: BASIC d2VibWFzdGVyOnpycW1hNHY=
```

The value decodes into `webmaster:zrma4v`.

Cookie

`Cookie: name=value`

Contains a name/value pair of information stored for that URL. Multiple cookies can be specified, separated by semicolons. For browsers supporting Netscape persistent cookies; not included in the HTTP standard. See the discussion of cookies later in this chapter for more information.

From

`From: email_address`

Gives the email address of the user executing the client.

Host

`Host: hostname[:port]`

Specifies the host and port number of the URI. Clients must supply this information in HTTP 1.1, so servers with multiple hostnames can easily differentiate between ambiguous URLs.

If-Modified-Since

`If-Modified-Since: date`

Specifies that the URI data is to be sent only if it has been modified since the date given as the value of this header. This is useful for client-side caching. If the document has not been modified, the server returns a code of `304`, indicating that the client should use the local copy. The specified date should follow the format described under the `Date` header.

If-Match

`If-Match: entity_tag`

A conditional requesting the entity only if it matches the given entity tags (see the `ETag` entity header). An asterisk (`*`) matches any entity, and the transaction continues only if the entity exists.

If-None-Match

`If-None-Match: entity_tag`

A conditional requesting the entity only if it does not match any of the given entity tags (see the `ETag` entity header). An asterisk (`*`) matches any entity; if the entity doesn't exist, the transaction continues.

If-Range

`If-Range: entity_tag | date`

A conditional requesting only the portion of the entity that is missing if it has not been changed, and the entire entity if it has. Must be used in conjunction with a `Range` header. Either an entity tag or a date can identify the partial entity already received; see the `Date` header for information on the format for dates.

If-Unmodified-Since

`If-Unmodified-Since: date`

Specifies that the URI data is to be sent only if it has not been modified since the given date. The specified date should follow the format described under the `Date` header.

Max-Forwards

`Max-Forwards: n`

Limits the number of proxies or gateways that can forward the request. Useful for debugging with the `TRACE` method, avoiding infinite loops.

Proxy-Authorization

`Proxy-Authorization: credentials`

Used for a client to identify itself to a proxy requiring authorization.

Range

`Range: bytes=n-m`

Specifies the partial range(s) requested from the document. Multiple ranges can be listed, separated by commas. If the first digit in the comma-separated byte range(s) is missing, the range is assumed to count from the end of the document. If the second digit is missing, the range is byte *n* to the end of the document. The first byte is byte 0.

Referer

`Referer: url`

Gives the URI of the document that refers to the requested URI (i.e., the source document of the link).

User-Agent

`User-Agent: string`

Gives identifying information about the client program.

Server Response Headers

The response headers described here are used in server responses to communicate information about the server and how it may handle requests.

Accept-Ranges

`Accept-Ranges: bytes|none`

Indicates the acceptance of range requests for a URI, specifying either the range unit (e.g., `bytes`), or `none` if no range requests are accepted.

Age

`Age: seconds`

Indicates the age of the document in seconds.

Proxy-Authenticate

`Proxy-Authenticate: scheme realm`

Indicates the authentication scheme and parameters applicable to the proxy for this URI and the current connection. Used with response `407` (`Proxy Authentication Required`).

Retry-After

`Retry-After: date|seconds`

Used with response code `503` (`Service Unavailable`). It contains either an integer number of seconds or a GMT date and time (as described by the `Date` header formats). If the value is an integer, it is interpreted as the number of seconds to wait after the request was issued. For example:

```
Retry-After: 3600
Retry-After: Sat, 18 May 1996 06:59:37 GMT
```

Server

`Server: string`

Contains the name and version number of the server. For example:

```
Server: NCSA/1.3
```

Set-Cookie

`Set-Cookie: name=value [; options]`

Contains a name/value pair of information to retain for this URL. For browsers supporting Netscape persistent cookies; not included in the HTTP standard. See the discussion of cookies later in this chapter for more information. Options are:

`expires=`*date*
: The cookie becomes invalid after the specified date.

`path=`*pathname*
: The URL range for which the cookie is valid.

`domain=`*domain_name*
: The domain name range for which the cookie is valid.

`secure`
: Return the cookie only under a secure connection.

Vary

`Vary: * | headers`

Specifies that the entity has multiple sources and may therefore vary according to a specified list of request header(s). Multiple headers can be listed, separated by commas. An asterisk (*) means that another factor other than the request headers may affect the document that is returned.

Warning

`Warning: code host [:port] string`

Indicates additional information to that in the status code, for use by caching proxies. The *host* field contains the name or pseudonym of the server host, with an optional port number. The two-digit warning codes and their recommended descriptive strings are:

`10 Response is stale`
: The response data is known to be stale.

`11 Revalidation failed`
: The response data is known to be stale because the proxy failed to revalidate the data.

`12 Disconnected operation`
: The cache is disconnected from the network.

`13 Heuristic expiration`
: The data is older than 24 hours, and the cache heuristically chose a freshness lifetime greater than 24 hours.

`14 Transformation applied`
: The proxy has changed the encoding or media type of the document, as specified by the `Content-Encoding` or `Content-Type` headers.

`99 Miscellaneous warning`
: Arbitrary information to be logged or presented to the user.

WWW-Authenticate

`WWW-Authenticate: scheme realm`

Used with the `401 (Unauthorized)` response code. It specifies the authorization scheme and realm of authorization required from a client at the requested URI. Many different authorization realms can exist on a server. A common authorization scheme is BASIC, which requires a username and password. For example:

```
WWW-Authenticate: BASIC realm="Admin"
```

When returned to the client, this header indicates that the BASIC type of authorization data in the appropriate realm should be returned in the client's `Authorization` header.

Entity Headers

Entity headers are used in both client requests and server responses. They supply information about the entity body in an HTTP message.

Allow

`Allow: *methods*`

Contains a comma-separated list of methods that are allowed at a specified URI. In a server response, it is used with code `405` (`Method Not Allowed`) to inform the client of valid methods available for the requested information.

Content-Encoding

`Content-Encoding: *encoding_schemes*`

Specifies the encoding scheme(s) used for the transferred entity body. Values are `gzip` (or `x-gzip`) and `compress` (or `x-compress`). If multiple encoding schemes are specified (in a comma-separated list), they must be listed in the order in which they were applied to the source data.

Content-Language

`Content-Language: *languages*`

Specifies the language(s) the transferred entity body is intended for. Languages are represented by their two-digit code (e.g., *en* for English, *fr* for French).

Content-Length

`Content-Length: *n*`

This header specifies the length of the data (in bytes) of the transferred entity body. Due to the dynamic nature of some requests, the content length is sometimes unknown, and this header is omitted.

Content-Location

`Content-Location: *uri*`

Supplies the URI for the entity, in cases where a document has multiple entities with separately accessible locations. The URI can be either absolute or relative.

Content-MD5

`Content-MD5:` *`digest`*

Supplies a MD5 digest of the entity, for checking the integrity of the message upon receipt.

Content-Range

`Content-Range: bytes` *`n-m/length`*

Specifies where the accompanying partial entity body should be inserted and the total size of the full entity body. For example:

```
Content-Range: bytes 6143-7166/15339
```

Content-Transfer-Encoding

`Content-Transfer-Encoding:` *`scheme`*

Specifies any transformations that are applied to the entity body for transport over a network. Common values are: `7bit`, `8bit`, `binary`, `base64`, and `quoted-printable`.

Content-Type

`Content-Type:` *`type/subtype`*

Describes the media type and subtype of an entity body. It uses the same values as the client's `Accept` header, and the server should return media types that conform with the client's preferred formats.

ETag

`ETag:` *`entity_tag`*

Defines the entity tag for the `If-Match` and `If-None-Match` request headers.

Expires

`Expires:` *`date`*

Specifies the time when a document may change, or its information becomes invalid. After that time, the document may or may not change or be deleted. The value is a date and time in a valid format, as described for the `Date` header.

Last-Modified

`Last-Modified:` *`date`*

→

Specifies when the specified URI was last modified. The value is a date and time in a valid format, as described for the `Date` header.

Location

`Location: uri`

Specifies the new location of a document, usually with response codes `201` (`Created`), `301` (`Moved Permanently`), or `302` (`Moved Temporarily`). The URI given must be written as an absolute URI.

Cookies

Persistent-state, client-side cookies were introduced by Netscape Navigator to enable a server to store client-specific information on the client's machine and use that information when a server or a particular page is accessed again by the client. The cookie mechanism allows servers to personalize pages for each client, or remember selections the client has made when browsing through various pages of a site—all without having to use a complicated (or more time-consuming) CGI/database system on the server's side.

Cookies work in the following way: when a CGI program identifies a new user, it adds an extra header to its response containing an identifier for that user and other information the server may glean from the client's input. This header informs the cookie-enabled browser to add this information to the client's *cookies* file. After this, all requests to that URL from the browser will include the cookie information as an extra header in the request. The CGI program uses this information to return a document tailored to that specific client. The cookies are stored on the client user's hard drive, so the information remains even when the browser is closed and reopened.

The Set-Cookie Response Header

A cookie is created when a client visits a site or page for the first time. A CGI program looks for previous cookie information in the client request and, if it is not there, sends a response containing a `Set-Cookie` header. This header contains a name/value pair (the actual cookie) that comprises the special information you want the client to maintain. There are other optional fields you may include in the header.

The `Set-Cookie` header uses the following syntax:

```
Set-Cookie: name=value; expires=date;
path=pathname; domain=domain-name; secure
```

Multiple `Set-Cookie` headers may be included in the server response. The *name=value* pair is the only required attribute for this header, and it should come first. The remaining attributes can be in any order and are defined as follows:

HTTP

`name`=*value*

Both *name* and *value* can be any strings that do not contain either a semi-colon, space, or tab. Encoding such as URL encoding may be used if these entities are required in the *name* or *value*, as long as your script is prepared to handle it.

`expires`=*date*

This attribute sets the date when a cookie becomes invalid. The date is formatted in a nonstandard way, like this:

```
Wednesday, 01-Sep-96 00:00:00 GMT
```

After this date, the cookie becomes invalid, and the browser no longer sends it. Only GMT (Greenwich Mean Time) is used. If no `expires` date is given, the cookie is used only for the current session.

`path`=*pathname*

The `path` attribute supplies a URL range for which the cookie is valid. If `path` is set to `/pub`, for example, the cookie is sent for URLs in `/pub` as well as lower levels such as `/pub/docs` and `/pub/images`. A *`pathname`* of "/" indicates that the cookie will be used for all URLs at the site from which the cookie originated. No `path` attribute means that the cookie is valid only for the originating URL.

`domain`=*domain-name*

This attribute specifies a domain name range for which the cookie is returned. The *domain-name* must contain at least two dots (.), e.g., `.oreilly.com`. This value covers both `www.oreilly.com` and `software.oreilly.com`, and any other server in the *oreilly.com* domain.

`secure`

The `secure` attribute tells the client to return the cookie only over a secure connection (via SHTTP and SSL). Leaving out this attribute means that the cookie is always returned, regardless of the connection.

The Cookie Request Header

Each time a browser goes to a web page, it checks its cookies file for any cookies stored for that URL. If there are any, the browser includes a `Cookie` header in the request containing the cookie's *name=value* pairs.

```
Cookie: name1=value1; name2=value2; . . .
```

Returned cookies may come from multiple entries in the cookies files, depending on path ranges and domain ranges. For instance, if two cookies from the same site are set with the following headers:

```
Set-Cookie: Gemstone=Diamond; path=/
Set-Cookie: Gemstone=Emerald; path=/caves
```

when the browser requests a page at the site in the */caves* path, it returns:

```
Cookie: Gemstone=Emerald; Gemstone=Diamond
```

Both items share the same name, but since they are separate cookies, they both apply to the particular URL in */caves*. When returning cookies, the browser returns the most specific path or domain first, followed by less specific matches.

When the `Cookie` header is encountered, many servers pass the value of that header to CGI programs using the HTTP_COOKIE environment variable. See Chapter 12, for more information on CGI environment variables.

The preliminary cookies specification places some restrictions on the number and size of cookies:

- Clients should be able to support at least 300 total cookies. Servers should not expect a client to store more.
- The limit on the size of each cookie (name and value combined) should not exceed 4KB.
- A maximum of 20 cookies per server or domain is allowed. This limit applies to each specified server or domain, so *www.oreilly.com* is allowed 20, and *software.oreilly.com* is allowed 20, if they are each specified by their full names.

An issue arises with proxy servers in regard to the headers. Both the `Set-Cookie` and `Cookie` headers should be propagated through the proxy, even if a page is cached or has not been modified (according to the `If-Modified-Since` condition). The `Set-Cookie` header should also never be cached by the proxy.

Most web servers and clients still support the original cookie specification proposed by Netscape. Recently, the IETF has issued an Internet draft proposal for an updated cookie specification. This document describes new `Set-Cookie2` and `Cookie2` headers to eventually replace the original headers. They add additional attributes for comments and path specifiers.

Clients and servers that implement the new headers should be backwards-compatible with the original specification. The draft proposal can be found at the following URL:

```
http://www.ietf.org/internet-drafts/draft-ietf-http-state-man-mec-10.txt
```

Media Types and Subtypes

Media types are used to communicate the format of the content in HTTP transactions. Clients use media types in their `Accept` headers to indicate what formats they prefer to receive data in. Servers use media types in their `Content-Type` headers to tell the client what format the accompanying entity is in—i.e., whether the enclosed text is HTML that needs to be formatted, GIF or JPEG to be rendered, or PDF that requires opening an external viewer or using a plug-in.

Internet media types used by HTTP closely resemble MIME types. MIME (Multipurpose Internet Mail Extension) was designed as a method for sending attachments in email over the Internet. Like MIME, media types follow the format *type/subtype*.

Asterisks (*) represent a wildcard. For example, the following client header means that documents of all formats are accepted:

```
Accept: */*
```

The following client header means that all `text` format types are accepted, regardless of the subtype:

```
Accept: text/*
```

Servers and CGI programs are expected to examine the format types reported by the `Accept` header and return data of an acceptable type when possible. Most servers determine the format of a document from its filename suffix—for example, a file ending with *.htm* or *.html* is assumed to be HTML format, so the server sends the document with a `Content-Type` of `text/html`. When calling a CGI program, servers cannot know the format of the data being returned, so the CGI program is responsible for reporting the content type itself. For that reason, every CGI program needs to include a `Content-Type` header such as:

```
Content-Type: text/html
```

Table 17-1 lists commonly used media types, along with the filename suffixes recognized by most servers. These servers can be easily configured to recognize additional suffixes as well.

Table 17-1: Media Types and Subtypes

Type/Subtype	*Usual Extension*
application/activemessage	
application/andrew-inset	
application/applefile	
application/atomicmail	
application/cals-1840	
application/commonground	
application/cybercash	
application/dca-rft	
application/dec-dx	
application/EDI-Consent	
application/EDIFACT	
application/EDI-X12	
application/eshop	
application/hyperstudio	
application/iges	
application/mac-binhex40	
application/macwriteii	
application/marc	
application/mathematica	
application/msword	doc
application/news-message-id	
application/news-transmission	

Table 17-1: Media Types and Subtypes (continued)

Type/Subtype	*Usual Extension*
application/octet-stream	bin
application/oda	oda
application/pdf	pdf
application/pgp-encrypted	
application/pgp-signature	
application/pgp-keys	
application/pkcs7-mime	
application/pkcs7-signature	
application/pkcs10	
application/postscript	ai, eps, ps
application/prs.alvestrand.titrax-sheet	
application/prs.cww	
application/prs.nprend	
application/remote-printing	
application/riscos	
application/rtf	rtf
application/set-payment-initiation	
application/set-payment	
application/set-registration-initiation	
application/set-registration	
application/sgml	sgm, sgml, gml, dtd
application/sgml-open-catalog	soc, cat
application/slate	
application/vemmi	
application/vnd.$commerce_battelle	
application/vnd.3M.Post-it-Notes	
application/vnd.acucobol	
application/vnd.anser-web-funds-transfer-initiation	
application/vnd.anser-web-certificate-issue-initiation	
application/vnd.audiograph	
application/vnd.businessobjects	
application/vnd.claymore	
application/vnd.comsocaller	
application/vnd.dna	
application/vnd.dxr	
application/vnd.ecdis-update	
application/vnd.ecowin.chart	
application/vnd.ecowin.filerequest	
application/vnd.ecowin.fileupdate	
application/vnd.ecowin.series	
application/vnd.ecowin.seriesrequest	
application/vnd.ecowin.seriesupdate	

Table 17-1: Media Types and Subtypes (continued)

Type/Subtype	*Usual Extension*
application/vnd.enliven	
application/vnd.epson.salt	
application/vnd.fdf	
application/vnd.ffsns	
application/vnd.FloGraphIt	
application/vnd.framemaker	
application/vnd.fujitsu.oasys	
application/vnd.fujitsu.oasys2	
application/vnd.fujitsu.oasys3	
application/vnd.fujitsu.oasysprs	
application/vnd.fujitsu.oasysgp	
application/vnd.fujixerox.docuworks	
application/vnd.hp-hps	
application/vnd.hp-HPGL	
application/vnd.hp-PCL	
application/vnd.hp-PCLXL	
application/vnd.ibm.MiniPay	
application/vnd.ibm.modcap	
application/vnd.intercon.formnet	
application/vnd.intertrust.digibox	
application/vnd.intertrust.nncp	
application/vnd.is-xpr	
application/vnd.japannet-directory-service	
application/vnd.japannet-jpnstore-wakeup	
application/vnd.japannet-payment-wakeup	
application/vnd.japannet-registration	
application/vnd.japannet-registration-wakeup	
application/vnd.japannet-setstore-wakeup	
application/vnd.japannet-verification	
application/vnd.japannet-verification-wakeup	
application/vnd.koan	
application/vnd.lotus-wordpro	
application/vnd.lotus-approach	
application/vnd.lotus-1-2-3	
application/vnd.lotus-organizer	
application/vnd.lotus-screencam	
application/vnd.lotus-freelance	
application/vnd.meridian-slingshot	
application/vnd.mif	
application/vnd.minisoft-hp3000-save	
application/vnd.mitsubishi.misty-guard.trustweb	
application/vnd.ms-artgalry	

Table 17-1: Media Types and Subtypes (continued)

Type/Subtype	*Usual Extension*
application/vnd.ms-asf	
application/vnd.ms-excel	
application/vnd.ms-powerpoint	
application/vnd.ms-project	
application/vnd.ms-tnef	
application/vnd.ms-works	
application/vnd.music-niff	
application/vnd.musician	
application/vnd.netfpx	
application/vnd.noblenet-web	
application/vnd.noblenet-sealer	
application/vnd.noblenet-directory	
application/vnd.novadigm.EDM	
application/vnd.novadigm.EDX	
application/vnd.novadigm.EXT	
application/vnd.osa.netdeploy	
application/vnd.powerbuilder6	
application/vnd.powerbuilder6-s	
application/vnd.rapid	
application/vnd.seemail	
application/vnd.shana.informed.formtemplate	
application/vnd.shana.informed.formdata	
application/vnd.shana.informed.package	
application/vnd.shana.informed.interchange	
application/vnd.street-stream	
application/vnd.svd	
application/vnd.swiftview-ics	
application/vnd.truedoc	
application/vnd.visio	
application/vnd.webturbo	
application/vnd.wrq-hp3000-labelled	
application/vnd.wt.stf	
application/vnd.xara	
application/vnd.yellowriver-custom-menu	
application/wita	
application/wordperfect5.1	
application/x-bcpio	bcpio
application/x-cpio	cpio
application/x-csh	csh
application/x-dvi	dvi
application/x-gtar	gtar
application/x-hdf	hdf

HTTP

Table 17-1: Media Types and Subtypes (continued)

Type/Subtype	*Usual Extension*
application/x-latex	latex
application/x-mif	mif
application/x-netcdf	nc, cdf
application/x-sh	sh
application/x-shar	shar
application/x-sv4cpio	sv4cpio
application/x-sv4crc	sv4crc
application/x-tar	tar
application/x-tcl	tcl
application/x-tex	tex
application/x-texinfo	texinfo, texi
application/x-troff-man	man
application/x-troff-me	me
application/x-troff-ms	ms
application/x-troff	t, tr, roff
application/x-ustar	ustar
application/x-wais-source	src
application/xml	xml, dtd
application/x400-bp	
application/zip	zip
audio/32kadpcm	
audio/32kadpcm	
audio/basic	au, snd
audio/vnd.qcelp	wav
audio/x-aiff	aif, aiff, aifc
audio/x-wav	wav
image/cgm	cgm
image/g3fax	
image/gif	gif
image/ief	ief
image/jpeg	jpeg, jpg, jpe
image/naplps	
image/png	png
image/tiff	tiff, tif
image/vnd.dwg	
image/vnd.dxf	
image/vnd.fpx	
image/vnd.net-fpx	
image/vnd.svf	
image/vnd.xiff	
image/x-cmu-raster	ras
image/x-portable-anymap	rpnm

Table 17-1: Media Types and Subtypes (continued)

Type/Subtype	*Usual Extension*
image/x-portable-bitmap	pbm
image/x-portable-graymap	pgm
image/x-portable-pixmap	ppm
image/x-rgb	rgb
image/x-xbitmap	xbm
image/x-xpixmap	xpm
image/x-xwindowdump	xwd
message/external-body	
message/http	
message/news	
message/partial	
message/rfc822	
model/iges	
model/mesh	
model/vnd.dwf	
model/vrml	
multipart/alternative	
multipart/appledouble	
multipart/digest	
multipart/form-data	
multipart/header-set	
multipart/mixed	
multipart/parallel	
multipart/related	
multipart/report	
multipart/voice-message	
text/enriched	
text/html	html, htm
text/plain	txt
text/richtext	rtx
text/sgml	sgm, sgml, gml, dtd
text/tab-separated-values	tsv
text/xml	xml, dtd
text/x-setext	etx
video/mpeg	mpeg, mpg, mpe
video/quicktime	qt, mov
video/vnd.vivo	
video/vnd.motorola.video	
video/vnd.motorola.videop	
video/x-msvideo	qvi
video/x-sgi-movie	movie

HTTP

PART VIII

Server Configuration

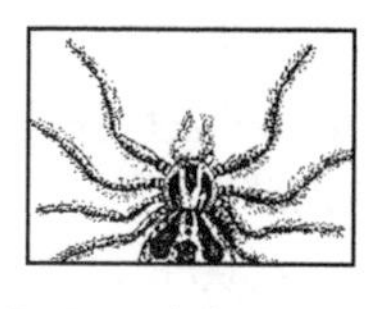

CHAPTER 18

Apache Configuration

Apache is the most widely used web server on the Internet. The Apache server was developed from an early version of the original NCSA server with the intent of providing further improvement while maintaining compatibility. Since then, all development efforts on the NCSA server have ceased. Apache has since earned the title of reigning king among web servers, and it isn't hard to see why: the base distribution is fast, free, and full-featured. You can pick up a copy of the Apache server and its documentation from the Apache home page: *http://www.apache.org*. This chapter covers Version 1.3 of the Apache server.

Understanding Apache

The Apache distribution consists of source for a core binary, *httpd*, which you can compile for your particular server architecture. By itself, *httpd* doesn't do very much. However, you can also include any number of Apache *modules*, either at compile-time or at runtime, depending on the version. These modules, written in C, define much of the behavior of the Apache server. Apache will call on each module to perform a dedicated task, such as user authentication or database queries.

At startup, Apache reads several configuration files. You can modify the behavior of Apache and its modules by inserting or modifying the runtime directives into one or more configuration files. Each file outlines how the Apache server will perform in specific areas. The files are:

httpd.conf
: The server configuration file, which specifies the basics of the server's operation.

srm.conf
: The resource configuration file, which specifies how the server should treat local resources when responding to a request.

access.conf

The access configuration file, which specifies what operations should be allowed on what files and by whom.

In addition, the Apache server uses another file, *mime.types*, to determine what MIME types should be associated with what file suffixes (see Chapter 17, *HTTP*).

In addition to the directives themselves, the configuration files may contain any number of blank lines or comment lines beginning with a hash mark (#). Although directive names are not case-sensitive, we use the case conventions in the default files. Example copies of each of these files are included with the server software distribution, which you can refer to for more information.

Apache Basics

The first file Apache uses to configure itself is *httpd.conf.* This file should be used to enable any modules the server needs, as well as provide directives used to configure the server itself. After that, Apache searches for the files *srm.conf* and *access.conf* in the same directory, which tell the server how to handle local resources and information access, respectively. If you wish, you can use the `AccessConfig` and `ResourceConfig` directives to override the default filenames.

Here is an example of the runtime directives you might find in the *httpd.conf* configuration file:

```
ServerType standalone
Port 80
ServerAdmin webmaster@oreilly.com
User nobody
Group nobody
```

Note that each directive specifies a property of the server's configuration and binds it to a default setting or value.

Handling Requests

Apache always starts itself as a system superuser. In Unix, this is often done at startup through entries in the system initialization files. Once started, Apache's job is to listen for requests on any address and port to which it has been configured. When handling a request to a specific client, Apache spawns a separate process to handle the connection. This spawned process, however, doesn't run as the superuser; for security reasons, it instead runs as a restricted user that serves files to the client.

Apache normally has five such processes waiting for connections; hence, after startup, you will see one process (*httpd*) running as root and five processes owned by the Apache user ID, which stand to service requests. You can reconfigure that number, as well as the minimum and maximum number of service processes allowed with the `StartServers`, `MinSpareServers`, and `MaxSpareServers` directives. Each process handles specific HTTP requests for the client, such as GET or POST, which affect content on the server.

All resources accessible to visiting browsers (HTML documents, images, etc.) reside under a base directory on the local disk. This location serves as the root directory of the web document tree. Apache uses the `DocumentRoot` directive to specify the location of the document directory for the server in question.

Within this directory structure, Apache searches for *.htaccess* files in each directory. These files, often called *access control files*, contain the same runtime directives as the base *access.conf* file and act as a security measure to indicate who is allowed access. Although the default name of each file is *.htaccess*, you can reset the name using the `AccessFileName` directive.

Typically, the local *.htaccess* files perform one or more of the following functions:

- Specifies the name of the password file where valid usernames and passwords are stored
- Specifies the name of the group file where valid groups of users are listed
- Sets the limits on who can access files in the directory and with what methods
- Specifies which advanced features are performed within a directory

It is not unusual for webmasters to restrict certain directories on the server to authorized users, where authorization is typically granted by username/password combinations, client IP addresses, or a combination of both. The group of directories a user can safely navigate through once authorization is granted is known as the user's *authorization realm*. There are a number of runtime configuration directives in Apache to support simple or complex variations of this behavior.

This is an example of a global *access.conf* configuration file:

```
<Directory /projects>
 Options All
 AuthType Basic
 AuthUserFile /usr/local/etc/httpd.conf/.htpasswd
 AuthGroupFile /usr/local/etc/httpd.conf/.htgroup
 <Limit GET>
   order allow,deny
   allow from all
 </Limit>
</Directory>

<Directory /projects/golf>
  <Limit GET>
   order deny,allow
   deny from all
   allow from .golf.org
  </Limit>
</Directory>

<Directory /projects/golf/team>
 AuthName For Team Players Only
 <Limit GET>
  require group golfteam
 </Limit>
</Directory>
```

```
<Directory /projects/golf/team/captain>
 AuthName Captain Only
 <Limit GET>
  require user captain
 </Limit>
</Directory>
```

This example shows the various ways in which access control can be implemented. The global *access.conf* file uses the `Directory` sectioning directives to enclose access information for different directories (wildcards may also be used to designate a set of directories). The `Directory` settings for each directory apply to that directory and all of its subdirectories unless overridden in a lower directory's specifications.

Per-directory *.htaccess* files typically contain the same information as `<Directory> ... </Directory>` sections, except without the `Directory` tags. Use of per-directory *.htaccess* files is controlled by the `AllowOverride` directive within `<Directory>` sections in the global *access.conf* file.

Password and Group Files

A password file is needed for user and group-level authentication. The location and name of the password file are specified with the `AuthUserName` directive. The easiest and most common way to create a password file is to use the *htpasswd* program that is distributed with the server. To create a new password file to store a new username and password, use this command:

```
htpasswd -c pathname username
```

The `-c` option tells the program to open a file with the given pathname. The program asks you to type the password you wish for the given username twice, and the username and encrypted password are stored in the new file. Other users can be added to the file using the same command and pathname without the `-c` option.

Password files created with *.htpasswd* are similar to Unix password files. Keep in mind, however, that there is no correspondence between valid users and passwords on a Unix server, and users and passwords on an Apache web server. You do not need an account on the Unix server to access the web server.

You can bundle several users into a single named group by creating a group file. The location and name of the group file are specified with the `AuthGroupFile` directive. Each line of a group file specifies the group name, followed by a colon, followed by a list of valid usernames that belong to the group:

```
groupname: username1 username2 username3 ...
```

Each user in a group needs to be entered into the Apache password file. When a group authentication is required, the server accepts any valid username/password from the group.

The *.htpasswd* user authentication scheme is known as the *basic* authentication method for HTTP servers. Apache allows other types of authentication methods, which are configured with a similar set of directives.

Virtual Hosting

Apache also has the ability to perform *virtual hosting*. This allows a single *httpd* process to serve multiple IP addresses or hostnames. Virtual hosting seems like a complicated procedure; however, it really isn't as bad as it seems. In each configuration file, you can structure directives that apply only to virtual hosts. For example, you can specify separate ServerRoot directives for each virtual machine, such that someone connecting to *www.oreilly.com* is served one set of documents, while another client connecting to *www.songline.com* receives another, even though the content for each of these sites is served by the same server on the same machine.

To create a virtual server, simply enclose *httpd.conf* directives related to the server in a <VirtualHost> directive. Here is an example *httpd.conf* configuration that will set up two virtual servers:

```
ServerName www.oreilly.com
AccessConfig /dev/null
ResourceConfig /dev/null

<VirtualHost www.oreilly.com>
ServerAdmin webmaster@oreilly.com
DocumentRoot /usr/local/www/virtual/htdocs/oreilly
ServerName www.oreilly.com
ErrorLog /usr/local/www/virtual/htdocs/oreilly/error_log
TransferLog /usr/local/www/virtual/htdocs/oreilly/transfer_log
</VirtualHost>

<VirtualHost www.songline.com>
ServerAdmin webmaster@songline.com
DocumentRoot /usr/local/www/virtual/htdocs/songline
ServerName www.songline.com
ErrorLog /usr/local/www/virtual/htdocs/songline/error_log
TransferLog /usr/local/www/virtual/htdocs/songline/transfer_log
</VirtualHost>
```

Log Files

Finally, Apache maintains two or more log files webmasters can use to determine server hits and errors:

access_log
: The server access log, which indicates which clients have made HTTP requests of the server

error_log
: The server error log, which reports a user-configurable number of errors Apache encountered when executing

You can control the locations of these files with the ErrorLog and TransferLog directives.

Basic Server Configuration: Core Directives

The following section contains core directives that are independent of modules and can be used in the Apache server at all times. With each directive, we indicate any version constraints that are required, as well as the *context* the directive should appear in. Contexts include:

server config
: The directive is allowed in the *httpd.conf* or *srm.conf* configuration files.

`<VirtualHost>`
: The directive can appear inside a `<VirtualHost>` subsection, stating that the directive applies to a virtual server.

`<Directory>`
: The directive can appear inside a `<Directory>` subsection, stating that the directive applies to a specific directory tree on the server.

.htaccess
: The directive can appear inside the per-directory

Directives pertaining to specific Apache modules are covered in Chapter 17.

AccessConfig

`AccessConfig` *`filename`*

[*server config* or within `<VirtualHost>`]

Specifies the location of the access configuration file, either as an absolute path (with a beginning slash) or as a relative path from the `ServerRoot` directory. For example:

```
AccessConfig conf/access.conf
```

(All)

AccessFileName

`AccessFileName` *`filename filename`* `. . .`

[*server config* or within `<VirtualHost>`]

Specifies the names of one or more per-directory access control files. The default is:

```
AccessFileName .htaccess
```

(All; more than one filename in Apache 1.3 or later)

AddModule

`AddModule` *`module module`* `. . .`

[*server config*]

→

Specifies one or more modules that should be enabled when the server begins running. Each module can either be compiled into the Apache executable or can exist as an external module. The module should not be already enabled. For example:

```
AddModule mod_auth_db mod_auth_dbm
```

You should always add any nonenabled modules with this directive before Apache encounters a directive targeted at that module.

(Apache 1.2 or later)

AllowOverride

`AllowOverride` *`options`* `. . .`

[Within `<Directory>`]

Controls the extent to which local per-directory *.htaccess* files can override the defaults defined by access control files in higher directories. The directive takes one or more options, which can be:

`None`
: Access control files are unrecognized in this directory.

`All`
: Access control files are unrestricted in this directory.

`Options`
: Allow use of the `Options` and `XBitHack` directives.

`Indexes`
: Allow use of directory indexing directives (`FancyIndexing`, `AddIcon`, and `AddDescription`, etc.).

`FileInfo`
: Allow use of the directive relating to document type: (`AddType`, `AddEncoding`, `AddLanguage`, etc.).

`AuthConfig`
: Allow use of these directives: `require`, `AuthName`, `AuthType`, `AuthUserFile`, `AuthGroupFile`, or any other `Auth*` directives.

`Limit`
: Allow use of the `allow`, `deny`, and `order` directives.

If omitted, the default is:

```
AllowOverride All
```

(All)

AuthName

`AuthName` *`name`*

[Within `<Directory>` or *.htaccess*]

→

Server Configuration

Sets the name of the username/password authorization realm for this directory. The value is a short name describing this authorization realm; it can contain spaces.

(All)

AuthType

`AuthType` *`type`*

[Within `<Directory>` or *.htaccess*]

Sets the type of authorization used in this directory. **`Basic`** authorization is the most commonly used method. If used, this directive should be followed by `AuthName`, `require`, `AuthGroupFile`, and `AuthUserFile` directives, which better describe the authorization realm.

(All)

BindAddress

`BindAddress` *`hostname`*

[*server config*]

Specifies the network addresses this server will listen for connections on. Either an IP address or DNS name can be used. In addition, you can also specify an asterisk (*) to have the server listen on all the server IP addresses. Here are some examples:

```
BindAddress www.oreilly.com
BindAddress *
```

The former will listen for clients connecting on the IP address that maps to `www.oreilly.com`, which the server occupies. The latter will listen for connections on every IP address that the server occupies. Only one `BindAddress` directive may be declared.

(All)

BS200AuthFile

`BS200AuthFile` *`authfile`*

[*server config*]

This directive is used for BS2000 machines only; it defines a password file that changes the task environment of Apache to the account specified by the `User` directive. This prevents CGI scripts from accessing the resources of the user that started the server.

(Apache 1.3 or later)

ClearModuleList

`ClearModuleList`

[*server config*]

Clears the list of enabled modules Apache uses at startup. If you use this directive, use the `AddModule` directive to reinstate any modules you wish to add to the server.

(Apache 1.2 or later)

ContentDigest

`ContentDigest on|off`

[*server config*, within `<VirtualHost>`, within `<Directory>`, or *.htaccess*]

Computes an MD5 (Message Digest 5) hash of the body content of core data sent to the client. This value is stored in a header that looks like:

```
Content-MD5: AyTr28784eSp2k67d98n28a=
```

The receiver can use this hash value to determine whether the contents of the page have been altered in transit. The hash values are not cached for each page sent; hence, they must be recalculated each time data is requested.

(Apache 1.1 or later)

CoreDumpDirectory

`CoreDumpDirectory` *`directory`*

[*server config*]

Specifies which directory Apache should dump a core file to when it encounters an unrecoverable error. A core file is typically written to the directory specified by `ServerRoot`; this directive overrides it.

(All)

DefaultType

`DefaultType` *`mime_type`*

[*server config*, within `<VirtualHost>`, within `<Directory>`, or *.htaccess*]

Establishes a default MIME type to be returned to a browser if mappings in the *mime.types* file fail to successfully identify a document or file type. The default is `text/html`.

(All)

<Directory>

`<Directory>...</Directory>`

[*server config* or within `<VirtualHost>`]

`<Directory>` is a sectioning directive that identifies the directory (and its subdirectories) to which contained access-control directives apply. This directive cannot be used in a per-directory

```
<Directory dir>
```

where *dir* is the absolute pathname of the directory. You can include wildcard characters (such as `*` and `?`) to designate a set of directories or even use regular expressions if preceded by a tilde (~).

(All)

<DirectoryMatch>

`<DirectoryMatch>...</DirectoryMatch>`

[*server config* or within `<VirtualHost>`]

`<DirectoryMatch>` is a sectioning directive that identifies the directory (and subdirectories) to which contained access-control directives apply. It cannot be used in a per-directory *.htaccess* file. The start tag has this format:

```
<DirectoryMatch regex>
```

where *regex* is a regular expression that designates one or more directories the enclosed directives apply to.

(Apache 1.2 or above)

DocumentRoot

`DocumentRoot directory_path`

[*server config* or within `<VirtualHost>`]

Specifies the root of the server document tree. For example:

```
DocumentRoot /usr/local/etc/httpd/htdocs/
```

This specifies that HTML documents for this server will reside in the given directory and its subdirectories. The default is:

```
DocumentRoot /usr/local/apache/htdocs/
```

(All)

ErrorDocument

`ErrorDocument code filename|string|URL`

[*server config*, within `<VirtualHost>`, within `<Directory>`, or *.htaccess*]

→

Allows you to customize the response sent by your server when an error is encountered. The error code is an HTTP status code as listed in Chapter 17. Possible values are:

filename
: A local file to return upon encountering this error

string
: A message to return upon encountering this error; the string must be surrounded by quotes

URL
: A local or remote document to redirect the user to upon encountering this error

Example usage:

```
ErrorDocument 404 /errors/notfound.html
ErrorDocument 408 "Sorry, the server timed out
 - try again later"
ErrorDocument 402 http://www.oreilly.com/payment/
```

(All; `<Directory>` and *.htaccess* in Apache 1.1 or later)

ErrorLog

`ErrorLog` *`filename`*

[*server config* or within `<VirtualHost>`]

Specifies the location of the error log file, either an absolute path or relative path to the `ServerRoot` directory if an opening slash (/) is omitted. The default setting is:

```
ErrorLog logs/error_log
```

Beginning with Apache 1.3, you can specify `syslog` if the system supports logging via `syslogd`.

(All)

<Files>

`<Files>...</Files>`

[*server config*, within `<VirtualHost>`, or *.htaccess*]

The `<Files>` directive is a sectioning directive that identifies the file or files to which contained access-control directives apply. The start tag has this format:

```
<Files filename>
```

where *filename* is the name of any file that should have restrictions placed on it. Note that *filename* may include wildcard characters (such as `*` and `?`) to designate a set of files. In addition, you may place it inside a `<Directory>`

Server Configuration

→

directive to further restrict which files are affected. You can also specify regular expressions by preceding them with a tilde (~).

(Apache 1.2 or above)

<FilesMatch>

`<FilesMatch>...</FilesMatch>`

[*server config*, within `<VirtualHost>`, or *.htaccess*]

The `<FilesMatch>` directive is a sectioning directive that identifies the file or files to which contained access-control directives apply. The start tag has the following format:

```
<FilesMatch regex>
```

where *regex* is a regular expression that designates one or more files the enclosed directives apply to. Note that you may place this directive inside a `<Directory>` directive to further restrict which files are affected.

(Apache 1.3 or above)

Group

`Group groupname`

[*server config* or within `<VirtualHost>`]

Specifies the group you want the server to process requests as. Either a group name or group ID can be specified; a group ID should be preceded by a hash mark (#). Setting this option to the same group as the superuser (i.e., `root`) is highly discouraged. Many administrators use the group `nobody` for the Apache server.

(All)

HostNameLookups

`HostNameLookups on|off|double`

[*server config*, within `<VirtualHost>` or `<Directory>`]

Enables whether the server should perform hostname lookups on clients instead of simply recording the IP address in the connection logs. If the *double* option is specified, the server performs a forward and reverse DNS lookup; this ensures that the client hostname maps to its IP, as well as the IP mapping to the DNS name. The *double* option is available only in Apache 1.3. The default with Apache 1.2 and below is `on`, while the default with Apache 1.3 is `off`.

(All; `double` option in Apache 1.3 or above)

IdentityCheck

`IdentityCheck on|off`

[*server config*, within `<VirtualHost>` or `<Directory>`]

Specifies whether the server should attempt to learn the user identity for each request by querying an *identd* process running on the user's machine. By default, identity checking is `off`.

(All)

<IfDefine>

`<IfDefine>...</IfDefine>`

[All]

A sectioning directive for specifying directives that apply if a given define is entered on the command line. For example:

```
<IfDefine MD5Digest>
LoadModule mod_digest libexec/moddigest.so
</IfDefine>
```

This directive is executed if the Apache server is started using the following command line parameter:

```
httpd -DMD5Digest ...
```

Note that you can place an exclamation mark in front of the `<IfDefine>` parameter to include such directives if a definition is *not* made on the command line.

(Apache 1.3.1 or later)

<IfModule>

`<IfModule>...</IfModule>`

[All]

A sectioning directive for specifying directives that apply if a given module has been compiled into the Apache server. For example:

```
<IfModule mod_cgi>
LoadModule mod_speling libexec/modspelling.so
</IfModule>
```

This directive is executed if Apache is compiled with the `mod_cgi` module. Note that you can place an exclamation mark in front of the module name to include such directives if a module is not included in the Apache server build.

(Apache 1.2 or later)

Include

`Include` *`filename`*

[*server config*]

Tells the server to include a specified file as part of its configuration.

(Apache 1.3 or later)

KeepAlive

`KeepAlive on|off`

[*server config*]

Tells the server to allow persistent connections using the same TCP connection. The default is on. See also `KeepAliveTimeOut` and `MaxKeepAliveRequests`.

(Apache 1.2 and above)

KeepAliveTimeOut

KeepAliveTimeOut *`seconds`*

[*server config*]

Specifies the number of seconds to wait for the next request before closing a persistent connection. Used only when persistent connections are enabled with the `KeepAlive On` setting. The default is 15.

(Apache 1.1 or later)

<Limit>

`<Limit>...</Limit>`

[Any]

`<Limit>` is a sectioning directive that applies to the specified access methods (GET, POST, etc.). This directive restricts the boundaries of the access methods specified; if you wish to apply restrictions globally, omit the `Limit` directive completely. The start tag has the following syntax:

```
<Limit method1 method2 ...>
```

where a *method* is one of the following:

GET
: Allows clients to retrieve documents and execute scripts with the GET request method.

POST
: Allows clients to use scripts and resources using the POST request method (mostly CGI programs).

→

PUT

Allows clients access to documents and resources using the PUT request method.

DELETE

Allows clients access to documents and resources using the DELETE request method.

CONNECT

Allows clients access to documents and resources using the CONNECT request method.

OPTIONS

Allows clients access to documents and resources using the OPTIONS request method.

The `order`, `deny`, `allow`, and `require` directives are the usual inhabitants of the `Limit` sectioning directive.

(All)

Listen

`Listen [`*`IP_address:`*`]`*`port`*

[*server config*]

Tells the server to listen for requests on the specified port for the specified IP address (if supplied), instead of that specified by the `BindAddress` and `Port` directives. Multiple `Listen` directives can be used to bind the server to more than one port or address/port combination.

(Apache 1.1 or Later)

ListenBacklog

`ListenBacklog` *`backlog`*

[*server config*]

Sets the length of the pending connection queue. Increasing this may be useful when the server is flooded with an unusually large number of pending connections. The default is 511.

(Apache 1.2.0 and above)

<Location>

`<Location> . . . </Location>`

[*server config* or within `<VirtualHost>`]

A sectioning directive for specifying directives that apply to a given URL. Basically just a more specific version of `<Directory>`. Wildcards and regular expressions are allowed.

(Apache 1.1 or later)

Server Configuration

<LocationMatch>

`<LocationMatch>...</LocationMatch>`

[*server config* or within `<VirtualHost>`]

A sectioning directive for specifying directives that apply to a given URL. Basically, it's just a more specific version of `<DirectoryMatch>`.

(Apache 1.1 or later)

LockFile

`LockFile` *`filename`*

[*server config*]

Sets the path to the lockfile Apache uses while running. The lockfile must be on the local disk and cannot be NFS-mounted. This file should never be placed in a world-writable directory.

(All)

LogLevel

`LogLevel` *`level`*

[*server config* or within `<VirtualHost>`]

This directive sets the verbosity of the Apache error logs. The level can be one of the following:

`emerg`
: Logs errors that cause the server to fail.

`alert`
: Reports alerts from program execution that had unexpected errors. The server may or may not perform correctly after such an error.

`crit`
: Reports critical conditions from server execution.

`error`
: Reports error conditions in Apache execution.

`warn`
: Reports warnings in Apache execution.

`notice`
: Reports common, noteworthy conditions.

`info`
: Reports informational items.

`debug`
: Reports simple debug-level items.

(Apache 1.3 or later)

MaxClients

`MaxClients` *number*

[*server config*]

Specifies the maximum number of slave processes, and hence the number of client connections, the Apache server can support at a given time. The default is 256.

(All)

MaxKeepAliveRequests

`MaxKeepAliveRequests` *number*

[*server config*]

When persistent connections are enabled with `KeepAlive On`, the `MaxKeepAliveRequests` directive specifies the number of requests the server allows per persistent connection. If set to 0, the server allows unlimited connections. The default is 100.

(Apache 1.2 or later)

MaxRequestsPerChild

`MaxRequestsPerChild` *number*

[*server config*]

Specifies how many requests a slave process may handle for a client during its life. If set to 0, the slave process may handle an unlimited number of connections; the default is 0. For example:

```
MaxRequestsPerChild 1000
```

This allows the slave process to handle up to 1000 requests per connection before the process dies, and the client is forced to reconnect to the server.

(All)

MaxSpareServers

`MaxSpareServers` *number*

[*server config*]

Specifies the upper range for how many idle slave processes the server should keep to handle requests. The default is 10.

(All)

MinSpareServers

`MinSpareServers` *`number`*

[*server config*]

Specifies the lower range for how many idle slave processes the server should keep around to handle requests. The default is 5.

(All)

NameVirtualHost

`NameVirtualHost` [*`IP_address:`*]*`port`*

[*server config*]

Specifies the name or address a virtual host on the server should resolve to. In addition to the address, you can also specify the port that should be used. For example, if you are accepting connections on the server under the IP 123.23.23.123, port 8001 (in addition to others), you would specify:

```
NameVirtualHost 123.23.23.123:8001
```

(Apache 1.3 or later)

Options

`Options` *`options ...`*

[*server config*, or within `<VirtualHost>` or `<Directory>`, or *.htaccess*]

Controls the degree of advanced features that you wish to allow on your server. One or more options may be listed on the `Options` line, separated by spaces. Valid entries are:

`None`
: No features are enabled in this directory.

`Indexes`
: Allows clients to request a formatted index of this directory if no `DirectoryIndex` has been specified.

`Includes`
: Server-side includes are enabled in this directory.

`IncludesNoExec`
: Server-side includes (SSIs) are enabled in the directory, but the *exec* feature and the *include* of CGI scripts is disabled.

`ExecCGI`
: Execution of CGI scripts is allowed in this directory.

`MultiViews`
: Content-negotiated multiviews are allowed in this directory.

→

`FollowSymLinks`
: The server follows symbolic links in this directory. The pathname is not altered to reflect to the new location.

`SymLinksIfOwnerMatch`
: The server follows symbolic links only if the target file/directory is owned by the same user ID as the link.

`All`
: All features are enabled in this directory.

The `Options` directive can be used in both the global *access.conf* and in per-directory *.htaccess* files. There can be only one `Options` directive per `Directory` segment. If omitted, the default is:

```
Options All
```

(All)

PidFile

`PidFile` *`filename`*

[*server config*]

Specifies the location of the file into which the server should place its process ID when running in standalone mode, either as an absolute path or as a relative path from the `ServerRoot` directory if an opening slash (/) has been omitted. The default is:

```
PidFile logs/httpd.pid
```

(All)

Port

`Port` *`number`*

[*server config*]

Specifies the server's port, with a default of 80. Many servers assign their ports to other values; 8001 is common. Note that this directive does not apply to a server acting as one or more virtual hosts.

(All)

---

require

`require` *`entity names`* `. . .`

[Within `<Directory>`, or *.htaccess*]

Specifies which authenticated users or groups can access a given directory, typically in a `<Limit>` section of an access control file. A `require` line requires that all of the appropriate `Auth*` directives are specified for the directory. *entity* is one of the following:

→

`user`
: Only the named users can access this directory with the given methods. Each name is therefore a username that exists in the `AuthUserFile` (specified password file).

`group`
: Only users in the named groups can access this directory with the given methods. Each name is therefore a group name that is listed in the specified group file.

`valid-user`
: All users listed in the `AuthUserFile` (specified password file) are allowed access upon providing a valid password.

For example, the following restricts access to a directory to a few key users:

```
require user jdoe msmith
```

(All)

ResourceConfig

`ResourceConfig` *`filename`*

[*server config*, or within `<VirtualHost>`]

Specifies the location of the resource configuration file, as an absolute path or as a relative path from the `ServerRoot` directory. This file is read after the *httpd.conf* file. The default is:

```
ResourceConfig /conf/srm.conf
```

(All)

RLimitCPU

`RLimitCPU` *`limit`*`[`*`limit`*`]`

[*`server config`*, or within `<VirtualHost>`]

Specifies the soft resource limit and optionally the maximum resource limit of CPU time, in seconds per slave process.

```
RLimitCPU 5 5
```

In place of each parameter, you can also use the `max` keyword, which sets it to the maximum allowed by the host operating system.

(Apache 1.2 or later)

RLimitMEM

`RLimitMEM` *`limit`*`[`*`limit`*`]`

[*server config*, or within `<VirtualHost>`]

→

Specifies the soft resource limit and optionally the maximum resource limit of memory, in bytes per process.

```
RLimitMEM 65535 65535
```

In place of each parameter, you can also use the `max` keyword, which sets it to the maximum allowed by the host operating system.

(Apache 1.2 or later)

RLimitNPROC

`RLimitNPROC` *`limit`*`[`*`limit`*`]`

[*server config*, or within `<VirtualHost>`]

Specifies the soft resource limit and optionally the maximum resource limit of slave processes that the server can create.

```
RLimitNPROC 20 20
```

In place of each parameter, you can also use the `max` keyword, which sets it to the maximum allowed by the host operating system.

(Apache 1.2 or later)

Satisfy

`Satisfy any|all`

[Within `<Directory>`, or *.htaccess*]

Specifies an access policy if access is restricted by both username-password and host address. The `any` parameter allows access if the client satisfies either the username-password or host address requirements. The `all` parameter requires that the client satisfy both.

(Apache 1.2 or later)

ScoreBoardFile

`ScoreBoardFile` *`filename`*

[*server config*]

Specifies the location of the server status file, used by the server to communicate with slave processes. The location is specified as an absolute path, or as a relative path from the `ServerRoot` directory if the opening slash (/) is omitted. The default is:

```
ScoreBoardFile logs/apache_status
```

(All)

SendBufferSize

`SendBufferSize` *`bytes`*

[*server config*]

Resets the TCP buffer size, typically over the OS default.

(All)

ServerAdmin

`ServerAdmin` *`email_address`*

[*server config*, or within `<VirtualHost>`]

Specifies the email address to which complaints, suggestions, and questions regarding your server should be sent. Used when the server sends error messages in response to failed requests. This directive has no default. It may be specified as follows:

```
ServerAdmin webmaster@oreilly.com
```

(All)

ServerAlias

`ServerAlias` *`virtual_hostname real_hostname`*

[Within `<VirtualHost>`]

Specifies an alternate name for a server virtual host.

(Apache 1.1 or later)

ServerName

`ServerName` *`hostname`*

[*server config*, or within `<VirtualHost>`]

Allows you to specify a preferred hostname for your server. This must be a valid, fully qualified DNS name for the server in question.

(All)

ServerPath

`ServerPath` *`pathname`*

[Within `<VirtualHost>`]

→

Specifies a pathname for a virtual host; that is, requests for this hostname are automatically routed to the specified pathname. For use within <VirtualHost> sections.

(Apache 1.1 or later)

ServerRoot

`ServerRoot` *`directory_path`*

[*server config*]

Specifies the directory in which all the server's associated files reside. This path is used as the root directory when relative paths are specified with other directives. For example:

```
ServerRoot /etc/httpd/
```

(All)

ServerSignature

`ServerSignature on|off|EMail`

[*server config*, or within `<VirtualHost>` or `<Directory>`, or *.htaccess*]

Creates a footer line under all documents to identify the exact server this document originated from. This is useful in the event that there is a series of proxies, any one of which can return a specific document or error message. The default is `off`. If the `on` option is specified, the footer creates a line with the `ServerName` and version number. If the `EMail` option is used, the server creates a name and version number as well as a "mailto:" reference to the `ServerAdmin`.

(Apache 1.3 or later)

ServerTokens

`ServerTokens Minimal|OS|Full`

[*server config*]

Specifies which type of header field is returned to clients when the information is requested. There are three options, listed with the appropriate formats:

`Minimal`

```
Server: Apache/1.3.1
```

`OS`

```
Server: Apache/1.3.1 (Unix)
```

`Full`

```
Server: Apache/1.3.1 (Unix) PHP/3.0 MyMod/1.2
```

(Apache 1.3 or later)

ServerType

`ServerType standalone|inetd`

[*server config*]

Specifies whether your server is run standalone or from the *inetd* daemon. If the server is run from *inetd*, it's restarted each time a connection is made; hence, using this option is discouraged. The default is to run standalone.

(All)

StartServers

`StartServers` *number*

[*server config*]

Specifies the initial number of slave processes at server startup. The default is 5. This directive has no effect under the Windows platform.

(All)

ThreadsPerChild

`ThreadsPerChild` *number*

[*server config*]

Specifies the maximum number of threads each child process can spawn. This directive is used only on Windows platforms. For example:

```
ThreadsPerChild 100
```

(Apache 1.3.1 or later)

TimeOut

`TimeOut` *seconds*

[*server config*]

Specifies the number of seconds to wait before closing a presumably defunct connection. The default is 300 seconds.

(All)

UseCanonicalName

`UseCanonicalName on|off`

[*server config*, or within `<Directory>` or `<VirtualHost>`, or *.htaccess*]

Used to build a self-referential URL. If on, Apache uses the `<ServerName>` and `<Port>` directives to build a URL representing itself. If `off`, Apache attempts

→

to construct its URL from the client parameters, which is typical when using the VirtualHost directive to represent different addresses.

(Apache 1.3 or later)

User

User *username*

[*server config*, or within <VirtualHost>]

Specifies the user you want the Apache server to process requests as. Either a username or user ID can be specified; a user ID should be preceded by a hash mark (#). Setting this to root is highly discouraged. Many administrators create a user nobody for Apache.

(All)

<VirtualHost>

<VirtualHost> . . . </VirtualHost>

[*server config*]

Used when the Apache server services multiple hostnames. Each hostname is given its own <VirtualHost> directive.

<VirtualHost> has a beginning and ending directive, with other configuration directives for the virtual host entered in between. Most directives are valid within <VirtualHost> except the following: BindAddress, GroupId, MaxRequestsPerChild, MaxSpareServers, MinSpareServers, Listen, NameVirtualHost, PidFile, ServerType, ServerRoot, StartServers, TypesConfig, and UserId. This is essentially a segmenting directive that applies directives solely to the virtual host specified. For example:

```
<VirtualHost sales.oreilly.com>
ServerAdmin webmaster@oreilly.com
DocumentRoot /ora/sales/www
ServerName sales.oreilly.com
ErrorLog /ora/sales/logs/error_log
TransferLog /ora/sales/logs/access_log
</VirtualHost>
```

(All)

Server Configuration

CHAPTER 19

Apache Modules

Modules are a key part of Apache. They provide much of the functionality administrators expect in a modern web server, including user tracking, CGI scripting, and authentication. However, we should warn you up front that not all the modules presented here are compiled by default into the Apache server; this can be configured by the administrator when the distribution is first compiled.

Table 19-1 describes the standard Apache modules.

Table 19-1: Apache Modules

Module	*Compiled*	*Description*
`mod_access`	Yes	Access control
`mod_actions`	Yes	CGI scripting
`mod_alias`	Yes	Aliasing and filesystem mapping
`mod_asis`	Yes	Provides for *.asis* (as is) files
`mod_auth`	Yes	User authentication
`mod_auth_anon`	No	Anonymous user authentication
`mod_auth_db`	No	User authentication with DB files
`mod_auth_dbm`	No	User authentication with DBM files
`mod_autoindex`	Yes	Automatic directory listings
`mod_browser`	No	Setting of environment variables (obsolete)
`mod_cern_meta`	No	Support for CERN metafiles
`mod_cgi`	Yes	Execution of CGI scripts
`mod_cookies`	No	User tracking (obsolete)
`mod_digest`	No	MD5 user authentication
`mod_dir`	Yes	Simple directory handling
`mod_dld`	No	Runtime linking of object modules (obsolete)
`mod_dll`	No	Runtime linking of object modules (obsolete)

Table 19-1: Apache Modules (continued)

Module	*Compiled*	*Description*
mod_env	No	Environment variable handling
mod_example	No	Example of Apache API usage
mod_expires	No	Automatic expire headers
mod_headers	No	Modification of HTTP response headers
mod_imap	Yes	Image map handling
mod_include	Yes	Server-side includes
mod_info	No	Server information
mod_isapi	Yes	Support for ISAPI extensions in Windows
mod_log_agent	No	Logs client user agents
mod_log_common	Yes	Standard server logging
mod_log_config	Yes	Configurable logging
mod_log_referer	No	Referer document logging
mod_mime	Yes	MIME handling
mod_mime_magic	No	MIME handling via magic numbers
mod_mmap_static	No	Memory mapping of files
mod_negotiation	Yes	Content negotiation
mod_proxy	No	Proxy capabilities
mod_rewrite	No	URL rewriting
mod_setenvif	Yes	Conditional setting of environment variables
mod_so	No	Dynamic loading of modules and libraries
mod_speling	No	Spelling corrections
mod_status	No	Server status pages
mod_userdir	Yes	User HTML directories
mod_unique_id	No	Unique server request identifiers
mod_usertrack	No	User tracking (cookies)

This chapter presents an overview of the runtime directives used with the Apache modules. Each of the directives listed in this chapter are grouped in association with the module they relate to.

mod_access

The mod_access module resolves which clients are allowed to access server directories based on their IP address or hostname.

allow

```
allow from hostname hostname ...
```

[Within <Directory> or *.htaccess*]

The allow directive specifies which hosts can access a given directory in the site. The *hostname* can be any of the following:

→

Server Configuration

Domain

A domain name, like *.oreilly.com*. Only hosts from the domain are permitted access.

Hostname

A full hostname.

Full

An IP address of a host.

Partial

The first 1 to 3 bytes of an IP address, for subnet restriction.

Network

A full network address, followed by a full netmask. (i.e., 192.168.220.110/255.255.255.0)

Network

A full network address, followed by an abbreviated netmask. (i.e., 192.168.220.110/24 is equivalent to 192.168.220.110/255.255.255.0)

`all"`

Using this option means that all hosts are allowed.

There can be only one `allow` directive per section. If omitted, there is no default.

(All)

---

allow

`allow from env=`*`variable`*

[Within `<Directory>` or *.htaccess*]

The `allow from env` directive sets whether access to a directory should be granted if a specific environment variable exists. For example, the following grants access to the `secret` directory if the client is using Version 5.0 of the "InternetStar" browser, via a user-agent string:

```
BrowserMatch ^InternetStar/5.0 ACCESS_GRANTED
<Directory /secret>
order deny, allow
deny from all
allow from env=ACCESS_GRANTED
</Directory>
```

(Apache 1.2 or later)

---

deny

`deny from hostname` *`hostname`* `. . .`

[Within `<Directory>` or *.htaccess*]

The `deny` directive specifies which hosts are denied access to a directory. The *hostname* can be one of the following:

→

Domain
: A domain name, like *.oreilly.com.* Hosts from that domain are denied access.

Hostname"
: A full hostname.

Full
: The IP address of a host.

Partial
: The first 1 to 3 bytes of an IP address, for subnet restriction.

Network
: A full network address, followed by a full netmask. (i.e., 192.168.220.110/255.255.255.0)

Network
: A full network address, followed by an abbreviated netmask. (i.e., 192.168.220.110/24 is equivalent to 192.168.220.110/255.255.255.0)

`all`"
: Using the word `all` means that all hosts are denied access.

deny

`deny from env=`*`variable`*

[Within `<Directory>` or *.htaccess*]

The `deny from env` directive sets whether access to a directory should be denied if a specific environment variable exists. For example, access to the `secret` directory is denied if the client is using Version 4.0 of the "InternetStar" browser, via a user-agent string:

```
BrowserMatch ^InternetStar/4.0 ACCESS_DENIED
<Directory /secret>
order deny, allow
deny from env=ACCESS_DENIED
allow from all
</Directory>
```

(Apache 1.2 or later)

order

`order` *`order`*

[Within `<Directory>` or *.htaccess*]

The `order` directive specifies the order in which `deny` and `allow` directives are evaluated. The `order` directive can take one of the following forms:

`order`
: `deny` directives are evaluated before `allow` directives (this is the default).

Server Configuration

→

`order`
: `allow` directives are evaluated before `deny` directives.

`order`
: This setting means that any host appearing on the `allow` list is allowed, and any host listed on the `deny` list is denied. Finally, any host not appearing on either list is denied.

mod_actions

The `mod_actions` module is responsible for handling the execution of CGI scripts based on content type. It is available only in Apache 1.1 and later.

Action

`Action` *`mime_type cgi_script`*

[*server config*, within `<VirtualHost>` or `<Directory>`, or *.htaccess*]

Directs the server to trigger the script *cgi_script* whenever a file of the specified MIME type is requested, sending the requested URL and file path as the `PATH_INFO` and `PATH_TRANSLATED` environment variables, respectively.

(Apache 1.1 or later)

Script

`Script` *`method cgi_script`*

[*server config*, within `<VirtualHost>` or `<Directory>`]

Specifies a script *cgi_script* to be executed when a given HTTP request is used. The directive sends the requested URL and file path as the `PATH_INFO` and `PATH_TRANSLATED` environment variables, respectively, to the CGI script. The *method* can be GET, POST, PUT, or DELETE.

(Apache 1.1 or later)

mod_alias

The `mod_alias` module assists filesystem mapping and URL redirection.

Alias

`Alias` *`symbolic_path real_path`*

[*server config*, within `<VirtualHost>`]

Creates a virtual name or directory by mapping a symbolic path that is used in a URL to a real path on the server. Aliasing is useful for organizing server

→

documents, keeping URLs simpler for users, and hiding the structure of a filesystem. For example, the icon directory is aliased in the default configuration file:

```
Alias /icons /usr/local/etc/httpd/icons
```

With this setting, a request for */icons/image.gif* is handled by sending back the file */usr/local/etc/httpd/icons/image.gif.* If you specify a trailing slash on the *symbolic path*, the client must also enter that slash for the alias to take effect.

(All)

AliasMatch

`AliasMatch` *`regex real_path`*

[*server config*, within `<VirtualHost>`]

Similar to `Alias` but uses regular expressions. This option creates a virtual name or directory by mapping a symbolic pathname that matches the standard regular expression, *regex*, to a real path on the server. For example:

```
AliasMatch ^/images(.*) /etc/httpd/server/images$1
```

(Apache 1.3 or later)

Redirect

`Redirect` *`[status] pathname url`*

[*server config*, within `<VirtualHost>` or `<Directory>`, or *.htaccess*]

Tells the server to forward clients that request a given directory or document, *pathname*, to a new location, specified by *url*. This new location must be a complete path, unless the *status* given is gone, in which case the new location must be omitted. The `Redirect` directive supersedes any `Alias` or `AliasMatch` directives that are specified.

The *status* variable can be one of the following:

`permanent"`
: This option uses an HTTP status 301 to indicate to the client that the redirect should be considered permanent.

`temp"`
: This option uses an HTTP status 302 to indicate to the client that the redirect is only temporary. This is the default.

`seeother"`
: This option uses an HTTP status 303 to indicate to the client that the resource requested has been superseded or replaced.

`gone"`
: This option uses an HTTP status 410 to indicate to the client that the resource has been removed.

(Apache 1.2 or later)

RedirectMatch

`RedirectMatch [status] regex url`

[*server config*, within <VirtualHost>]

Similar to `Redirect` but uses standard regular expressions. This option tells the server to forward clients that request a directory or document matching the regular expression *regex* to a new location, specified by *url*. For example:

```
RedirectMatch (.*).jpg http://imageserver.mycorp.com$1.jpg
```

(Apache 1.3 or later)

RedirectPermanent

`RedirectPermanent url-path url`

Equivalent to `Redirect` with a status of `permanent`.

(Apache 1.2 only)

RedirectTemp

`RedirectTemp url-path url`

Equivalent to `Redirect` with a status of `temp`.

(Apache 1.2 only)

ScriptAlias

`ScriptAlias symbolic_path real_path`

[*server config*, within <VirtualHost>]

Creates a virtual directory of CGI programs by mapping a symbolic pathname that is used in a URL to a real directory of executable CGI programs on your server. Instead of returning a document in that directory, the server runs a requested file within a CGI environment and returns the output. For example:

```
ScriptAlias /cgi-bin/ /usr/local/frank/cgi-bin/
```

See Chapter 12, *CGI Overview*, for more information on CGI.

(All)

ScriptAliasMatch

`ScriptAliasMatch regex filename`

[*server config*, within <VirtualHost>]

Similar to `ScriptAlias`, but uses regular expressions. This option creates a virtual directory of CGI programs by mapping any symbolic pathnames that

→

match the standard regular expression *regex* to a real directory of executable CGI programs on the server. For example:

```
ScriptAliasMatch ^/cgi-bin(.*) /usr/local/frank/cgi-bin$1
```

See Chapter 12 for more information on CGI.

(Apache 1.3 and later)

mod_auth

The mod_auth module provides for user authentication using ordinary text files. Its directives override any core authentication directives given.

AuthAuthoritative

`AuthAuthoritative on|off`

[Within <Directory>, or *.htaccess*]

Decides at which level authentication and authorization can be performed. If off is specified, and there is no user ID matching the requester, authentication and authorization are passed to lower-level modules, which allow access to their respective content based on individual settings. The default is on.

(All)

AuthGroupFile

`AuthGroupFile filename`

[Within <Directory>, or *.htaccess*]

Specifies the user group filename, either as a fully qualified filename or relative to ServerRoot. For example:

```
AuthGroupFile /WWW/Admin/.htgroup
```

The format of the file should list on each line a group name, followed by a colon (:), followed by one or more users that belong to that group.

```
authors: robert stephen val
```

(All)

AuthUserFile

`AuthUserFile filename`

[Within <Directory>, or *.htaccess*]

Specifies a file that contains a list of users and passwords for user authentication, either as a fully qualified filename or relative to the ServerRoot. The password file is typically created with the *htpasswd* support program, which

→

Server Configuration

comes with the Apache distribution. It is best to place the password file outside the DocumentRoot for security purposes. For example:

```
AuthUserFile /etc/admin/.htpasswd
```

(All)

mod_auth_anon

The mod_auth_anon module determines which clients can access parts of the server anonymously. A standard anonymous connection uses the user anonymous with the client user's email address as password. Use of this module allows the server to track visitors and what pages they have requested.

Anonymous

`Anonymous` *`user1 user2 . . .`*

[Within <Directory>, or *.htaccess*]

Specifies a list of users who do not require password authentication to access documents in this realm. The user IDs are case-insensitive. For example:

```
Anonymous anonymous guest "Some User"
```

(All)

Anonymous_Authoritative on|off

`Anonymous_Authoritative on|off`

[Within <Directory>, or *.htaccess*]

Decides at which level authentication and authorization can be performed. If off is specified, and there is no user ID matching the requester, authentication and authorization are passed to lower-level modules, which allow anonymous access to their respective content based on individual settings.

(All)

Anonymous_LogEmail on|off

`Anonymous_LogEmail on|off`

[Within <Directory>, or *.htaccess*]

If set to on, logs the anonymous password entry (the requested email address) to the error log. The default is on.

(All)

Anonymous_MustGiveEmail on|off

`Anonymous_MustGiveEmail on|off`

[Within `<Directory>`, or *.htaccess*]

If set to on, prohibits blank passwords from being used. The default is on.

(All)

Anonymous_NoUserID on|off

`Anonymous_NoUserID on|off`

[Within `<Directory>`, or *.htaccess*]

If set to on, allows the user ID entry to be empty. The default is `off`, which specifies that the client must enter a user ID.

(All)

Anonymous_VerifyEmail on|off

`Anonymous_VerifyEmail on|off`

[Within `<Directory>`, or *.htaccess*]

If set to on, verifies that the password entered contains a `@` and a `.` character. The default is `off`.

(All)

mod_auth_db

The `mod_auth_db` module allows user authentication using Berkeley-style DB files. Its directives override any core authentication directives specified.

AuthDBAuthoritative on|off

`AuthDBAuthoritative on|off`

[Within `<Directory>`, or *.htaccess*]

Decides at which level authentication and authorization can be performed. If `off` is specified, and there is no user ID matching the requester, authentication and authorization are passed to lower-level modules, which allow access to their respective content based on individual settings. The default is on.

(All)

Server Configuration

AuthDBGroupFile

`AuthDBGroupFile filename`

[Within <Directory>, or *.htaccess*]

Specifies the group filename as a Berkeley DB-style file, either as a fully qualified filename or relative to `ServerRoot`. For example:

```
AuthDBGroupFile /www/admin/.groupdb
```

(All)

AuthDBUserFile

`AuthDBUserFile filename`

[Within <Directory>, or *.htaccess*]

Specifies the file that contains a list of users and passwords for user authentication, using either as a fully qualified filename or a pathname relative to the `ServerRoot`. For example:

```
AuthDBUserFile /WWW/Admin/.passwddb
```

(All)

mod_auth_dbm

The `mod_auth_dbm` module allows user authentication using DBM files. Its directives overrides any core authentication directives specified.

AuthDBMAuthoritative

`AuthDBMAuthoritative on|off`

[Within <Directory>, or *.htaccess*]

Decides at which level authentication and authorization can be performed. If `off` is specified, and there is no user ID matching the requester, authentication and authorization are passed to lower-level modules, which allow access to their respective contents based on individual settings. The default is on.

(All)

AuthDBMGroupFile

`AuthDBMGroupFile filename`

[Within <Directory>, or *.htaccess*]

→

Specifies the group filename as a DBM file, using either a fully qualified filename or a path relative to `ServerRoot`. For example:

```
AuthDBMGroupFile /www/admin/.groupdbm
```

(All)

AuthDBMUserFile

`AuthDBMUserFile` *`filename`*

[Within `<Directory>` or *.htaccess*]

Specifies the DBM file that contains a list of users and passwords for user authentication. For example:

```
AuthDBMUserFile /WWW/Admin/.passwddbm
```

(All)

mod_autoindex

The `mod_autoindex` module assists with automatic listings of server directory contents. This module can create icons and descriptions for each of the files in the directory, as well as display file content before and after the index itself.

AddAlt

`AddAlt` *`string filenames|suffixes ...`*

[*server config*, within `<VirtualHost>` or `<Directory>`, or *.htaccess*]

Specifies alternative text for icons used with a given file listing in a directory index. The alternative text is used if the client is unable to load the image for any reason or has disabled the display of images. The text is used as the first argument to the directive, followed by one or more file extensions or names. For example:

```
AddAlt "Image" .gif .jpg .png
AddAlt "Logo" logo.gif
```

See also `FancyIndexing`.

(All)

AddAltByEncoding

`AddAltByEncoding` *`string mime-encoding ...`*

[*server config*, within `<VirtualHost>` or `<Directory>`, or *.htaccess*]

Similar to `AddAlt`, except that it specifies alternative text based on the MIME content encoding of the file being listed. For example, to specify the string

Server Configuration

→

"gzip" for a file encoded using the *gzip* compression program, the directive would be:

```
AddAltByEncoding "gzip" x-gzip
```

See also `FancyIndexing`.

(All)

AddAltByType

`AddAltByType` *`string mime-type ...`*

[*server config*, within `<VirtualHost>` or `<Directory>`, or *.htaccess*]

Similar to `AddAlt`, except that it specifies alternative text based on the media type of the file being listed. For example, to use the alt text "image" for all GIF files, the directive would be:

```
AddAltByType "image" image/gif
```

See also `FancyIndexing`.

(All)

AddDescription

`AddDescription` *`string file ...`*

[*server config*, within `<VirtualHost>` or `<Directory>`, or *.htaccess*]

Used to associate a descriptive text phrase with a particular type of file. The text appears to the right of the filename in a directory index. The descriptive text must be surrounded by quotes and should be fairly short. Files can be associated by extension or name. For example:

```
AddDescription "GIF image file" .gif
AddDescription "The bottom of Hoover Dam" /home/user/vacation1.gif
```

See also `FancyIndexing`.

(All)

AddIcon

`AddIcon` *`icon name ...`*

[*server config*, within `<VirtualHost>` or `<Directory>`, or *.htaccess*]

Specifies an icon image to be displayed with a given type of file in a directory index. For example:

```
AddIcon /icons/image.gif .gif .jpg .png
```

An optional syntax lets you specify alternative text in this directive as well:

```
AddIcon (IMAGE,/icons/image.gif) .gif .jpg .png
```

→

Three values can be used for the file extensions in the AddIcon directive:

^^DIRECTORY^^
The icon is used for subdirectory names.

.. The icon is used for the parent directory.

^^BLANKICON^^
The icon is used only for spacing in the header of the page.

See also FancyIndexing.

(All)

AddIconByEncoding

AddIconByEncoding *icon mime-encoding . . .*

[*server config*, within <VirtualHost> or <Directory>, or *.htaccess*]

Specifies an icon to be displayed with a file in a directory index based on the file's encoding. For example:

```
AddIconByEncoding /icons/gzip.gif x-gzip
AddIconByEncoding (GZIP,/icons/gzip.gif) x-gzip
```

See also FancyIndexing.

(All)

AddIconByType

AddIconByType *icon mime-type*

[*server config*, within <VirtualHost> or <Directory>, or *.htaccess*]

Specifies an icon to be displayed with a file in a directory index based on the file's media type. For example:

```
AddIconByType /icons/image.gif image/*
AddIconByType (IMAGE,/icons/image.gif) image/*
```

See also FancyIndexing.

(All)

DefaultIcon

DefaultIcon *url*

[*server config*, within <VirtualHost> or <Directory>, or *.htaccess*]

Specifies the default icon to use when no icon image has been assigned by one of the AddIcon* directives.

See also FancyIndexing.

(All)

FancyIndexing

`FancyIndexing on|off`

[*server config*, within <VirtualHost> or <Directory>, or *.htaccess*]

Specifies that the server should create a fancy index for a directory listing, including filenames and icons representing the files' types, sizes, and last-modified dates. By default, fancy indexing is `off`. If it's `on`, the module looks to other directives in this module to determine how to display the directory.

(All)

HeaderName

`HeaderName` *`filename`*

[*server config*, within <VirtualHost> or <Directory>, or *.htaccess*]

Specifies a file to be inserted at the top of the listing when generating a directory index. The example file uses the following setting:

```
HeaderName index.html
```

The server looks for this filename first with an *.html* extension and, failing that, without an extension to display at the top of the directory index.

(All)

IndexIgnore

`IndexIgnore` *`filename ...`*

[*server config*, within <VirtualHost> or <Directory>, or *.htaccess*]

Tells the server to ignore (hide) certain files when automatically building a directory index on the fly. The files are specified as full server paths, and you can use the wildcards `*` and `?` with their usual meanings. Thus, to ignore all hidden files (i.e., files whose names begin with a period) at every level, you could use the following setting:

```
IndexIgnore */.?*
```

Any number of `IndexIgnore` directives may be included.

(All)

IndexOptions

`IndexOptions` *`option ...`*

[*server config*, within <VirtualHost> or <Directory>, or *.htaccess*]

Specifies a number of options to use when creating a directory index on the fly. Possible options are:

→

`FancyIndexing`
: Equivalent to `FancyIndexing On`. Unless fancy indexing is turned on by either method, the other index options (except `None`) are ignored.

`IconsAreLinks`
: Make the icons link to the documents (in addition to making the names link).

`IconWidth[=Pixels]`
: Include a `WIDTH` attribute in the image tag for the file icon.

`IconHeight[=Pixels]`
: Include a `HEIGHT` attribute in the image tag for the file icon.

`ScanHTMLTitles`
: Scan any HTML files in the directory, extract their titles, and use them as descriptions for the files.

`SuppressLastModified`
: Omit the last-modified date from the fancy index.

`SuppressSize`
: Omit the size from the fancy index.

`SuppressDescription`
: Omit the description from the fancy index.

`SuppressHTMLPreamble`
: Deactivate the automatic generation of HTML preambles that accompany the `HeaderName`.

(All)

ReadmeName

`ReadmeName` *`filename`*

[*server config*, within `<VirtualHost>` or `<Directory>`, or *.htaccess*]

Specifies a file to be appended to the end of a file listing when generating a directory index. The example file uses the following setting:

```
ReadmeName README
```

The server looks for this filename first with an *.html* extension and, failing that, without an extension. In this case, it will find the file *README* with such an extension.

(All)

---

mod_browser

The `mod_browser` module is no longer in general use. Its purpose was to set environment variables based on user agent strings passed in by the browser. Its directives, `BrowserMatch` and `BrowserMatchNoCase`, are superseded by the directives in the `mod_setenvif` module.

mod_cern_meta

The `mod_cern_meta` module emulates the CERN web-server metafile semantics. The options listed here are correct as of Apache 1.3. This module is no longer in general use.

MetaDir

`MetaDir` *`directory`*

[*htaccess.conf*]

Indicates the directory in which metafiles can be found. For example:

```
MetaDir .hidden
```

(Apache 1.3 or later)

MetaFiles

`MetaFiles on|off`

[*htaccess.conf, server config* before Apache 1.3]

Indicates whether metafiles should be used on a directory-by-directory basis.

(Apache 1.1 or later)

MetaSuffix

`MetaSuffix` *`suffix`*

[*htaccess.conf, server config* before Apache 1.3]

Indicates the suffix of the file or files that contains the meta information.

(Apache 1.1 or later)

---

mod_cgi

The `mod_cgi` module provides for execution of CGI scripts, including the handling of environment variables and logging. When a CGI script is started, this module creates an environment variable called `DOCUMENT_ROOT` that mimics the `Document-Root` directive. It also sets the `REMOTE_HOST`, `REMOTE_IDENT`, and `REMOTE_USER` environment variables if appropriate.

ScriptLog

`ScriptLog` *`filename`*

[*server config*]

→

Sets the name of the CGI-script error log, either as a fully qualified filename or relative to ServerRoot. All CGI errors are written out to this file. Note that there is no default log file; if this directive is omitted, the log file isn't created, and all errors are discarded.

(All)

ScriptLogLength

`ScriptLogLength size`

[*server config*]

Specifies the maximum length of the CGI-script error log file. This is essentially a safety precaution. If the error log file exceeds this length, no more data will be written to it. The default is 10385760 bytes.

(All)

ScriptLogBuffer

`ScriptLogBuffer size`

[*server config*]

Specifies how much data at a time can be logged to the CGI-script error log with an HTTP PUT or POST command. The default is 1024 bytes.

(All)

mod_cookies

This module is obsolete. It previously performed user tracking with Netscape cookies but has since been replaced by the mod_usertrack module.

mod_digest

The mod_digest module performs authentication using the MD5 digest. As of this writing, neither Netscape nor Internet Explorer supports this feature.

AuthDigestFile

`AuthDigestFile filename`

[Within <Directory> or *.htaccess*]

Specifies the name of the file that contains a list of usernames and passwords for authentication using the MD5 digest. This file can be created using the *htdigest* tool that comes with the Apache distribution.

(Apache 1.1 or later)

mod_dir

The `mod_dir` module assists in locating various URL addresses that resolve to a directory or begin with a trailing slash.

DirectoryIndex

`DirectoryIndex` *`url`* `. . .`

[*server config*, or within `<VirtualHost>` or `<Directory>` or *.htaccess*]

Specifies the files that should be searched for when the client requests a directory with a trailing slash. All *url* entries must be local to the server machine but do not have to be relative to `ServerRoot`. The server uses the first *url* entry that is found. If no entry is found, the server attempts to list the directory.

(All)

mod_dld

The `mod_dld` module is obsolete. It previously handled runtime linking with GNU object files. It has been replaced with `mod_so`.

mod_dll

The `mod_dll` module is obsolete. It previously handled runtime linking with Windows DLL files. It has been replaced with `mod_so`.

mod_env

The `mod_env` module manages how environment variables are passed to CGI/SSI scripts from the shell running the `httpd` server. It contains three straightforward directives.

PassEnv

`PassEnv` *`variable`* `. . .`

[*server config* or within `<VirtualHost>`]

Passes one or more environment variables to the server CGI scripts.

```
PassEnv HOME
```

(Apache 1.1 or later)

SetEnv

`SetEnv` *`variable value`*

[*server config* or within `<VirtualHost>`]

Sets one or more environment variables in the context of a server CGI script.

```
SetEnv HOME /home/mike
```

(Apache 1.1 or later)

UnsetEnv

`UnsetEnv` *`variable ...`*

[*server config* or within `<VirtualHost>`]

Unsets (removes) one or more environment variables from the context of a server CGI script.

```
UnsetEnv HOME
```

(Apache 1.1 or later)

mod_example

The `mod_example` module provides an example module from which Apache module developers can learn the Apache API.

Example

`Example`

[*server config*, or within `<VirtualHost>` or `<Directory>`, or *.htaccess*]

Used to activate the example module, which provides server calling information for Apache module developers.

(Apache 1.3 or later)

mod_expires

The `mod_expires` module allows for the generation of HTTP `Expires` headers for server content. This prevents a document retrieved from the server from being cached and reused on the client machine for any duration past the stated expiration date.

ExpiresActive

`ExpiresActive true|false`

[*server config*, or within `<VirtualHost>` or `<Directory>`, or *.htaccess*]

Activates an expiration header for the documents in this realm. The default is `false`.

(All)

ExpiresByType

`ExpiresByType` *`mime-type`* `<A|M>`*`seconds`*

[*server config*, or within `<VirtualHost>` or `<Directory>`, or *.htaccess*]

Specifies the mime-type of a document and the number of seconds the document should expire in. For example:

```
ExpiresByType text/html A300000
ExpiresByType image/jpg M300000
```

The *seconds* field should be preceded by either the letter `A` or `M`. An `A` indicates that the resource should expire the specified number of seconds after the client's access. An `M` indicates that the the resource should expire the specified number of seconds after the last modification date of the document as it resides on the server. The default is specified by the `ExpiresDefault` directive below; this directive overrides the default.

(All)

ExpiresDefault

`ExpiresDefault <A|M>`*`seconds`*

[*server config*, or within `<VirtualHost>` or `<Directory>`, or *.htaccess*]

Specifies the default type of expiry and the number of seconds that document in a specified realm should be cached before it expires. See `ExpiresByType` above.

(All)

mod_headers

The `mod_headers` module allows administrators to merge, remove, or replace customizable HTTP response headers to be distributed with documents from the server.

Header

`Header <set|append|add|unset>:`*`header [value]`*

[*server config*, or within `<VirtualHost>` or `<Directory>`, or *.htaccess*]

This directive allows administrators to merge, remove, or replace HTTP headers that are transmitted with server documents. The header action performed is specified after the `Header` directive; it can be one of four choices:

`set`
: The header specified is reset to the value specified.

`append`
: A header is appended to the specified response header, if it exists. The new value is listed after the old value and is separated by a comma.

`add`
: A new header is created and added to the response headers, even if one already exists.

`unset`
: This option deletes the first occurrence of the header in question.

Headers such as `Date` and `Server` cannot be overridden using this directive.

(All)

mod_imap

The `mod_imap` module provides support for *.map* files and imagemaps. Imagemaps allow a server to respond to clicks in various "hot zones" of an image, without creating an explicit link to redirect the client.

ImapBase

`ImapBase map|referer|url`

[*server config*, or within `<VirtualHost>` or `<Directory>`, or *.htaccess*]

Specifies the default base for imagemap files, if there is no `base` directive in the imagemap file itself. A URL can be specified, or one of the following options can be used:

`map`
: Uses the URL of the imagemap file.

`referer`
: Uses the referring document or the `ServerRoot` if a `Referer` header is not specified.

(Apache 1.1 or later)

Server Configuration

ImapDefault

`ImapDefault error|nocontent|map|referer|URL`

[*server config*, or within `<VirtualHost>` or `<Directory>`, or *.htaccess*]

Specifies the default action for imagemap files, if there is no `default` directive in the imagemap file itself. A URL can be specified, or one of the following options can be used:

`error`
: Fails with a server response code of 500 (see Chapter 17, *HTTP*).

`nocontent`
: Sends a server response code of 204, telling the client to keep the same page displayed (see Chapter 17).

`map`
: Uses the URL of the imagemap file.

`referer`
: Uses the referring document, or the server root if a `Referer` header is not specified.

(Apache 1.1 or later)

ImapMenu

`ImapMenu none|formatted|semiformatted|unformatted`

[*server config*, or within `<VirtualHost>` or `<Directory>`, or *.htaccess*]

Under Apache, if an imagemap is called without valid coordinates, the server can return a menu of the items in the imagemap file. The `ImapMenu` directive configures that menu. Options are:

`none`
: No menu is created. The action specified with `ImapDefault` is taken.

`formatted`
: A formatted menu is generated, with a listing of the possible links.

`semiformatted`
: A menu with comments from the imagemap file and simple breaks is generated, with a listing of the possible links.

`unformatted`
: A menu with the text of the imagemap file, unformatted. Useful if map files are written as HTML.

(Apache 1.1 or later)

mod_include

The mod_include module provides support for server-side includes (SSIs). See Chapter 13, *Server Side Includes*, for further explanation.

XBitHack

`XBitHack` *`status`*

[*server config*, or within <VirtualHost> or <Directory>, or *.htaccess*]

Specifies the parsing of executable HTML documents. Options are:

`on`
: Files that are user-executable are treated as a server-parsed HTML document (SPML).

`off`
: Executable files are treated as regular files.

`full`
: Files that are both user- and group-executable have the last modified time altered to match that of the returned document.

(All)

mod_info

The mod_info module allows for addition information links to be placed in various documents sent by the server.

AddModuleInfo

`AddModuleInfo` *`module string`*

[*server config*, or within <VirtualHost>]

Places the text specified by *string* as a link for additional information for the module specified. For example:

```
AddModuleInfo mod_include.c 'See <A HREF="/docs/mod/mod_include.html">
the following link </A> for more information.
```

(Apache 1.1 or later)

mod_isapi

The mod_isapi module provides for ISAPI extensions when the server is running under Microsoft Windows. This module is compiled into the server by default if the target platform is Microsoft; otherwise, the module is left out. There are no directives in this module.

mod_log_agent

The mod_log_agent module allows logging of client user agents.

AgentLog

AgentLog *file|pipe-command*

[*server config*, or within <VirtualHost>]

This directive specifies the name of the file relative to ServerRoot the server logs user-agent information in. If you wish, you can specify a pipe (|) followed by a shell command in place of the filename; the program runs as the user that started the *httpd* server and receives the log information as standard input. For example:

```
AgentLog |"grep email >>.emaillog"
```

The default file is logs/agent_log.

(All)

mod_log_common

The mod_log_common module provides logging of common requests made to the server. It is now obsolete and has been replaced by the mod_log_config module.

mod_log_config

The mod_log_config module provides logging of requests made to the server. See the Apache documentation for an explanation of the logging format.

CookieLog

CookieLog *filename*

[*server config*, or within <VirtualHost>]

Specifies the location of the file where cookie requests can be logged, relative to the ServerRoot. This directive is deprecated.

CustomLog

CustomLog *file format*

[*server config*, or within <VirtualHost>]

Specifies the location of the file where logs can be recorded, either as a fully qualified filename or relative to the ServerRoot. You can instruct the server to use a specific format to log the records using the *format* parameter. In

→

addition, you can specify a formatting nickname as defined by the LogFormat directive.

(Apache 1.3 or later)

LogFormat

LogFormat *format [nickname]*

[*server config*, or within <VirtualHost>]

This sets the default format of the log file specified by the TransferLog directive. If you wish, you can also use the directive to declare a nickname for a format. If you specify a nickname, the command does not apply the format as the default. Log formats are defined using the "Common Log Format," which is explained in greater detail in the Apache documentation.

(Apache 1.2 or later)

TransferLog

TransferLog *file|pipe-command*

[*server config*, or within <VirtualHost>]

Specifies a default log file using a format dictated by the LogFormat command. If you wish, you can specify a pipe (|) followed by a shell command in place of the filename; this program runs as the user that started the *httpd* server and receives the log information as standard input. For example:

```
TransferLog |"grep PUT >>.putlog"
```

(Apache 1.2 or later)

mod_log_referer

The mod_log_referer module allows administrators to configure information on referer logs. A referer is an outside document that references other documents on your server.

RefererIgnore

RefererIgnore *string ...*

[*server config*, or within <VirtualHost>]

Specifies one or more strings to ignore in the referer headers. If it is encountered, no information is written to the referer log.

(All)

Server Configuration

RefererLog

`RefererLog filename|pipe-command`

[*server config*, or within `<VirtualHost>`]

Specifies the location of the referer log file. It may be specified either as an absolute path or as a relative path from the `ServerRoot` directory. All referer headers are logged at this location. The default is:

```
RefererLog logs/referer_log
```

If you wish, you can specify a pipe (|) followed by a shell command in place of the filename; this program runs as the user that started the *httpd* server and receives the log information as standard input.

(All)

mod_mime

The `mod_mime` module contains directives that help to organize various MIME types on the server.

AddEncoding

`AddEncoding encoding extension ...`

[*server config*, or within `<VirtualHost>` or `<Directory>`, or *.htaccess*]

Allows you to specify which MIME encodings should be associated with documents from your server. Encodings beginning with `x-` are used for unofficial encodings. For example:

```
AddEncoding x-gzip gz
```

(All)

AddHandler

`AddHandler handler-name extension ...`

[*server config*, or within `<VirtualHost>` or `<Directory>`, or *.htaccess*]

Maps one or more filename extensions to a specific handler for the server. For example, for CGI scripts, you might use the following:

```
AddHandler cgi-script cgi
```

(Apache 1.1 or later)

AddLanguage

`AddLanguage` *`mime-lang extension ...`*

[*server config*, or within `<VirtualHost>` or `<Directory>`, or *.htaccess*]

Specifies that a certain extension should be associated with a specific language for purposes of content negotiation. For example, to associate the extension *.francais* with French documents, use the following setting:

```
AddLanguage fr .francais
```

(All)

AddType

`AddType` *`mime-type extension`*

[*server config*, or within `<VirtualHost>` or `<Directory>`, or *.htaccess*]

Specifies a MIME type and subtype to be associated with certain file extensions. For example, if you want to serve a Microsoft Word document:

```
AddType application/msword .doc
```

`AddType` directives overrides any extension-to-type mappings in your *mime.types* file.

(All)

ForceType

`ForceType` *`mime_type`*

[Within `<Directory>`, or *.htaccess*]

Specifies that all files in this directory should be served with the specified type. Appropriate for inclusion in *.htaccess* files or within `<Directory>` section directives.

SetHandler

`SetHandler` *`handler`*

[Within `<Directory>`, or *.htaccess*]

Specifies that all files in the directory should be passed through the specified handler. Values are:

`cgi-script`
: All files treated as CGI scripts (see Chapter 12)

`imap-file`
: All files treated as imagemap files

Server Configuration

→

`send-as-is`
: All files sent as is without additional server-supplied HTTP headers

`server-info`
: All files sent with server configuration information

`server-parsed`
: All files parsed as server-side includes (see Chapter 13)

`type-map`
: All files parsed as type map files for content negotiation

(Apache 1.1 or later)

TypesConfig

`TypesConfig` *`filename`*

[*server config*]

Specifies the location of the MIME types file. As with other configuration paths, the location may be given as either an absolute path or a relative path to the `ServerRoot` directory. The default is:

```
TypesConfig conf/mime.types
```

(All)

---

mod_mime_magic

The `mod_mime_magic` module enables looking up of specific MIME types by its initial contents, such as scanning for magic numbers.

MimeMagicFile

`MimeMagicFile` *`file`*

[*server config* or `<VirtualHost>`]

Enables the `mod_mime_magic` module for this realm with the specified file. A default file is located at `conf/magic`.

(Apache 1.3 or later)

---

mod_mmap_static

The `mod_mmap_static` module allows the administrator to cache various files in memory, thus cutting the amount of time the server needs to retrieve its contents.

MMapFile

```
MMapFile file
```

[*server config*]

This command maps one or more files into system memory at server startup. This can be helpful if a specific document is frequently requested from the server, which allows Apache to transmit it from memory instead of repeatedly fetching it from disk. For example:

```
MMapFile /usr/local/apache/local/server/index.html
```

(Apache 1.3 or later)

mod_negotiation

The `mod_negotiation` module performs content negotiation between the server and the client.

CacheNegotiatedDocs

```
CacheNegotiatedDocs
```

[*server config*]

Tells the server to allow remote proxy servers to cache negotiated documents. By default, Apache does not allow caching of negotiated documents.

(Apache 1.1 or later)

LanguagePriority

```
LanguagePriority language ...
```

[*server config*, within `<VirtualHost>` or `<Directory>`, or *.htaccess*]

Allows you to specify a ranking of languages, which is used in the event that a user's preferences are equal among language choices. For example:

```
LanguagePriority de it
```

specifies German before Italian.

(Apache 1.1 or later)

mod_proxy

The `mod_proxy` module handles a multitude of proxying and caching capabilities for the server. *Proxies* enforce security by screening and relaying requests made by a client; *caches* help to optimize transfer by storing recently requested information.

CacheDefaultExpire

`CacheDefaultExpire` *`time`*

[*server config* or within `<VirtualHost>`]

This sets the default expiry time, in hours, of a document in the cache, assuming an expiry has not already been set. The default is one hour. After the document has been expired, the client must refetch it directly from the server.

(Apache 1.1 or later)

CacheDirLength

`CacheDirLength` *`length`*

[*server config* or within `<VirtualHost>`]

This directive sets the number of characters a directory can contain in the proxy cache.

```
CacheDirLength 1024768
```

(Apache 1.1 or later)

CacheDirLevels

`CacheDirLevels` *`level`*

[*server config* or within `<VirtualHost>`]

This directive sets the number of subdirectories in the cache.

```
CacheDirLevels 10
```

(Apache 1.1 or later)

CacheForceCompletion

`CacheForceCompletion` *`percentage`*

[*server config* or within `<VirtualHost>`]

This directive specifies the minimum percentage of a document required in order for it to be cached. This is useful in the event a document is canceled before completing a transfer. The default is 90 percent.

(Apache 1.3.1 or later)

CacheGcInterval

`CacheGcInterval` *`time`*

[*server config* or within `<VirtualHost>`]

This directive instructs the server to garbage-collect the cache if the space usage is greater than the size specified by the `CacheSize` directive. The collection is performed every *time* hours. You can specify a noninteger for the *time* if you want to perform garbage collections between hours.

(Apache 1.1 or later)

CacheLastModifiedFactor

`CacheLastModifiedFactor` *`factor`*

[*server config* or within `<VirtualHost>`]

This directive estimates an expiry date for a document by multiplying the *factor* specified by the time since the last modification. This is effective only if an expiry date for a document has not been set already. If the expiration date is greater than `CacheMaxExpire`, `CacheMaxExpire` is used instead.

(Apache 1.1 or later)

CacheMaxExpire

`CacheMaxExpire` *`time`*

[*server config* or within `<VirtualHost>`]

This directive specifies the maximum amount of time a document should remain active. Once past this time, it is considered "expired" and should be reloaded directly from the server.

(Apache 1.1 or later)

CacheRoot

`CacheRoot` *`directory`*

[*server config* or within `<VirtualHost>`]

This directive sets the name of the directory that will contain cache files.

(Apache 1.1 or later)

CacheSize

`CacheSize` *`size`*

[*server config* or within `<VirtualHost>`]

→

This directive sets the maximum size, in kilobytes, of the cache. Once this size is exceeded, no more data is written to the cache.

(Apache 1.1 or later)

NoCache

`NoCache` *`word|host|domain list`*

[*server config* or within `<VirtualHost>`]

This directive specifies a matching of documents that are not cached by the server. You can use one of three options:

`word`
: The server searches for any such word in the title of the document. If one is found, the document is not cached.

`host`
: A document that originates from the target host isn't cached.

`domain`
: Documents originating from any domain in the list are not cached.

For example:

```
NoCache abc.com def.com ghi.com
NoCache somecompany
NoCache *
```

Note that you are allowed to use wildcards. The last example forcees the server not to cache any documents at all.

(Apache 1.1 or later)

NoProxy

`NoProxy` *`domain|subnet|ip|hostname`*

[*server config* or within `<VirtualHost>`]

Specifies a list of intranet addresses or domains the proxy should not attempt to intermediate between. The parameter can be one of the following:

domain
: A domain name, like *.oreilly.com*; hosts from the domain can bypass the proxy

hostname
: A full hostname that can bypass the proxy

IP
: An IP address of a host that can bypass the proxy

subnet
: A subnet of addresses that can bypass the proxy

→

For example, the following disables the proxy for all addresses in the subnet 192.168:

```
NoProxy 192.168.0.0
```

(Apache 1.3 or later)

ProxyBlock

`ProxyBlock` *`word|host|domain list`*

[*server config* or within `<VirtualHost>`]

Specifies a list of intranet addresses or domains which the proxy should block access to any documents on the server. The parameter can be one of the following:

`word`
: The server searches for any such word in the title of the document. If one is found, the document is blocked.

`host`
: A document that originates from the target host will be blocked.

`domain`
: Documents originating from any domain in the list are blocked.

For example, the following blocks all requests for documents from `dirtyrotten.com` and `hackers.com`:

```
ProxyBlock dirtyrotten.com hackers.com
```

(Apache 1.2 or later)

ProxyDomain

`ProxyDomain` *`domain`*

[*server config* or within `<VirtualHost>`]

This directive specifies the default domain of the proxy. For example:

```
ProxyDomain .oreilly.com
```

(Apache 1.3 or later)

ProxyPass

`ProxyPass` *`path url`*

[*server config* or within `<VirtualHost>`]

This directive translates requests for a specific *path* to be redirected to the corresponding *url*. This allows remote servers to act as if they existed in the

Server Configuration

→

local filesystem. Note that this directive takes place regardless of whether the ProxyRequests directive is activated. For example:

```
ProxyPass /mydir http://www.otherserver.com/mydir
```

(Apache 1.1 or later)

ProxyPassReverse

ProxyPassReverse *path url*

[*server config* or within <VirtualHost>]

Handles redirects made by a server pointed to by the ProxyPass directive by modifying the Location header in the HTTP redirect response. This directive alters redirect references to a specific *path* to the corresponding *url*.

(Apache 1.3beta6 or later)

ProxyReceiveBufferSize

ProxyReceiveBufferSize *bytes*

[*server config* or within <VirtualHost>]

Specifies the networking buffer size for outgoing connections through the proxy. The value must be greater than 512. However, you can use the value 0 to indicate that the system's default buffer size should be used. For example:

```
ProxyReceiveBufferSize 4096
```

(Apache 1.3 or later)

ProxyRemote

ProxyRemote *match remote-server*

[*server config* or within <VirtualHost>]

This directive specifies a remote proxy that should be used under user-definable conditions. The *match* parameter is either a URL scheme (http, ftp, etc.) that the server supports, or a partial URL which should be redirected to the remote proxy. The *remote-server* parameter should be organized as a fully qualified URL, as shown below:

```
ProxyRemote ftp http://ftpproxy.oreilly.com:8080
ProxyRemote * http://handle.everything.oreilly.com:9001
```

Currently, http is the only scheme supported for the *remote-server* parameter.

(Apache 1.1 or later)

ProxyRequests

ProxyRequests on|off

[*server config* or within <VirtualHost>]

This directive activates or deactivates proxy serving. The default is:

```
ProxyRequests Off
```

Note that even though proxy requests are deactivated, the **ProxyPass** directives are still valid.

(Apache 1.1 or later)

mod_rewrite

The mod_rewrite module allows for rewriting URLs for clients based on specific rules. This is a powerful module with many rewriting features (too many to list here) that perform their functions on the fly.

RewriteBase

RewriteBase *url*

[Within <Directory> or *.htaccess*]

Sets the base directory for rewrites. This specifies a portion of the URI that will not be modified by any subsequent rewriting, even if the URI maps to a different filesystem. For example:

```
RewriteBase /files
```

This directive tells the rewriting engine to ignore the files directory in the URI when rewriting.

RewriteCond

RewriteCond *string condition*

Defines a rule condition for URI rewriting. See the Apache documentation for more information.

(Apache 1.3 or later)

RewriteEngine

RewriteEngine on|off

[*server config*, within <Directory> or <VirtualHost>, or *.htaccess*]

Server Configuration

→

This directive enables or disables the rewriting engine of this module. The default setting is:

```
RewriteEngine off
```

(Apache 1.2 or later)

RewriteLock

`RewriteLock` *`filename`*

[*server config* or `<VirtualHost>`]

Sets a filename to serve as the lockfile used by the rewriting engine. It is recommended that this file reside on the local drive and not on an NFS-mounted drive.

(Apache 1.3 or later)

RewriteLog

`RewriteLog` *`filename`*

[*server config* or `<VirtualHost>`]

This directive specifies the name of the log file to which it records any URL rewriting activities. *filename* can be a fully qualified filename or relative to the `ServerRoot` directive. For example:

```
RewriteLog "logs/rewrite.log"
```

(Apache 1.2 or later)

RewriteLogLevel

`RewriteLogLevel` *`level`*

[*server config* or `<VirtualHost>`]

Sets the amount of reporting that is done to the rewriting log file, a number between 0 and 9. The default is `RewriteLogLevel 0`. For example:

```
RewriteLogLevel 3
```

It is recommended that levels greater than 2 be used only for debugging purposes, as they can generate large amounts of data in a short period of time.

(Apache 1.2 or later)

RewriteMap

`RewriteMap` *`name type:source`*

[*server config* or `<VirtualHost>`]

→

Declares the rewriting map and its type. The map file performs substitutions for various URIs. The *name* parameter makes up the given name of the mapping. The *type* and *source* variables are determined by the *type*:

`txt`
: A plain-text file, with the *source* pointing to a regular file

`rnd`
: A plain-text file with a random mapping choice; the *source* variable points to a regular file

`dbm`
: The *source* variable points to a DBM-formatted file

`int`
: An internal Apache function; the *source* variable can be one of two functions: `toupper` or `tolower`

`prg`
: A program. The *source* variable points to a Unix executable

Here is an example that shows how to use a text-based rewriting file:

```
RewriteMap real-host txt:/usr/local/maps/mymap.txt
```

(Apache 1.3 or later)

RewriteOptions

`RewriteOptions` *`option`*

[*server config*, within `<VirtualHost>` or `<Directory>`, or *.htaccess*]

Sets options for the rewriting engine in this context. Currently, the only option available is:

`inherit`
: This option instructs the current rewriting configuration to inherit the values of its parent directory's access control file.

(Apache 1.2 or later)

RewriteRule

`RewriteRule` *`pattern substitution`*

[*server config*, within `<VirtualHost>` or `<Directory>`, or *.htaccess*]

Defines a single rewriting rule. See the Apache documentation for further information.

(Apache 1.3 or later)

Server Configuration

mod_setenvif

The `mod_setenvif` module sets environment variables based on the client's browser or other information.

BrowserMatch

`BrowserMatch` *`regex var[=value] var[=value] ...`*

[*server config*]

Sets environment variables based on the client's browser type. If the `User-Agent` HTTP header matches the regular expression specified by *regex*, set one or more environment variables as follows:

`var`
: The environment variable is defined and given the value of 1.

`!var`
: The environment variable is deleted.

`var=value`
: The environment variable is set to an initial value.

Here is an example of how to locate various browsers. The first sets `compatible` if the client is connecting with Versions 2 through 4 of Netscape. The second sets `microsoft` if Internet Explorer is detected:

```
BrowserMatch ^Mozilla/[2-4] compatible !microsoft
BrowserMatch MSIE microsoft
```

(Apache 1.3 or later)

BrowserMatchNoCase

`BrowserMatchNoCase` *`regex var=value var=value ...`*

[*server config*]

Identical to `BrowserMatch`, except that matching is now case-insensitive. For example, the following would still work to detect Internet Explorer:

```
BrowserMatch msie microsoft
```

(Apache 1.3 or later)

SetEnvIf

`SetEnvIf` *`attribute regex var[=value] var[=value] ...`*

[*server config*]

Sets environment variables based on the attributes of an HTTP request. Some of the more common attributes are:

→

`Remote_Host`
: The hostname of the client, if known

`Remote_Addr`
: The IP address of the client

`Remote_User`
: The user which is making the request, if known

`Request_Method`
: The name of the HTTP method being used to request information

`Request_URI`
: The latter portion of the URL, after the host information

`Referer`
: The URI of the referring page, if known

For example, the following sets the environment variable `SOMEONE_FROM_OREILLY` if the remote host resolves to the domain *oreilly.com*:

```
SetEnvIf Remote_Host oreilly.com SOMEONE_FROM_OREILLY
```

(Apache 1.3 or later)

SetEnvIfNoCase

`SetEnvIfNoCase` ***`attribute regex var[=value] var[=value] ...`***

[*server config*]

Identical to `SetEnvIf`, except that attribute matching is now case-insensitive.

(Apache 1.3 or later)

mod_so

The `mod_so` module assists in loading shared object files into the server at startup. This includes modules and other shared libraries, including Dynamic Link Libraries (DLLs) and Unix `.so` shared libraries. See the Apache documentation for information on creating DLL modules for Windows.

LoadFile

`LoadFile` ***`filename ...`***

[*server config*]

This directive loads one or more specified object libraries when the server is started. The *filename* can be an absolute pathname or can be relative to `ServerRoot`.

(Apache 1.3 or above)

LoadModule

`LoadModule module filename`

[*server config*]

This directive loads the given *filename* as a given module, adding it to the list of active modules. For example:

```
LoadModule status_module mod_stat.so
```

(Apache 1.3 or above)

mod_speling

The mod_speling module (spelled with one "l") attempts to correct various spelling errors a user can make while requesting a document on the server.

CheckSpelling

`CheckSpelling on|off`

[*server config*, within <VirtualHost> or <Directory>, or *.htaccess*]

This directive enables or disables the spelling assistance.

(Apache 1.1 or above)

mod_status

The mod_status module enables server status pages to be generated, documenting the usage of the Apache server. If this module is compiled into the Apache server, you can enable server status reports with the following directives:

```
<Location /server-status>
SetHandler server-status

order deny,allow
deny from all
allow from .foo.com
</Location>
```

This automatically generates an HTML status page that is located in the server-status subdirectory of your document tree.

ExtendedStatus

`ExtendedStatus on|off`

[*server config*]

→

This directive enables or disables the extended status information.

(Apache 1.3.2 or later)

mod_userdir

The mod_userdir module provides automatic mapping to user directories for requested addresses.

UserDir

UserDir *directory|filename*

[*server config*, or within <VirtualHost>]

Translates a username to a specific directory and default filename. The default is the user's home directory in the subdirectory *public_html*, loading the file *index.html*. Alternatively, you can specify the enabled or disabled keyword followed by a series of usernames you wish to enable or disable access. For example:

```
UserDir enabled robert stephen
UserDir disabled john linda
```

(Apache 1.3 or later)

mod_unique_id

The mod_unique_id module generates an environment variable, UNIQUE_ID, which is guaranteed to be a unique number for each request given to the server. The variable consists of an encoding of the 32-bit IP address of the server, the httpd process ID, the current UTC time stamp, and an independent counter.

mod_usertrack

The mod_usertrack module tracks various users who have accessed documents and other information from the server. Information is stored is a log file using the CustomLog directive.

CookieExpires

CookieExpires *period*

[*server config*, or within <VirtualHost>]

→

This specifies the number of seconds a cookie should exist before it is considered "expired." You can also specify the expiry period in a format such as:

```
5 weeks 4 days 12 hours
```

Otherwise, the cookies last only for the current browser session.

(Apache 1.2 or later)

CookieTracking

`CookieTracking on|off`

[*server config*, within `<VirtualHost>` or `<Directory>`, or *.htaccess*]

This directive enables or disables cookie tracking. If the directive is set to `on` for a directory, the Apache server sends cookies for all new HTTP requests. The default is `off`.

(Apache 1.2 or later)

CHAPTER 20

Server Performance

While there are literally thousands of things you can do to help web performance, here are 10 areas that will provide large and quick performance improvement for your efforts.

Turn Off Reverse DNS Lookups

Reverse DNS maps IP numbers to machine names. The web server uses reverse DNS for two things: writing a machine name rather than simply an IP address in the web servers logs, and giving CGI programs easy access to the client machine name. The CGI program can access the client machine name via the REMOTE_HOST environment variable if reverse DNS is on.

The problems with reverse DNS are that it can take a long time and is generally implemented as a blocking system call. This means that the current process or thread can do no further work until the call either returns with an answer or times out. While the time required generally isn't a problem for a single HTTP request, it rapidly becomes the server bottleneck if there are more than a few users making requests.

Fortunately, you don't really need reverse DNS to be turned on in your web server. First of all, your CGI program may not even use the REMOTE_HOST environment variable. If the CGI does need to know the client DNS name, it can make the DNS call itself. And while it is more enlightening for a human to see DNS names rather than IP addresses in the server logs, server logs can be processed offline and the mapping of IP to DNS name done then.

Here is how your CGI can get machine names from IP numbers. In C under Unix, call the *gethostbyaddr()* function. See the *gethostbyaddr* manpage for more information. In Perl, use the *gethostbyaddr* function. It is explained in the Perl documentation. And in Java, you can use the *java.net.InetAddress.getHostName()* method. See the JDK documentation.

To parse access log files and insert the DNS names, use the *logresolve* program that is part of the Apache distribution.

Here's how to turn off reverse DNS in Apache and Netscape. For Apache, in the *httpd.conf*, include this line: `HostnameLookups off`. As of Netscape Enterprise 3.5, DNS lookups are off by default, but if you have an older Netscape server, in the *magnus.conf* file, put `DNS off` and in the `AddLog` directive in *obj.conf* put `iponly=1`. In Java Web Server, reverse DNS is apparently always `off`.

Use the Most Recent Version of Your Server

Web server performance has improved dramatically in the short time since the creation of HTTP. The latest generation of servers are more than 10 times faster than the earliest servers. And they're still getting better.

inetd Spawned Servers

The first generation of web servers were just another Unix service launched on demand from *inetd*, the Internet daemon. *inetd* reads */etc/services* and */etc/inet/inetd.conf* when it starts at boot-time and listens to the ports specified. When a request comes in on one of *inetd*'s ports, it launches the program specified in */etc/inet/inetd.conf* to deal with requests on that port.

This mechanism is intended to conserve system resources by running daemons only when they're needed, providing better performance for everything else. And it works that way, if you need the service only occasionally.

For example, watch the list of processes running on your system—say, with *top*. Start an FTP session to your own machine. When the request comes in on port 21, *inetd* launches *ftpd*, and you will see *ftpd* appear in the list of processes. When the FTP session is over, the *ftpd* process goes away.

Originally, *httpd* was launched the same way but from port 80, the standard port for HTTP. It worked fine at light loads, but trouble started when servers were loaded above one or two hits per second. Remember that a single HTML page can have many embedded images. Therefore, one page can quickly generate a burst of HTTP operations, reaching the maximum rate at which *inetd* can launch new copies of the web server to deal with the requests. Overall system load is actually increased and performance reduced by the many startups of *httpd* when the server load increased beyond a very minimal level.

The reason *inetd*-spawned servers are inefficient is that launching a new program requires calling the *fork()* and *exec()* system calls, which are expensive. *fork()* clones *inetd* to get process space and then *exec()* writes over that process with the desired executable. This method of process creation is flexible; it's just not high-performance.

Forking Servers

A step up from using *inetd* to *fork()* and *exec()* is to use an instance of *httpd* to simply *fork()* another copy of itself to handle the request, with no need for an *exec()*. This was the original intent behind the *fork()* system call and works reasonably well for the client-server world, where the new copy of the server process hangs around for a long time servicing a single client. Unfortunately, because HTTP requests arrive so frequently and are of such short duration, the time spent in creating a new *httpd* process is larger than the time spent actually servicing the request. The early CERN and NCSA servers were forking servers.

Preforking Servers

Another improvement came with the preforking server. The Apache server is preforking. For example, when Apache 1.2.4 *httpd* starts up, it immediately starts five additional servers by default to handle multiple simultaneous requests from one browser or from several concurrent clients. Each of the *httpd* processes continue to live and wait for new requests. Apache increases the number of preforked server processes in response to a heavier load, and this works quite well, even for very large sites, but is memory- and CPU-intensive.

Apache gives you the option to launch from *inetd*, but now you know that it's probably not a good idea. Run a standalone server instead. Configure Apache's *httpd.conf* like this:

```
# ServerType is either inetd, or standalone.
ServerType standalone
```

Threaded Servers

To match the lightweight and transient nature of an HTTP connection, server programmers have created threaded web servers. Threads are independent streams of execution within a single process. Thread creation and thread context switching is on the order of 10 times faster than for spawning processes. Still, once you have a process created and ready to handle a connection, as Apache does, the bottleneck is in servicing the request rather than the overhead of managing server processes or threads, so you don't see a full ten-fold increase in the performance of threaded servers over preforking servers. Netscape Enterprise 2.0 and later are threaded servers and can serve several thousand connections per second on the best hardware.

Keepalive Servers

An additional improvement in performance is available by keeping TCP connections open for serving multiple files in one request. This technique is informally known as *keepalive* and is part of the HTTP 1.1 standard. The formally correct name is "persistent connections," to distinguish from the TCP keepalive timeout, which is something else. Most browsers and servers now understand keepalives, even if they don't fully implement HTTP 1.1. Browsers will indicate they understand keepalive connections by sending a "Connection: keepalive" header with their request, or by explicitly telling the server to use HTTP 1.1. Both pre-forking and threaded servers use keepalives, but they are used only when the content length is exactly known before the transfer starts, so they aren't used with most CGI scripts.

There is a performance hazard to keepalives in that clients may disconnect without notifying the server, which then has an open connection consuming resources until the TCP keepalive timeout finally removes it. To prevent too many such connections from accumulating, most implementations of keepalive come with a timeout parameter that closes unused connections. A keepalive timeout of 15 seconds should be a sufficient timeout parameter if your customers are generally coming from a LAN, or 30 seconds for modem customers.

Keepalive is turned on in Apache 1.1 by default. Here is the Apache directive to limit total connection time to 15 seconds:

```
# Limit keepalive connections to 15 seconds.
KeepAliveTimeout 15
```

Keep HTML Content and HTTP Logs on Different Disks

For the best performance, your web server should have at least two disks: one for content and the OS, and another one for web server logging. The reason is that accessing content causes essentially random disk access, while writing to the log file causes the disk arm to move sequentially. If you keep the log file writes sequential by confining them to their own disk, they'll be very fast. Another reason to keep logs on another disk is to keep the system from crashing if the log file grows to take essentially the whole disk before being truncated or reset by the system administrator. You can also increase performance further by using another disk for your swap space. While you're at it, consider yet another disk for the operating system itself because it has its own disk-usage patterns.

If you have separate disk controller cards for all these disks, their operations can proceed in parallel. If you use a single controller for several disks, make sure it has a maximum transfer rate equal to or better than the sum of the maximum transfer rates of all the disks connected to it.

Solid-state disks are now on the market. These disks use nonvolatile memory—either "flash" RAM or battery-backed RAM—but use a SCSI or other disk interface and so appear to the system to be an ordinary disk. There are no moving parts, so they are quite unlikely to ever break, unlike ordinary disks. Access time is thousands of times faster than rotating physical disks but not as fast as system memory. The main disadvantage to solid-state disks is cost, which is comparable per megabyte to that for system memory, less than $10/MB at this writing, compared to 20consideration is that system RAM is faster than solid-state disks because of the overhead of the SCSI protocol. So if you have the money, you'd get more performance spending it on system memory. Still, if you have filled your web server to its maximum with memory, a solid state disk could be more cost-effective than upgrading the web server machine itself.

The standard disk you get with a PC is known as an Integrated Drive Electronics (IDE) disk. This is the commodity sort of disk, not very expensive, but without high performance, reliability, or scalability. IDE disks should be fine for your web logging needs, but they are not suitable for a high-performance web content disk or database.

As an example, here are the mount points showing how you might break up your filesystem onto four different disks:

```
/
/home/content
/var/log/web
/swap
```

Keep Content as Small as Possible

The network doesn't know or care what type of content you are serving. Bits are bits. Size is all that really matters for network transfer time. Keeping file size down also means that your server can handle more requests. The following table shows the theoretical limits for the number of HTTP requests your server can process based on network connection and average file size. In the real world, the numbers will be considerably less, depending on a number of factors.

Connection	*Average File Size (KB)*		
	1K	*10K*	*100K*
14,400 bits/sec	1.8	0.2	0.0
28,800 bits/sec	3.6	0.3	0.0
56 Kbits/sec	7.0	0.7	0.1
64 Kbits/sec	8.0	0.8	0.1
128 Kbits/sec	16.0	1.6	0.2
1.5 Mbits/sec	187.5	18.7	1.8
10 Mbits/sec	1250.0	125	12.5
45 Mbits/sec	5625	562	56.2
100 Mbits/sec	12500	1250	125.0
155 Mbits/sec	19375	1937	193
622 Mbits/sec	77750	7775	777.0

The basic performance principle is therefore to send fewer bits and make fewer requests. Try to think of size in terms of download time rather than absolute bits because how short a time a human being has to wait is the ultimate measure of success. If most of your users are on 28.8 modems, make a rule that no image can be larger than 10 seconds. Ten seconds is about 35K if the 28.8 modem is running perfectly.

A slight amount of waste is intrinsic to HTML because HTML is written in ASCII text. ASCII is defined as using only 7 bits of each byte, so 1 bit in 8, or 12.5%, is wasted. A larger waste is due to the fact that text is highly compressible, but no compression is used for most HTTP transfers. It is normal for a text compression program to reduce the size of a text file by half, meaning that the file can then be downloaded in half the time. Right now, transmission bandwidth is the bottleneck and CPU power for decompression is cheap, so compressing web pages seems to make sense, even if it would make debugging problems harder.

This lack of compression is not an issue for small pages since network transit time will be negligible, but large text pages will be sent significantly more quickly in compressed format to a browser that understands *gzip* compression, for example. I believe that Mosaic is the only popular browser that understands *gzip*. Another option is to compress your content and configure your web server to use a certain type of MIME type for that compressed content, but you would then have to ask your users to configure their browser to launch the decompression utility when a file with a certain content type is received. This requires a bit of work on both the client and server side.

Performance Tips for HTML Authors

Make It Easy on the Server

When composing HTML, try to keep pathnames short, both in number of directories in the path and in the length of each directory name. Keep the target file name short, too. Make your links explicitly refer to *index.html* files or end directory references with `/`. More on this later.

You can scale static content easily by partitioning the content across multiple servers and using HTML links to the different servers. To start out partitioning, consider using one server for images, another for HTML, another for applets, etc. Also keep in mind that your HTML can refer quite easily to other web sites for embedded content, entirely removing the load from your servers but creating a dependency on the other server and making for twisty copyright issues. For example, the Gamelan (*http://www.gamelan.com/*) applet directory does not have applets itself but simply links to the sites that do, with the authors' consent. There has recently been some legal action against a site that was embedding news from other web sites in frames and selling its own advertising in a top frame.

Going the other way, if you need to have a link on your page to a site known to be very slow, consider asking the site's administrator for permission to mirror the page or site on your own web server.

If your content is a huge number of files with a fairly even distribution of access—say, in a large archive—then your OS' buffer cache and the web server's cache aren't going to be effective. Items will be copied to the cache but won't be accessed again before getting pushed out by new items. In this situation, you'll have to hit the disk for most accesses, so don't spend all your money on RAM, but rather, get the fastest disks or disk arrays you can afford, concentrating on the seek time. Disk striping should help considerably.

Make it easy on the network

The most important thing to do with content from the network's point of view is to keep the size down. If you have a large document, the user may appreciate getting the whole thing and not having to click and wait to get more. However, it may be wise to give just a summary and the first part to see if they really want the whole thing. HTTP 1.1's "byte-range" downloads are capable of downloading part of a document at first, and then the rest when the user requests it. This requires a browser and server that understand HTTP 1.1. Typical HTML size is 4K, which is about two pages of text in a browser. You might want to make the text fit into the MTU if you know it, so that you will get it all in one packet. If your MTU is 1500 bytes, which is common on Ethernet LANs, you'll see better performance from 1460-byte HTML pages than from 1461-byte pages. There will 20 bytes of TCP overhead and 20 bytes of IP overhead.

Make It Easy on the Browser

Parsing HTML is compute-intensive, so you want to make it easy on the browser. You can do this by eliminating redundant or useless tags, using few fancy features like nested tables or frames, and giving the browser information it would otherwise have to calculate itself, such as image sizes. Also, word-processing programs that generate HTML tend to do a rather bad job, often using extra tags that format blank lines. It is simple to clean this up by hand, but time-consuming, so it's worthwhile to write a few simple Perl scripts that will do some substitutions or eliminations for you. Here's an example of a one-line Perl script that removes <br> tags that are alone on a line. These tags are often an artifact of using a graphical page-composition tool.

```
perl -pi -e 's/^<br>$//i' *.html
```

Don't put much in the <head> of the page because that part must be parsed and acted on before the rest of the page can be displayed. In particular, don't put extensive JavaScript scripts in the <head>. Put the majority of the script near where it is used—for example, within a form that is being validated with JavaScript.

Background images are loaded before the text of the page, so keep them simple or eliminate them. A large single background image can make scrolling painfully slow on an old PC. Background images composed of repeating small elements render much faster.

Use the image size option to the <img> tag to tell the browser the size of the image. It saves the browser some processing time and allows it to lay out the HTML before receiving all of the images. Here is an example:

```
<img src="/images/demo.gif" height="150" width="100">
```

Some versions of the Unix *size* command will give the size of images, and therefore can be used in a Perl script to examine images in HTML source and insert their sizes. There are some publicly available utilities to do this, such as *wwwis* (*http://bunge.jump.com/~ark/wwwis/*), or you can write your own. You can scale an image in HTML by including a size that is different from the image's true size in pixels or using percentage of screen width for the values, but it is rather wasteful to use a size smaller than the pixel size. Scaling an image upward works, but it takes a bit of the browser's time, and the image gets coarser.

Multiple nested frames take significant time to retrieve and render. There are examples of recursive abuse of frames around the Web (no examples given here).

Be warned that these pages will try to use up all the browser's memory and either crash it or make it so slow as to be useless.

You can use IP addresses rather than domain names in your links to avoid DNS lookups. For HTML page links, this puts the IP rather than the server's domain name in the browser's Location box, which might be confusing to the user. For links that include images from other sites, the user won't notice anything, but the image loads slightly faster. Make sure to watch for changed IP addresses, as domains can jump around from address to address.

Make It Easy on the User

The first thing the browser displays is the text within the `<title> . . . </title>` tags, so try to make it descriptive enough that users know whether they want to wait for the entire page to load. Many people don't notice the title, so give them a nice clear label on the page in `<h1> . . . </h1>` tags too.

Make every site's home page load lightning fast because it sets the tone for entire site. Users will wait longer for detail pages further in the site, but if they can't get in the front door right away, they may assume the site is down or go away because they're annoyed. You might want to dedicate a server just to the initial home page.

For every image that is a link, be sure to provide a text link as well, in case the user has images turned off or is using a text-only browser. Many sites are useless without images because no planning was done for text-only browsing. An alternative to putting a text link under each graphic is to offer a link from the home page to a parallel tree of light graphics or to a text-only menu. You can use cookies to track whether the user wants a light-graphics version of the site, but cookie-recognition puts a burden on the server, and a parallel content tree just adds more content to track, so there is some cost either way.

Always provide the `alt` attribute of image tags so users know if an image is worth waiting for or if images are off. Making all of your site available via text is also nice for blind people surfing the Web with text-to-audio converters.

Similarly, use alternative functionality between `<applet> . . . </applet>` tags so that the user can turn off Java if he needs to for bandwidth reasons. The default action of HTML is to ignore tags it doesn't understand, and if Java is turned off, the `<applet>` tag is no longer understood. The net result is that you can put any valid HTML between `<applet>` tags and it will be parsed and displayed only if Java is off. This can be used to provide an alternative CGI form for a Java program. The form did the same thing as the applet that was the alternative. The difference was that the applet was more interactive and fun, but it took longer to download.

Don't tell the user about an FTP site or an email address without providing an *ftp://* or *mailto:* link. It's much faster for the user to just click rather than type in a URL or email address.

Change your web server's `404 - file not found` HTML page to contain a map of your site so that the user doesn't have to hit the back button to figure out what his alternatives are on your site. This is also a performance issue because it saves the user time. If the bad link as defined by the HTTP_REFERER in your logs shows that one link within your site failed to find another page on your own site, set up the server to mail the webmaster about the errors. For more info on HTML, read the Usenet group *comp.infosystems.www.authoring.html.*

Graphics

The typical web graphic is 10KB to 20KB, so they are much larger than typical 4KB HTML in a page. The challenge with graphics is again mostly how to make them smaller without losing much quality.

Weight Watching

Make images small by reducing size in the number of pixels and colors (8 bits is usually enough) and by using a format with compression appropriate to the image. JPEG has better compression than GIF for photos but is lossy, meaning that an image compressed into JPEG format cannot be recovered exactly. The compression is good enough that most users will not know that any information is missing. GIF has better compression than JPEG for line-oriented images because it compresses line by line of pixels. GIF is not lossy. The new Portable Network Graphics format is available in NS4.0 and IE4.0. PNG has yet better compression than JPEG or GIF.

Java is often put down for its long startup time and relatively large memory footprint, but large graphics composed of simple shapes will consume less network bandwidth as simple Java class files rather than as bitmap images. I have used Java's *drawPolygon()* method in an applet to display a map of all of the rail tracks in the eastern United States as sets of points connected by lines. This was not only smaller than a bit map, but had the added flexibility of easy zooming and scrolling, which would not have been possible with a static image.

Consolidation

Consolidate images to avoid the overhead of sending multiple images when you can combine them into one to save download time as well as display time. If the images are each links, you can make the composite into an image map and retain the link functionality. Use a client-side image map, where the URL is chosen by the client, rather than a server-side image map, where the URL is deduced from the click coordinates by a process on the server side. Use a cached image map in place of a frame for navigation to save the download of a master frame and navigation subframe.

Reuse

Reuse graphics where ever possible. The browser's cache is smart enough to find them if you reference them in exactly the same way.

Psychology

A common trick is to put your graphics toward the bottom of the page so the user doesn't notice that they're loading while reading the top of the page. Be sure to include the image size in the IMG tag, or you will just delay display of the entire page until Netscape gets the image and figures out its size. 640x480 is still a very common screen size, so if you're designing on a much higher-resolution monitor, it's easy to forget that and create something that users will have to scroll horizontally in order to see. This makes it harder to view your site.

Animation

Animation using either "client pull" or "server push" are now both obsolete, replaced by animated GIFs, which not only download quickly but run without any network interaction. Animated GIFs are also quicker to download and start than Java applets, though of course their functionality is limited to displaying a series of images, while Java applets can do far more. The downside to animated GIF's is that they use up a great deal of the client's CPU, even if the user switches from the browser to another application.

VRML

Support for the Virtual Reality Modeling Language (VRML), is now supported in many versions of Netscape with SGI's Cosmo Player plug-in. VRML downloads quickly relative to the level of detail you get, but it requires a very high-performance machine on the client side to be useful.

Preprocess Queries and Cache the Results

Do you ever wonder how the network news programs can have a detailed obituary story ready within hours of the death of a celebrity? What looks like superhuman performance is actually preprocessing. The TV networks keep preprepared obituaries of major celebrities, especially seriously ill ones. The networks don't know when anyone is going to die, but since there are only a limited number of people whose death is considered newsworthy, the networks have the resources to write stories on all of them. The principle here is that the more you limit the input parameters, the fewer possible results there are. A smaller result set means you can do more effective caching of responses. While the point of a CGI is to output different HTML depending on user input and state information, if the number of possible input and state combinations is small, it makes sense to run the CGI for all possible input offline and cache each result in a plain HTML file. As another example, if a CGI can inform you of tomorrow's weather forecast in 100 cities around the United States, you will certainly get better performance and scalability by regenerating 100 static HTML pages every night than by running a CGI in response to every query.

Even if there are a huge number of possible inputs, if there are a few common combinations of input it makes sense to dynamically cache those. Keep a server-side cache of frequently requested CGI output and have a stub CGI merely return an HTTP `Location:` response pointing to a static HTML page if the page is in the cache.

AltaVista users can input a query containing any string at all, currently up to 800 characters. Because the data set (all web pages in the AltaVista database) and what the user wants are potentially huge, the effort required to deal with this uncertainty is also huge. But that doesn't mean that they have to do a linear search through their entire data set for each query. Like most large databases, the AltaVista database is indexed so that the server can simply use the input keywords as an index into the data set and return any result. An index is not always faster than a linear search. A linear search has the advantage that the disk heads move very little, just from one track to the next during the search, while an indexed retrieval may require the heads to jump around a great deal. If the answer was to be found at the beginning of a linear search, it would probably have been faster. Which is better is very dependent on the size of your index and data set. The Alta Vista web server also caches the results of the most frequent queries.

As an example of effective use of indexing, consider a CGI that needs to search through the server's filesystem for a particular file, named, say *desiree*. While it is easy to have the CGI run the Unix *find* command, it is far more efficient to search a prebuilt index of the filesystem. To build an index of your entire filesystem, you can simply do this:

```
find / > index
```

Now the two approaches to finding the file are these:

```
find / -name desiree
```

and:

```
grep desiree index
```

You can time how long it takes these commands by prefixing them with the Unix *time* command. For example:

```
time find / -name desiree
```

You want to look at the "real" or "elapsed" time in the output of the time command. Use the *man time* command for more information about your system's output format. You should see that the grep of the index is 10 to 100 times faster. This is the benefit of indexing.

One other thing you should notice is that if you run either command again soon, it will run more quickly than it did at first. Why is this? It's because your program has been loaded into RAM and probably has not been swapped out, and because the part of the filesystem you were accessing is also now cached in RAM. This is just how Unix operates, and it works automatically to your advantage.

Another feature of Unix related to caching is the fact that the "text" segment which is the executable code part of programs is shared between concurrent instances. For a quick example of the kind of speedup you get by shared code, start a copy of Netscape and note how long it takes. Then go to Netscape's menubar and choose `File -> New Web Browser`. It will start in a flash. The key is that the code or "text segment" is already loaded and ready to run. So when you start getting many hits on the same CGI in a short time frame, the second and subsequent hits will use the same text segment as the first, meaning the RAM needed to run the second and subsequent copies is smaller than that for the first copy. This also reduces the risk of paging or swapping. So for all these reasons, the second and subsequent copies will usually run faster than the first.

Use Servlets or Server APIs

If you have to generate dynamic content, user your server API or Java servlets rather than slow CGI. CGI depends on forking user processes for each request. This works well with light loads, but becomes a bottleneck as the load gets heavier, for the same reason that inetd-spawned servers don't scale well. Servlets and server API's scale better.

CGI Internals and Performance Problems

Though the CGI mechanism for generating dynamic web content is very versatile, the basic structure of CGI limits its performance. The main performance penalty is that a new instance of the program is executed for each user's request. This process exits immediately after sending its output back to the web server for forwarding to the browser. If the CGI program opens a database connection, the database connection must be reopened for the next instance of the CGI. This load on the operating system severely limits the number of CGI requests that can be serviced per second. CGI execution time is likely to be the bottleneck under any but the lightest loads. CGIs typically take far more CPU and other resources than serving HTML pages.

Let's take a closer look at the sequence of events in starting a CGI program and where the performance problems are. When a CGI request comes in, the web server must parse the input URL and the request headers, recognize that the user desires to execute a CGI program, and begin the CGI with the *fork()* and *exec()* system calls. The parsing and the *fork()* and *exec()* are where much of the cost of CGI is. The server sets up the environment variables and the standard I/O for the child process. Then it begins to write the URL-encoded data to the CGI's standard input. The CGI reads the data, stopping when it has read the number of bytes specified in the CONTENT-LENGTH environment variable. The CGI may also read URL-encoded command-line arguments, which are given by placing them after the script name in the URL, like this:

```
http://www.nowhere.com/script.cgi?cmd_line_arg
```

It is then up to the CGI to decode the data and decide what to return to the browser. This is the meat of the CGI and varies widely in complexity. When the CGI is done, it outputs its results to the web server, which adds on HTTP headers and forwards everything to the browser. The CGI then exits. There is a rather dated, but still accurate, illustration of CGI events at *http://www.ansa.co.uk/ANSA/ISF/1506/1506prt4.html.*

CGI is also problematic because communication between browser and server is limited to parameters that the browser sends and the result the server returns.

Ongoing communication within the same connection is difficult to implement. Given that CGI performance is poor and that all it can do is reply to a request and close the connection, why does anyone use CGI? In fact, there is a migration to Java and CORBA underway already, allowing code on the browser to directly call methods on remote Java objects. Still, there are a number of good reasons that CGI is popular and will probably be around for at least a few more years.

- CGI is conceptually simple.
- CGI is an open standard supported by most web servers, regardless of hardware or operating system. So your CGI scripts are portable.
- CGIs are easy to write and can be written in almost any programming language.
- CGIs won't crash a web server because they run as separate processes.
- There are many freely available CGI scripts.

Server APIs, such as the Apache API, NSAPI, and IISAPI, are a huge performance win over CGI at the expense of portability. Once you've written a program for a server's API, there is a cost to porting it to another server, unlike CGI or Java. But on the other hand, there is no cost of a separate CGI process. Programs written using the API run as part of the web server process. Note that some databases are also web servers, eliminating even the overhead of the separate *httpd* process. Java servlets fall between CGI and native server APIs in performance, but are very portable, running on any server that supports servlets.

Increase RAM and Bandwidth

The worst thing short of total failure that can happen to your server is a memory shortage serious enough to start the swapping of entire processes out to disk. When that happens, performance drops quickly, and users wonder if it's worth their time to wait for your content. It is better simply to refuse the excess connections you cannot handle well than for all of your users to get unacceptable performance. Servers that run as multiple processes, such as Apache, have a configurable limit to the number of processes and simultaneous connections per process. Multithreaded servers provide limits to the number of active threads. You can limit incoming connections by setting the TCP listen queue small enough that you are assured of being able to service the users who have connected.

A system that is short of memory may show high CPU utilization because the operating system constantly needs to scan for pages of memory to move out to disk. In such a case, adding CPU power won't help. You should add more memory or reduce memory usage. Look at the rate of page scanning with *vmstat* under Solaris or the Performance Monitor under NT. Under Solaris, the "sr" column tells you the scan rate. Sustained scanning is an indication of a memory shortage. Under NT, the clue is that your processor time will be high and almost identical to privileged time, meaning that the CPU is doing almost no work on behalf of the web server, only on behalf of the OS itself.

There is a limit to the amount of memory any particular machine physically has room for. Be aware that this is a hard limit on scalability for that machine. When you hit that limit, you have to either replace the machine or offload some of the processing—for example by using FastCGI, which is described in Chapter 12, *CGI Overview*.

Memory for the Operating System

First let's just consider the operating system. Linux 2.0 can run well in less than 8MB, while you should budget 32MB for Solaris 2.6 or NT 4.0 unless you know your configuration requires less. And that's just for the operating system, not the web server or applications. Also, it is ironic but true that your OS will require slightly more memory itself when you have more memory. This is because the kernel uses memory to keep tables that track memory usage.

One reason more RAM helps very busy web servers is that impolite clients that disconnect abruptly leave open TCP connections, which consume RAM in the kernel until they eventually time out. Each of these connections requires on the order of 50KB of TCP/IP socket buffer memory. The number of such connections can rapidly accumulate on busy web servers. The Unix *netstat -a* command is an easy way to see how many connections exist at the moment. The "keepalive" timeout parameter determines how long it will be before the OS clears out the unused connections. Another reason more RAM helps very busy web servers is that many actively used connections can accumulate due to the bandwidth limitations of the Internet.

Memory for httpd

Now you should budget for the number of server daemons you have running on top of the memory you have for the OS. Allocate 1MB or 2 MB per server daemon running as a separate process; you can see memory usage of *httpd* processes with *top* or *ps*, but you cannot tell exactly how much is shared and how much is used per additional process. For threaded servers, Adrian Cockcroft, a Sun performance expert, made a rough recommendation of 1M per server process plus 100K per thread, because he measured Netscape 2.0 processes, which can spawn up to 32 threads, and found that they used about 1M when idle and grew to be 3M to 4M when busy, probably due to caching of content. From this it can be assumed that the 32 threads took up 3M, so that's about 100K each. You should also allocate about 50K for each network connection, the number of which will be the same as the number of threads running.

Memory for Content

Another rule of thumb is to provide enough RAM to hold all the content that you expect will be accessed within a five-minute interval. This should prevent the web server from having to access the content disk more than once in any five-minute interval. Many servers cache recently accessed pages in memory, even though the pages may already be in the buffer cache. This caching by the server may improve performance slightly over the use of the buffer cache alone, but it could also double your memory usage. You can try turning off the web server's cache and compare performance and memory usage. You may save on memory and not lose any performance.

Memory for CGIs

To budget memory for CGIs, you need to know how many CGIs will be running concurrently. To really know the number of concurrent CGIs you'll be running, you need to know the number of requests to run the CGI per second and the time each CGI takes to complete. But that completion time depends on how many are running! The recursive math quickly gets daunting.

The safe thing is to budget enough memory to run as many CGI processes as you have server threads or daemons, on the assumption that each thread or daemon may run a CGI concurrently with all the others. CGI processes can easily require more memory than the *httpd* process itself, especially if the CGI is written in an interpreted language, which requires loading the interpreter, or if the CGI accesses a database, which often has large connection libraries that must be loaded before a connection can be made. The use of transaction processing monitors can help performance by managing a pool of open database connections rather than opening a new connection for each CGI. See Chapter 12 for additional hints on how to reduce CGI executable sizes.

The number of different CGI executables that you run has an impact on the amount of memory you need, since the code segment can be shared between concurrent instances of the same program, though the heap and stack cannot. Use the Unix `size` program to determine the size of the text (i.e., code), data, and bss segments of your CGI. The data and bss give you a lower limit for how much additional RAM each instance of the CGI will use. The CGI can and probably will use more memory than that as it runs. Use *ps* and *top* to see how much unshared memory is really being used for a typical copy of the CGI. Budget RAM for one copy of the text segment of the CGI, plus RAM for stack and heap for each concurrent user you expect. Then consider that you need more RAM if users are connecting over 28.8 than over a LAN because the connections are around longer (since the user can't get his data out as fast). This means more concurrently running connections and CGIs. A slow CPU has a similar effect, requiring more RAM.

Look for Excessive TCP Retransmits

TCP has many parameters that can be adjusted to affect network performance. A primary concern is avoiding retransmissions of packets when they have been received intact, only delayed because of the latency inherent in the Internet. The default settings may work just fine on a low-latency LAN but then wind up causing unneeded retransmission on the Internet. Under Solaris, many TCP/IP parameters can be changed in a running kernel with the *ndd* command. The *ndd* timing parameters are in milliseconds. You can see *ndd* parameters even if you are not root, using the command *ndd /dev/tcp \?*, but you can't change anything with *ndd* unless you are root.

If TCP does not receive a segment acknowledgment within a certain interval of time, it considers the segment lost and sends another copy. The default timeout is 200 milliseconds, which is fine on a LAN but sometimes inadequate for the much larger latencies of the Internet. If you simply use the default, you may end up sending several identical packets when you could just be sending one. A reasonable setting for a high-latency environment like the Internet is 1000 milliseconds. The Unix *snoop* utility can give you a feel for how your network is running and whether you are retransmitting unnecessarily. The Mac TCP Monitor tool is a good way to see retransmissions on the client side if your clients are Macs. The retransmission delay parameter is known as RTOmax on Windows.

The tradeoff with retransmission delay is that an increase in the timeout will make a lossy connection run more slowly than it otherwise would. It is usually best to leave the settings as they are by default under Solaris 2.6. A more precise way to monitor the number of retransmissions under Solaris is to use the command:

```
netstat -s
```

In the output from the command, compare `tcpOutDataSegs` to `tcpRetransSegs` and `tcpOutDataBytes` to `tcpRetransBytes`. If you are retransmitting more than 20% of the segments or bytes, try setting the retransmission interval higher and re-examine the netstat output. Here is how you change the retransmission interval under Solaris:

```
/usr/sbin/ndd -set /dev/tcp tcp_rexmit_interval_initial 1000
```

Use the Same TCP MTU as Your ISP

If you're talking in the same size packets as your ISP, there will be less time spent splitting up packets or putting them back together.

The maximum IP packet size is 64KB, so most HTTP transfers could fit easily in a single packet, given that the average HTTP transfer is 10KB. This does not mean that only one packet gets sent per request or reply; the TCP setup and teardown are complex and requires multiple packet exchanges. In addition, most web servers use Ethernet connections to their router. Ethernet has a frame size limit of 1500 bytes, forcing larger IP packets to be broken up into 1500-byte fragments.

Even with a 1500-byte limit, packets are subject to fragmentation into yet smaller pieces to fit routers along the path with a maximum transmission unit (MTU) of less than 1500 bytes or to reach clients with an MTU of less than 1500 bytes. The IP header and TCP header are both 20 bytes, so the maximum TCP data segment can be only the MTU—40 without fragmentation. Fragmentation slows a transfer because the originator has to resend in smaller chunks, and because fragments have to be reassembled into a coherent whole at the client. A well-tuned intranet will have the same MTU from end to end, but there is not much you can do about small MTUs on the Internet as a whole. When a packet size exceeds the MTU of the sender, it must be broken up and re-sent as multiple packets.

You can get the source code for a version, of *traceroute* that finds MTUs along a route from the code associated with Stevens' *TCP/IP Illustrated*, Vol 1. The code is at *ftp://ftp.uu.net/published/books/stevens/tcpipiv1.tar.Z*. There is a standard for

MTU "discovery" now, specified in RFC-1191. MTU discovery works by a machine's sending out a large IP packet with the DF (Don't Fragment) option set in the IP header. When the packet hits a router or bridge with a lower MTU, the router generates an ICMP "Can't Fragment" reply. The sending machine gets the reply and then tries a smaller MTU. This continues until an MTU that works along the entire route is discovered. Note that Solaris 2.x includes MTU discovery in the kernel. DNS and TFTP (Trivial FTP) use packets of only 512 bytes maximum because fragmentation is guaranteed not to occur for packets of less than 576 bytes. On an Ethernet LAN, the MTU is generally set to be 1500 bytes, and this is the way many clients such as Windows 95 are configured by default, but on the Internet it is sometimes a better idea to set the MTU to 576. You can use the modified *traceroute* program mentioned earlier to find out about the MTU between yourself and points you commonly visit.

Use a Trailing Slash When Requesting a Directory

A URL pointing to a directory is technically supposed to end in a slash to indicate that it refers to a directory and not explicitly to a file. Nonetheless, most users leave off the slash, leaving it up to the server to figure out that the user is requesting a directory. Servers figure it out, but they have to go through the step of looking for an ordinary file which they don't find, and this slows things down. They could then give you the index file for the directory you gave them. In practice, servers just respond with a redirect to the client, adding to network traffic and delaying the eventual response. It would be better for your server if users provided the correct syntax to the server, so if you publish a URL or embed links in HTML, use the correct syntax, e.g. *http://www.oreilly.com/catalog/*. For example, Apache 1.2.4 responds with an HTTP redirect, i.e., sending a `Location:` URL back to the client, to the same URL but with a slash appended. If we request a directory named *dir* without the trailing slash from a server at *www.oreilly.com*, this is what we would see on the network:

```
% telnet www.oreilly.com 80
Trying 127.0.0.1...
Connected to www.oreilly.com.
Escape character is '^]'.
GET /catalog HTTP/1.0
HTTP/1.1 301 Moved Permanently
Date: Thu, 14 May 1998 03:41:58 GMT
Server: Apache/1.2.4
Location: http://www.oreilly.com/catalog/
Connection: close
Content-Type: text/html
<HTML><HEAD>
<TITLE>301 Moved Permanently</TITLE>
</HEAD><BODY>
<H1>Moved Permanently</H1>
The document has moved <A HREF="http://www.oreilly.com/catalog/">here</A>.<P>
</BODY></HTML>
Connection closed by foreign host.
```

Index

D

F

I

J

M

O

P

Q

R

S

T

U

V

W

X

Y

Z

About the Authors

Stephen Spainhour is a writer for O'Reilly & Associates. He coauthored the first edition of *Webmaster in a Nutshell*, as well as *Perl in a Nutshell*, and contributed to many other O'Reilly titles. He is an avid fan of professional tennis, and when he's not checking for tennis scores on the Web, he enjoys cooking, electronic music, and watching too much television.

Robert Eckstein enjoys dabbling with just about anything related to computers. From rendering to electronic commerce to compiler construction to fuzzy logic, most of his friends agree that Robert spends far too much time in front of a computer screen, and is the world's largest consumer of caffeine.

Robert has recently coauthored *Java Swing* for O'Reilly, and in his spare time is known to provide online coverage for popular conferences. He holds honors degrees in computer science and communications from Trinity University in San Antonio, Texas. In the past, Robert has worked for the USAA insurance company and more recently spent four years with Motorola's cellular software division. He now lives in Austin, Texas, with his wife Michelle; they hope to adopt a talking puppy soon.

Colophon

Our look is the result of reader comments, our own experimentation, and feedback from distribution channels. Distinctive covers complement our distinctive approach to technical topics, breathing personality and life into potentially dry subjects.

A crab spider is featured on the cover of *Webmaster in a Nutshell*. Like the crustaceans after which they are named, crab spiders walk sideways or backwards. They feed on bees and other pollenizing insects, often laying in wait for them by hiding on flowers. Some species of crab spider can, over a period of several days, change color from white to yellow and back again to blend into the flower on which they are sitting. The spider can grab its prey quickly with its forward facing legs. It then injects its victims with a fast-acting, highly-poisonous venom, in this way protecting itself from the bee's sting.

Spiders are similar to, but not the same as, insects. They belong to the class *Arachnida*, named after Arachne, a maiden in Greek mythology. She defeated the goddess Athena in a weaving contest. In a fury of anger, Athena destroyed Arachne's weaving and beat her about the head. In utter disgrace, Arachne hanged herself. A regretful Athena changed Arachne into a spider so she could weave forever.

While they are certainly not going to win any popularity contests, spiders' insect-eating habits are extremely helpful to humans. Every year, billions of spiders do away with large numbers of disease-carrying and crop-destroying insects. If every spider ate one a day for just a year, those insects, piled in one spot, would weigh as much as 50 million people. Spiders are, by far, the most important predator of insects in the world.

Mary Anne Weeks Mayo was the production editor for *Webmaster in a Nutshell, Second Edition*; Sheryl Avruch was the production manager; Clairemarie Fisher O'Leary and Maureen Dempsey provided quality control. Audrey Doyle was the copyeditor. Lenny Muellner provided troff technical support. Seth Maislin wrote the index.

Edie Freedman designed the cover of this book, using a 19th-century engraving from the Dover Pictorial Archive. The cover layout was produced with Quark XPress 3.32 using the ITC Garamond font. Whenever possible, our books use RepKover™, a durable and flexible lay-flat binding. If the page count exceeds RepKover's limit, perfect binding is used.

The inside layout was designed by Alicia Cech and implemented in groff by Lenny Muellner. The text and heading fonts are ITC Garamond Light and Garamond Book. The illustrations that appear in the book were produced by Robert Romano and Rhon Porter using Macromedia FreeHand 8 and Adobe Photoshop 5. This colophon was written by Clairemarie Fisher O'Leary, with help from Elaine and Michael Kalantarian.

More Titles from O'Reilly

Web Authoring and Design

Designing with JavaScript

By Nick Heinle
1st Edition September 1997
256 pages, Includes CD-ROM
ISBN 1-56592-300-6

Written by the author of the "JavaScript Tip of the Week" web site, this new Web Review Studio book focuses on the most useful and applicable scripts for making truly interactive, engaging web sites. You'll not only have quick access to the scripts you need, you'll finally understand why the scripts work, how to alter the scripts to get the effects you want, and, ultimately, how to write your own groundbreaking scripts from scratch.

Information Architecture for the World Wide Web

By Louis Rosenfeld & Peter Morville
1st Edition January 1998
226 pages, ISBN 1-56592-282-4

Learn how to merge aesthetics and mechanics to design web sites that "work." This book shows how to apply principles of architecture and library science to design cohesive web sites and intranets that are easy to use, manage, and expand. Covers building complex sites, hierarchy design and organization, and techniques to make your site easier to search. For webmasters, designers, and administrators.

HTML: The Definitive Guide, 3rd Edition

By Chuck Musciano & Bill Kennedy
3rd Edition August 1998
576 pages, ISBN 1-56592-492-4

This complete guide is chock full of examples, sample code, and practical, hands-on advice to help you create truly effective web pages and master advanced features. Learn how to insert images and other multimedia elements, create useful links and searchable documents, use Netscape extensions, design great forms, and lots more. The third edition covers HTML 4.0, Netscape 4.5, and Internet Explorer 4.0, plus all the common extensions.

Photoshop for the Web

By Mikkel Aaland
1st Edition April 1998
238 pages, ISBN 1-56592-350-2

Photoshop for the Web shows you how to use the world's most popular imaging software to create Web graphics and images that look great and download blazingly fast. The book is crammed full of step-by-step examples and real-world solutions from some of the country's hottest Web producers, including *HotWired*, c|net, *Discovery Online*, *Second Story*, *SFGate*, and more than 20 others.

Web Navigation: Designing the User Experience

By Jennifer Fleming
1st Edition September 1998
288 pages, Includes CD-ROM
ISBN 1-56592-351-0

This book takes the first in-depth look at designing Web site navigation through design strategies to help you uncover solutions that work for your site and audience. It focuses on designing by purpose, with chapters on entertainment, shopping, identity, learning, information, and community sites. Comes with a CD-ROM that containing software demos and a "netography" of related Web resources.

PNG: The Definitive Guide

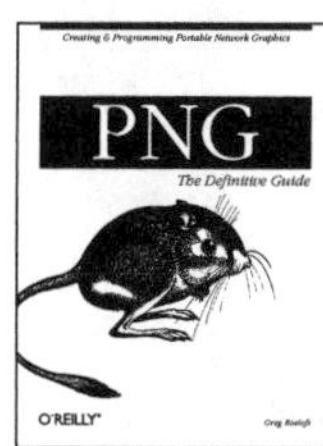

By Greg Roelofs
1st Edition June 1999 (est.)
504 pages (est.), ISBN 1-56592-542-4

PNG: The Definitive Guide addresses the needs of graphic designers who want to get the most out of this next-generation graphics file format and programmers who want to add full PNG-support to their own applications. It focuses on implementing PNG with the libpng C library and discusses improvements, such as gamma correction and the standard color spaces for precise reproduction of image colors on a wide range of systems.

In a Nutshell Quick References

Web Design in a Nutshell

By Jennifer Niederst
1st Edition November 1998
580 pages, ISBN 1-56592-515-7

Web Design in a Nutshell contains the nitty-gritty on everything you need to know to design Web pages. Written by veteran Web designer Jennifer Niederst, this book provides quick access to the wide range of technologies and techniques from which Web designers and authors must draw. Topics include understanding the Web environment, HTML, graphics, multimedia and interactivity, and emerging technologies.

WebMaster in a Nutshell, Deluxe Edition

By O'Reilly & Associates, Inc.
1st Edition September 1997
374 pages, includes CD-ROM & book
ISBN 1-56592-305-7

The Deluxe Edition of *WebMaster in a Nutshell* is a complete library for web programmers. It features the Web Developer's Library, a CD-ROM containing the electronic text of five popular O'Reilly titles: *HTML: The Definitive Guide*, 2nd Edition; *JavaScript: The Definitive Guide*, 2nd Edition; *CGI Programming on the World Wide Web*; *Programming Perl*, 2nd Edition—the classic "camel book"; and *WebMaster in a Nutshell*, which is also included in a companion desktop edition.

AOL in a Nutshell

By Curt Degenhart & Jen Muehlbauer
1st Edition June 1998
536 pages, ISBN 1-56592-424-X

This definitive reference breaks through the hype and shows advanced AOL users and sophisticated beginners how to get the most out of AOL's tools and features. You'll learn how to customize AOL to meet your needs, work around annoying idiosyncrasies, avoid unwanted email and Instant Messages, understand Parental Controls, and turn off intrusive advertisements. It's an indispensable guide for users who aren't dummies.

Internet in a Nutshell

By Valerie Quercia
1st Edition October 1997
450 pages, ISBN 1-56592-323-5

Internet in a Nutshell is a quick-moving guide that goes beyond the "hype" and right to the heart of the matter: how to get the Internet to work for you. This is a second-generation Internet book for readers who have already taken a spin around the Net and now want to learn the shortcuts.

ASP in a Nutshell

By A. Keyton Weissinger
1st Edition February 1999
426 pages, ISBN 1-56592-490-8

This detailed reference contains all the information Web developers need to create effective Active Server Pages (ASP) applications. It focuses on how features are used in a real application and highlights little-known or undocumented aspects, enabling even experienced developers to advance their ASP applications to new levels.

Perl in a Nutshell

By Stephen Spainhour, Ellen Siever & Nathan Patwardhan
1st Edition January 1999
674 pages, ISBN 1-56592-286-7

The perfect companion for working programmers, *Perl in a Nutshell* is a comprehensive reference guide to the world of Perl. It contains everything you need to know for all but the most obscure Perl questions. This wealth of information is packed into an efficient, extraordinarily usable format.

How to stay in touch with O'Reilly

1. Visit Our Award-Winning Site

http://www.oreilly.com/

★ "Top 100 Sites on the Web" —*PC Magazine*
★ "Top 5% Web sites" —*Point Communications*
★ "3-Star site" —*The McKinley Group*

Our web site contains a library of comprehensive product information (including book excerpts and tables of contents), downloadable software, background articles, interviews with technology leaders, links to relevant sites, book cover art, and more. File us in your Bookmarks or Hotlist!

2. Join Our Email Mailing Lists

New Product Releases

To receive automatic email with brief descriptions of all new O'Reilly products as they are released, send email to:
listproc@online.oreilly.com
Put the following information in the first line of your message (*not* in the Subject field):
subscribe oreilly-news

O'Reilly Events

If you'd also like us to send information about trade show events, special promotions, and other O'Reilly events, send email to:
listproc@online.oreilly.com
Put the following information in the first line of your message (*not* in the Subject field):
subscribe oreilly-events

3. Get Examples from Our Books via FTP

There are two ways to access an archive of example files from our books:

Regular FTP

- ftp to:
  ftp.oreilly.com
  (login: anonymous
  password: your email address)
- Point your web browser to:
  ftp://ftp.oreilly.com/

FTPMAIL

- Send an email message to:
  ftpmail@online.oreilly.com
  (Write "help" in the message body)

4. Contact Us via Email

order@oreilly.com
To place a book or software order online. Good for North American and international customers.

subscriptions@oreilly.com
To place an order for any of our newsletters or periodicals.

books@oreilly.com
General questions about any of our books.

software@oreilly.com
For general questions and product information about our software. Check out O'Reilly Software Online at **http://software.oreilly.com/** for software and technical support information. Registered O'Reilly software users send your questions to:
website-support@oreilly.com

cs@oreilly.com
For answers to problems regarding your order or our products.

booktech@oreilly.com
For book content technical questions or corrections.

proposals@oreilly.com
To submit new book or software proposals to our editors and product managers.

international@oreilly.com
For information about our international distributors or translation queries. For a list of our distributors outside of North America check out:
http://www.oreilly.com/www/order/country.html

O'Reilly & Associates, Inc.
101 Morris Street, Sebastopol, CA 95472 USA
TEL 707-829-0515 or 800-998-9938
(6am to 5pm PST)
FAX 707-829-0104

International Distributors

UK, Europe, Middle East and Africa (except France, Germany, Austria, Switzerland, Luxembourg, Liechtenstein, and Eastern Europe)

INQUIRIES

O'Reilly UK Limited
4 Castle Street
Farnham
Surrey, GU9 7HS
United Kingdom
Telephone: 44-1252-711776
Fax: 44-1252-734211
Email: josette@oreilly.com

ORDERS

Wiley Distribution Services Ltd.
1 Oldlands Way
Bognor Regis
West Sussex PO22 9SA
United Kingdom
Telephone: 44-1243-779777
Fax: 44-1243-820250
Email: cs-books@wiley.co.uk

France

Orders

GEODIF
61, Bd Saint-Germain
75240 Paris Cedex 05, France
Tel: 33-1-44-41-46-16 (French books)
Tel: 33-1-44-41-11-87 (English books)
Fax: 33-1-44-41-11-44
Email: distribution@eyrolles.com

Inquiries

Éditions O'Reilly
18 rue Séguier
75006 Paris, France
Tel: 33-1-40-51-52-30
Fax: 33-1-40-51-52-31
Email: france@editions-oreilly.fr

Germany, Switzerland, Austria, Eastern Europe, Luxembourg, and Liechtenstein

Inquiries & Orders

O'Reilly Verlag
Balthasarstr. 81
D-50670 Köln
Germany
Telephone: 49-221-973160-91
Fax: 49-221-973160-8
Email: anfragen@oreilly.de (inquiries)
Email: order@oreilly.de (orders)

Canada (French language books)

Les Éditions Flammarion ltée
375, Avenue Laurier Ouest
Montréal (Québec) H2V 2K3
Tel: 00-1-514-277-8807
Fax: 00-1-514-278-2085
Email: info@flammarion.qc.ca

Hong Kong

City Discount Subscription Service, Ltd.
Unit D, 3rd Floor, Yan's Tower
27 Wong Chuk Hang Road
Aberdeen, Hong Kong
Tel: 852-2580-3539
Fax: 852-2580-6463
Email: citydis@ppn.com.hk

Korea

Hanbit Media, Inc.
Sonyoung Bldg. 202
Yeksam-dong 736-36
Kangnam-ku
Seoul, Korea
Tel: 822-554-9610
Fax: 822-556-0363
Email: hant93@chollian.dacom.co.kr

Philippines

Mutual Books, Inc.
429-D Shaw Boulevard
Mandaluyong City, Metro
Manila, Philippines
Tel: 632-725-7538
Fax: 632-721-3056
Email: mbikikog@mnl.sequel.net

Taiwan

O'Reilly Taiwan
No. 3, Lane 131
Hang-Chow South Road
Section 1, Taipei, Taiwan
Tel: 886-2-23968990
Fax: 886-2-23968916
Email: benh@oreilly.com

China

O'Reilly Beijing
Room 2410
160, FuXingMenNeiDaJie
XiCheng District
Beijing
China PR 100031
Tel: 86-10-86631006
Fax: 86-10-86631007
Email: frederic@oreilly.com

India

Computer Bookshop (India) Pvt. Ltd.
190 Dr. D.N. Road, Fort
Bombay 400 001 India
Tel: 91-22-207-0989
Fax: 91-22-262-3551
Email: cbsbom@giasbm01.vsnl.net.in

Japan

O'Reilly Japan, Inc.
Kiyoshige Building 2F
12-Bancho, Sanei-cho
Shinjuku-ku
Tokyo 160-0008 Japan
Tel: 81-3-3356-5227
Fax: 81-3-3356-5261
Email: japan@oreilly.com

All Other Asian Countries

O'Reilly & Associates, Inc.
101 Morris Street
Sebastopol, CA 95472 USA
Tel: 707-829-0515
Fax: 707-829-0104
Email: order@oreilly.com

Australia

WoodsLane Pty., Ltd.
7/5 Vuko Place
Warriewood NSW 2102
Australia
Tel: 61-2-9970-5111
Fax: 61-2-9970-5002
Email: info@woodslane.com.au

New Zealand

Woodslane New Zealand, Ltd.
21 Cooks Street (P.O. Box 575)
Waganui, New Zealand
Tel: 64-6-347-6543
Fax: 64-6-345-4840
Email: info@woodslane.com.au

Latin America

McGraw-Hill Interamericana
Editores, S.A. de C.V.
Cedro No. 512
Col. Atlampa
06450, Mexico, D.F.
Tel: 52-5-547-6777
Fax: 52-5-547-3336
Email: mcgraw-hill@infosel.net.mx

O'REILLY®

O'Reilly & Associates, Inc.
101 Morris Street
Sebastopol, CA 95472-9902
1-800-998-9938

Visit us online at:
www.oreilly.com
order@oreilly.com

O'REILLY WOULD LIKE TO HEAR FROM YOU

Which book did this card come from?

____

Where did you buy this book?
- ❑ Bookstore
- ❑ Computer Store
- ❑ Direct from O'Reilly
- ❑ Class/seminar
- ❑ Bundled with hardware/software
- ❑ Other ____________________

What operating system do you use?
- ❑ UNIX
- ❑ Macintosh
- ❑ Windows NT
- ❑ PC(Windows/DOS)
- ❑ Other ____________________

What is your job description?
- ❑ System Administrator
- ❑ Programmer
- ❑ Network Administrator
- ❑ Educator/Teacher
- ❑ Web Developer
- ❑ Other ____________________

❑ Please send me O'Reilly's catalog, containing a complete listing of O'Reilly books and software.

Name __________ Company/Organization __________

Address __________

City __________ State __________ Zip/Postal Code __________ Country __________

Telephone __________ Internet or other email address (specify network) __________

Nineteenth century wood engraving of a bear from the O'Reilly & Associates Nutshell Handbook® *Using & Managing UUCP.*

PLACE
STAMP
HERE

NO POSTAGE
NECESSARY IF
MAILED IN THE
UNITED STATES

BUSINESS REPLY MAIL

FIRST CLASS MAIL PERMIT NO. 80 SEBASTOPOL, CA

Postage will be paid by addressee

O'Reilly & Associates, Inc.
101 Morris Street
Sebastopol, CA 95472-9902